PLANNING EFFECTIVE CURRICULUM
for GIFTED LEARNERS

Joyce VanTassel-Baska

College of William and Mary

D0714025

LOVE PUBLISHING COMPANY®
Denver, Colorado 80222

Chapter Contributors

Agnes Donovan
Teachers' College, Columbia University

Lori Korinek
College of William and Mary

Virginia Laycock
College of William and Mary

Gail McEachron-Hirsch
College of William and Mary

I would like to acknowledge with gratitude the careful assistance provided by my faithful secretary, Cathy Prigge, in the typing and revising of this manuscript, and the expertise of Dr. A. Harry Passow for his thoughtful and constructive critique of an early draft of this book.

Library of Congress Catalog Card Number 91-077051

Copyright © 1992 Love Publishing Company
Printed in the U.S.A.
ISBN 0-89108-218-2

Contents

APPENDIX
Sample Curriculum Units

To my sprite, Ariel

Introduction: Gifted Education at the Crossroad

Gifted education is now at a critical crossroad in respect to its next stage of development. Since the middle 1970s, growth of the field at the grassroots level and at the state level has been phenomenal. Even in the face of no federal visibility or support during the Reagan years, the field managed to grow in the area of direct service to gifted learners and in opportunities for training teachers and other school personnel. As we look ahead, however, what will make gifted education viable is highly dependent on its capacity to establish linkages with the existing structures in education, to form partnerships in key areas, and to take advantage of the best that general education* research and best practices have to offer us as a field.

The field of gifted education historically has used the special education model as the basis for nascent efforts in program development. Identification and assessment practices, teacher training and administrative program models have been derived from special education. Gifted education also has attempted to incorporate much of the special education rhetoric in its advocacy role for gifted children, speaking of the special needs of the population, appropriate placements, and categorical considerations. Use of these special education models has led us to grow and develop as a field. Yet the special education model itself

---

* By *general education,* I mean the educational curriculum practices used for the majority of students in our schools, including all basic or core curriculum requirements. *Special education* refers to the field of education that specializes in exceptionalities related to handicapping conditions.

may be limited in the very areas in which gifted education is in greatest need of development currently — the areas of curricula, instructional materials, and evaluation.

If we are to advance as a field, we shall have to embrace the world of general education, its models and its curriculum reforms, while not forsaking totally the exceptionality concept that defines the nature of the gifted population. We can begin to establish sound curriculum practices for gifted learners, built on a research base of the latest developments in teaching and learning, motivation, and child development, as well as on an organizational base constructed out of the effective schools movement.

Thus, gifted education must relate to two educational worlds: (a) the special education world, representing the continuum of services necessary for exceptional learners, and (b) the general education world, representing the curriculum and organizational support structures that underlie schooling for all learners. Figure I.1 graphically depicts this concept and some program development issues in each of the two realms. Our task is to find ways to appropriately negotiate these worlds so that program development efforts for the gifted can move to a higher level of operation.

Elementary program models in gifted education have used almost exclusively the special education paradigm for development. In the push to build programs, curriculum intervention was frequently the last consideration. At the secondary level, however, mild content acceleration and enrichment has been the point of departure in the scheme of program design, often thwarting further development beyond the established honors concept in specific disciplines of study. This elementary/secondary split in gifted curriculum development illustrates the uncomfortable straddling of these educational worlds that we have attempted in gifted education.

Linkage to the curriculum reform movement on the part of gifted educators requires embracing the traditional content dimensions as core areas of learning for the gifted at all levels K-12 rather than treating these areas as peripheral, especially at the elementary level. There are several valid reasons for moving to a content-based instructional model for the gifted. Schools are organized by basic content areas, and to deviate significantly from these areas is to be outside a predominant organizational pattern that aids communication on gifted issues within the school system. It also provides the natural context for planning curriculum, because school systems, even those with self-contained programs for the gifted, are obligated to show mastery of basic skills for gifted students in these subject matter areas. Moreover, gifted students are spending the majority of their instructional time in the traditional subject matter disciplines. Thus, the impact of programs for the gifted is limited severely by ignoring content, as is the appropriateness of a significant amount of learning time.

At a social level, knowledge is organized in discipline-specific ways. We study disciplines in college, and we organize our professions around key learning

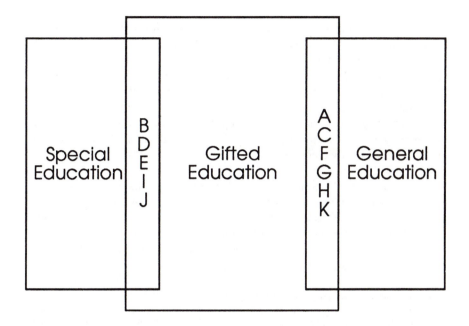

Program Development Issues in Gifted Education

A		philosophy and goals	G	=	materials and resources
B	=	identification and assessment	H	=	instructional processes
C	=	program approaches	I	=	teacher training
D	=	program administration	J	=	advocacy
E	=	grouping strategies	K	=	evaluation
F	=	curriculum			

Figure I.1
**KEY LINKAGES OF SPECIAL EDUCATION AND GENERAL EDUCATION
IN PROGRAM DEVELOPMENT FOR THE GIFTED**

areas. Clearly our knowledge producers are content experts. Nobel prizes are given in physics, chemistry, and literature, not in constructing an electrical car. Many significant products of civilization are discipline-specific (the best novel, the most beautiful piece of music, the most wondrous painting). Society continues to organize learning and define societal progress around distinct knowledge bases or domains.

Our current research base on conceptions of giftedness also lends credence to a content-specific curriculum model of organization. Gardner (1983), Feldman (1986), and Bloom (1985) all conceptualize giftedness as domain-specific. Our studies of eminence further speak to contributions in a given area of talent.

Research on teaching and learning also suggests the importance of embedding thinking skills in content to maximize transfer effect (Perkins & Saloman, 1989). The argument for discipline-specific curricula for the gifted creates an added rationale for strong linkages to the curriculum reform movement because innovative opportunities for curriculum development will come through these same disciplines.

To effect positive change in curriculum development for the gifted, key aspects of general education must be taken into consideration. Three areas that can be clearly identified are:

1. The curriculum reform movement and its implications for gifted education.
2. Basic research on teaching and learning that increases our understanding of how students learn, especially those studies that carry direct implications for working more effectively with the gifted.
3. The effective schools research and related areas of informed practice that are shaping the current organizational structure of schools in profound ways.

THE CURRICULUM REFORM MOVEMENT

Volumes have been written about the curriculum reform movement of the 1980s and of its negligible effects so far on improving the nation's schools. Cuban (1990) argued for the inevitability of educational reform movements in the United States, driven by dominant social groups to address social problems, and the shared value perception that schools promote social mobility and make good citizens. Passow (1989) observed that the reform movement may be harmful to gifted education in its imposing a common curriculum for all learners with a common standard of performance. Yet the message of curriculum reform is one of excellence, an attempt to raise the standard for all learners. This context provides gifted education an opportunity to demonstrate that curricula appropriate for able learners may in fact be "filtered down" in a variety of ways for all learners. And the curriculum reform movement offers an unprecedented opportunity for curriculum development and experimentation with differing models, especially in the areas of mathematics and science (VanTassel-Baska & Kulieke, 1987; Wheatley, 1988).

The curriculum reform movement emphasizes some key areas in which gifted education has already demonstrated a leadership role. These provide important pathways to further collaborative work with general educators. One is the *focus on mathematics, science, and technology,* which has stressed stiffer graduation requirements, the development of new courses, and teacher training and early involvement of women and minorities in a career track. This emphasis in the reform movement emanates from international studies showing United States students lagging behind those of many other nations in achievement in these core areas, and creates concern about the United States competing successfully in the future. Top students in the United States show even greater gaps in achievement when compared to top students in Russia, Japan, and West Germany.

In response to the reform issue, gifted education has developed several programs and services that address this national concern directly. These efforts include:

— the establishment of academies and residential schools for the gifted, with a focus on mathematics and science.
— the provision of advanced opportunities early to talented students in these content areas through the talent search program available through five universities across the country.
— the development of programs that link scientists and mathematicians to the schools and students through mentorships and internships.

A second focus of the reform movement has been on *internationalizing education* — increasing awareness of other cultures, languages, and world geography. This interest has emerged from a recognition of global interdependence, of multinational interests, and the importance of being competitive in a world trade market. Because gifted students are likely to constitute the leadership of tomorrow in all spheres of influence, a strong education in global issues is important. As a field, our response to this general education effort has been to provide:

— earlier intervention in foreign language; encouragement to learn two languages in addition to English.
— special programs organized around global issues and concerns.
— seminars and special course opportunities in international studies.

A third direct linkage between gifted education and curriculum reform is in the *infusion of thinking skills* into the core curriculum. National assessment results from 1982 indicate that reasoning capacities of high school students are severely deficient. For example, only 14% could handle a simple inference and deductive reasoning problem (Darling-Hammond, 1990). This points to a need to enhance critical thinking and to help students utilize more thinking processes. For years gifted education has focused on teaching thinking skills. Our response to this general curriculum trend must still be to provide direct teaching of alternative thinking processes (critical, creative, metacognitive) to the gifted and to develop programs organized around thinking processes, especially analysis, synthesis, evaluation, and divergent skills appropriately differentiated for the gifted. At the same time, we are in a unique position to assist general education staff development and curriculum development promoting the infusion model of thinking into the curriculum for all learners.

A strong *accountability* movement, using tests as benchmarks of educational progress and standards of learning as evidence of minimum levels of competency, also characterizes the reform movement in schools. A 20-year decline in test scores of school-aged populations, particularly on the Scholastic Aptitude Test

(SAT) and other competency-based achievement measures, has prompted educational critics to call for better results. As we try to embrace this aspect of the reform movement, we have to refocus the core skill areas of the curriculum at maximum competency levels. This implies curriculum adaptation in core content areas, and evaluation models responsive to differentiated curriculum goals and objectives.

Moreover, the curriculum reform recommendations emanating from curriculum organizations, such as the National Science Teachers' Association (NSTA) and the National Council of Teachers of Math (NCTM), substantively call for *problem-solving approaches* to current curriculum issues, consonant with gifted education strategies and approaches. Generic concerns across curriculum groups have highlighted issues such as the information and knowledge explosion, too much review of material that should have been mastered at an earlier stage of development, passive learning dispensed in the form of facts, the rigidity of disciplines, and separate curricula based on ability (Association for Supervision and Curriculum Development, 1990). Solutions cited by these same curriculum groups have been endorsed by gifted education for some time.

- *Reorganizing content according to essential elements.* This solution to the knowledge explosion has long been suggested as a strategy for gifted students because of their ability to grasp underlying concepts readily if information is presented in a condensed, economical fashion. It also paves the way for limiting the number of similar problems to which students are to apply the concept, because the gifted typically need fewer examples to internalize a concept.
- *Using diagnostic-prescriptive procedures to reduce drill and practice on learned materials.* Just as mathematics educators have decried the 20% to 60% overlap in math learning from year to year in basal texts (Hershfield, 1986), so, too, have educators of the gifted long decried the repetition of old learning for the gifted, instead advocating a diagnostic-prescriptive approach that allows for continuous progress (George, Cohn & Stanley, 1979).
- *Active learning through an emphasis on problem-solving and thinking strategies.* Perhaps in no area of gifted education has more been done than in promoting problem-solving and thinking skills with gifted learners. It has been a major focus of staff development workshops and graduate coursework, and the basis on which many pull-out resource programs for the gifted have been organized. This solution represents a real strength of gifted education and a potential avenue for the strongest linkage to general education reform.
- *Applying integrative approaches and connections in curriculum areas.* As in thinking skills, gifted education strongly advocates a major emphasis on curriculum development processes that are organized by issues, themes, and ideas and a resulting curriculum that is both intra- and interdisciplinary. Moreover, we have actively encouraged team teaching and block scheduling — both important administrative structures to support an interdisciplinary model of curricula. This represents another commitment parallel with general education.

- *Providing common core curricula for all students.* Although some educators of the gifted could argue for differentiated curricula as something totally different from what other learners are receiving, many from general education, too, would support this concept. As long as the translation of the common core would not be expected to occur at the same grade level for all learners, would not be taught in the same way, or would not limit gifted learners to the common core, disagreement with this concept would surely be minimal. With these caveats, the relationship that might be forged to mainstream curricula again is clear. Linking general learner outcomes to more appropriate outcomes for gifted learners, taking these principles into consideration, has been attempted already (VanTassel-Baska, 1990).

These types of connections should be viewed as important prototypes for further development of gifted programs in consonance with the initiatives of general education. We have much to gain from an alliance such as this, and nothing to lose by collaborative efforts in these domains. As Maeroff (1989) cited in a paper urging collaboration with colleges, businesses, and practitioners in all areas: "The time is right to reach these people. The vehicles are in place. There may never again be so much opportunity for coalition building" (p. 5).

CURRENT RESEARCH ON TEACHING AND LEARNING

Ongoing strands of research in general education seem important to our conceptual framework for understanding appropriate curricula for the gifted. Curriculum planners for the gifted need to be mindful of the optimal match between learner capacity and level of experiences provided. Consequently, the best curriculum intervention may occur when both personal skill level and challenge level are correspondingly high, as found in recent studies of both gifted and nongifted adolescents (Csikszentmihalyi, 1987).

Recent *research on creativity* (Amabile, 1983) reinforces the idea of working with learning in content-specific areas as a prelude to teaching creativity-relevant skills. Picasso was creative in art because he knew it well as a domain, had practiced it assiduously from an early age, and was deeply interested in it as a field of inquiry. Recognizing that sophistication in a content area precedes creative accomplishments in that area is a key understanding for curriculum planners in gifted education.

Research on motivational theory also provides important bridges to gifted education, and a real need exists for relating new findings in this area to curriculum and instructional planning. Research has demonstrated that children who have learning goals rather than performance goals use obstacles as a cue to increase efforts, change strategies, and improve performance (Ames, 1984; Dweck, 1986; Nicholls, 1984). Studies of the relationship of ability to motivation have suggested that children's actual competence does not strongly predict confidence in future attainment. For gifted girls, a negative correlation has been found between actual ability and maladaptive patterns such as low expectancies, challenge avoidance, and debilitation under failure (Licht & Dweck, 1984). Understanding individual differences on the motivation dimension within the gifted population, and especially sub-populations such as girls, the disadvantaged, and minority populations, is critical in planning appropriate curricula for them.

Studies of thinking also contribute to understanding curriculum directions for the gifted. Expert-novice comparisons in various fields (Berliner, 1985; Sommers, 1980) have yielded differences favoring experts in metacognitive acts such as planning and revising. Yet, a collection of research on expertise has revealed that successful utilization of these skills may be content-specific. Rabinowitz and Glaser (1985) found that expert performance entails a large knowledge base of domain-specific patterns, rapid recognition of situations to which these patterns apply, and forward reasoning based on pattern manipulation to reach solutions. Further support for domain-specific research comes out of studies using general context-independent cognitive strategies and finding no clear benefits outside the specific domains in which they are taught (Pressley, Snyder, & Cariglia-Bull, 1987). Thus, research on transfer suggests that "thinking at its most effective depends on specific context-bound skills and units of knowledge that have little application to other domains" (Perkins & Saloman, 1987, p. 119).

The implication for gifted education then might be to wed heuristic thinking models such as creative problem solving and creative thinking to specific domains of inquiry where they could be effectively utilized. Further, it implies the need to uncover the paradigms for thinking embedded in traditional subject matter.

Curriculum planners for gifted learners have to be sensitive to the research in this area so they can adapt methods and approaches to teaching the gifted based on a firm grounding in relevant areas. Clearly, the studies cited offer noteworthy data for educators of the gifted at all levels of schooling.

EFFECTIVE SCHOOLS: RESEARCH AND PRACTICE

The emphasis on effective schools has coincided with the curriculum reform movement in a purposeful way to provide contexts of support for innovations and change to occur in education. For probably the first time since the individually guided education (IGE) model of the 1960s, educators have concentrated on changing the organizational structure of classrooms and schools with a heavy emphasis on collaborative approaches to both teaching and learning. We witness this phenomenon through the focus on cooperative learning models, peer tutoring and coaching models for students and teachers, and shared governance models for administering schools.

What are we learning about effective schools from the spate of studies in this area? Much of the research has centered on urban schools with sizable populations of lower socioeconomic status (SES) students (Lezotte & Bancroft,

1985; Mann, 1985; Maskowitz & Hayman, 1976; Ornstein, 1983). In an extensive review of what is known about educating for minority achievement, Ornstein (1983) cited several studies indicating that the quality of school is an important factor in outcomes for students. He listed leadership, supervision of teachers, teacher morale, emphasis on reading instruction, and communication with parents as influential factors. Other studies revealed that expectations of principals and instructional support are related to achievement in reading and mathematics. Murphy (1986) found that structured learning environments, emphasis on math and reading, staff development, parental involvement and, again, active, motivated leadership are more likely present in schools that are successful. Mann (1985) found matching instruction to the child's learning style and ensuring overlap between what is taught and what is tested to be important school factors. These issues get theoretical support from other studies as well (Lezotte & Bancroft, 1985).

How might gifted education interpret these elements of effective schools? Strong instructional leadership by the principal is an overall positive trend, but it may create undue focus on these elements of "effective schools" at the risk of other successful emphases for the gifted, such as ability grouping and acceleration. Teachers' high expectation for student achievement is often cited as another characteristic of effective schools. Because it has been based on studies showing that low-achieving students are neglected, this factor may direct teachers' attention away from gifted learners who already are achieving at or above expectancy levels. Emphasis on mastery of common objectives in the curriculum, especially basic skills, could easily lead to low-level work and drill-and-practice workbooks for the gifted.

An antidote must be found in differentiating student learning objectives for gifted learners in core skill areas. Frequent and systematic evaluation of students could be a problem if inappropriate measurement devices are used to document progress and if more emphasis is placed on testing than on learning. Also, evaluation designs should provide a link to gifted learner outcomes that are differentiated from generic learner outcomes based on grade level.

SPECIAL ISSUES

The Middle School Organization

The effective schools research has been used as a basis for middle school organizational shifts that may be defined as:

— a strong affective component (teams of students and teachers).
— an interdisciplinary focus on content.
— a curriculum emphasis on student-based inquiry experiences.
— flexible scheduling.
— a movement toward heterogeneous grouping/mainstreaming of all students.

Table I.1
IMPLICATIONS OF MIDDLE SCHOOL TRENDS
FOR GIFTED LEARNERS

Trends in Middle School Education	Potential Effects on the Gifted	
	Positive	Negative
Cooperative learning	Enables small-group efforts organized around a problem	Lacks attention to instructional grouping by abilities/interests; lacks appropriate level problems
Peer tutoring	Offers opportunities for social interaction, leadership, and self-efficacy	Overuse could impair the gifted child's own learning of appropriate material
Teacher empowerment	Effective curricula and instruction for gifted students relies on teacher's judgment about student needs	Could be interpreted only as a shared governance model at the school level rather than a mandate to engage in educational decision making about individual children
Heterogeneous grouping	Provides a mechanism for all learners to access the same learning opportunities	Fails to account for discrepant individual needs at middle school level
Emphasis on affective development	Provides a balance in emphasis between traditional elementary and secondary views of education and the learner	Could be overemphasized to the detriment of needed cognitive development and oversimplified in practice
Team teaching/ Interdisciplinary curriculum	Could lead to enhanced learning of key issues, themes, and ideas across the curriculum	Could be organized at too low a level to benefit the gifted, and delivered without instructional modifications for gifted learners

These features have been the basis for differentiating middle school from more traditional junior high models of organization (Clift & Waxman, 1985; Mergendeller & Mitman, 1985). Table I.1 explores their potential positive and negative effects. If middle school educators and gifted educators could map out a plan to ensure balance and flexibility in implementing these organizational strategies, the hard lines of perceived disagreement between the two special interest groups might be overcome.

Collaborative planning at the middle school level is essential to ensure that gifted learners are not left to stagnate in an unresponsive environment primarily geared to the needs of other groups of learners. Useful approaches to consider in effecting collaborative planning might be:

— the use of teachers/specialists of the gifted as cooperative teachers in heterogeneous classrooms to focus on the needs of the gifted.
— collaborative planning among educators on a regular basis to tailor curricula appropriately to the needs of the gifted and other special needs learners.
— staff development and training of middle school teachers in adapting regular curricula to individual needs, managing differentiated instructional plans, and using inquiry-based strategies.
— the application of grouping and regrouping techniques within and across grade levels that would honor individual differences in instructional learning level for key areas of the curriculum.
— the development of a myriad of cocurricular opportunities that all students could access based on interest (e.g., centers, chess, theatre, conceptual art).
— a system of curriculum and instructional monitoring that would promote better understanding of the impact of middle school innovations on teaching and learning in the classroom.
— movement away from a single text toward multiple resources for classroom use that would allow for greater student choice and alternatives in learning, and enhanced opportunities for interest-based inquiry projects.
— differentiated staffing in the middle school that would enable teacher specialists in content areas to work with the most able learners in these areas in some model of instruction.

For each of these approaches, translations from theory to practice will provide the best view of helpful or harmful effects of an innovation on any given group of learners. Consequently, middle school educators should be open to trying various adaptations of the possibilities suggested.

Ability Grouping

Perhaps no aspect of school reform is as troublesome to those in gifted education as the trend toward eliminating ability grouping. Although ability grouping has been abused in many school settings, the belief that doing away with it can benefit the achievement level or the self-concept of any student is highly questionable. To suggest that evidence supports the elimination of grouping gifted students is to ignore the existing body of research. Studies suggest that:

- The achievement of gifted students at both elementary and secondary levels is enhanced by a variety of ability grouping forms including instructional grouping in core academic areas, cross-grade grouping, and special-interest grouping (Slavin, 1986). Moreover, the achievement of other groups of learners seems to be unaffected by grouping the gifted in these ways (Kulik & Kulik, 1987).
- Grouping by ability produces no significant effect on the self-esteem or general school attitude for any group of students, at either the elementary or the secondary level. Yet grouping by ability produces a positive attitude toward subject matter for all groups of learners (Kulik & Kulik, 1982).
- Ability grouping without special instructional provisions has no effect on any group of learners (Slavin, 1986). Thus, the benefits of ability grouping are activated only through a differentiated instructional plan based on student level of readiness.
- Cooperative learning models do not enhance achievement of the gifted unless some form of ability grouping is employed. Mixing low-ability and high-ability students typically results in no growth for the high-ability group (Slavin, 1986).
- Low-ability students do not model after gifted students (Shunk, 1987). The argument that mixing ability groups provides advantageous learning models for less able children cannot be supported.
- Educators cannot effectively differentiate instructional plans for gifted learners without ability grouping in some form. In effect, to eliminate ability grouping for all is to eliminate special programs for the gifted and talented.

Educational and political groups that have a strong stake in educational reform have not ignored these findings. The nation's governors, while challenging educators to eliminate widespread ability grouping and tracking, specifically indicated that eliminating these practices should not mean ending special opportunities for gifted and talented students. Moreover, the Policy Perspectives publication on at-risk students (McPartland and Slavin, 1990, p. 21) states that educators should "Retain separate offerings for gifted students, limited English proficient students, and special education students at each grade level, along with the program [a] of limited tracking." Thus, the educational movement to reduce the practice of ability grouping in general should not be construed to mean that gifted students should not continue to be grouped in various ways or that programming for gifted and talented learners is inappropriate.

Educators in responsible positions should not think naively that anyone would benefit from dismantling grouping practices necessary to provide gifted and talented programs. Educational reform is not about allowing able learners to stagnate in age-grade lockstep classrooms. If schools were willing to adopt flexible models of grouping, allowing for student needs, rather than administrative fiat or fashions of the time, to dictate practice, the needs of all children might be better met. If schools were willing to alter instruction based on need as readily as they are willing to move children around administratively, the needs of all children might be better met. The problem is not ability grouping but, instead, a lack of flexibility and imagination in applying educational principles in practice.

Minority Achievement

Improving the quality of education for all requires that we be sensitive to the needs of all and plan educational experiences accordingly. Equality of opportunity and equality of treatment in education, however, are not the same — nor should they be. In any profession, the client's needs dictate the nature of the prescription. High-quality services should be available to all, but the nature and organization of those services should vary based on diagnosed need. Education can ill afford to level its services lest the bitter pill of mediocrity be absorbed into the bloodstream of all our students.

Implicit in the argument against ability grouping is the inference that gifted and talented programming takes away from or negatively affects minority achievement, as if these two issues were at opposite poles. Gifted students come from all socioeconomic, racial, and ethnic groups. Some African-American writers have eloquently spoken to the need for developing what they called "the talented tenth," the group of students that is the most promising within the culture to carry out leadership roles. Minority achievement programs would do well to heed DuBois's advice and focus some of their resources on enhancing the development of high-achieving minority students, just as gifted education has recently done.

The current federal allocation of money for the gifted has targeted identification and programming of underrepresented groups such as minority students, low-income students, and students with disabilities as a priority need. Actually, developing the potential of gifted students from diverse cultural groups should be a major priority for education in general, as these students will become this country's leaders of the next generation. The interests of minority students are and can be well served in the context and fabric of gifted education, not separate from it. Serving these students effectively, however, requires even more attention to individual differences and needs, not less.

Minority educators speak of a multicultural curriculum, attention to individual learning style, and appreciation of a child's cultural and class background as essential in responding to the needs of minority learners. Only a small percentage of schools and teachers across the United States currently employ differentiated instructional plans for *any* learner based on a diagnostic assessment of individual learning needs. How can we believe that less grouping and more heterogeneous classrooms will enhance the learning process for *any* student with special needs?

IMPLICATIONS OF CURRENT EDUCATIONAL REFORM

The rhetoric associated with the educational reform movement revolves around organizational reform and curriculum reform issues. Unfortunately, much of the rhetoric has not been realized in practice, and the major "reform" initiatives have been translated into a faddish emphasis on administrative changes such as heterogeneous grouping, cooperative learning, site-based management, and outcome-based education for all. This translation approach, without an underlying substantive base of change in classroom teaching and learning behaviors, is doomed to be more ineffective than earlier models because it fails to account sufficiently for the interactive nature of learning. One can change organizational shells, but the activity of the organism inside is still what will dictate the nature and extent of productivity and desired results.

Until schools are willing to accept that several aspects of the educational enterprise must be changed simultaneously, we have little reason to think that educational reform has meaning. These simultaneous changes should include:

— profound changes in the development and use of curriculum materials.
— instructional strategies that complement these changes and demonstrate effectiveness with a variety of gifted learners.
— teacher attitudes and behaviors that accept the importance of curriculum and instructional change for the gifted and are capable of executing it.
— models for understanding the conditions under which these three dynamics work together to effect positive change for gifted learners.

Even though all groups of students are likely to feel the effects of the problems associated with educational reform, the children most directly impacted by the limited organizational translations of theory to practice will be those groups requiring the greatest amount of individual attention and adaptation in their learning plan: the at-risk and the gifted. Because these groups tend to function farthest from the "norm" in a regular classroom, they tend to be more in need of individualized techniques and processes. Yet, staff development programs have not addressed the key skills regular classroom teachers must be trained to use if these groups are to receive an appropriate education in our schools.

A training program for regular classroom teachers must address key issues that allow for appropriate tailoring of curriculum experiences. Teachers in the regular classroom must:

— be able and willing to assess the child's level of knowledge and appropriate instructional level.
— know how to select appropriate instructional materials to facilitate optimal challenge.
— be able to handle effectively small- and large-group instruction and individual learning.
— be willing to accommodate varying learning styles.
— be knowledgeable about and willing to use various methods of advancement.
— apply problem-centered approaches and open-ended learning.
— teach to varying modalities (auditory, visual, kinesthetic).

In addition, if gifted students are to be well served in regular classroom contexts, the instructional pattern must include:

— pacing (e.g., cutting time in half for instruction, providing less explanation: "What are the three most important points?"
  - Assume that students can learn material quickly.
  - Omit review: "Does anyone need a review on this?"
  - Limit drill and practice).
— question asking (more time spent in asking questions than in explaining).
— asking more open-ended questions (e.g., What if you were President Bush? How would you have handled Iraq's defiance in the face of sanctions?).
— using inquiry-based models (hands-on/problem-solving/discovery).
— providing students access to advanced resources (materials, people, places).

In sum, the direct impact on gifted education of the overall educational reform movement is likely to be negative for all the reasons suggested. The farther removed we become from learners' direct characteristics and individual needs, the more faulty is our perspective on providing an appropriate education for all children. Curriculum flexibility and balance must prevail in all school settings to ensure that educational practice is responsive to individual differences and sensitive to the importance of valuing those differences.

SUMMARY AND CONCLUSION

Curriculum reform efforts, current research in teaching and learning, and organizational innovations to promote effective schools are vital considerations as we seek to provide educational opportunities for gifted learners. Special issues include the middle school organization, ability grouping, and minority achievement, in relation to their impact on gifted education efforts. Now, more than ever, practitioners in gifted education must take seriously the need to collaborate with each other, and with content specialists, school administrators, support personnel, and regular classroom teachers in new configurations that will allow the special needs of gifted learners to be appropriately met.

The age of educational reform and all of its trappings are clearly with us. We must find ways to adapt without compromising the entire enterprise of gifted education in the process. The intent of this book is to provide a blueprint for curriculum planning that carefully considers the current climate of educational reform. It does not supply easy answers, but it does present curricular patterns that can make gifted programs more credible and stable than they currently are. Deliberate collaborative efforts and linkage with general education and special education, I hope, will result in enhanced services to the gifted and greater support for gifted education at all levels of schooling.

16   *Introduction*

REFERENCES

Amabile, T. (1983). *The social psychology of creativity*. New York: Springer-Verlag.

Ames, C. (1984). Achievement attributions and self instruction under competitive and individualistic goal structure. *Journal of Educational Psychology, 69*, 1–8.

Association for Supervision and Curriculum Development. 1990. *Update*. Alexandria, VA.

Berliner, D. (1985). Presidential address to American Educational Research Association, San Francisco.

Bloom, B. (1985). *Developing talent in young people*. New York: Ballantine.

Clift, R. T., & Waxman, H. C. (1985). Some neglected elements of effective schools research: A review of literature. *Journal of Classroom Interaction, 20*(2), 2–11.

Csikszentmihalyi, M. (1987). *Intrinsic motivation*. Paper presented at Northwestern University Phi Delta Kappa research symposium, Evanston, IL.

Cuban, L. (1990). Reforming again, again, and again. *Educational Researcher, 19*(1), 3–13.

Darling-Hammond, L. (1990). Achieving our goals: Superficial or structural reforms. *Phi Delta Kappan, 72*, 286–295.

Dweck, C. (1986). Motivational processes affecting learning. *American Psychologist, 41*(10), 1040–1048.

Feldman, D. (1986). *Nature's gambit*. New York: Basic Books.

Gardner, H. (1983). *Frames of Mind*. New York: Basic Books.

George, W., Cohn, S., and Stanley, J. (Eds.). (1979). *Educating the gifted: Acceleration and Enrichment*. Baltimore: Johns Hopkins University Press.

Kulik, C. C., & Kulik, J. A. (1982). Effects of ability grouping on secondary school students: A meta-analysis of evaluation findings. *American Educational Research Journal, 19*(3), 415–428.

Kulik, J. A., & Kulik, C. C. (1987). Effects of ability grouping on student achievement. *Equity & Excellence, 23*(1-2), 22–30.

Lezotte, L. W. & Bancroft, B. A. (1985). School improvement based on effective schools research: A promising approach for economically disadvantaged and minority students. *Journal of Negro Education, 54*(3), 301–311.

Licht, B. & Dweck, C. (1984). Determinants of academic achievement: The interaction of children's achievement orientations with skill areas. *Developmental Psychology, 20*, 628–636.

Maeroff, G. (1989, April). *Educational Partnerships*. Paper presented to TAG Policy Conference, San Francisco.

Mann, D. (1985). Effective schools for children of the poor. *Education Digest, 51*, 24–25.

Maskowitz, G., & Hayman, J. T. (1976). Success strategies of inner city teachers: A year long study. *Journal of Education Research, 69*, 283–289.

McPartland, J. M., & Slavin, R. E. (1990). *Policy perspectives: Increasing achievement of at-risk students at each grade level*. Washington DC: U.S. Department of Education, Office of Educational Research and Improvement.

Mergendeller, J. R., & Mitman, A. L. (1985). The relationship of middle school program features, instructional strategy, instructional performance, and student engagement. *Journal of Early Adolescence, 6*(2), 183–196.

Murphy, D. M. (1986). Educational disadvantagement. *Journal of Negro Education, 55*(4), 495–507.

Nicholls, J. (1984). Conceptions of ability and achievement motivation. In R. Ames & C. Ames (Eds.), *Research on motivation in education*. (Vol. 1, pp. 39-73). New York: Academic Press.

Ornstein, A. C. (1983). Educating disadvantaged learners. *Educational Forum, 47*(2), 225–247.

Passow, H. (1989). Critical issues in curriculum for the gifted: Implications of the national reports. Chapter in J. VanTassel-Baska & P. Olszewski-Kublilius (Eds.), *Patterns of influence on gifted learners* (pp. 169-177). New York: Teachers College Press.

Perkins, D., & Saloman, G. (1989). Are cognitive skills context bound? *Educational Research, 18*(1), 16–25.

Pressley, M., Snyder, B., & Cariglia-Bull, T. (1987). How can good strategy use be taught to children? Evaluation of six alternative approaches. In S. M. Cormier & J. D. Hagman (Eds.), *Transfer of learning: Contemporary research and applications* (pp. 81–120). New York: Academic Press.

Rabinowitz, M., & Glaser, R. (1985). Cognitive structure and process in highly competent performance. In F. D. Horowitz & M. O'Brien (Eds.), *The gifted and talented: Developmental perspectives* (pp. 75–98). Washington, DC: American Psychological Association.

Shunk, D. H. (1987). Peer models and children's behavioral change. *Review of Educational Research, 52*(2), 149–174.

Slavin, R. W. (1986). Best-evidence synthesis: An alternative to meta-analytic and traditional reviews. *Educational Researcher, 15*(9), 5–11.

Sommers, N. (1980). Revision strategies of student writers and experienced writers. *College Composition & Communications, 31*, 378–387.

VanTassel-Baska, J. (1990). *English curriculum for gifted 9-12*. Atlanta: Georgia Department of Education.

VanTassel-Baska, J., & Kulieke, M. (1987). The role of the community in developing scientific talent. *Gifted Child Quarterly, 31*(3), 115–119.

Wheatley, G. (1988). Mathematics for the gifted. Chapter in J. VanTassel-Baska et al., *Comprehensive Curriculum for Gifted Learners*. Boston: Allyn & Bacon.

PART ONE

General Issues in the Design and Development of Appropriate Curricula for the Gifted

The sign of intelligence is the ability to hold
two contradictory ideas at the same time.

— F. Scott Fitzgerald

In planning and developing curricula for gifted learners, educators have to hold onto several seemingly contradictory ideas simultaneously. We have to be able to filter ideas, beliefs, and values about an appropriate education for the gifted through the lenses of various stages of the curriculum and instructional design process. In doing so, the differential models for gifted education become wedded to traditional design elements. And each of these design elements must be adapted to the demands of the population of learners being considered. Though these elements are the basic ones, the modifications are uniquely derived from the nature of gifted learners and their atypical capacity to learn quickly and well at all levels of the educational enterprise.

Beyond these basic adaptations are two others with which we must be concerned. One is the *developmental appropriateness* of curriculum experiences for gifted learners at each stage. Certainly these learners progress more rapidly than typical learners through Piagetian stages, and we have some evidence that they can move more rapidly to a next level of development as well (Feldman, 1986). But it is presumptuous to assume that all gifted learners are capable of these developmental spurts or leaps. Even if they were, the timing of developmental events has an unevenness that precludes the kind of curriculum planning advocated in this book. Consequently, we must be responsive to developmental differences at two levels — one in respect to the advanced capacity of many gifted learners to handle more abstract concepts at younger ages, particularly in a domain of strength, and, second, to the individual variations among gifted learners in the developmental transitions and the variations in timing regarding these transitions. For example, a gifted child might be reading at the third-grade level in May of her kindergarten year even though she did not find the key to reading until February. Developmental spurts such as this are imperceptible to educational practitioners if we are not attuned to them and the tremendous possibilities they bring for challenging a learner at a propitious moment.

A second concern, which converges with the first to some extent, relates to the *curricular needs of special populations*. Half of this book is devoted to considerations surrounding this issue. We should see these individual and group variations within the gifted population as another filter through which we plan appropriate curriculum and instruction. The adaptations we make are grounded in the characteristics and needs of the given population under consideration. Thus, gifted minority students, learning disabled gifted students, and low socioeconomic status (SES) gifted students all should receive curricular attention that parallels their special needs.

KEY ELEMENTS IN CONSTRUCTING CURRICULA

The first part of this book lays out a process for examining and planning appropriate curriculum experiences for gifted learners K-12, through shifting the focus from one key consideration in curriculum design to the next. Figure P1.1 presents the total set of lenses used for viewing the curriculum and instructional development process. This total design model provides a means to study up close several key aspects or views. These are briefly iterated here and explicated more fully in each of the succeeding chapters in Part One of the book.

Characteristics and Needs of the Learner

Gifted learners require differential treatments in curriculum and instructional patterns of delivery. Chapter 1 attempts to show that the characterological behaviors defining the gifted learner are both cognitive and affective, so curriculum responses must consider both dimensions in planning actual experiences. Major approaches currently used to articulate differentiated curricula for the gifted illustrate the relationship of curricula to the stated characteristics. This focus on

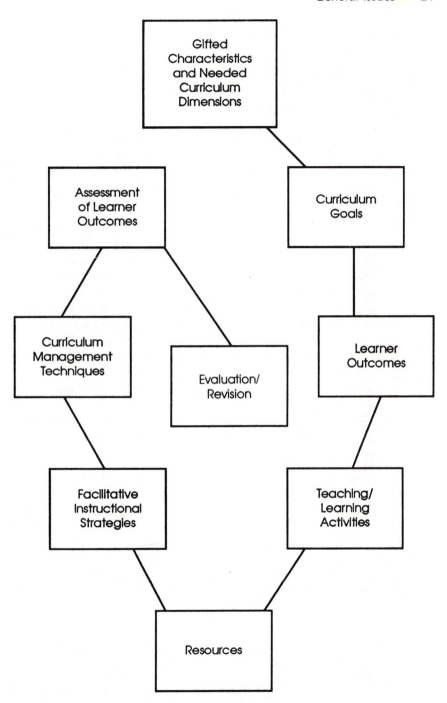

Figure P1.1
CURRICULUM/INSTRUCTIONAL DESIGN MODEL
FOR CONSTRUCTING CURRICULUM FOR GIFTED LEARNERS

the learner and his or her curriculum needs is an important starting point for further curriculum inquiry.

Philosophy and Goals

Once we have a firm grasp of the nature of curricular needs of the gifted learner, we can begin formulating a philosophical orientation toward programs and services in the context of schools. This philosophy and resulting goal statements set the direction for specific curriculum planning and define the general scope of the enterprise. Just as the gifted learner is multifaceted, so, too, the curriculum goals should reflect the multiple domains and facets of giftedness that any school population is likely to display. Thus, goal statements should reflect considerations for the cognitive, affective, aesthetic, and social/behavioral domains.

Learner Outcomes

As the philosophical direction of the program becomes distinct, we then can turn to the issues associated with major outcomes of learning. This lens must be focused on several issues simultaneously. There is the issue of content mastery required for all learners in the core curriculum. How can we adapt this more appropriately to the gifted learner's needs? There is also the issue of infusing all core curricula with higher-level thinking skills and product development opportunities. How can we affect the infusion process as we are raising the complexity level of the core content? Last there is the issue of interdisciplinary connections. How do we suffuse our adapted core curricula with relevant issues, themes, and ideas that will allow gifted learners pathways among the halls of knowledge domains? The level of learning objectives is probably where these issues should become synthesized into the curriculum design process.

Teaching/Learning Activities

As we are capable of defining learning outcomes, we are ready to develop, adapt, or select meaningful activities for gifted learners to experience in a variety of settings. These activities should be challenging, diverse, and reflect a clear balance among stated objectives. Major activity clusters for gifted learners should include oral presentations, writing, assignments, reading, discussion, project work, and variations on each of these major elements. Moreover, the activities should reflect good differentiation principles of curriculum for the gifted, for this is the level of the design model at which these distinctions should be most apparent and defensible.

Resources

Linked to appropriate activities for the gifted are key resources that allow flexibility to both teacher and learner in the learning process. To engage the gifted in a topic from several perspectives, use of diverse materials is essential. Multiple resources are also necessary to differentiate instruction adequately for these learners, because basal materials tend to treat themes and higher-order skills at a superficial level. Moreover, using human as well as material resources enhances their capacity to understand, reflect, and ultimately generate new ideas about an issue. Gifted learners also must have access to high-powered human resources in the form of mentors or outside contexts, or both, that allow for internships or apprenticeships.

Instructional Strategies

Also inextricably linked to both activities and resources are the instructional strategies we use to highlight, exemplify, demonstrate, illustrate — in short, to teach gifted learners. These strategies further require diversification in technique and type. At the level of strategies, teachers must engage most carefully in decision making, because the success of the educational enterprise rests with their ability to translate the ideas, concepts, and skills into meaningful dynamic learning situations. The teacher must be a good facilitator of the learning process for small-group and independent activities and to stimulate and challenge the gifted with higher-order and open-ended questions in all types of learning experiences.

Management Techniques

Just as strategies are the vehicles to convey dynamism in the teaching-learning process, so effective curriculum management techniques allow the teacher to group and regroup, to individualize, to physically reorganize space in the classroom, and to establish the routines of learning that will enhance the instructional process. These techniques should be flexible enough to accommodate a wide range of abilities, interests, and creative spurts that gifted learners often display in schools. An important underpinning to curriculum management for the gifted is the use of learning centers or stations both inside and outside the classroom, to facilitate the delivery of different instructional plans.

Assessment of Learning Objectives

As one moves beyond the lenses of classroom-level concerns with activities/resources, strategies, and management techniques, we turn to the lens of assessment. How do we know that gifted learners have benefited from specialized treatment? How do we know that they have mastered the objectives of learning we had defined at an earlier stage of the curriculum development process? Assessment must bring these questions into focus if we are to be able to defend what we do with gifted learners. We need to develop more authentic testing approaches that better approximate the desired behaviors of gifted learners and at the same time recognize the importance of multiple approaches to assessment. Our approach to, and choices in, measuring gifted student learning and instrumentation are crucial at this phase of curriculum development.

Evaluation and Revision

After we are able to answer the questions posed by the assessment process and demonstrate the extent of student learning, we must reflect on what the assessment results mean. We may reenter the design model to determine which lens should be refocused to produce a more positive outcome with gifted learners or to increase the challenge level. We can tinker a bit with each lens or focus on the one that appears to be most responsible for the assessment results. In this way, curriculum evaluation becomes linked to curriculum improvement — the desired next step in the process, and the one that reactivates the entire system of curriculum design and development.

FOUNDATIONAL CONCERNS

The curriculum development process may be perceived as dynamic and ongoing. But special considerations underlie the process, foundational concerns that affect the dynamism of the model. These concerns are treated in the last three chapters of Part One. One is curriculum alignment — how to ensure that all of the lenses fit together in a congruent manner. A second concern is for the overall framework of the curriculum, its articulation in a scope and sequence model. The third concern regards implementation of new curricula in the context of a school system — how it impacts on staff and how it has to impact on teacher evaluation and staff development systems.

Part One of this book should guide the reader through a series of curriculum adventures with a hand lens that allows for pausing and reflecting on elements of design along the pathway of curriculum development. The path is marked, but the route may be traversed from any direction with longer pauses at certain stations if desired. Through the lens, one can study the relevant elements in curricula for gifted learners. Through the thoughtful and careful analysis of these design elements, appropriate and effective curricula will be constructed for gifted learners.

REFERENCES

Feldman, D. (1986). *Nature's gambit*. New York: Basic Books.

CHAPTER ONE

Scope and Sequence in Curricula for the Gifted

T he process of curriculum planning and development is complex, dynamic, and generative in nature, and our approach to the task should reflect that reality. An emphasis on comprehensive planning of an appropriate curriculum for gifted learners is called for to activate the curriculum development process on a large scale and to ensure its relevancy within a given school district. This sort of K-12 curriculum planning is a relatively recent phenomenon for gifted educators who historically ascribed to program development at more narrowly prescribed grade levels. Just as expert problem solvers spend more time on planning than on any other aspect of the problem-solving process, so we in gifted education must become expert at planning and organizing a meaningful scope and sequence of curriculum experiences for our most talented learners.

ASSUMPTIONS ABOUT GENERAL CURRICULA

Certain underlying assumptions about the general curriculum must be stated before we begin the work of developing scope and sequence in curricula for gifted learners.

1. *General school curricula are inappropriate for gifted learners.* We recognize that the needs of gifted learners are atypical in respect to several core areas: rate of learning (Keating, 1976), capacity for in-depth learning (Renzulli, 1977), ability to manipulate conceptual schemata (Sternberg, 1985), and need

for diversity and challenge in learning experiences (Passow et al., 1982). This leads us to realize that school curricula organized around the needs of typical learners, with its spiral effect of incremental learning modules coupled with heavy doses of reinforcement around a given skill or concept, is the pattern for basic text materials as well as the dominant mode for classroom instruction. One of the first issues to be addressed in developing curricula for the gifted, then, is how to modify or adapt the general curriculum within core areas to better respond to their atypical needs. Clearly, if the core curriculum is to be meaningful for the gifted during their K-12 experience, accelerative, enriched, and conceptual reorganization must occur.

2. *Appropriate differentiation of the curriculum in one area and at one grade level affects all areas and levels.* Curriculum development for the gifted, then, has to be viewed as a long-term process involving adaptation of the current curriculum, infusion of appropriate extant curricula for the gifted, and the development of new curricula. Most curriculum work that has been done for the gifted has taken an isolationist perspective — conceptualized and written with the idea of being "the curriculum for the gifted." Consequently, committees of writers struggled with key models and concepts as they strove to create a "new" curriculum, appropriate only for the gifted in some special setting. What that approach has fostered is a fragmentation of curriculum experiences for the gifted, and frequently the curriculum is organized from a faulty understanding of the models and concepts it purports to convey.

   Some of the best curricula used with the gifted was not written for them deliberately. The major curriculum projects of the 1960s in science, mathematics, English, and social studies (MACOS) have proved highly useful with gifted populations even though they were not so intended. The *Junior Great Books Program* and *Philosophy for Children,* both widely used curricula in gifted programs, were not developed expressly for the gifted. Tested curriculum materials like these can save districts the time and expense of trying to reinvent what would clearly be an inferior wheel. And more effort should be expended in bridging the district core curriculum to appropriate adaptations of it for gifted learners. To conceptualize curriculum development as a short-term activity is to misunderstand the nature and scope of the process that should be undertaken.

3. *A curriculum plan for the gifted must be written down and communicated appropriately within a school district.* A curriculum has a recognizable shape or form only when it is written. What goes on in a classroom between teacher and learner is evanescent if the experiences are not recorded. What curriculum planning provides is a sense of purpose and direction in areas of educational value that both teacher and student explore. A curriculum for the gifted should give educational personnel and the community an understanding of what areas of investigation are valuable and why, how students will meet their learning objectives, and by what means they will be evaluated. A curriculum for the

gifted emphasizes purpose, means, and ends somewhat equally and in a manner that the lay public can understand. The obligation to communicate what is distinct about a program for the gifted is paramount, and the strength of that distinction lies in effective curriculum planning.

If we believe these assumptions to be true, we must advocate a curriculum planning effort that will allow for comprehensive and articulated curriculum experiences for gifted learners at all stages of their development. Unfortunately, many school districts have chosen to approach curriculum development at the level of unit development, in which individual teachers organize a teaching unit on a topic of interest and need in the gifted program. This work is termed "unfortunate" in that a great deal of teacher time and energy, as well as district financial resources, are required to consummate the curriculum products, and in the end the school district typically ends up with idiosyncratic pieces of curricula that can be interpreted and taught only by the teacher who developed them. No real curriculum planning or development has occurred — only the random act of writing unrelated individual units.

PURPOSES OF SCOPE AND SEQUENCE DEVELOPMENT

Although working on individual units of instruction is a worthy task for teachers at the classroom level of instruction, it is inappropriate in building an entire school district effort. Rather, scope and sequence development is helpful as a starting point. Scope and sequence developmental work can serve several inter-locking purposes for a school district:

1. It can be a planning tool to define curriculum direction.
2. It can help define gaps in current curriculum materials and resources.
3. It can serve to define student expectation levels in curriculum areas that can be evaluated.

DEFINITIONS

In beginning to consider the tasks associated with developing scope and sequence in curricula for gifted learners, it may be useful to examine what we mean by the terms "scope" and "sequence," and the decision criteria for each. *Scope* refers to the expansiveness and comprehensiveness of any given curriculum. Criteria to consider in deciding the scope of a given curriculum might be:

- *What are the important knowledge, skills, concepts, and attitudes for the gifted learner to master?* We can teach the gifted many things, but we have limited time. Given the parameters of time and developmental readiness, what are the broad areas of study to which they should be exposed at the K-12 levels of schooling?

- *How broadly should various skills and concepts be presented?* We must consider how topics are treated in a curriculum for gifted learners. Should we treat some topics at a survey level and others in greater depth? What decision criteria should guide our thinking on this issue?
- *What critical exposures to new content should the gifted learner have?* In a time of knowledge explosion, a curriculum for the gifted should promote opportunities for understanding whole fields such as biochemistry, systems analysis, and computer graphics. How do we systematically ensure that our content is continually being updated?
- *How much time will be needed to engage in various topics at an appropriate depth?* As we grapple with decisions of scope, we must be mindful of the interaction effect of time. Teaching less at a given stage of development may be preferable if it is taught well and at an appropriate depth. Brief coverage of many topics may be far less meaningful.
- *Is the teaching staff capable of delivering the nature and extent of the proposed curriculum for the gifted learner?* The more we expand curricula for the gifted, the more we stretch existing resources to handle it. Teachers of the gifted need to feel confident in their skills to deliver a particular type of curriculum before it should become a part of the plan. Staff development can assist in this endeavor, but it is not a substitution for being well grounded in a curriculum area one is expected to teach.

Sequence

Sequence refers to the organizing and ordering of curriculum experiences to maximize learner effects. Questions to be asked by curriculum planners about sequence include:

- *At what stages is the gifted learner ready for certain curriculum experiences?* Most gifted learners show advanced development in key curriculum areas, so the idea of setting upper-level expectations by grade level changes for this population. But we don't really know what the appropriate upper limits might be without more experimentation. Thus, we need to carefully consider readiness of this population in each core area of the curriculum.
- *What are appropriate developmental transitions in shaping curricular order?* Schools are organized along elementary, middle, and secondary components. Curricula for the gifted shift dramatically as students move from one school context to the next. How can we smooth out these transitional points to allow for greater continuity and challenge in curricula for the gifted at each stage?
- *What is the desired cumulative effect of gifted learners' engagement in specified curriculum experiences?* We should be able to answer the question of what outcome expectations we have for students who have been in specialized programs for 12 years. Should not these expectations be both greater and different from those of students not participating in those experiences? The cumulative effect of gifted programs should be stated and used as a reference point for developing a reasonable sequence of curriculum experiences.

■ *What contents, processes, and products constitute logical extensions of the curriculum at key points in the schooling process?* When curricula are organized at high levels to begin with, it is difficult to know what the next logical area to study might be. For example, should students move from one type of writing to another or become more proficient in one as they move from grade 6 to grade 7? This type of sequencing issue is difficult to make decisions about, yet it is central to continuing to challenge gifted learners.

A PROCESS FOR DEVELOPING SCOPE AND SEQUENCE IN CURRICULA

In addition to asking key questions about the definitional structure of scope and sequence in curricula for gifted learners, a process for engaging in development is essential. This entails several steps.

1. *Conduct a curriculum needs assessment.* This initial step in the process provides a school district with basic planning information that can help direct the curriculum effort productively. Being able to articulate what the current curriculum is for gifted learners, how it differs from what is available for all learners, and where the gaps are is a key part of developing meaningful curriculum products.

2. *Develop an overall curriculum framework of K-12 process and product goals.* Once a school district has determined "what is" in its curriculum for gifted learners, educators are in a better position to fashion "what might be" in the curriculum so it is cohesive from kindergarten through 12th grade. At this stage of the process, product or outcome goals should be developed for gifted students, a clear set of expectations based on their participating in a program for 13 years. Along with this, process goals for teachers should be developed, strategies that will enable them to help students reach the stated expectation levels. These goal statements should be translatable to content, process-product, and "great ideas" interdisciplinary curricula — all necessary approaches in a comprehensive program for the gifted learner.

3. *Develop goals and learner outcomes K-12.* After the framework has been conceptualized, goals and learner outcomes have to be delineated for all areas of the school curriculum. The general school curriculum is to be used as a touchstone in this effort so the resulting product circumscribes what is required for all learners, but is reorganized and enriched more appropriately for the gifted. Particular attention must be paid to the alignment process linking goals to learner outcomes in a coherent fashion but also linking learner outcomes across grade-level clusters at increasing levels of complexity.

4. *Decide on an appropriate coding format for representing scope and sequence work to various publics.* Once goals and student learner outcomes have been delineated, it is useful to consider how best to translate scope and sequence work to various groups. Many states require the learner outcome framework for their general curricula, but some gifted educators may wish to depart from

that format and take an approach that links immediately to classroom materials, activities, or teaching units.

5. *Write a K-12 outline for each major curriculum strand.* Many gifted programs use curriculum content that is not formally a part of the general school curriculum. These areas have to be well defined at each stage of development, and linked in a scope and sequence model. One of the central issues in doing this for an area such as thinking skills, for example, is the choice of paradigm and the consistency of its use across grade levels. A second issue relates to the complexity of the assigned tasks at each stage. Deductive reasoning can be taught at increasing levels of difficulty, but some designation of how that is occurring is necessary to understand that progressive development in that thinking skill area is going on.

6. *Align all goals and outcomes with exemplary activities and resources/materials.* It is insufficient to stop the scope and sequence process short of aligning learner outcomes to actual teaching units, resources, and activities. Only by including this step can we be satisfied that the curriculum in the classroom reflects the general direction desired. This is the level of alignment at which the ideal curriculum plan merges with the real classroom lesson plan.

7. *Identify areas within the scope and sequence for curriculum unit development.* The next stage in developing scope and sequence is to identify gaps in teaching units and curriculum materials. Typically, as one completes the alignment process, an imbalance between what should be taught and what is being taught becomes apparent. The reason for the gap is often a lack of "hands-on" material. This issue can now be addressed systematically.

8. *Implement the scope and sequence model with staff and gifted students.* At this final stage of the process, several new initiatives must be begun, for scope and sequence work now has to relate to the larger ongoing systems of staff development and evaluation in a given school district. Three major tasks might be identified:

    a. Structure staff development sessions.
    b. Monitor implementation.
    c. Evaluate student progress at requisite grade levels.

Curriculum Issues

Assessment of written curricula in several districts suggests the need for more internal consistency in curricular products to meet students' specific individual needs and interests. This assessment also reveals a number of critical issues to be considered in future planning and curriculum development:

- Providing for continuity and articulation in curricula for the gifted.
- Systematic planning to improve curricula for the gifted.
- Developing a comprehensive plan for curriculum development.
- Moving from the development of curricula at the micro level of unit development to the macro level of scope and sequence development.

Curriculum Alignment

One of the major difficulties in developing written curricula for gifted learners is to make curriculum documents relevant at two levels of the program simultaneously. First, the design model must reflect broad program goals and learner outcomes across the span of K-12. Second, the model must at the same time adequately represent and be aligned with what is actually taking place with gifted learners in the classroom. Thus, broad-level planning must be congruent with more specific planning at the level of classroom implementation.

Organization of Curriculum Products

Undue concern about the form a curriculum product takes can absorb valuable time and energy. Yet the shape of the product can predestine its usability within the school system itself. Because most states have developed state-wide learner outcomes, which local school districts are to adopt or modity, this same framework seems reasonable to illustrate adaptations for gifted learners.

Even though individual teachers may prefer curriculum representation by activity clusters or key materials and texts, the purpose of the broader level of specificity is central to the curriculum development task. In an attempt to ensure curriculum alignment, however, documents should always be cross-coded to specific teacher activities at requisite grade levels, curriculum resource units used with the gifted program, "packaged" programs such as *Junior Great Books,* and key materials and texts. In that way, elements of the design process will be linked at all levels of the curriculum development process, from the characteristic

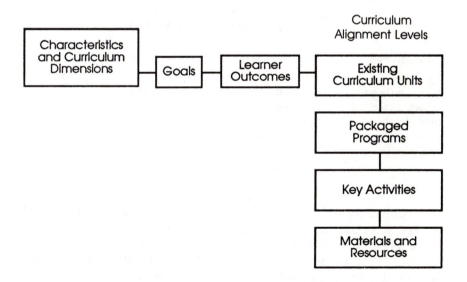

Figure 1.1
LEVELS OF SPECIFICITY IN CURRICULUM ALIGNMENT

and curriculum dimensions all the way down to classroom activities and materials and resources. The levels of specificity in curriculum alignment are depicted in Figure 1.1.

In preparing well aligned and articulated curriculum products, teachers must be involved in the curriculum work in various organizational patterns. Grade-level clusters should be identified according to natural grouping patterns in a given school district program. The following levels give examples of typical points to specify anticipated learner outcomes for the gifted. This specification also pre-shapes the levels at which student progress might be measured.

Level I	K–3	cluster defined by cross-disciplinary teaming and common core
Level II	4–6	cluster defined by cross-disciplinary teaming and common core
Level III	7–8	subject specific classes in all core areas, special classes, interdisciplinary offerings
Level IV	9–12	subject specific honors, advanced placement, and dual enrollment in selected areas; seminars; independent study options, etc.

The curriculum alignment model shown in Table 1.1 summarizes the nature of the process.

Table 1.1
CURRICULUM ALIGNMENT MODEL

Program Level	Alignment Needs and Issues	Classroom Level
Goals and learning objectives by grade-level clusters (K-3, 4–6, 7–8, 9–12)	Grade-level objectives Sub-objectives Curriculum units Packaged programs Instructional processes	Activities Materials Resources Delivery systems

Many existing state and local scope and sequence documents are organized by key goals and learner outcomes for all learners. Therefore, this basic framework should be adapted for gifted learners, with an alignment process allowing all classroom teachers at all grade levels to understand how their work with gifted learners fits into the larger schema. This also allows curriculum developers to spot weak links in the overall process, leading to decision points about the curriculum. These decisions might include:

- Developing teaching units to help bridge where the program should be rather than where it is at the classroom level.
- Implementing existing packaged gifted programs to fill gaps in the model at the classroom level.
- Selecting key materials to assist in carrying out the curriculum plan at the classroom level.

Through the process of alignment, one can more easily determine where curriculum needs may lie, and make more intelligent decisions about how to proceed to meet them.

The alignment process might employ numerous approaches. One is to analyze carefully the sub-components of a given learner outcome. Figure 1.2 illustrates a learner outcome conceptualized for mastery by gifted students at the end of eighth grade, when students should be able to use appropriate texts such as fiction, nonfiction, poetry, letters, directions, and reference material to accomplish the various purposes for reading. By breaking down the desired outcome

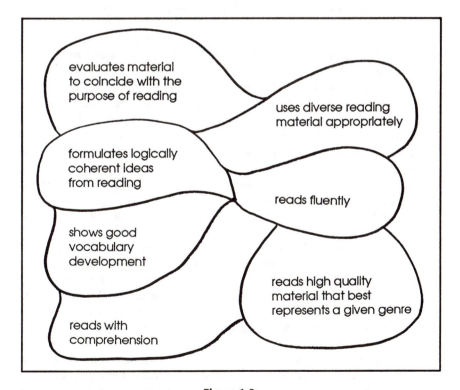

Figure 1.2
ANALYSIS OF THE SUB-COMPONENTS OF A SAMPLE LEARNER OUTCOME

into constituent parts, we can begin to see where individual grade level emphasis might be. (An extended example is given in the Appendix to Chapter One.)

Organizing for Curriculum Alignment

How might we best organize to accomplish curriculum alignment in school districts? One model is to form grade-level cluster teams of teachers of the gifted so K-3 teachers, for example, could "work down" from the learner outcome conceptualized for mastery at the end of grade 3. In like fashion, 4-6, 7-8, and 9-12 teams can be organized. The task for teams is to generate the necessary sub-outcomes, activities, and key resources at each level in order to align the outcomes for relevant content areas and special strands in the curriculum. A standard outline may be provided to ensure consistency in form. Another needed alignment task is to ensure levels of specificity across grade levels for sub-objectives, consonance of language, and comparable numbers of activities and resources across the clusters. In this way, the curriculum document can be perceived as somewhat standardized, even though several different individuals developed pieces of it.

Other approaches also could work. Team leaders at the elementary level and department chairpersons at the secondary level, for example, could provide this function. One issue to consider, however, is the extent to which the individuals working with the curriculum alignment process understand the relevant components of the outcome and are sufficiently knowledgeable about what goes on in the classroom at each requisite level.

Teachers' involvement with curriculum development, especially at their level of operation, is an advantageous process that sets the stage for greater acceptance and use of the curriculum being developed. Teachers also must be integrally involved with writing down these linkages, because they represent the internal workings of the program that only they know. Teacher involvement in the process is crucial to its success.

Another important concern in alignment is in matching the gifted program goals, outcomes, and activities/resources to those in the general curriculum. This task in itself is monumental, because many school districts do not have written curriculum guides specifying major learner outcomes by content areas. As each state has moved to develop learner outcomes, however, more uniformity and standardization around basic curricula are taking place. Every school district could use a state document of this nature, as the foundation for aligning the gifted curriculum to the basic curriculum. One way to attempt this is to match, in a column model, the major goals and outcomes within a given area, for easy comparison. Table 1.2 provides an example in the area of reading, within language arts.

This approach visually allows even a casual reader to discern the differences between the focus of the gifted reading curricula and that of the general curricula in reading. The "match-up" conveys the necessary relationships between the two curricula. Some school districts prefer to use a coding format that merely keys

Table 1.2
**MAJOR GOALS AND OUTCOMES IN EXAMPLE GIFTED PROGRAM AND
BASIC EDUCATION PROGRAM**

Gifted Program Goal in Language Arts and Underlying Outcomes	Basic Education Goal in Language Arts and Underlying Outcomes
To develop critical reading behaviors*	To develop reading skills
The gifted learner will be able to:	The typical learner will be able to:
a. analyze material read from high quality children's literature and selected classical and contemporary adult literature	a. read with fluency selected material
b. interpret reading material in various genres	b. develop vocabulary at appropriate levels
c. evaluate authors' perspective and point of view	c. read with comprehension
d. draw inferences based on selected reading	d. appropriately use various genres of reading material
e. use deductive reasoning to understand arguments in written form	e. develop library reference skills
f. develop analogical reasoning skills based on reading	f. develop analytical and interpretive skills in reading

* Basic reading goal and underlying outcomes will be tested at each appropriate level in the gifted program to ensure mastery. The *emphasis* of the program, however, is best reflected in the outcomes given here.

by number and letter the relationship of the gifted and the general curricula. Using this shorthand method, column 1 in Table 1.2 could be referenced as Goal 2, Outcomes a-f. Seeing the comparisons juxtaposed, however, serves best. The explanatory note at the bottom of column 1 is significant in that it describes how the two columns interface. Without it, a reader might assume that the basic skills of reading are not addressed at all in the gifted program and that accountability for mastery of these basic skills is missing. Relationships to the general or basic curriculum have to be made patent so that educators can understand the differences in educational focus between general education and gifted education in key content areas.

SUMMARY

Scope refers to the comprehensiveness of a curriculum. Sequence is the organizing and ordering of curriculum experiences to maximize learner effects.

In developing scope and sequence for gifted learners, educators have to assume that the general school curriculum is inappropriate for the gifted; that curriculum development for the gifted is a long-term process encompassing all areas and all grade levels; and that the curriculum plan must be written and understood throughout the school district. Scope and sequence development can serve as a planning tool, can define gaps in curriculum materials and resources, and can define student expectation that can be evaluated.

The process involved in developing scope and sequence is to (a) conduct a curriculum needs assessment, (b) develop an overall framework of process and product goals, (c) develop goals and learner outcomes, (d) determine how to make it understandable to those involved, (e) write a K-12 outline for each major strand, (f) align goals and outcomes with activities and resources, (g) identify areas for unit development, and (h) implement.

Curriculum alignment means making curriculum documents relevant across the entire K-12 span and adequately representing what is occurring in the classroom. Thus documents should be cross-referenced to goals, learner outcomes, and specific activities and resources at each grade level. This can be accomplished by generating sub-outcomes, activities, and key resources at each level to align the outcomes for content areas and strands in the curriculum. Specificity can be encouraged through sub-objectives, consonance of language, and comparable emphases. One model may be found in the Gary Language Arts Scope and Sequence that follows.

QUESTIONS FOR REFLECTION

1. What would you predict a curriculum needs assessment might reveal in a school district? How might it be used to encourage change?
2. What is your understanding of how curriculum decisions are made? How might this process be improved?
3. What are the benefits of developing a scope and sequence document from K-12?
4. What procedures for curriculum alignment need to be undertaken for ease of communication and understanding of the total curricular structure? How might teachers best be involved in the process? Administrators? Parents?

REFERENCES

Keating, D. (1976). *Intellectual talent*. Baltimore: The Johns Hopkins University Press.
Passow, A. H., et al. (1982). LTI List of Differential Curriculum Principles for Gifted Programs. Committee Report to the National/State Leadership Training Institute on the Gifted and Talented. Office of the Superintendent of Schools, Ventura County, California.
Renzulli, J. (1977). *The enrichment triad*. Wethersfield, CT: Creative Learning Press.
Sternberg, R. (1985). *Beyond IQ*. New York: Basic Books.

A Scope and Sequence of the Gary (Indiana) Community School District Language Arts Curriculum K–12

LANGUAGE ARTS GOALS K-12

As a result of K-12 gifted programs, students will be able to:

1. Develop critical reading behaviors.
2. Develop critical listening skills.
3. Develop proficiency in grammar and usage.
4. Develop proficiency in oral communication.
5. Analyze and evaluate various literary forms (genres) and ideas (themes) in world literature.
6. Develop expository and technical writing skills.
7. Develop cross-cultural understanding through studying the literature, art, and music of selected African, Oriental, Indian, and European cultures.

Goal #1
Develop Critical Reading Behaviors

By the end of grade 3, gifted students should be able to:

A. Read fluently at least two grade levels above placement.
B. Comprehend stories read to them.
C. Understand character, plot sequencing, and setting in stories.
D. Interpret the meaning of stories/passages they read.
E. Write stories based on reading experiences.

F.   Master vocabulary two grade levels above placement.
G.   Participate effectively in literary discussion.
H.   Manage independent writing.
I.   Demonstrate proficiency in the skills of comprehension, application, and classification.

By the end of grade 6, gifted students should be able to:

A.   Read fluently at least two grade levels above placement.
B.   Interpret the meaning of stories read.
C.   Understand the literary structures of motivation, theme, climax, and story development.
D.   Compare and contrast stories/passages read according to content and form.
E.   Write essays, based on original ideas.
F.   Master vocabulary two grade levels above placement.
G.   Evidence skills in the inquiry process of discussion.
H.   Manage independent reading projects.
I.   Demonstrate proficiency in the skills of analysis, synthesis, and evaluation.

By the end of grade 8, gifted students should be able to:

A.   Comprehend advanced (adult) reading material on diverse topics.
B.   Analyze, interpret, and evaluate literature read.
C.   Recognize and understand characteristics of all literary forms and genres.
D.   Conduct debates/panel discussions on readings, using a thesis or key question.
E.   Critique selected readings orally and in writing.
F.   Make valid inferences based on reading selections.
G.   Demonstrate proficiency in recognizing and creating analogies.
H.   Generalize from specific data.

By the end of grade 12, gifted students should be able to:

A.   Analyze and interpret adult reading material in any content domain.
B.   Synthesize ideas about an author's form and content.
C.   Master advanced adult vocabulary.
D.   Critique a reading selection according to a given set of criteria or standards.
E.   Develop an essay that compares key elements used by one author in several works to another author's work.
F.   Demonstrate proficiency in working with inference, inductive and deductive reasoning, analogies, assumptions, and evaluation of arguments.

Goal #2
Develop Critical Listening Skills

By the end of grade 3, gifted students should be able to:

A. Identify verbal and nonverbal cues to meaning.
B. Identify different points of view in oral messages.
C. Recognize cultural differences based on communication behaviors.
D. Listen attentively to various media presentations of appropriate length.
E. Use appropriate audience/listener responses.
F. Follow multi-step oral directions.

By the end of grade 6, gifted students should be able to:

A. Identify relevant information, bias, and details from oral messages.
B. Understand point of view in an oral message.
C. Demonstrate ability to concentrate on listening, given a moderate level of distraction.
D. Provide a summary of an oral presentation.
E. Focus and sustain attention during an oral presentation of 30 minutes.
F. Take accurate notes on underlying ideas presented orally.

By the end of grade 8, gifted students should be able to:

A. Identify criteria for evaluating oral presentations.
B. Make valid inferences and judgments about an oral message.
C. Demonstrate interactive listening skills.
D. Provide constructive feedback at appropriate times in oral discourse.
E. Focus and sustain attention during an oral presentation of 45 minutes.
F. Develop a content outline of oral presentations heard.

By the end of grade 12, gifted students should be able to:

A. Analyze the content of oral presentations of varying lengths.
B. Judge the effectiveness of an oral argument (debate) according to predetermined criteria.
C. Evaluate purposes in oral messages.
D. Analyze the effectiveness of various techniques used to present ideas orally.
E. Demonstrate communication behavior consonant with purpose and intent.
F. Demonstrate interactive listening skills in various settings.
G. Focus and sustain attention during an oral presentation of 60 minutes.
H. Analyze differing perspectives and points of view.

Goal #3
Develop Proficiency in Grammar and Usage

By the end of grade 3, gifted students should be able to:

A. Understand the various purposes of oral and written communication (e.g., describe, persuade, debate).
B. Use correct symbols of capitalization and punctuation appropriate to level.
C. Spell common words correctly.
D. Correct errors in written and oral communication.
E. Recognize nouns, verbs, and adjectives.
F. Create simple, compound, and complex sentences.
G. Use reference tools as needed for developing communication (e.g., dictionary, thesaurus).
H. Design written and oral messages for a variety of purposes (e.g., to entertain, to express feelings, to share information).

By the end of grade 6, gifted students should be able to:

A. Write for various purposes and audiences.
B. Use correct symbols of capitalization and punctuation in all contexts.
C. Use all forms of words correctly.
D. Recognize and use all basic sentence patterns.
E. Correct common usage errors.
F. Write a coherent theme free of mechanical errors.

By the end of grade 8, gifted students should be able to:

A. Write and speak using conventional forms of standard English.
B. Use multiple resources to develop communications.
C. Manipulate grammatical aspects of a theme to achieve a desired effect.
D. Expand and reduce sentence elements for either elaboration or clarity.
E. Analyze complicated sentence structure.
F. Analyze uncommon usage problems.

By the end of grade 12, gifted students should be able to:

A. Proofread, edit, and revise written and oral communications.
B. Apply grammar and usage principles in the writing and oral presentation of coherent ideas.
C. Discriminate choice of style and content based on audience need/demand.
D. Evaluate effective word choice, sentence structure, and passage appropriateness in a variety of contexts.
E. Recognize usage errors in all forms of written and spoken communication.
F. Analyze the evolution of language syntax and usage within a culture.

Goal #4
Develop Proficiency in Oral Communication
By the end of grade 3, gifted students should be able to:

A. Demonstrate poise when speaking before a group.
B. Organize an effective presentation of 5 minutes in length.
C. Use oral communication to create dramatic scenes and situations.
D. Express feelings about self and others in oral form.
E. Demonstrate appropriate language use when speaking.
F. Use voice and physical gestures to create a desired effect.
G. Send and receive oral messages in various forms (e.g., directions, information, ideas, actual and invented dialogue).
H. Use oral communication to enhance social interaction.

By the end of grade 6, gifted students should be able to:

A. Use appropriate articulation, pronunciation, volume, rate, and intonation when speaking before an audience.
B. Adapt language usage to audience setting.
C. Use nonverbal cues to emphasize meaning and enhance oral presentations.
D. Use multiple media in an effective manner.
E. Demonstrate a variety of oral presentation purposes (e.g., to inform, to entertain, to feel, to imagine).
F. Organize an effective presentation of 10 minutes in length.
G. Use oral communication to enhance social relationships.

By the end of grade 8, gifted students should be able to:

A. Use differing organizational patterns for oral presentations, based on purpose and audience.
B. Master parliamentary procedure.
C. Prepare an agenda and lead a group discussion.
D. Use multiple sources to support ideas in oral communications.
E. Demonstrate mastery of the fundamental rules of debate.
F. Use oral communication to express creative ideas and feelings.
G. Use oral communication to enhance social situations.
H. Analyze and evaluate oral presentations of peers.

By the end of grade 12, gifted students should be able to:

A. Participate effectively in a debate structure.
B. Lead a group discussion on a self-selected topic.
C. Prepare and deliver a 15-minute oral presentation on a pre-assigned topic.

D.　Create and act out an original dramatic scene expressing an idea, emotion, or event.
E.　Demonstrate proficiency in extemporaneous speaking.
F·　Analyze and evaluate the effectiveness of any example of oral communication.
G.　Use oral communication to enhance social relationships and situations.
H.　Participate effectively in a panel discussion.

Goal #5
Analyze and Evaluate Various Literary Forms (Genres) and Ideas (Themes) in World Literature

By the end of grade 3, gifted students should be able to:

A.　Identify the basic literary forms of drama, poetry, short stories, nonfiction, letters, myths and fables, biography, and autobiography.
B.　Compare and contrast literary forms at appropriate levels.
C.　Compare and contrast ideas from selections read.
D.　Identify the literary structures of character, plot, setting, and theme in each literary form studied.
E.　Compare and contrast literary devices.
F.　Identify character behavior in selected literature.
G.　Evaluate the effectiveness of alternative endings to selected pieces of literature.
H.　Create a "literary piece" in a given form at the appropriate level.

By the end of grade 6, gifted students should be able to:

A.　Identify the literary devices important to each literary form (e.g., poetry — use of imagery, simile, metaphor, rhyme, alliteration, onomatopoeia).
B.　Compare and contrast literary forms at appropriate levels.
C.　Compare and contrast literary structural elements from two selections read.
D.　Create a piece of literature in any form or style, based on a given idea.
E.　Infer ideas from literary works studied.
F.　Analyze the use of symbols in selected pieces of literature.
G.　Create a "literary piece" in a self-selected form at the appropriate level.

By the end of grade 8, gifted students should be able to:

A.　Analyze and interpret form and idea in "moderately difficult" literary selections.
B.　Compare and contrast literary works from different periods based on a common theme.

C. Employ appropriate critical reading behaviors in encountering new reading material (e.g., finding the main idea, making appropriate inferences, evaluating data given, discerning author's tone).
D. Interpret character motivation in selected literature.
E. Compare literary structural elements from at least four selections read.
F. Create "literary pieces" in at least three different forms.
G. Demonstrate mastery of the creative problem-solving process as it applies to developing an independent/group project.

By the end of grade 12, gifted students should be able to:

A. Analyze and interpret form and idea in "difficult" literary selections.
B. Compare and contrast disparate works of literature according to form, style, ideas, cultural milieu, point of view, historical context, and personal relevance.
C. Evaluate any new piece of literature encountered.
D. Create a piece of literature in a chosen form that successfully integrates form and meaning.
E. Evaluate the potential impact of selected literary works on individual/ collective value systems and philosophies.
F. Create a "literary piece" in a self-selected form at a level appropriate for contest submission.

Goal #6
Develop Expository and Technical Writing Skills
By the end of grade 3, gifted students should be able to:

A. Use at least five forms of public and personal writing (e.g., public-expository essay; report writing, narrative account; private-journal writing, letters).
B. Tailor writing for various audiences.
C. Write about a single event or idea.
D. Demonstrate an understanding of sequence in writing.
E. Illustrate ideas through word choice, graphic representation, and use of space on a page.
F. Exhibit ideational fluency in written form.

By the end of grade 6, gifted students should be able to:

A. Use multiple sources in preparing research reports.
B. Develop a content outline for a report.
C. Prepare a bibliography and use footnotes appropriately.
D. Use descriptive details, reasons for an opinion, concrete examples of a solution to a problem in written form.

E.   Write in narrative, expository, descriptive, and persuasive styles.
F.   Develop effective paragraphs that illustrate appropriate use of chronology, contrast, and cause-and-effect relationships.
G.   Demonstrate basic competency in the writing process (pre-writing, writing, editing, revision).

By the end of grade 8, gifted students should be able to:

A.   Prepare a technical report of 10 pages that follows a standard format (e.g., outline, footnote, bibliography, multiple sources).
B.   Prepare an expository essay of 250 words or more that shows proficiency in idea development, organization, and mechanics.
C.   Use journal writing techniques for weekly entries.
D.   Demonstrate mastery of punctuation, capitalization, grammar, and usage in the context of written work.
E.   Use advanced vocabulary in the context of written work.
F.   Use the workshopping technique with peers to improve individual pieces of writing.
G.   Use appropriate techniques to facilitate the writing process (e.g., visualization, note taking, organizing).

By the end of grade 12, gifted students should be able to:

A.   Prepare a technical report of 20 pages that follows a prescribed format.
B.   Prepare an expository essay of 500 words or more that reflects competency in the blend of form and idea.
C.   Use journal writing techniques for a variety of purposes.
D.   Demonstrate competency in the editing process.
E.   Revise written work to meet the needs of various audiences and purposes.
F.   Use peer review for improvement of individual writing.

Goal #7
Develop Cross-Cultural Understanding Through Studying the Literature, Art, and Music of Selected African, Oriental, Indian, and European Cultures

By the end of grade 3, gifted students should be able to:

A.   Discuss similarities and differences between stories, myths, or folk tales representing two different cultures.
B.   Re-create an artistic piece in the style of a given culture studied.
C.   Create a musical composition reflecting the style of a given culture studied.
D.   Cite similarities and differences in social customs, clothing, and beliefs of two cultures as depicted in their literature, art, and music.

E.   Conduct research on key aspects of a given culture.
F.   Create a "cultural exhibit" demonstrating one dimension of a culture.

By the end of grade 6, gifted students should be able to:

A.   Compare and contrast archetypal literature studied from African, Indian, Oriental, and European traditions.
B.   Compare and contrast art forms studied from African, Indian, Oriental, and European traditions.
C.   Compare and contrast sample musical compositions studied from African, Indian, Oriental, and European traditions.
D.   Conduct research that compares two cultures on key criteria.
E.   Compare and contrast language differences among the cultural traditions studied.
F.   Create a "cultural exhibit" demonstrating two dimensions of two different cultures.

By the end of grade 8, gifted students should be able to:

A.   Analyze and interpret common themes and ideas found in the literature, art, and music of a given culture.
B.   Conduct research on a key idea as it is reflected in the art, literature, and music of a given culture.
C.   Analyze cultural artifacts to derive an elemental understanding of a culture.
D.   Express similar ideas and feelings in two languages.
E.   Analyze differences among artistic forms represented by at least three cultures.
F.   Create a "cultural exhibit" demonstrating multiple dimensions of two different cultures.

By the end of grade 12, gifted students should be able to:

A.   Analyze and interpret key ideas represented by selected literature, art, and music of any given culture.
B.   Create a montage of literature, art, and music in the style of a given culture and period.
C.   Use an understanding of cultural "motifs" to enhance oral and written communication.
D.   Display oral and written proficiency in a second language that reflects a cultural tradition different from America.
E.   Demonstrate an understanding of global interdependence as evidenced by the similarities in cultural traditions, artifacts, etc.
F.   Use appropriate problem-solving strategies in focusing on world problems, highlighted in literature read.

SAMPLE LANGUAGE ART ACTIVITIES KEYED TO GOALS AND OBJECTIVES BY LEVEL

Goals and Objectives	Goal Level
Have the students write about their interpretations of the theme, mood or tone, author's style, descriptive language, and point of view in a book.	Goal 5A intermediate
Have students select a book to read and choose a special follow-up project to do (e.g., oral book report, taped book report, imaginary interview with the author or a character, a poster advertising the book, a skit about a favorite scene, a puppet show, or a cartoon strip).	Goal 1H intermediate
Develop group definitions of literary criticism.	Goal 1E junior high
Research the time period, clothing, or customs of a book.	Goal 7E primary
Use a character's words and actions to write about a character's feelings.	Goal 6E intermediate
Relate causes and effects of a character's problems with problems of students.	Goal 5F primary
Have students make outlines and flow charts to develop sequencing skills.	Goal 6D primary
Engage in role playing and creative dramatics to understand relationships.	Goal 4D high school
Visit an art museum.	Goal 7A high school
Attend various ethnic festivals.	Goal 7F junior high
Present skits or puppet plays.	Goal 4C primary
Listen to tapes to make comparisons, judge the qualifications of a speaker, evaluate what is being said, and judge for bias and methods of delivery.	Goal 2A intermediate
Listen critically to a variety of sources such as television, sociodramas, assembly programs, radio	Goal 2B junior high

broadcasts, dramatizations, and dialogues to
evaluate ideas and values transmitted.

Chart the characteristics of a good listener.	Goal 2C junior high
Keep a journal in which to write ideas about the events that occur in the world around you.	Goal 6C junior high
Make a list of feelings you've experienced today.	Goal 6C high school
Write your ideas of friendship and put them in a letter to a friend.	Goal 6E intermediate
Write an editorial showing the logic steps you used to reach a conclusion.	Goal 1G high school
Present choral readings.	Goal 4C primary
Stage radio and television broadcasts to satirize current shows.	Goal 4D high school
Write haiku and cinquain poetry.	Goal 5F junior high
Create rebus stories.	Goal 5G intermediate
Study the origins of the English language and its changes through the years.	Goal 3F high school
Play word classification games, using the parts of speech.	Goal 3C intermediate
Paint prepositions for art as abstractions (e.g., across, under, down).	Goal 3C intermediate
Study adjectives by making a game of developing descriptive phrases.	Goal 3E primary
Make a "wordbook" in which students focus their attention on the interaction of different forms of words and their functions by drawing cartoons or animated word pictures.	Goals 3C/D intermediate
Do an independent project on the author's time period or cultural background of stories read.	Goal 1H intermediate

List events that happen in a story in the order in which   Goal 6D primary
they are most important to you. Explain why.

RESOURCE UNITS

The following topical units have already been developed for use at grades K-6 and appear in the existing curriculum guide for the Gary Community School District. These units are cross-referenced to each of the language arts goals delineated in the preceding section of this document.

Unit	Goal
1. Oral language	4
2. Dictation	4
3. Journal writing	6
4. Choral speaking and rhythm instruments	2, 4
5. At the concert (listening skills)	2
6. Water animals	1, 2, 4, 6
7. Public speaking	4
8. Indian dunes	1, 2, 4, 6

Key Packaged Programs Used

Junior Great Books has been cited as a key resource for use at all levels of the gifted program in elementary and junior high. No other set of packaged materials developed for use with the gifted learner has been cited.

CHAPTER TWO

Correspondence Between Gifted Learner Characteristics and Curricula

T he beginning point for all meaningful curricula for the gifted must be their individual and group characteristics and needs. Existing curricula found to be effective with them have evolved primarily from this understanding (VanTassel-Baska et al., 1988; Maker, 1982). Although most effective approaches to curricula rely on introducing advanced skills and concepts at younger ages, thus tuning in to advanced cognitive development in specific domains, this approach demands sensitivity to the level and learning capacity of a student at a given stage of development.

COGNITIVE CHARACTERISTICS OF THE GIFTED

Characteristics and needs perceived as important for identification of the gifted are also indispensable for curriculum design. A few of these characteristics are related to curriculum considerations in the following discussion.

Manipulation of Abstract Symbol Systems, Rapid Learning of New Material

In the cognitive area, the ability to manipulate abstract symbol systems much better than average age peers obviates against a lockstep, incremental part-to-whole teaching-learning process, which is often the practice in the regular classroom. The rate and pace of gifted students' ability to learn material and the manner in which they can process large amounts of information point to the need for advanced work early. Many of the gifted are early readers, operationally two to six years ahead of their age peers. The power of intellectual thought of gifted students enables them to master concepts and systems of thought holistically rather than piecemeal, reducing the time needed to teach them any given topic. Their general quickness and alertness can be transformed into boredom and frustration when they are held back in a regular classroom situation, or when they are submitted to a start-and-stop method of reaching a given point in a set of materials and being told to wait until the rest of the class is ready to go on.

Affectively, many gifted learners are highly impatient. When appropriate pacing and what is actually happening in the classroom are disparate, their frustration is heightened. A greater degree of sensitivity, even mild hyperactivity and central nervous system reaction, can cause an internal reaction against the "braking mechanism" that tends to occur in learning when they are not allowed to move ahead at their own rate. Moreover, the socioemotional development of the gifted is impaired by lack of exposure to peers at their level. The only satisfactory balm for a gifted child who is ostracized in a typical classroom is to find "learning mates," even if they are imported from across a city or found two grade levels up.

Symbol system manipulation is probably first noticed in young gifted children who read early. Because language learning is a powerful key to other forms of learning, it becomes a good example of a crucial symbol system. The gifted tend to access this symbol system earlier and more intensely, and master it more rapidly than typical learners. They also are apt to rate reading as a favorite leisure-time activity during the secondary years (VanTassel-Baska, 1983). Should we focus on this *one* symbol system primarily, allowing the gifted to advance and be enriched in all their reading and related language arts experiences? If the answer to this curriculum question is yes, the following elements would seem beneficial as staples in a reading program for the gifted at all levels (VanTassel-Baska, 1991):

- Work out of core materials off-level.
- Literature program based on child-appropriate adolescent and adult literature.
- Writing program that encourages ideas from literature to be elaborated on in building stories and essays.
- Vocabulary development emphasis.
- Reading in the content areas and in biography.
- Use of multicultural literature.
- Sustained foreign language opportunities.
- Emphasis on logic and critical thinking behaviors.
- Diagnostic testing in reading skill areas, with instructional follow-up.
- Spelling work derived from both basal and literary reading selections.
- Storytelling, the reading of one's own stories, and discussing stories read.
- Creation of one's own books, journals, and so on.
- Free reading, based on student interests.

This list of reading program interventions with primary-level gifted learners is typical of the role that key characteristics should play in setting the curricular pattern in all content areas. Although the overall emphasis of the program is whole-language experience with a strong emphasis on enrichment of the basic curriculum, the underlying issue of appropriate level work is stressed through careful assessment of reading skill levels at various stages during the school year, through access to advanced reading materials, basal, literary, and content dimensions, and through a requisite vocabulary and spelling program that responds to reading level.

Without this set of interwoven responses to the advanced reading level of a gifted child, progress would be limited. The child would be working out of the basal worksheets provided rather than receiving direct instructional intervention to produce sustained growth. *Acceleration of content*, then, is a key intervention for all gifted learners at each succeeding stage of development in each area where they show advancement.

Mathematics is another field of study in which young gifted learners typically excel and show advanced behavior. Beyond assessment and intervention with basal materials at appropriate levels, the following should be considered in the curriculum:

- Attention to developing spatial skills and concepts through geometry and other media.
- A focus on problem-solving skills with appropriately challenging problems.
- An emphasis on the use of calculators and computers as tools in the problem-solving process.
- More emphasis on mathematical concepts and less on computation skills.
- A focus on logic problems that require deductive thinking skills and inference.
- Applications of mathematics in the real world through creation of projects that provide that experience.
- An emphasis on algebraic manipulations.
- Work with statistics and probability.

Again, the components of an appropriate mathematics curriculum are balanced between advanced content early and enrichment so that skills, concepts, and requisite materials are presented at a challenging level for the child rather than geared to grade level considerations. The child's capacity to manipulate symbol systems is recognized and responded to as a positive learning trait.

Power of Concentration, Diversity of Interests, Curiosity

The gifted tend to have high powers of concentration, wide diversity of interests, and much curiosity. Educators can manipulate learning time in such a way as to promote or impede these characteristics. Focusing on a topic for longer time periods but not every day may evoke a good response. Or the amount of time spent on advanced topics might be doubled. In a secondary English program, for example, more time and emphasis on composition might be warranted; a double period twice a week could be scheduled.

Manipulation of time is only one variable of importance here. In addition, we have to consider how to best nurture these characteristics. Students might be asked to make choices regarding tasks to be accomplished and topics to be studied. The students could be engaged in independent and small-group investigations based on an area of interest. These investigations typically follow a model of organization stressing the processes of problem finding and problem solving and also employing a project orientation. A typical student-generated project might consist of:

— topic negotiated between teacher and learner.
— work to be done planned by student.
— contract solidifying the learning to be accomplished.
— exploration of topic through multiple types of resources.
— mode of resultant product selected from set of alternative options (written, oral, graphic, etc.).
— product judged at a level of adult competence.
— use of higher-level thinking processes to stimulate project development.
— involvement of multiple media in product.
— consideration of marketability in product generation.

Often research skills are taught as a part of the background process for developing products. The following skills emphasize the level of intervention needed to have gifted students engage in research.

Affinity for Making Meaning, Good Perception of Relationships

The gifted have an interest in and capacity for constructing knowledge for themselves, an ability to generate new ideas and to creatively synthesize existing ideas. It is the characteristic that may be most powerful in any program in which gifted students are given the opportunity to explore an idea and make meaning out of it through alternative teaching-learning approaches. A few examples are:

▪ Given the theme of alienation in much of modern literature and art, create a personal statement of that theme in some mode of expression (e.g., poetry, painting, film).
▪ Using art, music, dance and literature, demonstrate the concept of "pattern" by:
— creating a skit.
— performing a play.
— making a film or video.
— developing an exhibit.
▪ Compose a short essay that discusses one of the following ideas about characters in literature:
a. They are blind to their faults.

b. They control their own fate.

c. They behave in foolish ways.

- Cite character examples from at least three different pieces of literature to support your point of view.
- Debate one of the following resolutions:
    a. Studying extinct and endangered species is important for understanding life on earth today.
    b. Studying our past will help us cope with the future. (Use multiple sources including surveys, interviews, and library sources.)

Baska (1989) compiled various cognitive characteristics of the gifted and corresponding needs and interventions, summarized in Table 2.1. This list further explicates the relationship of characteristics of the gifted and implications for curriculum interventions, providing a blueprint for adapting curriculum opportunities for gifted learners at various stages of development.

AFFECTIVE CHARACTERISTICS

Just as we can delineate cognitive characteristics and needs of the gifted, so too we can attend in our curricular planning to their affective needs. Major benefits of gifted programs lie in the affective arena: the opportunity to learn with others of like ability, interest, and temperament; the chance to be accepted for oneself and not perceived as a "nerd" or a "brain"; the feelings of self-worth that accrue from developing good social relationships with others, perhaps for the first time. These affective concerns can also be addressed in a systematic way through a planned curriculum.

In analyzing the relationship of the reading and writing processes to the counseling process, Bailey, Boyce, and VanTassel-Baska (1990) found many similarities. The use of books as cognitive therapy is a well established strategy in counseling circles, as well as in affective curricula for the gifted. Journal writing in particular has been found to be therapeutic for individuals in working through problems. The use of bibliotherapy and writing as curriculum interventions with gifted learners who have typical affective concerns and problems seems to be a way to define academic therapy. Table 2.2 delineates selected affective characteristics and needs of gifted learners and key aspects of the writing process and bibliotherapy that might specifically address them, illustrating the way in which a curriculum might be used to enhance affective development.

One key affective characteristic of the gifted, for example, is a tendency toward perfectionism, a need to perform at the top level in everything undertaken, to get all A's on a report card, and to get 100% on all work done in school. This tendency also produces a fear of failure in the gifted: Can I keep my record in place? Will I slip if I take a particular class or approach a task differently? Concerns of this nature often lead gifted learners to confuse performance with the process of learning; they only learn to be able to demonstrate peak performance

Table 2.1

THE RELATIONSHIP OF CHARACTERISTICS, LEARNING NEEDS, AND CURRICULA FOR THE GIFTED (COGNITIVE)

Characteristic	Learning Need	Curriculum Inference
Ability to handle abstractions	Presentation of symbol systems at higher levels of abstraction	Reorganized basic skills curricula Introduction of new symbol systems (computers, foreign language, statistics) at earlier stages of development
Power of concentration	Longer time frame that allows for focused in-depth work in a given area of interest and challenge	Diversified scheduling of curriculum work "Chunks" of time for special project work and small-group efforts
Ability to make connections and establish relationships among disparate data	Exposure to multiple perspectives and domains of inquiry	Interdisciplinary curriculum opportunities (special concept units, humanities, and the interrelated arts) Use of multiple text materials and resources
Ability to memorize and learn rapidly	Rapid movement through basic skills and concepts in traditional areas; organization of new areas of learning more economically	Restructured learning frames to accommodate capacities of these learners (speed up and reduce reinforcement activities) New curriculum organized according to its underlying structure
Multiple interests; wide information base	Opportunity to choose area(s) of interest in school work and go into greater depth within a chosen area	Learning center areas in the school for extended time use Self-directed learning packets Individual learning contracts

Source: From "Characteristics and Needs of the Gifted" by L. Baska, in J. Feldhusen, J. VanTassel-Baska, and K. Seeley, *Excellence in Educating the Gifted* (pp. 15–28), 1989, Denver: Love Publishing.

Table 2.2
AFFECTIVE NEEDS OF AND RESPONSES TO GIFTED LEARNERS

Selected Affective Needs of Gifted Learners	Responsive Strategies of the Writing Process	Selected Books to Read and Discuss
Dealing with perfectionism Fear of failure	Focusing on process that stresses and rewards rewriting-editing Assigning open-ended writing (in which format and content are not set — no standard for correct response)	Selected biographies of writers

Understanding giftedness
  Feelings of being
  different
  Coping skills
  Need for risk taking
	Clarifying and articulating experiences
	Publishing
	Striving for excellence
	Display of peer group talent
	Trying something new and different with writing techniques, ideas, format
		John Updike's *Selfconscious*

Developing relationships and and social skills	Conferencing and workshopping techniques with peers Sharing writing in a public forum/group setting Developing collaborative product (journal, newspaper collections of written stories)	*David Copperfield* by Charles Dickens
Introversion Communication	Allowing for individual expression of ideas in a protected environment Promoting one-to-one sharing of ideas with teacher Promoting reflection and introspection as part of the writing process Providing opportunity to articulate thoughts, get feedback, and to test ideas, feelings against another's reality	*Hamlet* by William Shakespeare
Too high expectations of self and others	Emphasis on improvement and development as an ongoing process rather than the value of a single product	*The Old Man and the Sea* by Ernest Hemingway
Getting in touch with inner self	Exploring experiences, feelings	*Catcher in the Rye* by J. D. Salinger
Sensitivity toward others Tolerance	Listening to another point of view Sharing time	*Beloved* by Toni Morrison

Source: From "The Writing, Reading, and Counseling Connection: A Framework for Serving the Gifted" by J. M. Bailey, L. N. Boyce, and J. VanTassel-Baska, in J. VanTassel-Baska (Ed.), *A Practical Guide to Counseling the Gifted in a School Setting* (2nd ed.), 1990, Reston, VA: Council for Exceptional Children.

on some task demand rather than to engage in the riskier business of learning for its own sake.

Two curricular strategies that can combat perfectionism are:

— the use of a writing process model that values editing, revision, and open-ended approaches to assignments. In this way the gifted learner can begin to progress as a writer and a learner through levels of reflection necessary for a quality product but also experience new learning along the way.
— the use of carefully selected reading materials, whether biographies or novels, to engage gifted learners in identifying with a character or person who has experienced these same feelings. Through guided discussion, gifted learners can understand a characteristic such as perfectionism as it is reflected in the lives of others and develop related coping strategies in their own lives.

CURRICULUM APPROACHES

The cognitive and affective characteristics of the gifted form the basis for the three major curriculum approaches taken in developing programs for them.

1. *Content-based instruction* at advanced levels, a staple of gifted curricula since the early years, has gained in popularity, particularly with middle school and secondary-level students through the national network of talent searches (Benbow & Stanley, 1983; Sawyer, 1982; VanTassel-Baska, 1985).
2. *Process skills as a basis of curriculum-making* for the gifted has been popularized through model curricula developed around higher-level thinking skills, creative thinking and problem solving (Feldhusen & Treffinger, 1977; Maker, 1982). An emphasis on product development has emerged with curriculum models that key on independent learning for the gifted, the gifted as practicing investigators of real-world problems, and generative learning practices resulting in creative products (Betts & Knapp, 1981; Kolloff & Feldhusen, 1981; Renzulli, 1977, 1986; Treffinger, 1986).
3. *Concept or theme-based curricula* for the gifted is derived from early work on the importance of students' understanding of the disciplines (Phenix, 1964; Schwab, 1964), later translation of these ideas to the field of gifted education (Ward, 1961, 1980), and the popularization of this approach in the context of training educators (Kaplan & Curry, 1985). Theme-based curricula for the gifted also receive support from general education ranks, as well through the ideas engendered in *Paedaeia Proposal* by Adler (1984).

Table 2.3 synthesizes these major ways to adapt curricula for the gifted. Each of the three models is delineated and described in respect to the manipulation process required for differentiation for gifted learners. Applications to curriculum context are provided to illustrate the process at work.

Table 2.3
A COMPARISON OF EFFECTIVE CURRICULUM MODELS
FOR THE GIFTED BY DIFFERENTIATION TECHNIQUES

Models	Differentiation Techniques	Description	Application
Content-based	Acceleration	Allowing students early access to advanced material and moving them through that material at a faster rate than the norm	Access to advanced reading and mathematics materials based on appropriate assessment
	Compression	Using diagnostic-prescriptive techniques to ensure maximum new learning and minimal reinforcement of already mastered materials	Use of subject proficiency tests at beginning of academic year to determine areas of mastery and concentration needs
	Reorganization	Organizing existing text material according to higher-order skills and concepts (i.e., making the "bits" of learning larger based on the underlying system of the discipline of study)	Study of mathematical operations ($+$, $-$, $\times$, $\div$) simultaneously rather than individually or studying all types of addition together (1-digit, 2-digit, 3-digit)
Process-Product based	Infusion and Application	Using a cognitive skill paradigm as a central organizer for selected content.	Application of Guilford-Torrance model of creative thinking in social studies content
		Setting up novel projects that reflect internalization of the cognitive skill paradigm addressed	Use of Parnes/Osborne creative problem-solving model as organizer for group project in ecology

Table 2.3
CONTINUED

Concept- or Theme-based	Integration	Interrelating ideas within domains of inquiry	Study of prediction as an idea in the sciences with applications in geology, biology, chemistry, and medicine
		Interrelating ideas across domains of inquiry	Study of prediction in the larger culture (astrology, tea leaves, social science models)

Another way to approach "differentiating" curricula for the gifted in the regular classroom is to appreciate the ways in which gifted students differ from their age peers in the context of school-based learning experiences. These differential characteristics should underlie curricular differentiation. Consequently, constructing a curriculum model based on an individual child's behavioral assessment profile is a way to define appropriate curriculum experiences for this population. In a model of behavioral assessment of gifted learners in the regular classroom, a curriculum has to be adapted to meet the behaviors manifest in learners.

At the level of the individual learner, Table 2.4 delineates the correspondence of gifted learner characteristics to curriculum emphasis. Thus we can see the direct correspondence between observed behaviors and desired curriculum treatment.

An understanding of key characteristics of the gifted learner is useful in making appropriate curriculum inferences. In addition, testing information and classroom performance tasks are helpful in regard to what is needed in a curriculum. Even though an underachieving child may not reveal her cognitive strengths in the classroom, for example, testing information offers an understanding of her intellectual capacity for challenging curricula. Individual testing of gifted students provides a context for observing these behaviors, through the test items themselves as well as through one-to-one interactions with the child. Careful individual testing of children is highly desirable for assessing their strengths and diagnosing appropriate curricular interventions.

Highly gifted learners are relatively heterogeneous, and the degree of intellectual power they possess is well beyond that of more mildly gifted students. Strengths, interests, and a predisposition toward learning in this population call for special attention on the part of educators, as the general provisions for gifted

Table 2.4
CORRESPONDENCE OF OBSERVED GIFTED CHARACTERISTICS
AND DESIRED CURRICULUM TREATMENTS

Gifted Learner Characteristics	Curricular Treatments
Ready manipulation of abstract symbol systems	Discipline-based systems of knowledge
Power of concentration Curiosity	Focus on interest-based inquiry
Advanced learning rate	Accelerated learning opportunities
Affinity for making meaning	Focus on issues, themes, and ideas within/across knowledge areas
Perfectionism	Creative opportunities that encourage risk taking
High expectations of self and others	Emphasis on learning goals rather than performance goals

learners are rarely sufficient in number or intensity for these students. Moreover, they demand a more individualized approach to planning that may require at least one of the following procedures, if not a combination:

- Development of an individual learning plan that is mutually derived between school and home.
- Development of a mentor relationship with an older student or adult.
- Collaboration with universities that sponsor special programs or offer dual enrollment opportunities.

SUMMARY

Gifted learners have key cognitive and affective characteristics from which curriculum inferences may be made. Cognitive characteristics include the ability to manipulate abstract symbols, rapid learning of new material, high powers of concentration, widely diverse interests, curiosity, an ability to construct knowledge and derive meaning from information, and a good perception of relationships among ideas. Affectively, gifted individuals are often perfectionists and fear failure. They feel "different," and therefore may have trouble developing social relationships with others. They are frequently introverted and introspective and have high expectations of themselves and others. At the same time, they tend to be sensitive and tolerant. A writing process model and selection of appropriate reading materials are key curricular strategies.

Curriculum approaches fall into three major categories: (a) content-based instruction; (b) process-based curricula; and (c) concept or theme-based curricula. Differentiation techniques for content-based instruction include acceleration, compression, and reorganization. Infusion and application are utilized in process-product-based approaches (creative thinking and problem-solving models). Theme-based curricula integrate ideas within and across domains of inquiry.

Highly gifted students call for even more challenging programs. Individualized learning plans, mentors, and collaboration with universities should be considered.

QUESTIONS FOR REFLECTION

1. How can characterological data be used more effectively as a basis for understanding the curriculum needs of the gifted?
2. How might educators systematically respond to the needs of the gifted for challenging curriculum experiences?
3. What major adaptations must be made in the core curriculum to respond effectively to gifted learners?
4. How can professional educators in other roles (e.g., classroom teachers, psychologists, curriculum specialists) help gifted educators plan effective curriculum experiences for the gifted learner?

REFERENCES

Adler, M. J. (1984). *The Paideia program. An educational syllabus.* New York: Macmillan Publishing.

Bailey, J. M., Boyce, L. N., & VanTassel-Baska, J. (1990). The writing, reading, and counseling connection: A framework for serving the gifted. In J. VanTassel-Baska (Ed.), *A practical guide to counseling the gifted in a school setting* (2d. ed.). Reston, VA: Council for Exceptional Children.

Baska, L. (1989). Characteristics and needs of the gifted. In J. Feldhusen, J. VanTassel-Baska, & K. Seeley, *Excellence in educating the gifted* (pp. 15–18). Denver: Love Publishing.

Benbow, C., & Stanley, J. (1983). *Academic precocity.* Baltimore: Johns Hopkins University Press.

Betts, G. T., & Knapp, J. K. (1981). Autonomous learning and the gifted. In A. Arnold et al (Eds.), *Secondary programs for the gifted/talented.* Ventura, CA: Office of Ventura County Superintendent of Schools.

Feldhusen, J., & Treffinger, D. (1977). *Teaching creative thinking and problem solving.* Dubuque, IA: Kendall-Hunt.

Kaplan, S., & Curry, J. (1985). [Presentation to graduate curriculum course.] Berkeley: University of California-Berkeley.

Kolloff, P. B., & Feldhusen, J. F. (1981). PACE (Program for Academic and Creative Enrichment): An application of the three-stage model. *Gifted Child Today, 18,* 47–50.

Maker, C. J. (1982). *Curriculum development for the gifted.* Rockville, MD: Aspen Systems.

Phenix, P. (1964). *Realms of meaning*. New York: McGraw-Hill.

Renzulli, J. (1977). *The enrichment triad*. Wethersfield, CT: Creative Learning Press.

Renzulli, J. (Ed.). (1986). *Systems and models for developing programs for the gifted and talented*. Mansfield Center, CT: Creative Learning Press.

Sawyer, R. N. (1982). The Duke University program to identify and educate brilliant young students. *Journal for the Education of the Gifted, 5*, 185–189.

Schwab, J. (Ed.). (1964). *Education and the structure of knowledge*. Chicago: Rand McNally.

Treffinger, D. J. (1986). Fostering effective independent learning through individualized programming. In J. S. Renzulli (Ed.), *Systems and models for developing programs for the gifted and talented* (pp. 429–460). Mansfield Center, CT: Creative Learning Press.

VanTassel-Baska, J. (1983). Profiles of precocity: The 1982 midwest talent search finalists. *Gifted Child Quarterly, 27*(3), 139–144.

VanTassel-Baska, J. (1985). The talent search model: Implications for secondary school reform. Special issue, *National Association of Secondary School Principals Journal, 69*(482), 39–47.

VanTassel-Baska, J. (1991). Identification of candidates for acceleration: Issues and concerns. In T. Southern & E. Jones, *The academic acceleration of gifted children* (pp. 148–161). New York: Teachers College Press.

VanTassel-Baska, J., Feldhusen, J., Seeley, K., Wheatley, G., Silverman, L., & Foster, W. (1988). *Comprehensive curriculum for gifted learners*. Boston: Allyn & Bacon.

Ward, V. (1961). *Educating the gifted: An axiomatic approach*. Columbus, OH: Charles E. Merrill.

Ward, V. (1980). *Differential education for the gifted*. Ventura, CA: Office of Ventura County Superintendent of Schools.

CHAPTER THREE

Philosophy and Goals
for a Gifted Program

D eveloping a philosophy of curricula for the gifted is highly dependent on a school district's belief system about all learners and its value system regarding exceptional learners. A general school district philosophy is a good point of departure to begin articulating a specialized philosophy for the gifted, keeping in mind three basic ideas fundamental to any statement of curriculum philosophy for the gifted:

1. The gifted have a right to an appropriate education, one grounded in the recognition of individual differences and unique learning needs.
2. The gifted need a curriculum responsive to their individual learning rate, style, and complexity.
3. The gifted learn best in an instructional environment that encourages and nurtures inquiry, flexibility, and divergent thinking.

Broadly stated, these ideas may be used to form the core of a differentiated philosophy for these learners, a philosophy concerned with a broad conceptual framework for developing curricula — not a recipe for what topics to include or what specific offering to provide at a given grade level.

In an attempt to design appropriate curricula, the question of purpose has to be central to the planning effort. Tyler (1962) urged educators to consider goals in terms of the question: "What are the educational purposes that schools seek to attain?" Without a clear sense of purpose, curriculum efforts for the gifted will be fragmented and diffused. Goals provide a sense of focus and

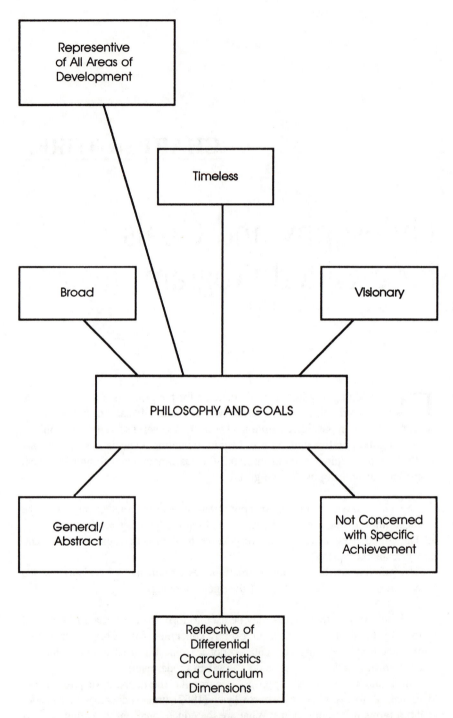

Figure 3.1
**A WEB OF CHARACTERISTICS OF PHILOSOPHY AND GOALS
FOR GIFTED PROGRAMS**

direction toward an ideal end. They should be visionary and not reflect a concern for specific achievement but, rather, point in the direction of maximum competency. They also should reflect a balanced view toward education of the gifted child, in respect to implied approach and potential end state. Figure 3.1 illustrates these interwoven characteristics. The goals should focus equally on areas such as the development of proficiency in core domains of knowledge, higher-order thinking skills, intra- and interdisciplinary concepts, and moral and ethical decision making.

DEVELOPING GOAL STATEMENTS

The development of appropriate goal statements for gifted curricula has received little attention in the field. DiNunno (1982) reported that goals are interpreted as processes around established programs rather than as desired student outcomes. The most common approach to goal development has been to take a list of differentiated principles regarding curricula and translate them into goals (see Passow et al., 1980).

Another approach has been to use a list of identified needs of the gifted as a basis for conducting a local needs assessment to determine consensus on goal emphasis (VanTassel, 1979). Student needs from which goals might be developed include:

A. Basic cognitive skills
   1. Critical thinking
   2. Creative thinking
   3. Problem solving
   4. Research
   5. Decision making
B. Basic affective skills
   1. Tolerance of self and others
   2. Constructive use of humor
   3. Coping with being different
   4. Discriminating between the real and the ideal
   5. Use of high-level sensitivity
C. To be challenged by mastery-level work in areas of strength and interest
D. To be challenged by exposure to new areas
E. To be challenged by the opportunity to see interrelationships
F. To be challenged by experiences that promote understanding of human value systems
G. To be challenged through discussions with intellectual peers
H. To be challenged by activities at complex levels of thought
I. To be challenged through opportunities for divergent production
J. To be challenged by the opportunity for real-world problem solving

Hickey (1988) did a Delphi study of student goals in gifted programs and found that experts in the field converged on only three goals at the elementary level:

1. To provide a learning environment that will permit and encourage the capable student to develop to his/her individual potential while interacting with intellectual peers.
2. To establish a climate that values and enhances intellectual ability, talent, creativity, and decision making.
3. To encourage the development of and provide opportunities for using higher-level thinking skills (analysis, synthesis, evaluation).

From the design perspective set forth in this book, educators might wish to derive a set of goals that correspond to each of the major curriculum dimensions described and then develop affective, social/behavioral, and aesthetic goals that would provide a comprehensive approach to goal setting. An example might be:

A. *Cognitive*
   1. To develop high-level proficiency in all core areas of learning
   2. To become an independent investigator
   3. To appreciate the world of ideas
   4. To enhance higher level thinking skills
   5. To encourage a spirit of inquiry
B. *Affective*
   1. To enhance self understanding
   2. To develop effective coping strategies for being labeled gifted
C. *Social/Behavioral*
   1. To develop appropriate social skills
   2. To enhance understanding of relationships
D. *Aesthetic*
   1. To develop an appreciation of the arts
   2. To enhance creative expression

Delineating Subject Matter Goals

Although defining goals is not always seen as a demanding task if undertaken individually, it can be quite challenging in the context of a school district effort to plan effectively for gifted programs because the success of any such undertaking lies in the ideas as they are shaped by the collective. *Vertical team planning* is essential to the success of goal setting. Articulated goals have to represent the thinking of the kindergarten teacher as well as that of the senior high school teacher. This requires "talking through" what a content-based curriculum should engender in gifted students.

In developing content-based goals for gifted curricula, the following issues should be considered:

- A goal represents an ideal state to be worked toward but not necessarily attained. Thus, content-based goal statements should be worthy enough to work on over 13 years of schooling.
- Content goals for gifted programs should be able to be compared to regular program goals and found to be more challenging, with a greater focus on advanced study, higher-level thinking processes, and interdisciplinary opportunities. Aspects of differentiation should be discernible already at this level of curriculum development.
- All goal statements should convey meaning at all grade levels.
- The goal statements should be comprehensive enough to subsume all worthy objectives and activities currently being addressed in the gifted program, as well as those conceptualized as ideal.
- The goal statements should adequately represent the focus and direction of the actual program.

The initial group session on reaching consensus in the goal statements can take several hours of discussion. The tentative list that emerges from such a planning session should be reworked by the group's facilitator in light of differentiation factors, and returned for a second discussion with the recast goals. After a second session, a set of goal statements that satisfy all criteria can emerge. A sample list of goals in the language arts area might be (from the language arts scope and sequence, Gary Community School Corporation, 1991):

1. Develop critical reading behaviors.
2. Develop critical listening skills.
3. Develop proficiency in grammar and usage.
4. Develop proficiency in oral communication.
5. Analyze and evaluate various literary forms (genres) and ideas (themes) in world literature.
6. Develop expository and technical writing skills.
7. Develop cross-cultural understanding through studying the literature, art, and music of selected African, Oriental, Indian, and European cultures.

Delineating Process Goals

A similar process might be used to decide on process goals for gifted learners, yet the nature of the consensual group make-up should be cross-disciplinary. The fundamental question becomes: Which higher-order skills in what areas do we want the gifted to develop through specialized programs? The answer to that question should be multidimensional in that it considers not only critical and creative thinking skills but also ethical decision-making skills, aesthetic judgment skills, and social skills. Thus, the matrix for decision making around process skill development in programs for the gifted would highlight all four of these dimensions in some way. It might look like this:

Dimensions	Process Goals of the Gifted Program
Cognitive	To develop critical thinking and logical reasoning.
	To develop creative problem-solving abilities.
Affective	To develop moral and ethical decision-making abilities.
Aesthetic	To develop moral judgment.
Social	To develop the skills of leadership.

Delineating Theme-based Goals

Just as gifted programs require content and process goals, they also must have some direction around themes expressed in goal form. Because a myriad of universal themes is available from which to choose, some current examples may be helpful.

The Individual Progress Program (IPP) in Seattle, Washington, has three central themes in its gifted program: origins, change, and systems. These themes are woven into curricula from grades 1–8 on a spiral model that revisits each theme every third year.

The following concept outlines, from the *Charleston High School Scope and Sequence Guide* (1987) in Charleston, West Virginia, have been articulated in the school district's social studies curriculum guide for the gifted:

By the end of grade 12, students will be able to:

1. Understand how the U.S. is not a purely independent entity, but that its present condition is interrelated with the historic, social, and economic development of the rest of the world.
2. Understand how change results out of conflict, individual struggle, leadership, new ideas, and accidental occurrences.
3. Know the major periods of history, including the prehistoric, ancient, classical, medieval, early modern, and contemporary, why these periods are defined as such, what elements of each led to or inhibited the arrival of the next, and the salient aspects that transcend these eras.

Delineating Affective Goals

Many programs for the gifted emphasize personal development, helping gifted learners develop as individuals. Yet, too frequently programs pay lip service to affective development but never articulate what outcomes they hope will accrue to gifted learners in this area. One approach toward affective goal development is to involve counselors and teachers as equal partners in reaching consensus on goals for this area. Again, the local context may dictate the specific goals derived. For example, a racially torn community may wish to institute a goal addressing this set of social problems: "To develop an appreciation of individual and group differences." Or a community that has experienced a recent bout of teen suicide might produce the goal statement: "To help gifted students construct meaning in their lives." A sample set of affective goals compiled from several school districts is:

By the end of the K-12 program, the student will:

1. Demonstrate effective social interactions by receiving a minimum of 80% score on an observation form.
2. Demonstrate understanding and application of coping strategies through the use of journal writing that reflects a good to superior level.
3. Demonstrate effective leadership in the context of peer teaching experiences rated on a 1–5 scale, with the attainment of a rating of 3.
4. Develop a plan that encompasses future academic and career goals that demonstrates long-range planning.
5. Demonstrate 85% proficiency in the acquisition of independent learning habits on a performance checklist.

Philosophy statements and goals set an important tone for curriculum development. Already at this stage of designing curricula, a school district has a unified and consensual focus that directs the course of further curriculum development work. Good goal statements are grounded in good practices of differentiation for gifted leraners and yet are sensitive to more localized concerns. Moreover, they attempt to define key emphases the curriculum will take at a level that students, parents, and other educators can understand and accept.

COMMUNICATING MEANING OF GOAL STATEMENTS

An important step beyond goal delineation must be done by the planning group: The meaning of the goals must be communicated in a way that the lay community can understand. In gifted education, we have developed an idiosyncratic jargon of specialized terms that mean different things to different educators. Curriculum planners must find a way to define terms such as "critical thinking" and "creative thinking" and "research skills" so they can be interpreted the same by all who are involved.

The Appendix to this chapter gives a course of study developed for use in Muskingum County, Ohio, by local and county directors of gifted programs (Muskingum County Board of Education, 1990). It provides an example of appropriate philosophy and goal statements for gifted programs and delineates a set of transitional objectives to help teachers, parents, and students better understand what the goals would mean in classroom practice.

The Appendix illustrates one way of handling the definition of terms: to translate each major goal into underlying objectives that represent constituent elements of the goal. Another approach might be to develop a glossary of terms.

The goal phase of curriculum development is critical for the transition to specific learning objectives, the next stage in the design model and the topic of the next chapter.

SUMMARY

An operative philosophy and a set of goal statements are fundamental to curriculum development because they provide direction and create a consensual perspective among constituent groups on what the curriculum should be. Philosophy and goals should be translated into written statements of purpose for a gifted program. They should be adopted by school boards, if possible, to give them the stature of policy.

There are different approaches to generating goals and different types of goals. From the student's perspective, the gifted have cognitive, affective, social/ behavioral, and aesthetic needs. Along this needs dimension, educators might develop content-based goal statements, process goals, theme-based goals, and affective goals. The key to successful implementation of goals is to communicate their meaning to students, parents, and educators.

QUESTIONS FOR REFLECTION

1. What do curriculum goals communicate about a gifted program?
2. How can we create goals that balance the concern for cognitive and affective development, for aesthetic appreciation and leadership skills, for creative productivity and proficiency in core areas?
3. How do values and beliefs shape thinking about curriculum goals in a school district?
4. How can a philosophy and set of goals be translated into action at the classroom level?

REFERENCES

Charleston High School Scope and Sequence Guide (1987). Charleston, WV.

DiNunno, L. (1982). *Curricular decision making in program development for the gifted and talented.* Unpublished dissertation, University of Virginia, Charlottesville.

Gary Community School Corporation (1991). *Language Arts Scope and Sequence Guide.* Gary, IN: Author.

Hickey, G. (1988). Goals for gifted programs: Perceptions of interested groups. *Gifted Child Quarterly, 32*(1), 231–233.

Muskingum County Board of Education. (1990). *Muskingum County Course of Study for the Gifted.* Zanesville, OH: Author.

Passow, A. H., et al. (1980). *LTI report on differentiated curriculum.* Ventura, CA: Office of the Ventura Superintendent of Schools.

Tyler, R. W. (1962). *Basic principles of curriculum and instruction.* Chicago: University of Chicago Press.

VanTassel, J. (1979). A needs assessment model for gifted education. *Journal for the Education of the Gifted, 2*(3), 141–148.

Muskingum County (Ohio) Course of Study for Gifted Students Position Statement

Gifted students have been identified as a population in our schools that requires a differentiated curriculum of greater challenge, more complexity and abstraction, and faster paced instruction. We recognize the diverse instructional levels of the individuals within the identified gifted population, and these differences make creating a common course of study a complex task. However, we believe to ensure learning progress on a continuum and to avoid a hit-and-miss approach to instruction, a course of study for the gifted can serve as an invaluable document.

The areas included in this course of study are multidisciplinary in nature and reflect the essential content defined in the Ohio Rules for School Foundation Units for Gifted Children. This course of study reflects the common needs of gifted children in the Superior Cognitive, Specific Academic, and Creative Thinking categories. Gifted students must be given opportunities to develop competence in the areas of creative thinking, critical thinking, creative problem solving, higher-level thinking (Bloom's taxonomy), logical thinking, research methods, oral and written expression, and social-emotional development. These essential areas are critical to enable gifted students to make full use of their capabilities and to enable them to perform at levels of excellence in their unique talent areas.

The purpose of this course of study is to guide and assist classroom teachers in serving the gifted child in the regular classroom. By including broad-based goals with sample objectives, teachers may use this document as a tool to develop challenging and appropriate curricula for the gifted at any level and within any core domain of inquiry. We support and encourage the teacher practice of prescriptive instruction, in which pre-assessment is used to determine the instructional levels of individual students. We also support the development of curricula for gifted students that progress at an appropriate pace and depth within a multidisciplinary framework based on the child's instructional level. The development of this curriculum must be ongoing and allow for evaluation and revision when appropriate.

Goal #1: The Student Will Develop Higher-Order Thinking Skills as Related to Bloom's Taxonomy

Student Objectives:
1. The student will develop the cognitive process of *analysis*.
2. The student will develop the cognitive process of *synthesis*.
3. The student will develop the cognitive process of *evaluation*.

Goal #2: The Student Will Think Critically in Response to Given Information

Student Objectives:
1. The student will demonstrate the ability to *define* and *clarify* given information.
2. The student will demonstrate the ability to *judge* given information.
3. The student will demonstrate the ability to *infer/solve* problems and *draw* reasonable conclusions.

Goal #3: The Student Will Reason Logically

Student Objectives:
1. The student will demonstrate the ability to apply basic argument forms.
2. The student will reason logically using deductive methods.
3. The student will reason logically using non-deductive methods.

Goal #4: The Student Will Develop Divergent Thinking Processes

Student Objectives:
1. The student will develop *fluency*.
2. The student will develop *flexibility*.
3. The student will develop *originality*.
4. The student will develop *elaboration*.

Goal #5: The Student Will Develop Competency in the Six Steps of Creative Problem Solving

Student Objectives:
1. The student will use *mess* finding to solve real and fictitious problems.
2. The student will use *data* finding to solve real and fictitious problems.
3. The student will use *problem* finding to solve real and fictitious problems.
4. The student will use *idea* finding to solve real and fictitious problems.
5. The student will use *solution* finding to solve real and fictitious problems.
6. The student will use *acceptance* finding to solve real and fictitious problems.

Goal #6: To Provide the Opportunity for the Students to Understand, to Appreciate, and to Practice the Science and the Art of Oral Communication

Student Objectives:
1. The student will recognize, prepare, and deliver the basic types of speeches.

2. The student will learn and demonstrate various forms of group communication (dyads, triads, etc.).
3. The student will understand and appreciate various aspects of drama.
4. The student will interpret and translate orally the meaning of selected works of art (linguistically, mathematically, musically, spatially, and/or kinesthetically).

Goal #7: The Student Will Develop Written Expression through Knowledge and Application of the Writing Process Model

Student Objectives:
1. The student will learn and apply *pre-writing* techniques to generate and clarify ideas.
2. The student will transfer pre-writing experiences in *drafting* forms.
3. The student will achieve clarity and precision in composing by learning and using strategies of *responding*.
4. The student will achieve clarity and precision in composing by learning and using strategies of *revising*.
5. The student will learn and apply *editing* strategies for conformity to standard American English.
6. The student will prepare written products in forms to be *published* for real and varied audiences.

Goal #8: The Student Will Learn and Apply Various Composing Strategies and Techniques

Student Objective:
1. The student will strengthen writing clarity and precision through the development of word meaning using formal and informal word study.

Goal #9: The Student Will Develop Written Expressions through Exposure to and Practice of the Various Forms of Writing

Student Objectives:
1. The student will learn and apply the techniques used in *personal writing*.
2. The student will learn and apply the techniques used in *functional writing*.
3. The student will learn and apply techniques used in *transitional writing*.
4. The student will learn and apply techniques used in *artistic writing*.

Goal #10: The Student Will Become Actively Involved in Inquiry into an Investigation of His/Her Own Selection and Design

Student Objectives:
1. The student will select a research question to be investigated through a method appropriate to the content area/core domain:
   — scientific method
   — historical approach

— case study approach
— survey approach
2. The student will share the product with an appropriate audience, including presentations at academic competitions.

Goal #11: The Student Will Demonstrate Facility in Using Various Sources of Information to Conduct Research

Student Objectives:
1. The student will experience library/media that go beyond the regular public school library's offerings:
— CD Rom
— microfiche
— ERIC system
— audiovisuals
— research journals
2. The student will refer to mentors and other experts for pertinent information.
3. The student will use computers when appropriate as tools for locating, organizing, storing, and analyzing information for use in the research process.

Goal #12: The Student Will Develop Appropriate Self-Expectations

Student Objectives:
1. The student will evaluate goals in terms of his/her personal abilities, performance, interests, and personality.
2. The student will deal effectively with success or lack of success.
3. The student will be aware of the impact of others' expectations on himself/herself.
4. The student will distinguish between boredom and lack of familiarity.
5. The student will develop willingness to undertake tasks that have uncertain outcomes.
6. The student will recognize stress and possess awareness of stress reduction behaviors.
7. The student will develop the techniques for time management.
8. The student will recognize patterns of perfectionism and possess awareness of strategies for addressing perfectionism.

Goal #13: The student will develop and maintain positive interpersonal relationships.

Student Objectives:
1. The student will recognize the influence of peer pressure.
2. The student will develop empathy and sensitivity for the feelings of others.
3. The student will develop appropriate ways to interact with authority.
4. The student will accept and offer constructive criticism.

CHAPTER FOUR

Gifted Learner Outcomes

T he practice of stating learning objectives in American education has always been linked to a strong behaviorist orientation (Bloom, Hastings, & Madaus, 1971; Mager, 1962). Recent thinking in curriculum matters considers stated learner outcomes* to be central to the teaching-learning enterprise (Shulman, 1987; Hunter, 1984). Most states have moved toward codifying overall learning outcome statements for all learners K–12. This has become the standard form for expressing overall curriculum expectations. Gifted education has the task of translating these typically minimum outcomes into more appropriate ones for gifted learners.

Learner outcomes constitute perhaps the most crucial part of the curriculum design model. They serve several functions in the curriculum:

1. Learner outcomes delineate student expectations. They specify how much and in what areas gifted students will be educated at a particular level.
2. Learner outcomes guide the assessment process by indicating what learning is valued and to what level of attainment students should aspire.
3. Learner outcomes guide the selection of key activities, materials, and strategies for use in classrooms with gifted learners. Without their specification, a curriculum for the gifted becomes a series of disconnected experiences, workbooks, and gimmicks.

Figure 4.1 graphically shows the functions of specifying learner outcomes.

---

* The term *learner outcomes* is used throughout this chapter to mean the specific stated purposes that justify any given learning experience. I view this term as loosely synonymous with *learning objectives*. Differences reside in the emphasis on the student and his or her assessment in learner *outcomes,* in contrast to the process emphasis in the term learning *objective.*

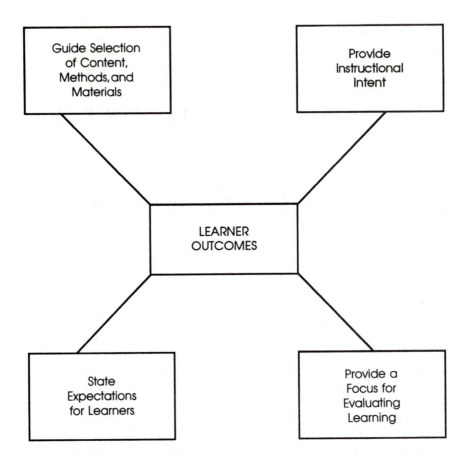

Figure 4.1
FUNCTIONS OF LEARNER OUTCOMES

A PROCESS APPROACH TO DEVELOPING
LEARNER OUTCOMES FOR THE GIFTED

A useful way to develop learner outcomes in districts that have ongoing gifted programs is for the teachers at each grade level to provide their version of what is occurring in the actual gifted program at each level, what materials are used, and what outcomes are expected. In this way, data can be synthesized accurately across all necessary levels of the curriculum to frame the cluster-level objectives. After the curriculum writer has developed the learner outcomes for each cluster within each goal statement, the draft outcomes are returned to the teachers for reaction and commentary. A follow-up session should be scheduled to talk through discrepancies, issues, concerns, and misinterpretations. Subsequent to

Table 4.1
SCHEDULE FOR DEVELOPING LEARNER OUTCOMES

Task	Time Frame
Grade-level teachers write up key outcomes, activities, and materials that address each goal statement	1–2 months
Curriculum writer synthesizes all teachers' submissions and distills them into learner outcomes by grade-level clusters.	2 months
Grade-level teachers review work.	1 month
Grade-level teachers and curriculum writer meet to clarify issues and resolve misinterpretations and discrepancies	1 day
Curriculum writer revises document based on mutual agreement with teachers.	1 month

this session, a revised set of outcomes can be prepared. The schedule for this phase is given in Table 4.1.

To illustrate the outcome of this process and to show the relationship of a goal to its corresponding learner outcomes, one example from a language arts scope and sequence document (VanTassel-Baska, 1988) is cited.

As a result of K-12 gifted programs, students will be able to analyze and evaluate various forms and ideas in significant literature representative of different cultures and eras.

Sequence of Learner Outcomes

I. By the end of *Grade 3*, gifted students should be able to:
  A. Identify the basic literary forms of drama, poetry, short stories, nonfiction, letters, myths and fables, biography, and autobiography.
  B. Compare and contrast literary forms.
  C. Compare and contrast ideas from selections read.
  D. Identify the literary structures of character, plot, setting, and theme in each literary form studied.
  E. Compare and contrast literary devices.
  F. Identify character behavior in selected literature.
  G. Evaluate the effectiveness of alternative endings to selected pieces of literature.
  H. Create a "literary piece" in each form.

II. By the end of *Grade 6*, gifted students should be able to:
   A. Identify the literary devices important to each literary form (e.g., poetry: use of imagery, simile, metaphor, rhyme, alliteration, onomatopoeia, etc.).
   B. Compare and contrast cultural differences revealed through works of literature read.
   C. Create a piece of literature in any form or style based on a given idea.
   D. Infer cultural issues from study of literary works.
   E. Analyze the use of symbols in selected pieces of literature.

III. By the end of *Grade 8*, gifted students should be able to:
   A. Analyze and interpret form and idea in "moderately difficult" literary selections.
   B. Compare and contrast literary works from different cultures and eras based on a common theme.
   C. Employ appropriate critical reading behaviors in encountering new reading material (e.g., finding the main idea, making appropriate inferences, evaluating data given, discerning author's tone).
   D. Interpret character motivation in selected literature.

IV. By the end of *Grade 12*, gifted students should be able to:
   A. Analyze and interpret form and idea in "difficult" literary selections.
   B. Compare and contrast disparate works of literature according to form, style, ideas, cultural milieu, point of view, historical context, and personal relevance.
   C. Evaluate any new piece of literature encountered.
   D. Create a piece of literature in a chosen form that successfully integrates form and meaning.
   E. Evaluate the potential impact of selected literary works on individual/collective value systems and philosophies.

Similarly, content goals and learner outcomes can be generated in all four core domains of learning within the same 6-month time period.

Another approach to delineating appropriate outcomes for gifted learners across several years is to use state or locally derived learner outcomes as a point of departure and then adapt them to appropriate outcomes for gifted learners at key stages of development. The example in Table 4.2 is derived from the Georgia State Department of Education (in press) resource guide for secondary English teachers. The core curriculum statements are given in the lefthand column; the corresponding outcome statements adapted for gifted learners appear in the righthand column, in which expectations for performance of gifted learners shifts to a higher and more complex level.

Table 4.2
EXAMPLE OF GENERAL OUTCOMES DIFFERENTIATED FOR THE GIFTED

Quality Core Curriculum for All Learners	Differentiation for Gifted Learners
• Uses literal comprehension skills (e.g., sequencing, explicitly stated main idea) • Uses inferential comprehension skills (e.g., predictions, comparisons, conclusions, implicitly stated main idea, propaganda techniques)	• Demonstrates proficiency in working with inference, inductive and deductive reasoning, analogies, assumptions, and evaluation of arguments in literature read
• Identifies and comprehends the main and subordinate ideas in a written work and summarizes ideas in own words	• Analyzes literary themes as they are developed within and across authors
• Recognizes different purposes and methods of writing; identifies a writer's point of view and tone • Interprets a writer's meaning inferentially as well as literally • Identifies personal opinions and assumptions in a writer	• Discusses and synthesizes ideas about an author's form and content • Develops an essay that compares key purposes and methods of writing used by one author to another author
• Comprehends a variety of materials	• Evaluates a given reading selection according to a set of criteria or standards
• Uses the features of print materials appropriately (e.g., table of contents, preface, introduction, titles and subtitles, index, glossary, appendix, bibliography)	• Creates a written product incorporating all major features of print materials that are one of the following: novel, biography, autobiography, poetry, short stories, book of essays
• Defines unfamiliar words by using appropriate word recognition skills	• Masters advanced adult vocabulary
• Is aware of important writers representing diverse backgrounds and traditions • Is familiar with mythology, especially Greek and Roman • Reads and compares world literature	• Compares and contrasts disparate works of literature according to form, style, ideas, milieu, point of view, historical context, and personal relevance

Table 4.2
CONTINUED

• Develops effective ways of telling and writing about literature • Is familiar with the structural elements of literature (plot, characterization, and so on)	• Creates a "literary piece" in a self-selected form at a level appropriate for contest submission, using appropriate structural elements and literary devices
• Judges literature critically on the the basis of personal response and literary quality	• Evaluates any new piece of literature encountered according to key criteria such as use of language, unity of purpose, characterization, credibility of main ideas, etc.
• Reads, discusses, and interprets book-length works of fiction and nonfiction	• Analyzes and interprets form and idea in "difficult" literary selections
• Selects and uses a variety of print and nonprint resources to become familiar with and compare literature	• Using multiple resources, creates a critical essay comparing two pieces of literature
• Is familiar with the similarities and differences of various literary genres • Reads a literary text analytically • Sees relationships between form and content	• Creates a piece of literature in a chosen form that successfully integrates form and meaning
• Develops an understanding of the chronology of American literature • Develops an understanding of the effect of history on American literature (e.g., literary movements and periods) • Reads and discusses representative works of American literature and American authors	• Analyzes and interprets key ideas represented by selected literature, art, and music of any given culture • Compares and contrasts the concepts of cultural identity, national identity, and global interdependence as evidenced by selected pieces of literature

Comparing the two columns in Table 4.2, we see several "differentiation" issues emerging. The gifted learner outcomes consistently:

— focus more on higher-level thinking tasks.
— provide more complex tasks.
— expect more sophisticated "products."

Table 4.3
COMPARISON OF LEARNER OUTCOMES BY TIME AND GRADE

Learner Outcomes	Time Unit	Grade Level of Outcome
By the end of the unit, gifted learners will be able to compare and contrast literary themes in selected short stories.	6 weeks	Upper Elementary
By the end of the unit, gifted learners will be able to evaluate the validity of an argument in written form	18 weeks	Middle School
By the end of the year, gifted learners will be able to construct an argument supporting any given important issue.	36 weeks	9th Grade
By the end of 4 years, gifted learners will be able to analyze and interpret any given passage from classical or contemporary literature	4 years	12th Grade

— achieve lower-level outcomes more readily.
— promote creative responses to material.
— broaden the scope of the learner's experience.
— emphasize multiple perspectives.
— provide for thematic exploration.

Learner outcomes should be stated in relationship to a specific time frame for attainment. Teachers may wish to key on a daily set of outcomes, a weekly set, unit outcomes over 9 weeks, an annual set of outcomes, or even multi-year outcomes. All of these time units are meaningful in curriculum implementation and correspond to the curriculum development "chunks" found in many gifted programs. Table 4.3 compares unit, annual, and multi-year examples of outcomes for gifted programs.

Learner outcomes also can be developed at a more specific level and grounded in a specific topic or content piece. Curry and Samara (1990) have developed an algorithm for developing these more specific learner outcomes, and they are also highly product-based.

In a study of _____, the students will be able to use what they have learned to _____ and will share their ideas through a _____, a _____, a _____, or a self-selected product.

Example:

   In a study of Shakespeare, the students will be able to use what they have learned to analyze famous Shakespearean women and will share their ideas through a performance, a videotape, an essay, or a self-selected product.

Moreover, learner outcomes can be written in behavioral terms from the outset so that criterion levels for evaluation are explicit. Two examples of this approach are:

- By the end of the year, 90% of gifted learners will increase their ability to handle inference problems by 20% as measured by the Cornell Test of Critical Thinking.
- By the end of the program, 100% of the gifted learners will complete a satisfactory research paper as judged by receiving 80 of 100 points on a predetermined assessment form.

LINKING LEARNER OUTCOMES TO ACTIVITIES

An aspect of curriculum design that may get overlooked is the linkage system among the various levels of learner outcomes, which becomes more specific in stated form as the outcomes approach the level of activities. The linkage system of learner outcomes to teaching activities is a critical one. Many times teachers have difficulty seeing the pathway between these two levels in the design process and may prefer to stay only at the level of teaching activities without an explicit statement about the desired outcomes for learners. Curriculum planners must find appropriate ways to express the relationship across these two levels. The model in Figure 4.2 illustrates alternative pathways connecting learner outcomes to teaching activities.

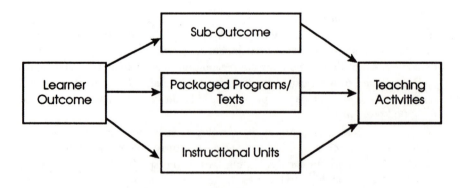

Figure 4.2
**ALTERNATIVE LINKAGES BETWEEN LEARNING OBJECTIVES
AND TEACHING ACTIVITIES**

Sub-Outcome Linkage

One pathway is to create sub-outcomes that provide greater specificity and direction for activities. This is often a good transition for gifted curricula because the framing of learner outcomes may be fairly broad and complex and span multiple years of work. Thus, sub-outcomes can clarify for grade-level teachers specific outcomes for which they are responsible, as illustrated in the following example at the elementary level, for language arts.

By the end of Grade 3, students should be able to use appropriate texts such as fiction, nonfiction, poetry, letters, directions, and reference material to accomplish the various purposes for reading.

Transition #1: Learner Sub-Outcomes
A. By the end of Grade 3, students should be able to use appropriate texts to read aloud.
B. By the end of Grade 3, students should be able to use appropriate texts to learn new vocabulary.
C. By the end of Grade 3, students should be able to use appropriate texts to understand the meaning of what they read.

Transition #2: Learner Sub-Outcomes at Specific Grade Level
A. By the end of Grade 1, students should be able to understand directions and act on them appropriately.
B. By the end of Grade 1, students should be able to read childen's literature and interpret meaning.
C. By the end of Grade 1, students should be able to read poetry aloud with expression and creative movement.

Learning Activities Needed for Grade 1 Sub-Outcomes
A. Students will read and interpret various signs and symbols.
B. Students will form literary groups to discuss selected children's literature.
C. Students will conduct poetry readings and dramatize individual poems.

Resources Needed for Specific Grade 1 Sub-Outcomes
A. Signs and Symbols Unit (teacher-developed)
B. *Junior Great Books,* Level 1
C. *Poetry for Young Children,* Tasha Tudor
D. Story and poetry tapes

Linkage Through Packaged Programs/Texts

A second pathway to teaching activities from learner outcomes is through the use of packaged programs or textbooks already organized around the desired outcomes. In fact, many programs for the gifted employ heavy use of text materials and packaged programs without a clear sense of how they might be adapted or used to highlight desired outcomes of the program. Typically this pathway links multiple outcomes to teaching activities. The example that follows illustrates how the organization of a packaged program, in this case *Junior Great Books,* fulfills major elements contained in three language arts outcomes for the gifted learner. Individual discussion activities based on a preselected set of readings then provide the core teaching activities that complete the linkage process.

Learner Outcomes
1. By the end of Grade 6, students should be able to use appropriate texts such as fiction, nonfiction, poetry, letters, directories, and reference material to accomplish the various purposes of reading.
2. By the end of Grade 6, students should be able to read and enjoy selected American literature and literature from other countries.
3. By the end of Grade 6, students should be able to summarize the important ideas of the text and the important supporting details.

Major Transitional Approach: Junior Great Books Program
1. Exposure to and understanding of classical and contemporary literature of various genres.
2. Development of interpretive literary skills that stress comprehension, careful textual reading, and analysis.
3. Development of discussion skills such as listening, summarizing ideas, using social cues, question-asking, and taking responsibility for contributing orally.

Linkage by Instructional Units

The third pathway one might choose to link learner outcomes to teaching activities is special instructional units constructed by teachers or others to deliberately address major outcomes in a gifted program. An example follows.

Gifted students will be able to improve their skills in solving inference problems and analogies as measured by an appropriate pre-post instrument.

A teacher may choose to develop an instructional unit on analogic and inference problems that provides short-term objectives and key activities, such as:

By the end of the unit, gifted students will be able to construct an argument using analogical reasoning.

1. Students will engage in group problem solving of complex analogies and derive the decisions-rules for solution.

2. Students will conduct library research on a current topic of interest and develop a position paper regarding the topic.
3. Students will construct an oral argument using analogies to present their position.

Each of these examples provides a linkage structure for learner outcomes and teaching activities to fit together. The technology of making explicit the stages of transition in this part of the curriculum design allows us to be more precise in our teaching of the gifted to ensure that outcome levels are as high as they might be. The fallacy of thinking that outcomes are irrelevant and only activities are important may be exposed for the shortsightedness it represents. A well planned curriculum for the gifted has no substitute. Criterial questions to consider in developing outcomes for a gifted program are:

1. Are they appropriate for gifted learners at the requisite stage of development?
2. Are they substantive and worthy?
3. Are they measurable?
4. Are they clearly stated?

SUMMARY

As learner outcomes are central to the teaching-learning process and as many states have codified objectives for general education, there is a need to translate these typically minimum outcomes into more appropriate ones for the gifted.

Learner outcomes are the most crucial piece of the curriculum because they delineate expectations and guide assessment and selection of activities, preventing the curriculum from being fragmented.

The process approach to developing learner outcomes for the gifted includes grade level teachers stating outcomes, activities, and material for each level, synthesis by a curriculum writer, review by teachers, meeting to clarify issues, and a revised set of outcomes written by the curriculum developer.

Another approach is to use state or local outcomes as a basis and then to adapt these for gifted, taking into account the following features of differentiated curriculum for the gifted: higher-level thinking; more complex, more sophisticated products; less time for lower-level objectives; promoting creative responses, broader scope, multiple perspectives, and a thematic orientation.

Learner outcomes for the gifted need to be stated relative to a specific time frame. Outcomes can be developed at a more specific level, grounded to a particular topic, and also can be written in behavioral terms so that criteria levels for evaluation are explicit.

The gap between learner outcomes and activities needs to be bridged by curriculum planners through suboutcomes, packaged programs or texts, or special instructional units. Bridging this gap increases outcome levels and prevents curricula from being sets of fragmented activities. Outcomes for the gifted should be appropriate for the gifted at a particular stage, substantive and worthy, measurable and clear.

QUESTIONS FOR REFLECTION

1. Do the outcomes meet the criteria listed above at more advanced levels than would normally be expected at the grade level or chronological age? Do they allow for variations in ability within the group of gifted by being flexible and allowing options?
2. Are they substantive and worthy? i.e., What relevance do the outcomes have for the students' future education or career or personal development? Are the outcomes more complex and thematic, or just novel and not normally covered within the regular curriculum?
3. Are they measurable? i.e., What is the student expected to do, demonstrate, pronounce, write, draw, produce, build, explain, synthesize, analyze, etc., and how is it related to the outcome?
4. Are they clearly stated? These questions should be answered by the outcomes: What is the student expected to do? How are they supposed to accomplish it? What prerequisites are there before the student does it? How will it be determined whether the student completed the outcome?
5. Can we set appropriate expectation levels for gifted students' learning, or does the nature of gifted learners defy such attempts? Explain.

REFERENCES

Bloom, B., Hastings, J., & Madaus, G. (1971). *Handbook on formative and summative evaluation of student learning*. New York: McGraw Hill.

Curry, J. & Samara, J. (1990). *Writing units that challenge: A guidebook for and by educators*. Portland, ME: Maine Educators of the Gifted and Talented.

Georgia State Department of Education Resource Guide for Secondary Teachers of the Gifted (in press). Atlanta, GA: Georgia State Department of Education.

Hunter, M. (1984). Knowing, teaching, and supervising. In P. Hosford, *Using what we know about teaching*. Alexandria, VA: Association for Supervision and Curriculum Development, 169–192.

Mager, R. (1962). *Preparing objectives for instructing*. Belmont, CA: Fearon.

Shulman, L. S. (1987). Assessment for teaching: An initiative for the professor. *Phi Delta Kappa, 69*, 38–44.

VanTassel-Baska, J. (1988). Developing a comprehensive approach to scope and sequence: Curriculum alignment. *GCT*, September-October, 42–45.

CHAPTER FIVE

Teaching-Learning Activities and Resources

n curriculum development, activities for gifted learners have often received the most attention, yet they represent a somewhat transitory level of concern. Even so, delineating some key issues may be helpful. These are also illustrated in Figure 5.1.

First is the importance of matching activities to a desired learner outcome. One way to ensure this is to develop an "outcome cluster" that includes at least four activities to be used in developing student learning in a given direction. The following cluster of activities is based on the sample outcome.

Learner Outcome:

The student will be able to demonstrate evidence of prejudice in news media presentations.

Activities:
1. Collect articles that reflect prejudice.
2. Trace placement of articles within the daily news.
3. Compare news weeklies, opinion magazines, and newspaper reports to see how news is reported.
4. Analyze the coverage of nightly television news programs, citing major stories, type of coverage, and potential biases.
5. Prepare a visual or written or performance product that illustrates how prejudice operates in the news media.

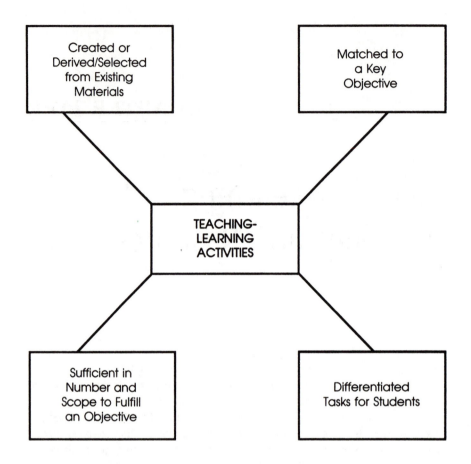

Figure 5.1
KEY FEATURES OF ACTIVITIES FOR THE GIFTED

Each activity progresses to fulfill the parameters of the outcome by relating to at least one aspect of the intent of the outcome. Developing activity clusters is a useful strategy for producing curriculum that is carefully articulated.

A second issue revolves around the question of how many activities and what types are necessary to fulfill the outcome statement. If the outcome is sufficiently differentiated, and therefore complex, one must be careful to discern and address all the components of the learner outcome. Many times a myriad of activities is necessary to fulfill the outcome. For example:

Gifted students will be able to analyze form and meaning in selected multicultural literature.

This objective implies the need for alternatives that address at least the following events:

1. Reading and discussion of key selections in multicultural literature, implying experience with at least three cultural literary traditions.
2. Understanding of and experience with different literary genres.
3. Study of universal themes of literature.
4. Expository writing skills that support the capacity to synthesize ideas.

A third issue is that of differentiation. At the level of an activity, we are faced with the most specific manifestation of stating differentiated tasks for gifted learners. Some key characteristics of differentiation tasks are:

- Use of a variety of resources.
- No upper limit on expectations.
- Facilitation emphasis by teacher.
- Study topics from multiple perspectives.
- More extended and involved.
- Higher-level thinking.
- Product alternatives.
- More open-ended (creative responses).
- More conceptual/abstract.
- More complex.
- More focused on analysis/interpretation.

A fourth issue concerns the source of activities for gifted learners. Though creating activities afresh may be useful in order to understand the principles of differentiation, it is not realistic to do so on a regular basis. This means that selecting or deriving appropriate activities from available resources becomes an important task. The need to identify key resources as bases for activities is an important concern in its own right in the curriculum development process and requires attention to the quality of resources selected.

DIFFERENTIATING APPROPRIATE ACTIVITIES FOR THE GIFTED

In constructing activities for gifted learners, a continuum model can be used to discern appropriateness. At some stages of development for some gifted learners, a fairly standard activity may be appropriate. The degree of differentiation required also relates to the aptitude of individual students and the degree of giftedness they display. To label any activity as "inappropriate" for the gifted is probably inappropriate. The continuum model allows us to apply the principles of differentiation without losing the flexibility necessary to make decisions about various activities with various gifted learners. Table 5.1 depicts a set of activities for secondary language arts students. The activities on the left are labeled "less appropriate" for gifted learners; the activities on the right are labeled "more appropriate."

In the literature example, the more appropriate activity requires gifted students to analyze two classic American short stories in respect to the complex literary elements of motivation and theme. The less appropriate activity demands only a vague discussion of basic literary elements in one short story.

The writing example that is more appropriate for the gifted requires students to engage in a more sophisticated writing form (the essay), be able to apply universal literary themes to their own reading, and convincingly defend their choices of characters, works of literature, and themes. This activity demand contrasts sharply with the less appropriate one requiring the student to engage in simple descriptive writing about a character of choice, using a simulation structure.

In the language example, the more appropriate activity requires students to master the linguistic system of form and function and apply it creatively in a self-generated written product. The less appropriate activity merely taps into students' ability to recall basic particularities of information related to a larger system.

The speaking example illustrates the appropriateness of the debate structure for engaging students in all forms of higher-level thinking, the issue approach to topics, and the need to perceive research as a broad-based and active enterprise. In contrast, the less appropriate speaking activity is vague about the structure of oral presentation, sets topics broadly, and defines research as library-based.

Another way of approaching differentiation of activities is to use prototypes such as case studies, simulations, or games that require both higher-level thinking and active learning on the part of gifted students. Simulations and dilemmas are particularly appropriate for gifted learners because these require higher-level thinking in a problem-centered context and use hypothetical situations for analysis that encourage relativistic thinking (see Perry, 1970). The example that follows illustrates a moral dilemma for use with gifted secondary students in science (Iozzi, 1984):

The following is adapted from Strunk *v.* Strunk, Court of Appeals, Kentucky, September 26, 1969, KY 445 S.W. 2nd 145:

Arthur L. Strunk, 54 years of age, and Ava Strunk, 52 years of age, of Williamstown, Kentucky, are the parents of two sons. Tommy Strunk is 28 years of age, married, an employee of the Penn State Railroad and a part-time student at the University of Cincinnati. Tommy is now suffering from chronic glomerulus nephritis, a fatal kidney disease. He is now being kept alive by frequent treatment on an artificial kidney, a procedure which cannot be continued much longer.

Jerry Strunk is 27 years of age, incompetent, and through proper legal proceedings has been committed to the Frankfort State Hospital and School, which is a state institution maintained for the feebleminded. He has an I.Q. of

Table 5.1
COMPARISON OF LESS AND MORE APPROPRIATE
LANGUAGE ARTS ACTIVITIES FOR GIFTED LEARNERS

Less Appropriate Activities for the Gifted	More Appropriate Activities for the Gifted
Literature Discuss plot, setting, and characters in the short story "A Rose for Emily."	*Literature* Compare and contrast the plot, setting, character motivation, and theme of "A Rose for Emily" and "The Bear."
Writing What if one of the characters we have read about were here? Write a description detailing what she looks like, how she behaves, and what kinds of things you would discuss with her.	*Writing* Compose a short essay discussing one of the following ideas about characters in literature: (1) They are blind to their faults. (2) They control their own fate. (3) They behave in foolish ways. Describe characters from at least three different pieces of literature to support your point of view.
Language Given a paragraph, have students identify basic parts of speech for key underlined words. Discuss.	*Language* Given a paragraph, have students: (1) identify form and function of underlined words, and (2) create a story using all basic sentence combinations.
Speaking Choose one of the following topics, and prepare an oral presentation using at least four library references: (1) Shakespeare's World (2) The American Dream in Fiction (3) Science Fiction	*Speaking* Debate one of the following resolutions, using literary works, criticisms, historical treatises, etc. as evidence: (1) Mankind is on a path toward progress. (2) Studying our past will help us cope with the future. Use multiple sources including surveys, interviews, and library sources to support your perspective.

approximately 35, which corresponds to the mentality of a six-year old. He is further handicapped by a speech defect, and has difficulty communicating with persons who do not know him well. Therefore, visits with his family, and especially his brother Tommy, with whom he identifies closely, are a very important element in his life.

When it was found that Tommy needed a kidney, doctors considered the possibility of using a kidney from a live donor. The entire family — his mother, father, and a number of relatives — was tested. Because of incompatibility of blood type or tissue, none were medically acceptable as live donors. As a last resort, Jerry was tested and found to be highly acceptable. This immediately presented the legal problem as to what, if anything, could be done by the family to procure a transplant from Jerry to Tommy. Since Jerry is officially a ward of the state, the mother petitioned the county court for authority to proceed with the operation.

Should the court permit the transplantation to take place? Why or why not?

Activities based on the dilemma can proceed from either set of the following questions. In this first set, the clear emphasis is on the dilemma. Activities could be structured to begin as a role-playing situation, followed by group discussion.

1. What is the basic dilemma the Strunks face?
2. What is the argument for Jerry's donating the kidney?
3. What is the argument against Jerry's donating the kidney?
4. Do you think Jerry's mental state should affect the decision?
5. If the situation was reversed, in the brothers, should the operation occur?
6. If you were the Strunks, what would you do? Why?
7. In your opinion, who should make the decision concerning the surgery?
8. How has scientific technology affected people's lives?
9. In your opinion, should we put greater emphasis on developing new technology or working through the human consequences of current technology?

In the second set of questions, the focus moves to the dilemma only after the teacher first emphasizes fundamental understanding of the scientific issues underlying the dilemma. Group problem solving for Level III deliberations may be an appropriate strategy to use.

Level 1: Knowledge
1. What is a kidney?
2. What does a kidney do?
3. What other organs do some of the same functions as the kidney?
4. What is a tissue?
5. What is blood type?

Level II: Application of Concepts
1. Why does each person have two kidneys?
2. What is the effect of receiving one kidney on the other?
3. What is diffusion?
4. How would diffusion be involved in dialysis?

5. Why test parents/siblings for blood type/tissue type?
6. Why not keep patients on dialysis over time?

Level III: The Dilemma
1. What are the benefits of the transplant?
   What might be the negative consequences?
2. The dilemma is concerned with the issue of human rights. What are the rights of each of the following in this case: the parents, the brothers, the courts?
3. Why do they have these rights?
4. Whose rights have priority?

Another highly appropriate type of activity for the gifted learner is to utilize a key resource or primary material as a basis for reading, then construct questions for discussion and some open-ended activities that build on the use of the resource. Two examples are presented here to illustrate the combination of recommended children's literature selections for the gifted with key questions for discussion and ideas for follow-up activities. Reading and discussion become primary activities as well as a basis for deriving additional extension activities.

If You Were a Writer
Joan Lowery Nixon

This book describes the process of being a writer as viewed from the perspective of a child learning from her mother. It is rich in descriptive language and uses hypothetical situations to facilitate understanding of the writing process.

I. Ideas for Using the Book
   - Use this book to introduce a Young Author's project.
   - Do an introductory brainstorming activity in which students list what they think the tasks of an author might be.
   - Read the book and have students list the writing activities mentioned in the book. Compare to brainstormed list.
   - Ask students to focus on the thinking aspects of writing.
   - Begin writing down ideas for a book.
   - Use this book for a career education activity tied to a Young Author's product. After reading and discussing this book, students could research various careers and the types of tasks or skills required of that profession. Next, students could write a book entitled *If I Were A* _____.
   - Share the books with the group and attempt some type of comparison/contrast of various professions through a listing, grid, or the like.

II. Questions
    A. Memory/Cognition
        1. Name the children in the family.
        2. What steps did Melia's mother lay out for being a writer?
        3. Where do words come from, according to Melia's mother?
    B. Convergent
        1. Why did Melia want to be a writer?
        2. How does a writer determine his/her writing success?
        3. How does the illustrator differentiate between reality and Melia's imagination?
    C. Divergent
        1. How would the story be different if Melia's mother had not been a writer?
        2. What if Melia's brothers and sisters wouldn't listen to her stories?
        3. Pretend you are Melia's career counselor. What elements do you believe are important for Melia to consider in thinking about a career?
    D. Evaluative
        1. In your opinion, is it good for children to follow in their parents' footsteps?
        2. In your opinion, should Melia become a writer?
        3. Which of Melia's story starters has the greatest potential for becoming an interesting story?
III. Follow-up Activity
    Select one story-starter and write a story.

Come Away from the Water, Shirley
John Burningham

This is a recommended book for gifted children at the primary level. It focuses on a family trip to the beach. Told primarily through pictures, the story centers on the contrast between Shirley's parents and their sedentary beach experience and her more active and imaginative experience.

I. Questions
    ▪ What do Shirley's parents do at the beginning of the story?
    ▪ How does Shirley's father spend his afternoon at the beach?
    ▪ Throughout the story, Shirley behaved differently to her parents' various responses. What are some of these behaviors?
    ▪ What do you think is going on in Shirley's mind when her parents advise her not to stroke the dog?
    ▪ Which of Shirley's imaginings were seeded by parental comments?

- In your opinion, which of Shirley's imaginings could be real and which could be only imagined?
- If you, like Shirley, were to find a chest full of treasures, what would be in it, and what would you do with it?
- Where do you think Shirley may have gotten the ideas for her adventure?
- Would you want to be Shirley? Why or why not? Would you feel "safer" at the shore *without* an imagination like Shirley's?
- Pretend you are Shirley. How would you react to her parents' concerns?
- If you were at the beach with your family, how would you behave different from Shirley? Write or act out, or both.

II. Activities
- Are there similarities between your life and Shirley's? List ways your life is the same and ways it is different.
- Divide into groups and dramatize another event in Shirley's life with her parents: at home, at the store, at a museum.
- Dramatize how Shirley may behave if she were the parent taking a child to the store.

BALANCE IN ACTIVITIES

Another consideration in developing learning activities for the gifted is the issue of balance in the types of activities used — between active and passive, oral and written, small-group and independent, instructional and self-study. Activities should require both convergent and divergent thinking, reading/discussion and products.

Active and Passive Activities

Gifted students are capable of absorbing large amounts of information in a short time. Using predominantly passive activities with these learners creates an imbalance and impedes more powerful learning opportunities that can accrue from lively interchange among the gifted, cooperative projects, and small-group problem solving. A good blend of active and passive activities is preferable so students can learn from each other, as well as from the teacher and themselves.

Oral and Written Activities

Teachers tend to prefer either the written or the oral mode for communication of student work. Gifted learners should have ample opportunities to participate in both types of activities. Expressive activities help them develop presentation skills. Written activities enhance thinking skills and precise use of language. Both are highly valued modes of communication in the world of professional work. Therefore, a strong balance in the use of these two modes is desirable.

Small-Group and Independent Activities

Gifted learners are often capable of working alone and, if unprompted, frequently choose to work alone. But learning to collaborate with others in activities is an important tool skill as well. Project work for the gifted might be best served by alternating between individual and group assignments. Typically, culturally diverse groups and gifted girls prefer more opportunities for working cooperatively. Attention to these special population distinctions also calls for a balance between the oral and written modes of learning.

Instruction and Self-Study

A popular myth says that gifted students need only facilitation, never direct instruction, in learning. Rather, these learners may need less direct instruction than other learners, geared at higher levels and provided at different times and in different areas of the curriculum. They also have a strong capacity to take charge of their own learning. Curricular activities should strive for balance between those that are teacher-directed and those that are student-directed. Mutual goal setting between teacher and gifted learner is one strategy to discern the appropriate balance.

Convergent and Divergent Thinking

As a field, gifted educators have long promoted divergent thinking over convergent thinking as a process skill to be taught to gifted learners. In reality, both modes are essential for creating anything worthwhile, whether it be a musical composition or an essay. Thus, deliberate emphasis on both styles of thinking should be incorporated in activities for the gifted. For example, ideational fluency activities can help students generate ideas in an exploratory context without imposing outside judgment. By the same token, at a later stage of thinking, these ideas should come under closer scrutiny and be evaluated according to key criteria for facilitating the goal of learning. A balanced focus on creative and critical thinking skills is necessary to enhance creative productivity.

Reading/Reflection and Project Work

We would do well to cultivate gifted learners who will become philosophers as well as those who will become marketing entrepreneurs. Thus, we should ensure a balance of activities that reward reading and discussion of ideas as much as we reward "products" in the tangible sense. In many fields the "production" of a new idea brought about by discussion in a small group of people can cause a paradigm shift more readily than can a project report detailing what happened and why. Developing a meaningful theory requires intellectual behavior and time to think prior to the conversion process to writing, speaking, or other forms of production. Gifted activities should reflect this balance, too.

Relative Emphasis

Another kind of balance that must be struck in the construction and choice of activities for gifted learners is in the relative emphasis given to one aspect of an activity over others. Table 5.2 outlines the major elements to be considered in developing language arts activities for the gifted and provides specific examples to consider as choices. Although the examples are only illustrative, they do represent an approach to giving each element some consideration. Using this table, curriculum developers can strike a balance among content, process skill, product, and concept development.

As we develop meaningful activities for the gifted, the activity prototype checklist in Figure 5.2 may be helpful in sufficiently differentiating appropriate activities for gifted learners. The checklist covers all the major issues raised in this chapter regarding activities for the gifted.

Table 5.2
ALTERNATIVE TEACHING/LEARNING ACTIVITY ELEMENTS
IN LANGUAGE ARTS

Activity Element	Alternative Examples
Themes	Patterns Change Space Signs and symbols Interdependence Systems Origins Reason
Topics	Colonial America Electricity Customs of France Fractions Popular composers Composition Poetry The brain
Content areas	Reading/Language arts Writing/Composition Math Science Social studies Art Music Foreign language

Table 5.2
CONTINUED

Literary genres	Poetry
	Short story
	Essay
	Novel
	Play
	Letter
	Biography
	Autobiography
Literary devices	Characterization
	Plot
	Setting
	Theme
	Motivation
	Climax
	Openings
	Denouement
Content resources	*Ozymandias* (poem by Shelley]
	The Lottery (short story by Shirley Jackson)
	Self-Reliance (Emerson essay)
	Old Man and The Sea (Novella by Ernest Hemingway)
	The Source (novel by James Michener)
	Self-Consciousness (autobiography by John Updike)
	Diary of Anne Frank
Thinking skills (critical)	Creative problem solving
	Deductive reasoning
	Inductive reasoning
	Setting up hypotheses
	Making inferences
	Creating metaphors/analogies
	Finding similarities/differences or advantages/ disadvantages
	Specific problem-solving heuristics
Thinking skills (creative)	Fluency (Name all the _____ you can in the next 10 minutes)
	Flexibility (How many different uses can you make of _____?)
	Elaboration (Add to the story/picture as much as you can.)
	Originality (Think of a _____ no one else has thought of. Represent it.)

Table 5.2
CONTINUED

Archetypal verbs for enhancing higher-order thinking	Analyze, compare/contrast, explicate, explain Set up criteria/standards Create, design, model, demonstrate Present, debate, write Evaluate, judge Critique, rate
Archetypal activities	Read and discuss Practice/apply skill or concept Respond to structured stimulus, orally or in writing, or act out Build stimulus to react to Conduct experiment Represent idea in some form Organize work plan/product
Archetypal discussion questions	Who? What? Where? When? Why/how did _____ happen? What would happen if _____? Which is better or best . . .? What are all the different ways that _____ _____? What did you like best/least about _____? Why? What does the following quotation mean? What was the author's tone, attitude, feeling about _____? How do you feel about _____?
Discussion questions for the fine arts/ humanities	What is it? What's it made of? What does it say? How do you respond to it? How good is it? When was it created? What do you see? Make a list. What ideas are conveyed? What feelings are evoked? If you were to identify with a character or object, what would it be, and why? How might you represent all of your reactions to the poem/painting/music/photograph? Respond in your preferred form.
Archetypal product tasks for groups and individuals	Create a collage Evaluate best uses, products, processes Write a story/poem/play Design an ad Act out/dramatize a scene Create a slide presentation Debate an issue Build/construct a model

Yes	No		
____	____	1.	Does the activity serve multiple purposes?
			Content purpose _____
			Process purpose _____
			Concept purpose _____
____	____	2.	Does the teacher's role in the activity facilitate learning?
____	____	3.	Does the activity promote critical thinking?
____	____	4.	Does the activity promote creative thinking, problem solving?
____	____	5.	Does the activity promote product-oriented, generative thinking?
____	____	6.	Does the teacher ask higher-level questions as part of the activity?
____	____	7.	Does the activity contain an element of choice?
____	____	8.	Is the activity interdisciplinary?
____	____	9.	Is the activity sufficiently advanced and complex for gifted learners?
____	____	10.	Does the activity promote opportunity for an open-ended response?
____	____	11.	Does the activity encourage students to seek multiple sources for understanding?
____	____	12.	Is the activity linked to a curriculum objective?

Figure 5.2
ACTIVITY PROTOTYPE CHECKLIST

RESOURCES FOR THE GIFTED

Appropriate activities are inextricably linked to appropriate resources. Many activities are derived from available books and materials, and human resources, too, are a vital part of any curriculum design.

Human Resources

Guest speakers, mentors, and community volunteers all represent viable avenues for potential assistance in a gifted program. Professionals such as practicing scientists, artists, and writers constitute a rich resource for many gifted programs across the country. In learning research skills, gifted learners should interview and interact with knowledgeable people in whatever area they are exploring.

This human side of resource utilization is fundamental to students' understanding of how knowledge is generated in the real world. Moreover, tapping into human resources adds the dimension of modeling: Here are individuals directly engaging in creative productivity from whom students can discern key qualities and skills necessary to function in a given field.

Material Resources

Materials of various types are essential to curricula for the gifted, and these must be selected carefully. Many materials that are superb for gifted programs do not carry a label identifying themselves as such, and many materials that do carry the label do not add anything of benefit to a curriculum plan.

Criteria in Resource Selection

Key criteria to consider in choosing resources for a gifted program are:

1. *The material addresses the major student learner outcomes of your program.* Many times teachers are enamored of materials because they are attractive, contain the appropriate buzz words, and emphasize hands-on activities. These criteria are insufficient as a basis for selecting materials in a program for gifted learners. The materials must be responsive to the desired learner outcomes or they will not be helpful in defining the curriculum according to your plan.
2. *Reading level is appropriate for gifted learners at the given stage of development.* Too many texts in all subject areas are "dummied down," frequently one to two grade levels below the stated level for which the material was intended. The result is low-level materials for the gifted. We need to be conscious of the reading level of all texts to ensure challenging reading behaviors in the gifted.
3. *The material is organized by key concepts rather than isolated skills.* Elementary materials tend to be organized by skills and not by ideas. Materials that offer a better balance of these two elements should be sought out.
4. *The material includes ideas for discussion at higher levels of thinking.* A key feature that would enhance material use with the gifted should be the inclusion of questions that tap into analytical, synthetic, and evaluative thinking.
5. *The material includes ideas for group and independent project investigations.* Materials that suggest self-generated activities for students are useful, because they can guide students to various alternative project opportunities.
6. *Problem sets are organized from simple to complex and allow gifted learners to extend off-level as appropriate.* The structure of materials should allow for students to deal with more complex problems or issues than the entry level. Although skill-based materials often provide this, materials geared only to the gifted often do not contain this developmental progression.
7. *The material provides alternative means to attain ends within the curriculum framework; it offers diversity in learning.* Materials for the gifted should offer choices to activate student interest through multiple suggestions for

activities leading to attainment of a desired learner outcome. Moreover, materials should provide various modes of inquiry and options for student-generated work.

8. *The material provides extension opportunities to understand other domains of inquiry.* Good resources for gifted learners allow for student development of multiple perspectives in various disciplines. Materials should make these connections for students.

9. *The material provides opportunities for creative thinking, for challenging assumptions, and for offering alternative solutions.* Materials should be grounded in the inquiry approach and sensitive to problem-based learning strategies. They should lead students to think about what they are learning rather than merely accepting it.

10. *The material encourages gifted learners to consult multiple resources on given topics.* Material for gifted learners should encourage further exploration of ideas. Good bibliographies and resource suggestions in both print and nonprint form are important.

These criteria may be useful in choosing core text materials for gifted learners, as well as in referring to other resources of merit. Textbook adoption committees would do well to use the list to ensure appropriate considerations for gifted students in district-wide adoptions.

Key Features as Curriculum

Regardless of target population, all good curriculum materials should contain:

— rationale and purpose.
— goals and objectives.
— curriculum content outline.
— activities.
— instructional strategies.
— evaluation procedures.
— materials/resources.
— extension activities.

In addition, materials can be reviewed in respect to what criteria educators in the disciplines perceive as critical content in an exemplary curriculum. An example of criteria from the discipline of science would include:

— presence of intra- and interrelations among scientific concepts.
— science research presented as practices in the real world of science.
— content base in key areas of science and technology.
— opportunities to hone scientific inquiry skills.
— opportunities for independent research.

— opportunities for collaborative work.
— presence of moral and ethical dimensions of science and technology.

Types of Materials

In the realm of bibliographic resources for programs for the gifted, several types are worth mentioning because they are so rich in challenging ideas for teachers and gifted learners alike. One group of resources could be labeled "interdisciplinary and idea-based." This type of resource is typically organized thematically and provides a broad scope of examples drawn from many disciplines to illustrate a given idea. Some excellent examples of this type of resource are:

Boorstein, D. J. (1985). *The Discoverers: A History of Man's Search to Know His World and Himself.* New York: Vintage Press.
Bronowski, J. (1973). *The Ascent of Man.* Boston: Little, Brown.
Burke, J. (1978). *Connections.* Boston: Little, Brown.
Burke, J. (1985). *The Day the Universe Changed.* London: British Broadcasting Corp.
Burger, D. (1965). *Sphereland.* New York: Harper & Row.
Challenge of the Unknown (1988) (math program with video). Bartlesville, OK: Phillips Petroleum.
Hofstadter, D. (1979). *Godel, Escher, Bach: An Eternal Golden Braid.* New York: Basic Books.
Jacobs, H. (1982). *Mathematics: A Human Endeavor.* New York: W. H. Freeman & Co.
Judson, H. (1974). *Search for Solutions.* Bartlesville, OK: Phillips Petroleum.
Sagan, C. (1980). *Cosmos.* New York: Random House.
Serra, M. (1989). *Discovering Geometry. An Inductive Approach.* Berkeley, CA: Key Curriculum Press.

Another type of valuable resource for gifted programs consists of materials that annotate additional resources for the gifted learner providing multiple options for reading or doing activities. A few superb examples of this type of resource are:

Baskin, B. H., & Harris, K. H. (1980). *Books for the Gifted Child.* New York: R. R. Bowker.
Halsted, J. (1988). *Guiding Gifted Readers From Pre-High School: A Handbook.* Columbus: Ohio Psychology Press.
Hauser, P., & Nelson, G. A. (1988). *Books for the Gifted (Vol. 2).* New York: R. R. Bowker.
Polette, N. (1982). *3 R's for the Gifted: Reading, Writing and Research.* Littleton, CO: Libraries Unlimited.
Saul, W., & Newman, A. (1986). *Science Fare.* New York: Harper & Row.

A third type of invaluable resource for use in gifted curricula is the "packaged" program. These materials have already been prestructured for classroom use and come with excellent teachers' guides — and often videotapes, filmstrips, or other multimedia to help implement the program. These resources require less inventiveness on the part of individual teachers to create activities. Sample materials of this sort include:

Bank Street College of Education. (1984). *The Voyage of the Mimi*. New York: Holt, Rinehart and Winston.
Challenge of the Unknown (1988) (math program with video). Bartlesville, OK: Phillips Petroleum.
The Good Books. Pleasantville, NY: Sunburst Publishing Company.
Junior Great Books. Chicago: Great Books Foundation.
Lego TC LOGO. Enfield, CT: Lego Systems.
MACOS (Man: A Course of Study). Washington, DC: Curriculum Associates.

Another type of material of interest to the gifted is biography and autobiography. Study of individuals who engage in an area of interest to them provides another whole dimension toward understanding a field of inquiry and relating to it as an individual. Some examples here are:

Baretta-Lorton, M. *Math Jobs*. Menlo Park, CA: Addison-Wesley.
Bell, E. T. (1965). *Men of Mathematics*. New York: Simon and Schuster.
Bruner, J. (1983). *In Search of Mind*. New York: Harper and Row.
Dillard, A. (1974). *Pilgrim at Tinker Creek*. New York: Harper's Magazine Press.
Fins, A. (1979). *Women in Science*. Skokie, IL: VGM Career Horizons.
Goodfield, J. (1981). *An Imagined World: A Story of Scientific Discovery*. New York: Harper and Row.
Keller, E. F. (1983). *A Feeling for the Organism: The Life and Work of Barbara McClintock*. New York: W. H. Freeman & Co.

All of these types of materials are invaluable in implementing an effective curriculum for gifted learners, for they provide a diverse set of opportunities for multiple activities and are responsive to the key issues cited earlier regarding qualities of good materials for the gifted. Above all, these materials stimulate teachers to improve, and gifted students to learn.

SUMMARY

Teaching-learning activities should be matched to learner outcomes, should be geared to differentiated tasks, must be sufficient to fulfill an objective, and should be created or derived from existing resources. An ideal balance should be sought between active and passive, oral and written, small-group and independent activities. These activities should encompass both convergent and divergent thinking, reading/discussion and products.

Appropriate resources are both human and material. Human resources include guest speakers, mentors, community volunteers, and professionals in various fields. Criteria for material resources include appropriate reading level, organization by key concepts, inclusion of ideas for higher-level thinking, alternative means to attain ends (diversity), and opportunities for creative thinking, among others.

Basic types of materials are: thematic and idea-based, those annotated for additional resources, packaged programs, and biography/autobiography.

QUESTIONS FOR REFLECTION

1. How can we organize teaching activities so that gifted learners regularly experience reading, discussion, simulations, project work, creative opportunities, and affective experiences regardless of age or area of study?
2. How might we ensure that all classroom activities contribute to the attainment of a stated objective?
3. If you were in charge of the gifted program in a school district, how would you organize the development of appropriate activities for the gifted?
4. What role should basal textbooks play in a gifted curriculum?
5. How can we ensure that multiple and diverse resources are used with gifted learners?

REFERENCES

Iozzi, F. (1984). *Dilemmas in bioethics*. New Brunswick, NJ: Rutgers University.

Perry, W. (1970). *Forms of intellectual and ethical development in the college years*. New York: Holt, Rinehart and Winston.

CHAPTER SIX

Instructional Strategies and Management Techniques

T eachers employ certain techniques and delivery systems in the classroom to provide appropriate curricula to gifted learners. Most instructional strategies have some value in working with the gifted, but those that allow for more open-ended, interactive, and generative learning behavior are probably most beneficial.

How do we know what strategies work? One way is to examine those used in exemplary programs that reflect positive growth gains for these learners. Three programs that meet this criterion are *Junior Great Books, Philosophy for Children,* and *Man: A Course of Study* (MACOS). Students exposed to these programs have demonstrated growth gains in critical thinking and interpretation of written material (Lipman, 1988; Norris, 1985; Sternberg and Bhana, 1986). The common instructional strategy across these programs is *inquiry*, questioning to stimulate and expand thinking about what students have read, experienced, or seen. Thus, gifted educators typically promote inquiry and question asking as key elements in gifted programs.

Another way to ascertain effective strategies is to observe what exemplary teachers of the gifted do to facilitate growth in their students. Martinson (1974) developed a scale of teacher behaviors to record these observations. Subsequent adaptations in that scale seek to extend our understanding of teacher behaviors based on general teacher education research as well as our understanding of what works with the gifted (VanTassel-Baska et al., 1988). A sample set of behaviors to evaluate teachers of the gifted in the Saturday and summer programs at the College of William and Mary consists of the following:

1. Plans curriculum experiences well.
2. Demonstrates understanding of the educational implications of giftedness.
3. Uses various teaching strategies effectively.
4. Selects questions that stimulate higher-level thinking.
5. Stimulates and models critical thinking skills in appropriate contexts.
6. Stimulates and models creative thinking techniques.
7. Stimulates and models problem-solving techniques.
8. Conducts group discussions well.
9. Encourages independent thinking and open inquiry.
10. Understands and encourages student ideas and student-directed work.
11. Synthesizes student assessment data and curriculum content effectively.
12. Provides for student extension activities outside of class.
13. Promotes a healthy teaching/learning climate.

Still another approach to examining effective strategies for the gifted is to focus on student outcomes first and then identify the desired *teacher* behaviors that would facilitate these outcomes. In his innovative assessment model, Shulman (1987) cited the importance of linking teacher behaviors to student outcomes. Using common outcome statements from typical gifted programs, Table 6.1 demonstrates this process.

GUIDELINES FOR CHOOSING APPROPRIATE STRATEGIES

Appropriate instructional strategies for gifted learners include all of the strategies deemed appropriate for other learners as well, and all teachers of the gifted should be comfortable using discussion, inquiry, small-group and individual consultation, and problem-solving approaches. But how does one choose the appropriate strategy in a given situation?

1. *Strategies should relate to instructional purposes, curriculum, and setting.* Effective strategies are dependent on the purpose of a given lesson and the nature of the curriculum being taught. For example, inquiry teaching is appropriate in many situations, but if the instructional purpose is to provide an overview of key ideas on China within an hour, inquiry may not be the best choice of strategy. We must carefully study the interrelationship of strategy with purpose, content, and time frames.
2. *Strategies should be diverse.* Research on instructional methods for the gifted currently points to the desirability of using a variety of techniques. Small-group cooperative learning strategies, independent learning models, and large-group instruction all have their place in the instructional pattern for the gifted. Striving for a good balance among these three instructional approaches may be optimal.
3. *Incorporate several strategies that are generative in nature.* Effective teachers of the gifted rely on strategies that involve the gifted as an active learner,

Table 6.1
EXPECTED STUDENT BEHAVIORS CORRELATED
WITH TEACHER BEHAVIORS

By the end of grade 4, gifted students will demonstrate enhanced ability to think creatively as evidenced by appropriate pre-post measures	1. Teacher employs brainstorming. 2. Teacher encourages flexible thinking. 3. Teacher asks students to elaborate ideas. 4. Teacher engages students in developing generative ideas and products.
By the end of grade 6, gifted students will improve their problem-solving skills as evidenced by pre-post application of novel problem sets.	1. Teacher employs creative problem-solving model. 2. Teacher uses problem-solving heuristics in presenting ideas. 3. Teacher asks students to define problems in a question form.
By the end of grade 8, gifted students will increase critical thinking skills in the areas of analysis and interpretation, inductive and deductive reasoning, and evaluation.	1. Teacher has students evaluate situations, problems, issues. 2. Teacher has students ask analytic questions. 3. Teacher has students generalize from concrete to abstract at advanced levels. 4. Teacher has students support generalizations in written and oral discourse. 5. Teacher has students interpret selected passages.

capable of generating new ideas and products of various kinds. A few key strategies that all teachers of the gifted should have in their arsenal include inquiry, problem solving, and discussion via careful question-asking techniques. If these techniques are not applied in gifted programs, students are cheated out of an important aspect of their learning.

4. *Strategies should provide a balance among active and passive activities.* Although having students work independently in the classroom has much value, it carries the potential problem of overloading students with passive types of activities in which they are merely receiving information by doing work in isolation. Many of their best insights can be gained from interacting with

each other and articulating ideas verbally. Consequently, educators of the gifted need to consider a balance in the activities employed.

5. *Strategies should consider cognitive style of both teacher and learners.* The individual learning styles of the gifted require a teacher's sensitivity to a student's cognitive style. At the same time, teachers often are superb at one instructional approach and only mediocre at another. Thus, teachers need to know their own strengths and try to capitalize upon them in classroom interactions. Recognition of cognitive style and attempts to respond to it help maximize the outcome of learning.

6. *Strategies should be subordinate to educational purpose.* Occasionally the strategy, instead of what is taught, becomes the purpose. For example, brainstorming may become more important than the ideas being considered; we lose sight of *why* the technique is important — namely, as a way of exploring an important idea. Group process is not an end in itself but, rather, must be tempered by relevant content for exploration.

PROGRAM STRATEGIES

Figure 6.1 identifies five program strategies that promote this type of generative learning with gifted learners.

The Pacing of Instruction

Activities must move at a rate that is comfortable for the gifted. I am often reminded of a student in my class many years ago. He was young for the seventh grade class and had an annoying habit of going under his desk whenever the pace of instruction slowed to accommodate others in the class. This went on for a few class sessions, with stern commentary from me regarding his appropriate physical placement in the classroom. Finally I made the connection between his behavior and the instructional pace. Once he was sub-grouped with other learners also capable of moving more rapidly, he became a different learner before my eyes — rapt, interested in the topics studied, and interactive with others.

Appropriate pacing of lessons also relates to limiting review of material already learned or providing a quick summary of key points at the beginning of a new lesson. The gifted typically enjoy a rapid pace that matches their mental quickness.

Obviously, however, there are some aspects of curricula where the pace should be deliberately slowed down to allow more time for thinking about ideas and processing information. Some activities, such as writing, require teacher sensitivity to gifted students' individual capacities and needs for longer work periods.

Use of Inquiry

At the most expansive level, inquiry means creating a climate of mutual investigation into a problem, issue, or idea worthy of attention. It requires

Figure 6.1
KEY STRATEGIES FOR USE WITH GIFTED LEARNERS

structuring a situation or activity in such a way as to elicit high-level thinking from learners. Asking open-ended and suggestive questions leads the learner to think through a problem, issue or idea in a deliberate way.

The use of inquiry techniques in gifted programs has long been supported in the literature as well as by enthusiastic teachers who see its effects with this type of learner. Why are inquiry approaches so successful with the gifted? First, gifted learners usually can handle formal operational thought more readily than can other learners, easily and quickly grasping the discovery approach to learning. The gifted have the insight to understand discrepant events in science within a class period, for example, rendering the instructional approach extremely doable in most learning contexts.

Inquiry techniques work well with this population also because of idiosyncratic knowledge of self. Educators can approach and carry out the learning task in many different ways, and thus accommodate to the varying cognitive styles of the gifted.

Last, inquiry approaches work because they are basically problem-centered. The gifted enjoy a good mystery, a puzzle, ambiguity, and paradox. Inquiry provides a learning context wherein the gifted learner's curiosity can roam unchecked, and it sets the stage for these learners to choose their own problems to be solved in future independent investigations.

A clarifying example may lead to a better understanding of the inquiry process.

A. *Stimulus Problem.* Each student is given a Japanese print that depicts a scene in nature, some with human figures, some without. The inquiry task is to study the picture and provide written commentary for each of the following questions:
   1. What objects do you see in your picture?
   2. What ideas does your picture convey?
   3. What feelings does your picture evoke?
   4. If you were to identify with an object in your picture, what would it be, and why?
   5. Based on your impressions, thoughts, and feelings about your picture, can you synthesize your reactions to the picture graphically or in written form?
B. Based on individual responses, each student shares his or her picture with two or three other students and discusses individual reactions. The group then responds to the following questions in a discussion context:
   1. What similarities and differences are present in your picture?
   2. Compare and contrast your individual reactions to each picture. What did you discover?
   3. Based on your experience, what generalizations might you make about the pictures?
   4. Based on your experience, what generalizations might you make about each other?
C. In a framework of group sharing, the total class engages in a debriefing of each group's perceptions. Pictures and ideas are shared across the five to six groups in the room. The total group then responds to the following questions:
   1. Based on your experiences with these prints, what do we know about the Japanese culture (its philosophy, its art, its geography, its religion, etc.)?
   2. What did we learn about each other from this experience?
   3. What important generalizations might you make about cultural understanding from this experience?
D. Key generalizations that might be derived from this inquiry lesson include:
   1. A culture is represented in its art at a symbolic level.

2. Studying artifacts (i.e., Japanese prints) helps us understand ourselves as well as others.
3. Cultural understanding is dependent on understanding multiple perspectives.
4. Knowing other people's perceptions about a given situation or problem helps us appreciate rather than denigrate individual differences.

This example of an inquiry lesson incorporates the nature of the activity, key questions, grouping arrangements, and anticipated outcomes of the lesson. The richness of the discovery, however, is left to individual gifted learners.

Questioning Techniques

Many educators of the gifted view effective questioning as employing a large number of higher-level questions. Other educators have successfully used techniques related to Socratic questioning, which forces the student to think more deeply about the heart of an issue and explore it from many sides. From the teacher's standpoint, the strategy calls for asking probing questions directed to central points.

The Junior Great Books Foundation, long a purveyor of key literature materials used in gifted programs, recommends focus on interpretive questions. It discourages teachers from asking either factual or evaluative questions and, rather, encourages the use of question clusters that direct the discussion along predetermined lines. Teachers are asked to read a story carefully and then single out the major aspect of interpretation, that area of the story that is intriguing to a reader because it has not been thoroughly explicated.

In Shirley Jackson's classic short story, "The Lottery," the plot culminates in the stoning by her neighbors of one Mrs. Henderson, who drew the black spot on her paper in the lottery process. The story is intriguing because (a) there is no real reason the lottery is being held; only tradition and rituals keep it going; (b) the townspeople have no reason to punish one of their own, for no crime has been committed against their society; thus (c) the sheer horror of the act is overwhelming to the reader. What is horribly open to interpretation in this story is why the townspeople stoned an innocent woman, and why this lottery ritual has been allowed to continue in the village. Thus, a question cluster for a 45-minute discussion with sixth-grade gifted students might be:

1. From the story, what do we know about Mrs. Henderson? About her husband? About others in her family?
2. Why, according to the author, does the town carry out a lottery?
3. What signs of foreboding does the story portend before the final act occurs?
4. What clues does the author provide that the ending of the story will be tragic?

5. Why do the townspeople carry out the stoning? What does this act reveal about their character?
6. A lottery usually represents "equality of opportunity"; in state lotteries, for example, people have equal opportunity to win prizes. How does Jackson treat this idea of "equality of opportunity" in the story?

In addition, many inquiry-based question paradigms have become popular. Sanders (1966) introduced several in his early book, and others including Barth and Shermis (1981) have modified preceding lists for "goodness of fit" with a specific content domain.

The Barth approach utilizes parts of the Guilford's structure of intellect model as the underlying organizer for developing the question set in social studies:

Question Type	Key Question
Memory/cognition	Who started the Civil War?
Convergent	Why was the conflict begun?
Divergent	What if the South had won the war?
	What might have occurred differently in the U.S. from 1865–1900?
Evaluative	In your opinion, who was the most impressive Civil War general? Why?

The model also can be applied easily to language arts and literature, as seen in the following question set for the charming African folktale, *Bringing the Rain to Kapiti Plain* by Verna Aardema.

Memory/Cognition
1. What caused the grass to turn brown?
2. What are some of the other things that happened as a result of no rain?
3. What did Kipat do to solve the problem of no rain?

Convergent
1. What important qualities did Kipat have?
2. Why did Kipat think of using a feather?
3. How does this story show the relationship of cause and effect in nature?
4. Why did the author end the story with Kipat's son tending the herds?

Divergent
1. Pretend you are a herdsman in Africa. What obstacles do you face in carrying out your job?

2. What if the cows had died? How might the story have been different?

Evaluative
1. Why do you think Kipat waited as long as he did to get married?
2. What did you think of the way the author used rhyme to tell the story?
3. In your opinion, what is the best part of the story? Why?

Another effective questioning strategy has been used in the Great Books study program. This model is particularly effective with secondary-level gifted students. Students begin by responding to hypothetical situations, then begin discussing the meaning of a given passage, and conclude by linking ideas in a particular work to the real world of applications.

Sample Reading Passage

Can poverty in the United States be abolished within the limits of the welfare state?

The answer is clear enough. The government's own figures demonstrate that the current antipoverty programs are basically inadequate. I do not, however, want to dismiss completely the government's antipoverty programs. Current serious discussion of poverty in this country is a gain which one owes in part to that program. But there is no point in pretending that a little more welfarism will do away with a national shame.

Today's poor are different from the pre-Second World War poor. The "old" poor lived at a time when economic opportunity was the national trend, when the net income from the growth of American manufacturing increased by 4,500 percent. It was the "old" poor, mostly Eastern European immigrants unified by language and culture, who created the big-city political machines and participated in the organization of unions and the political struggle for the New Deal. They had objective, realistic reason for hope.

An analysis of the first phase and second phase of the New Deal of the Roosevelt administration is quite relevant at this point. The first phase of the New Deal, supported by corporate dream — economy planned by business. The second phase of the New Deal (the source of today's welfare theory and antipoverty wisdom) moved away from the concept of planning and toward a "free market." The assumption was that in its intervention the government should not plan but should stimulate the economy and that the private sector and initiative would continue to be the mainspring of progress.

After the Second World War, the government started emphasizing training programs because some workers were not participating in the general economic advance. However, these training programs have missed the fundamental prob-

lem. The novelty of impoverishment today is that it takes place in a time of automation. The government offers education and training and at the same time admits that the jobs for its graduates are obsolete. Such hypocrisy reinforces the cynicism and resistance to organization which characterizes poor communities.

It is therefore crucial that the federal government generate jobs and create an environment of economic hope. The essence of the "third phase" of the New Deal would be social investment, a conscious and political allocation of resources to meet public needs. This New Deal would be dependent upon a coalition, which would include, but not be confined to, the poor, that would see to it that planning and social investment were extended in a democratic way.

Source: From the College Board, *10 SAT's* (p. 206), 1983, New York: College Entrance Examination Board.

Application of the Great Books Questioning Model

Opening Questions
1. Propose a title for the passage. What is your title?
2. What audience would be interested in reading the passage? Why do you think so?
3. How would President Bush react to this passage? Why?
4. What public figures would agree with the perspective in the passage? Would any of our American presidents?

Core: Examining Central Points
1. According to the passage, is it possible for:

Yes   No

Yes	No		
____	____	a.	poverty to be abolished?
____	____	b.	America to return to pre-World War II levels of economic opportunity?
____	____	c.	poverty to be reduced in the current free market atmosphere?
____	____	d.	job training programs to solve the problem of poverty?
____	____	e.	America's poor today to have economic hope?

2. How would you rank order the following ideas for dealing with poverty in America, based on the perspective of the author of this passage?

____ Be more competitive in the world marketplace.
____ Stimulate the economy.
____ Create coalitions of support for social investment.

_____ Return to earlier phases of the New Deal.
_____ Let business plan the economy.
_____ Reduce hopelessness among the poor.

Which did you rank first? Why?
Which did you rank last? Why?

Closing: Relating to the World

1. If fighting poverty requires "social investment," how might that approach be undertaken?
2. At what levels can this concept of "social investment" be employed? (neighborhoods, social community, states, at a global level)
3. How "marketable" is this idea in today's world?

These examples of questioning techniques represent many approaches that are effective with gifted learners. In making decisions about questions to be asked, practitioners should ask:

1. What is the purpose of each question and of the string or cluster of questions? Do they individually and collectively contribute to greater student understanding of the work under study?
2. Are the questions interesting to *you*? Would you like to discuss them?
3. Do the questions encourage students to think more deeply about a story or event?
4. Do the questions encourage discussion and dialogue?
5. Do the questions raise issues, themes, and problems central to the story or event?
6. Will the questions carry a discussion for 45 minutes, without the teacher having to intervene unduly?

Both of the approaches cited here have to be preceded by careful reading of assigned text material, for they are predicated on a student's basic knowledge and comprehension of reading material in order to be able to discuss ideas intelligently. Questioning strategies can be effective only if students are prepared to engage in the inquiry process.

Problem Solving

One of the most frequently used forms of problem solving has followed the model of creative problem solving, popularized by Parnes (1975) and by Feldhusen and Treffinger (1979). This model emphasizes equally the processes of problem finding and problem solving and allows students to develop a self-generated plan of action. Although the model is highly structured and moves from divergent to convergent inquiry with some regularity, it does provide an excellent context in which to teach the importance of both types of inquiry for generating a worthwhile "product." The model is delineated as follows (Parnes, 1975):

Creative Problem Solving

1. *Fact finding: gathering data in preparation for defining the problem*
   — Identify the problem by asking questions: Who? What? Where? When? Why?

2. *Problem finding: analyzing problematic areas in order to pick out and point up the problem to be attacked*
   — Question: "In what ways might I . . .?"
   — Gather data

3. *Idea finding: idea production — thinking up, processing, and developing numerous possible leads to solutions*
   — Put to other uses
   — Modify
   — Magnify
   — Rearrange
   — Combine
   — Adapt
   — Minimize
   — Substitute
   — Reverse

4. *Solution finding: evaluating potential solutions against defined criteria*
   — Establish criteria
   — Evaluate
   — Verify
   — Test

5. *Acceptance finding: adoption — developing a plan of action and implementing the chosen solution*
   — Implement
   — Prepare for acceptance

Source: From *Aha! Insights into Creative Behavior* by S. J. Parnes, 1975, Buffalo, NY: DOK Publishers.

An activity for gifted students using the model in a secondary English classroom might include the following guided inquiry:

I. *Problem Generation*
    A. What are all the problems faced by characters in important American novels we have read? (brainstorm problems)
    B. What are the most critical and general problems? (pick three, then one)

II. *Problem Clarification*
   A. Where are illustrations of the problem?
   B. What are things that cause the problem?
   C. What are further problems caused by the problem?

III. *Problem Identification*
   A. State the problem in light of Stage II discussion.
   B. State problems as a "how" question.

IV. *Idea Finding*
   A. What could the character do?
   B. Brainstorm solutions.

V. *Synthesizing a Solution*
   A. Pick out the best elements from Stage IV.
   B. Develop a comprehensive solution.
   C. Does it fit the problem statement?

VI. *Implementation*
   A. Who?
   B. How?
   C. What order of events?
   D. Precautions/obstacles
   E. How to overcome obstacles

USE OF BIBLIOTHERAPY

Key instructional approaches can be valuable in working with the gifted in the psychosocial domain, as in cognitive areas. Teachers and parents many times are in an excellent position to provide guidance to students in several areas of psychosocial development. These guidance techniques may be integral to other teaching and learning activities in the classroom. One of these approaches is bibliotherapy, the use of books to help learners reach important understandings about themselves and others. Deliberately choosing books that have a gifted child as a protagonist is an excellent way for students to begin identifying some of their own problems in others. Through discussion, gifted students can come to new awareness about how to cope with their problems. One example follows.

Problem identified: Understanding differences
Book: *Lord of the Flies*
Key questions:

- Why did the group ostracize Piggy?
- What might he have done to prevent this?
- According to the author, what happens to people who feel rejected?

- Can you think of a time when you have felt rejected? How did you respond or react? How might you have changed your behavior to obtain more favorable results?

(Write individually and then discuss as a group.)

An excellent teacher reference for this type of activity is a booklist from the National Council of Teachers of English entitled *The Gifted Child in Literature* (Tway, 1980).

A second area of psychosocial development that a teacher can help the gifted explore is their tendency toward perfectionism. By focusing on open-ended activities and leading students to engage in "safe" risk-taking behaviors, teachers can set a climate in which students are encouraged to accept that most situations in life do not require *one* right answer — rendering unimportant the standard the gifted often set to rate themselves and others on the way to "perfection." An example of an activity follows.

Pass out pictures (the same picture for every three students) that are impressionistic in style, and ask students to respond to these vital stimuli according to the following paradigm:

1. What did you observe in the picture? (Make a list of what you see.)
2. What ideas does your picture convey?
3. What feelings does your picture evoke?
4. If you were to identify with an object in your picture, what would you identify with and why?
5. Now spend a few minutes synthesizing your observations, ideas, feelings, and reactions to your picture in whatever form you wish. You may choose to write a poem, draw a picture, create a descriptive story, etc.

After each student has responded individually to these questions and activities, have the three students in each group discuss each other's perceptions of the pictures. Then, if you wish, ask individual students to share their pictures and their reactions to them. Follow-up may include whole-group discussion of similarities and differences in the pictures. This activity can also introduce a unit of study on cultural or individual differences.

A third area of exploration with the gifted involves forming meaningful relationships and developing friendships. For this area of psychosocial development, books such as *The Bunny Who Wanted a Friend,* by Joan Berg, is an example of a key tool with primary-age students. Questions such as the following can be used to elicit understanding of the strategies by which we gain friends:

1. What are all the reasons the bunny did not have a friend?
2. What was wrong with his method of making friends?
3. What was his "secret" to finally finding a friend?
4. What if you were the bunny? How would you have tried to get a friend?
5. Why were the bunny and the bird friends at the end of the story? List the reasons.

All of these bibliotherapy strategies are viable for use with the gifted in both home and school settings.

SELECTING INSTRUCTIONAL STRATEGIES

Instructional processes serve the important function of mediating the objective of any lesson and the receptivity level of students to that objective. Thus, the function of instruction, though not paramount, is critical to the enterprise of teaching and learning. And, it might be argued, the mode of instruction for gifted learners is less critical, given their ability to connect with content and master it usually quickly and well. Yet, even the gifted need high quality instruction to maximize their knowledge acquisition and minimize the time and energy needed to focus on lower-level work. If a teacher cannot mediate the knowledge acquisition process effectively for individual learners, the best curriculum plan and set of activities will go awry.

How does one go about mediation? Is it dependent on learned skills in areas such as discovery learning or inquiry or in asking the right level questions or in using teaching paradigms such as creative problem solving? Merely manipulating process is insufficient to mediate curricula for the gifted. We also must attend to manipulation of content in fundamental ways.

By way of example, one of the alternative activity sets from chapter 5, Table 5.1, representing a continuum from "less appropriate" to "more appropriate" is:

Discuss plot, setting and characters in the short story "A Rose for Emily."   *Compare and contrast the plot, setting, character motivation, and theme of "A Rose for Emily" and "The Bear."*

This pair of activities, geared for use at the secondary level, represents important distinctions. The more appropriate activity on the right engages learners in critical analysis as the foundational element of their manipulation of knowledge. Moreover, it seeks to have them use two stimuli to do so. Another distinction lies in the more complex and abstract task of manipulating theme and character motivation in addition to the basic elements of plot, character, and setting.

If we agree that the activity on the right is more appropriate for gifted learners, what instructional mediation would enhance its use? We could:

— hold a discussion in which students demonstrate their capacity to do the activity in oral form.
— have students develop an expository essay in class, and conference with them individually or in small groups regarding their analysis.
— lecture on key elements of short stories, and use the activity as a seatwork application of information for quizzing students on their understanding.
— develop panel discussion groups that allow students to discuss and present as a group their critical analysis of the two stories.
— engage students in "creating a representational visual product" that conveys their analysis of the stories — videotape, mobile, slides, collage, etc.
— assign the activity as homework — a direct follow-up to a class lecture and discussion on short story elements.

How does one make the choice among a list of options? Selecting the instructional process for this activity depends on several factors:

1. *Instructional time*. Given the relative importance of a specific activity, decisions about instructional process have to consider real time constraints. Some options are more time-consuming than others. If time is limited, a strategy that will work in the allotted time would be more prudent.
2. *Mixing of instructional processes*. Choice of a process to accompany any activity is somewhat dependent on what processes preceded this one and what will follow it as well. Various approaches work well with gifted learners.
3. *Student need for a particular approach*. The needs of gifted learners themselves sometimes affect a choice of instructional process. Perhaps they need more cooperative learning at a given point, or need to enhance expository writing skills, or be able to orally articulate a perspective. Such needs then may become a criterion for choosing the approach.
4. *Effectiveness of a given approach with gifted learners*. A meta-analysis of research on gifted learners has demonstrated a high effect size for increased homework, a moderate effect size for active questioning and discussion, and a moderate effect size for inquiry-discovery teaching (Walberg, 1990). To make intelligent choices of strategies, we have to examine what we know about what works. In the three strategies cited, recognizing the role that each could play in delivering curriculum would be an important perspective.
5. *The nature of the activity itself*. The choice of activity may make the choice of instructional process easier, for many activities call out for the use of particular strategies. For example, we might discern that our critical analysis activity is basically a reflective activity, one in which gifted learners need considerable time to think about the two stories in depth. Therefore, an instructional process that honors thinking time may be a better choice than one that emphasizes quick response or group interaction skills.

Instructional choice can be made once all factors have been considered. As in other aspects of this curriculum design model, the emphasis is on careful thinking and planning of what to do.

CURRICULUM MANAGEMENT STRATEGIES

An imperceptible line separates instructional strategies from management techniques. Yet, addressing the fundamental ways in which teachers need to organize classrooms to accommodate the gifted would seem to be important. Major curriculum management techniques include various grouping arrangements, individualized approaches including individualized education programs (IEPs), diagnostic-prescriptive approaches, and learning contracts and agreements, as shown in Figure 6.2 and discussed in the remainder of the chapter. Several writers have focused on the importance of these techniques in planning a curriculum for gifted learners (Parke, 1989; Parker, 1989; Feldhusen, 1986). Each technique offers opportunities for a differentiated program of study to be delivered to gifted learners.

Grouping Techniques

In the absence of grouping strategies, much of the power of any differentiated curriculum or instructional plan would be lost, for the grouping arrangement gives the gifted the potential to fully respond to any curriculum. Key grouping strategies are cooperative learning groups, cluster grouping, dyads and triads, learning centers, and cross-age grouping.

Cooperative Learning Groups

Cooperative learning has become popular in recent years. All students in the group contribute actively to the problem under study, and group energy propels learners toward mastery of the material. To make cooperative learning effective for the gifted, students' ability and interest must be considered in establishing the groups. Cooperative learning can be a powerful way to organize gifted learners for an English project in which each student has a role to perform. Examples include:

— writing skits.
— performing a play.
— developing an advertising campaign.
— organizing a literary exhibit.
— producing a literary magazine.
— conducting research on a topic from a multiple source/multiple viewpoint perspective.

Cluster Grouping

In cluster grouping, gifted students are assigned to one teacher as part of an overall class at a given grade level. The gifted can be grouped and regrouped

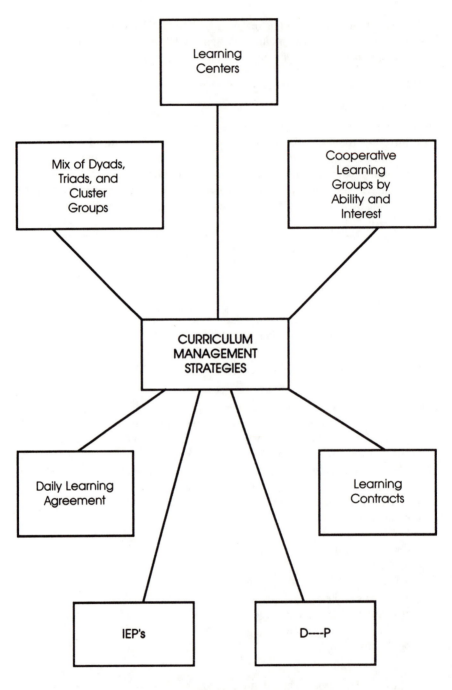

Figure 6.2
CLASSROOM ORGANIZATION OPTIONS

within the classroom to accommodate different instructional needs. For academic subjects, members of the cluster group work together on the same instructional plan while other students in the room follow a different plan.

Dyads and Triads

This grouping strategy allows gifted learners to find one or two true peers in the classroom with whom they can work effectively. Sometimes these pairings occur naturally, and other times they are carefully nurtured by an insightful teacher. This approach to learning is ideal for initiating independent projects and for having students move ahead somewhat independently in parts of the English curriculum. Rather than having an isolated student work alone on English grammar and usage or do an enrichment project, having two or three students do the assignment together is better, even if the ability levels are somewhat different. As long as the gifted learners are well motivated and interested in the learning task, some ability differences can be tolerated. This grouping approach also encourages social development beyond the classroom, in the form of study groups or less formal get-togethers.

Learning Centers

Many gifted classrooms establish learning centers and have students actively participate in center activities according to a rotating schedule throughout the week. Gifted learners are typically accommodated by either (a) extended activities in each center geared to their level of need or (b) a gifted center where all instructional activities are geared to their level. This approach provides instructional alternatives for all class members and enables students to develop responsibility for their own learning in selected areas of the curriculum. A center model can be organized in a high school library rather than a classroom. The important concept is the student's freedom in choice of activities and voluntary movement toward desired learning opportunities.

Cross-Age Grouping

Cross-age grouping allows gifted learners, within two or three grade levels of each other to work together in areas of strength and interest. Some high schools offer courses across grade levels. Others bring together groups of gifted students at predetermined times during the week. This technique is frequently used in small schools with few gifted children at each grade level.

All of these approaches should be considered in providing appropriate instructional options for gifted learners at the classroom level. Because even the most critical opponents of ability grouping voice support for instructional grouping (Slavin, 1986; Oakes, 1985), schools would be prudent to enhance their programs with variations of the grouping strategies discussed. Without grouping provisions, the gifted have limited access to appropriate challenges in the context of elementary and secondary classrooms and programs.

The Diagnostic-Prescriptive Approach

In the diagnostic-prescriptive approach, each gifted learner takes a diagnostic test at the beginning of the school year over subject matter to be studied that year. Based on this information, the student's instructional range is determined both for grade-level skill development or content-based knowledge and for the level of capacity to engage in concepts and problem solving in verbal, mathematical, and scientific domains. Students then are grouped in whatever configuration best matches their instructional range and are provided opportunities to move at a rate in the curriculum consonant with their tested level of competency and their aptitude to engage in more challenging curricula.

Expectations for annual accomplishment in the area are determined with each group by the teacher, based on a differential starting point. Thus, a group of fifth graders conceivably could be studying algebra or probability and statistics as their core math program. For less precocious math students, work in problem-solving heuristics and symbolic logic might accompany their work at appropriate levels in pre-algebra mathematics.

Learning Contracts/Agreements

Learning contracts or daily/weekly agreements can be used to help students manage their own curriculum plan according to a time frame that individual students might handle. Feldhusen (1986) recommends a weekly form on which gifted students plan each day's work and make choices in the areas of reading, mathematics, writing, and several other curriculum areas that could change daily. Options include (a) working out of programmed materials at an individual level, (b) working at a center in activities such as writing ads, poetry, or bookmaking in creative writing, (c) using a diagnostic-prescriptive model in basic materials, and (d) interacting in a group discussion after reading an assigned book. Students then make decisions about individual and sub-groupings in order to complete their work each day. Teachers monitor the completed work and its consonance with the choices made.

Individualized Education Programs

Developing IEPs as an annual process for differentiating curricula for the gifted is another management technique used in several states as a particularly effective way to serve the gifted learner in the regular classroom. IEPs vary considerably in terms of format and duration. A weekly learning agreement might be part of the IEP structure, but individualized record keeping may be most useful over a year's span. Typically, an IEP for the gifted would include:

— annual goals in learning (negotiated between teacher and learner).
— specific short-term objectives.
— activity options to lead to mastery of short-term objectives.

— a mechanism to evaluate student progress.

— assessment data emphasizing student strengths and weaknesses and major student interests.

All of these management techniques should be considered in classroom delivery and implementation of a planned curriculum. This is the level of the design process at which individual rather than group adaptations are made. Modifying a preplanned curriculum is an integral part of maintaining the necessary curriculum flexibility for individual gifted learners.

SUMMARY

Instructional strategies are crucial in delivering curricula for the gifted learner. No curriculum is likely to be judged effective with gifted learners without careful choices regarding strategies. Alternative strategies include small groups, individual consultation, inquiry, questioning techniques, pacing, and problem solving. Many educators cite the importance of linking teacher behaviors to student outcomes. Exemplary teachers plan curricula well, use various teaching strategies, select questions that stimulate higher-level thinking, foster critical thinking, creative thinking, and problem solving, encourage independent thinking and open inquiry, conduct group discussions well, promote student-directed work, and provide a healthy learning environment, among other behaviors.

Bibliotherapy — the use of books to further learning — is one strategy that is particularly effective with the gifted. Through books, they can gain insight by identifying their problems in others, exploring their tendency for perfectionism, and learning how to develop friendships.

In selecting which instructional strategies to use, the teacher has to consider the amount of time required, a mix of processes, individual need and effectiveness of a given approach with that learner, and the nature of the activity itself.

In curriculum management, grouping techniques include cooperative learning groups, cluster grouping, dyads and triads, learning centers, and cross-age grouping. Curriculum management can be undertaken also through the diagnostic-prescriptive approach, through learning contracts/agreements, and individualized education programs.

QUESTIONS FOR REFLECTION

1. How can gifted educators find effective ways to monitor teacher behaviors in the classroom to ensure high-level instruction for the gifted?

2. How might videotaping and peer coaching be employed to improve teaching strategies?

3. What combinations of strategies might maximize creative productivity for gifted learners?

4. How might we better organize classrooms to manage the instructional processes and management techniques advocated in this chapter?
5. "Gifted education is just good teaching." How would you respond to this
   statement?

REFERENCES

Barth, J. L., & Shermis, S. S. (1981). *Teaching social studies to the gifted and talented*. Indianapolis:
    Indiana State Department of Public Instruction; Lafayette: Purdue University Div. of Curriculum.
    (ED 212118)

Feldhusen, J. (1986). *Individualized teaching of gifted children in regular classrooms*. New York:
    DOK Publishing.

Feldhusen, J. & Treffinger, D. (1979). *Creative thinking and problem-solving*. Dubuque, IA: Kendall-
    Hunt.

Lipman, M. (1988). Critical thinking — What can it be? *Educational Leadership, 46*, 38–43.

Martinson, R. (1974). Martinson-Weiner rating scale of behaviors in teachers of the gifted. In *A Guide
    Toward Better Teaching for the Gifted*. Ventura, CA: Ventura County Superintendent of Schools.

Norris, S. P. (1985). Synthesis of research on critical thinking. *Educational Leadership, 42*, 40–45.

Oakes, J. (1985). *Keeping track: How schools structure inequality*. New Haven, CT: Yale University
    Press.

Parker, B. N. (1989). *Gifted students in regular classrooms*. Boston: Allyn & Bacon.

Parker, J. P. (1989). *Instructional strategies for teaching the gifted*. Boston: Allyn & Bacon.

Parnes, S. (1975). *Aha! Insights into creative behavior*. Buffalo, New York: DOK Publishing.

Sanders, N. M. (1966). *Classroom questions: What kinds*. New York: Harper and Row.

Shulman, L. A. (1987). Assessment for teaching: An initiative for the profession. *Phi Delta Kappan,
    69*, 38–44.

Slavin, R. (1986). *Educational psychology: Theory into practice*. Englewood Cliffs, NJ: Prentice-
    Hall.

Sternberg, R. J., & Bhana, K. (1986). Synthesis of research on the effectiveness of intellectual skills
    programs: Snake-oil remedies or miracle cures? *Educational Leadership, 44*, 60–67.

Tway, E. (1980). The gifted child in literature. *Language Arts, 57*(1), 14–20.

VanTassel-Baska, J., Feldhusen, J., Seeley, K., Wheatley, G., Silverman, L., & Foster, W. (1988).
    Comprehensive Curriculum for Gifted Learners. Boston: Allyn & Bacon.

Walberg, H. (1990). Presentation at Indiana Department of Public Instruction conference, Indiana-
    polis.

CHAPTER SEVEN

Assessing and Evaluating Curricula

A ssessment of the impact of a gifted program curriculum on learners is one of the most important aspects in curriculum design work. This is the stage of analysis at which one can begin to understand the learner's level of comprehension and knowledge of what we had hoped to teach. At this stage we have a sense of "learning receptivity" rather than "social receptivity" in the learner. The purpose of the assessment process is multidimensional. It provides insights into student progress in a curriculum and attempts to pinpoint future needs in a curriculum area for a learner. As such, it is a critical tool for ongoing curriculum planning. Moreover, assessment data instruct us about how well our deliberate planning and teaching of learner outcomes have fared. Under ideal circumstances, each stated learner outcome in a curriculum for the gifted would have a corresponding assessment technique so that each learning focus could be measured and evaluated. Figure 7.1 depicts these multiple purposes of assessment.

Because the emphasis of our educational enterprise with the gifted is different from that with typical learners, the match between learner outcomes and assessment approaches is all the more crucial. Standardized tests normed on typical populations tell us almost nothing about growth in learning for gifted populations.

Part of the problem in evaluating gifted learner outcomes lies with the evaluation methodology available to demonstrate effectiveness in gifted programs. Tests must be carefully selected and piloted for potential ceiling effects in which outcomes exceed those measured. A ceiling effect occurs when scores for a particular group cluster toward the top of a scale rather than in a more meaningful distribution, which would indicate growth gains. If a score is at the top of a scale before and after a particular educational treatment, nothing is known about the effects of the treatment. The gifted tend to score at the top of an in-grade standardized test at the outset, further growth cannot be measured with subsequent administrations of the same type of test.

Another part of the problem is understanding how evaluation results can be utilized to improve programs for the gifted. Too frequently evaluation reports are merely shelved. Callahan and Caldwell (1984) synthesized the literature on effective utilization of evaluation results and found that the conceptualization of

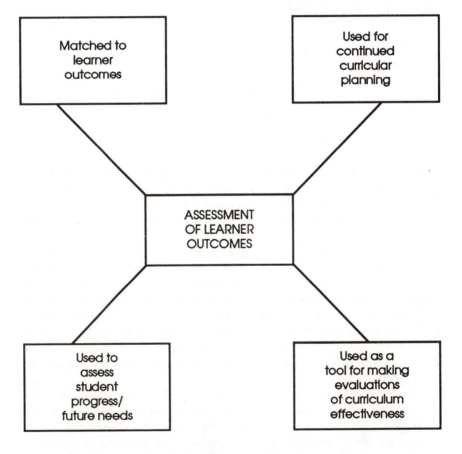

Figure 7.1
THE ROLE OF ASSESSMENT IN CURRICULUM DESIGN

the evaluation process, the credibility of information, the timing, and the feasibility of the evaluation are the most critical elements determining usefulness. Carter and Hamilton (1985) noted the problem of relying on attitudinal data rather than data on student growth or change to validate program effectiveness.

Approaches for evaluating gifted programs have also been delineated in the literature. Archambault (1984) advocated better quantitative designs in gifted education, to measure program outcomes as well as qualitative procedures. Some researchers have viewed naturalistic evaluation as useful in special program areas such as gifted education as long as systematic procedures are followed and triangulation of results is obtained from multiple data sources (Stake, 1975; Barnette, 1984). Trazler (1987) recommended early design of learning assessment procedures by an individual knowledgeable in assessment of learning.

GUIDELINES FOR BUILDING AN ASSESSMENT MODEL

In evaluating curriculum interventions with the gifted, the following principles should be considered in building an assessment model:

1. *The assessment model should use multiple measures and varied types of measures.* The most promising approaches in assessing gifted learner outcomes include portfolios of students' work, product evaluation, and observational checklists of student behaviors. (Sample forms that delineate key behaviors are included at the end of this chapter.)
2. *The assessment model should attempt to establish triangulation of perceived benefits.* When attempting to delineate student benefits from a special curriculum for the gifted, parents, students, and teachers should be asked the same questions, to establish triangulation of results from three different publics. If three different groups concur on the outcomes derived from the program, this can help take the edge off the subjectivity of the responses.
3. *The assessment model should work across three levels: curriculum validity, perceived benefit, and actual student outcomes.* Curriculum effectiveness can be analyzed at three levels, as depicted in Figure 7.2. At Level 1 we can establish content or face validity by subjecting initial curriculum development efforts to the scrutiny of trained curriculum specialists. At Level 2 we can obtain attitudinal/perceptual data on effectiveness, and at Level 3 we can more directly measure impact on student learning. Attention to all three levels ensures a systematic approach to revising curriculum efforts so that desired changes are fed back into the curriculum design process.
4. *The assessment model should incorporate long-term and short-term measures.* One interpretation of this idea suggests that frequent quizzes and less frequent tests taken in combination are more desirable than only one or the other approach. This idea has saliency for other types of evaluative tools as well. Short-term products combined with one long-term project reveal more of what has been learned than only short projects or only one long-term one.

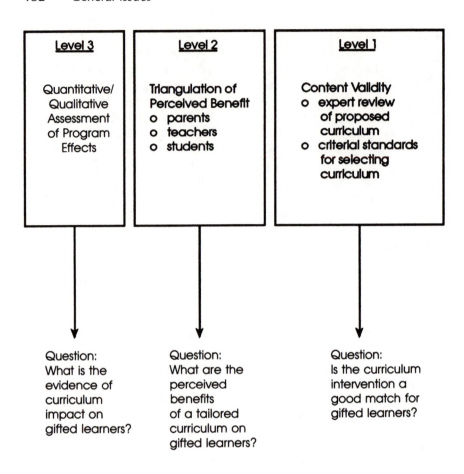

Figure 7.2
LEVELS OF ANALYSIS IN CURRICULUM EVALUATION

This combination honors the concept of time series as a mode of assessment. We want to know how the learner has progressed incrementally as well as where he or she has ended up at the end of 32 weeks of intervention.

5. *The assessment model should incorporate multiple approaches to evaluation design.* A good combination might be pre-post, time-series, and product assessment. Because gifted learner outcomes are geared to higher levels than typical student outcomes, relying on one approach to evaluation to achieve the outcomes desired becomes problematic. Moreover, gifted curricula/pro-

grams frequently have outcomes that are incompatible with the use of one design. Thus, a combinational approach is recommended. An overall assessment model for the College of William and Mary's Governor's School in Science and Technology, Table 7.1, illustrates well this issue of multiple design approaches.

Table 7.1
EVALUATION PLAN: 1990 GOVERNOR'S SCHOOL FOR SCIENCE AND TECHNOLOGY

Objective	Type of Data Gathering Instrument	Data Collection Methodology	Person(s) Responsible
1. Students will develop content knowledge in one of four domains of science: geology, physics, chemistry, biology.	Regular academic classwork.	Collect and assess classwork. Provide evaluators with student achievement.	Academic teams
2. Students will develop their ability to relate content knowledge *across* domains of science.	Cognitive structure task.	Pre-post during first and last week.	Evaluation team
3. Students will develop and demonstrate inquiry skills in an applied laboratory setting in geology, physics, chemistry, or biology.	Lab or field reports, or both	Collect and assess reports. Provide evaluators with student achievement.	Academic teams
4. Students will develop their understanding of the principles of the scientific method and their ability to apply these principles in the process of doing science.	Two experimental design problems.	Pre-post during first and last week.	Dorm counselors will distribute and collect.

Table 7.1
CONTINUED

5. Students will develop their ability to apply moral and ethical considerations to science and technology.	Hypothetical moral/ethical science-related dilemmas.	Pre-post during first and last week.	Dorm counselors will distribute and collect.
6. Students will develop cooperative and collaborative attitudes, work habits, and interaction skills in both academic and non-academic settings.	Checklist rating of interpersonal skill.	Post-test during last week.	Dorm counselors will rate students.
7. Students will develop and demonstrate their ability to take full advantage of the kinds of educational opportunities and resources afforded by a program like the Governor's School.	Self-rating student evaluation form.	Post-test during last week.	Dorm counselors will distribute and collect.

Source: From *Evaluation Report of the 1990 Governor's School Program* by G. Bass and R. Reis, 1991, Williamsburg, VA: College of William and Mary.

6. *The assessment model should be developed early, preferably at the time learner outcomes are designed.* For each learner outcome in a curriculum for the gifted, a requisite outcome assessment approach should be delineated. This is much easier to do while the overall planning process is evolving than after the instructional features have been delineated. The assessment approach also should influence choices made in the instructional pattern. Table 7.1 again highlights this principle.

7. *The assessment model should be seen as a basis for making evaluative judgments about the effectiveness of the curriculum design elements singly or in combination.*

A learner outcome may state:

90% of gifted students at grade 6 will increase their problem-solving abilities by 30% pre-post on a measure of mathematics and heuristic use. Only 40% of the students increased at the stated criterion level, whereas 50% of the students increased by 20%. For 30% of the students, no increases were noted. Yet the pre-post assessment also revealed that the 30% who showed no increase were already operating at the 75% or higher on the pre-test measure.

How should we interpret and therefore "evaluate" the outcome of this assessment? The standard interpretation would be to say that the outcome was not met, and therefore the teacher should work harder at this outcome another year. This, however, is a simplistic interpretation of the assessment data. Another interpretation, perhaps more valid, would be that the criterion level of 30% is inappropriate, given the nature of the outcome and the nature of the learner. Thus, we may evaluate the outcome of assessment by taking into account the relative difficulty in showing growth gains for a group already scoring very high on a pre-test. For another year, we may wish to alter the criterion level, change the substance of the outcome, or target activities more sharply to address the desired outcome. This decision must be based on careful consideration of all aspects of the design process, not just the end result.

Evaluation of student learner outcomes for gifted programs should be undertaken at least once each year. With some process outcomes, evaluation could occur less frequently, perhaps once every three years.

PERCEPTIONS OF BENEFIT BY RELEVANT GROUPS

Beyond assessing the face validity of curriculum materials for use with gifted learners at requisite stages of development, the materials should be piloted in classrooms as soon as feasible. After a curriculum unit has been studied, students and teachers should respond to questions like the following, based on their curriculum experiences.

Student Questions
- What new learning did you acquire as a result of the unit of study just completed?
- What aspects of the unit were repetitive or focused on things you already know?
- What in the unit was most interesting to you? Why?
- What aspects of the unit didn't you enjoy?
- What activities did you find most impactful?
- If you were to experience this unit of study again, what one change would you like to see?

Teacher Questions
- What do you perceive to be the major benefits to your students from the unit?
- What were the activities they found most motivating?

- What instructional strategies/management techniques worked the best in implementing the unit?
- What aspects of the unit didn't work for you?
- What aspect of the unit did you enjoy teaching the most? Why?
- How would you change the unit the next time you teach it?

CONTENT-BASED ASSESSMENT APPROACHES FOR STUDENT IMPACTS

Assessing learner outcomes allows us to get a clearer picture of the nature and extent of learning that has occurred in a special program. Consequently, gifted programs require multiple and diverse ways of assessing student progress in the absence of good standardized instruments.

For example, diverse approaches to evaluation are identified in Table 7.2 according to major strands in a language arts curriculum. Content area considerations, as well as type of emphasis in the program, dictate appropriate techniques for evaluation.

FORM A
Essay Evaluation Form

Directions: Rate each student on a 1 (low) to 5 (high) scale for each item number listed.

Technical Qualities

____ 1.   Thesis
      a.   Writer effectively expresses central idea in a clearly stated thesis.
      b.   Thesis clearly arises from an analysis of/encounter with the assigned topic (rather than a thesis arbitrarily imposed upon a subject).
      c.   Organization and development of essay are controlled by the focus and limits of the thesis.

____ 2.   Paragraph Unity
      a.   Each paragraph contains only those ideas relevant to the topic of the paragraph.
      b.   Sentences within each paragraph are sensibly ordered.
      c.   Sentences are connected with clear transitions.

____ 3.   Developmental Flow
      a.   Progression of paragraphs follows a sensible order.
      b.   Transitions are used as needed to clarify relationships among paper's major points.
      c.   Writer adequately develops major points with explanation, exemplification, and evidence. (Abstractions are made concrete; generalizations are supported with specific detail.)

_____ 4. Logic
    a. Writer has avoided conceptual errors [tautologies (circular reasoning), faulty cause and effect, contradiction, faulty identification — for instance, defining entities in terms of what they are not — unexamined, unsupported assumptions].
    b. Writer has avoided factual errors (misquotations, evidence out of context, misidentifications, insensitivity to or misappropriation of historical context).
    c. Writer has avoided syntactical errors (faulty parallel structure, excessive subordination or coordination, awkward shifts in grammatical structures).

_____ 5. Conclusions
    a. Writer brings essay to satisfying ending.
    b. Writer synthesizes main ideas.

_____ 6. Grammar and Mechanics
    Writer uses appropriate grammar and shows evidence of mechanical control.

_____ 7. Diction
    a. Writer consistently uses tone appropriate to audience addressed.
    b. Writer creates an authentic voice.
    c. Words chosen are precise and appropriate to context.
    d. Writer avoids needless repetition.
    e. Writer avoids wordiness and cliches.

FORM B
Sample Essay Evaluation Questions for Use in Literature Programs for the Gifted

1. Setting is the physical environment in which action occurs. It includes time and place.

   In many novels and plays, setting is used significantly. For example, the author may employ it as a motivating force in human behavior, as a reflection of the state of mind of characters, or as a representation of the values held by characters.

   Choose a novel or a play in which setting is important and write an essay in which you explain the uses the author makes of it.

2. "The struggle to achieve dominance over others frequently appears in fiction."

   Choose a novel in which a struggle for dominance occurs, and write an essay showing for what purposes the author uses the struggle.

   Do not merely retell the story.

3. Choose a complex and important character in a novel or a play of recognized literary merit who might — on the basis of the character's actions alone — be considered evil or immoral. In a well organized essay, explain both how and why full presentation of the character in the work makes us react more sympathetically than we otherwise might. Avoid plot summary.

4. In retrospect, the reader often discovers that the first chapter of a novel or the opening scene of a drama introduces some of the major themes of the work. Write an essay about the opening scene of a drama or the first chapter of a novel in which you explain how it functions in this way.

   In your essay do not merely summarize the plot of the work you are discussing.

5. A character's attempt to recapture or to reject the past is important in many plays, novels, and poems.

   Choose a literary work in which a character views the past with feelings such as reverence, bitterness, or longing. Show with clear evidence from the work how the character's view of the past is used to develop a theme in the work.

6. In some novels and plays certain parallel or recurring events prove to be significant. In an essay, describe the major similarities and differences in a sequence of parallel or recurring events in a novel or play and discuss the significance of such events. Do not merely summarize the plot.

Source: Excerpted from College Board Advanced Placement exams.

FORM C
Sample Student Evaluation Questionnaire
on a Thematic Unit

To help evaluate the unit just completed on the topic of The Unexpected,* please answer the following questions:

1. How useful are literature logs as preparation for discussion?
2. Did you find class discussions about the stories and poems stimulating (Did they make you think?) and did you learn from the discussions?
3. How challenging, creative, or interesting did you find the group problem solving/ dramatizations about the ballads? Did you learn anything?
4. How effective was the questioning technique about the modern paintings in making you reflect on the piece of art?
5. Was researching the artist and his works a valuable activity?
6. Did you learn anything from Mr. Girod's presentation about surrealism?
7. How would you rate the activity of writing a contemporary poem and illustrating it with surrealism?

* Included in the Appendix to this book.

8. How did you feel about the close reading and quizzes on "Our Exploits at West Poley?"
9. How useful was collaborating with someone to revise and elaborate on the essay about "George?"
10. Did writing the essays at the end of The Unexpected unit make you think and tie together the concepts presented in the unit?
11. Does peer response and editing help your writing?
12. What was your favorite activity in the unit?
13. What was your least favorite activity?
14. What would you change about the unit?

Source: Teacher-developed by Nancy Howard, Alexandria School Division, Alexandria, VA.

FORM D
Evaluation of Student-Led Discussions

Rate the quality of the discussion on a 1–5 scale (using the following criteria) by filling in the number in the space provided.

Leader

	1	2	3	4	5
1. Questions were interesting and pertinent, illuminating the ideas raised within the work.	—	—	—	—	—
2. Questions were clearly stated and effectively reworded when necessary.	—	—	—	—	—
3. Questions directed me to a clearer understanding of the work or concept.	—	—	—	—	—
4. Discussion introduced perspectives I had not already discovered.	—	—	—	—	—
5. Leader was assertive and in control of the discussion, keeping it focused on that material and maintaining its coherence.	—	—	—	—	—
6. Leader was well prepared and able to answer questions and correct errors and misinterpretations.	—	—	—	—	—
7. Leader was flexible, eliciting the expression of a variety of points of view.	—	—	—	—	—
8. Leader effectively summarized the major points of the discussion.	—	—	—	—	—

9. Leader created and maintained an
atmosphere conducive to the free
exchange of ideas.   ——   ——   ——   ——   ——

10. Individual leaders shared time with
one another and with students.   ——   ——   ——   ——   ——

TOTAL:

Make comments intended to help discussion leader improve his/her discussion skills.

For the leader: What did you learn about the material, your skills, or the difficulty
of the task? What would you do differently next time? What did you feel you did
particularly well?

Another helpful qualitative tool in assessing student impacts is the use of
student or parent direct statements about the program. VanTassel-Baska, Willis,
& Meyer (1989) collected data on how a gifted program curriculum affected
student "quality of learning" indicators.

Representative comments provided by parents of children verify what the
ratings suggested:

> The class creates a mutual competitiveness without fear of failure or (more impor-
> tant) the embarrassment of being "too smart."

> She has renewed interest in school and her ability to learn. She has developed a
> true feeling of belonging and closeness with the other students in the class.

> He has learned more responsibility. He has been academically challenged for the
> first time. Also his attitude toward school has improved. He hated it before.

Comments such as these provide another perspective on benefits to students
of special programs. Clearly, for some audiences the directness of student comments speaks more eloquently than levels of significance.

SUMMARY

Determining the effectiveness of what we do with gifted learners requires serious
attention at the front end of curriculum planning, but it also requires good
follow-up at the end, to assess what happened in the curriculum treatment. This
evaluation of student learning in gifted programs must be multileveled and considered an ongoing part of the curriculum development process.

Curriculum design should be (a) matched to learner outcomes, (b) used for
continuous curricular planning, (c) enable evaluation of curriculum effectiveness,
and (d) be used to assess student progress and future needs. Curricular assessment
should work across three levels: curriculum validity, perceived benefit, and
student outcomes. When analyzing student benefits from a curriculum, parents,

Table 7.2
DIVERSE APPROACHES TO EVALUATING STUDENT IMPACTS

Speaking/ Listening/ Language Development	Reading/ Literature	Writing	Thinking Skills
1. Criterial checklists to be completed by teacher or peers, or both	1. Teacher-constructed tests	1. Holistic grading based on predetermined criteria (Form A)	1. Pre-post use of Watson-Glaser Critical Thinking or Cornell Test of Critical Thinking
2. Holistic assessment of oral presentation	2. Sample Scholastic Aptitude Test (SAT) Reading Comprehension passages	2. Peer review based on workshopping model	2. Teacher-developed activities
3. Pre-post tests on grammar and usage	3. Holistic assessment of essay exams (Form B)		3. Simulations
4. Unit tests	4. Videotapes of discussion		
	5. Student evaluation of activities (Form C)		
	6. Peer evaluation of student-led discussions (Form D)		

students, and teachers should be asked the same questions, to establish triangulation of results.

QUESTIONS FOR REFLECTION

1. What areas of gifted student learning do you want to emphasize each year in the classroom? Make a list and think of appropriate approaches you might use to find out if students benefited from the special experiences provided.

2. How might we best assess theme-based or interdisciplinary learning in gifted programs?
3. If you were a school board member, what learner outcomes would you expect to see from a specialized curriculum for the gifted learner?
4. What mechanisms might schools employ to make assessment of learning easier to accomplish and more meaningful to ongoing curriculum development?

REFERENCES

Archambault, F. X. (1984). Measurement and evaluation concerns in evaluating programs for the gifted and talented. *Journal for the Education of the Gifted, 7,* 12–25.

Barnette, J. J. (1984). Naturalistic approaches to gifted and talented program evaluation. *Journal for the Education of the Gifted, 7,* 26–37.

Callahan, C., & Caldwell, M. (1984). Using evaluation results to improve programs for the gifted and talented. *Journal for the Education of the Gifted, 7,* 60–74.

Carter, K. R., & Hamilton, W. (1985). Formative evaluation of gifted programs: A process and model. *Gifted Child Quarterly, 29,* 5–11.

Stake, R. E. (1975). *Program evaluation* (Occasional paper series No. 5). Kalamazoo, MI: Western Michigan University Evaluation Center.

Trazler, M. A. (1987). Gifted education program evaluation: A national review. *Journal for the Education of the Gifted, 10,* 107–113.

VanTassel-Baska, J., Willis, G., & Meyer, D. (1989). Evaluation of a full-time self-contained class for gifted students. *Gifted Child Quarterly, 33*(1), 7–10.

CHAPTER EIGHT

Implementing a Curriculum for Gifted Learners

T oo frequently, new curriculum projects are viewed as isolated from the ongoing school district institutional processes that we believe may have greater value than curriculum development itself or to which we attach greater significance. The central purpose of this chapter is to relate the critical factors of curriculum implementation to existing structures in the school district that will ensure continued support for ongoing curriculum work. The proposed model for this process is illustrated in Figure 8.1.

Once curriculum has been codified systematically at all grade levels and in all content disciplines, many educators believe that curriculum development has ended and we move on to implementation. One crucial tenet to understand about curriculum development is its dynamic nature — some of it being engaged at an implementation level of piloting, monitoring, and revising, while at the same time some of it being written up and codified — and that each part of the process continuously feeds the other (VanTassel-Baska, 1988). Consequently, implementation should be viewed as a part of the overall curriculum development process and an important phase in continuing to impact written curriculum documents. Thus, the planning process for curriculum development must include the elements for keeping the process going beyond the time of special funding and outside consultants.

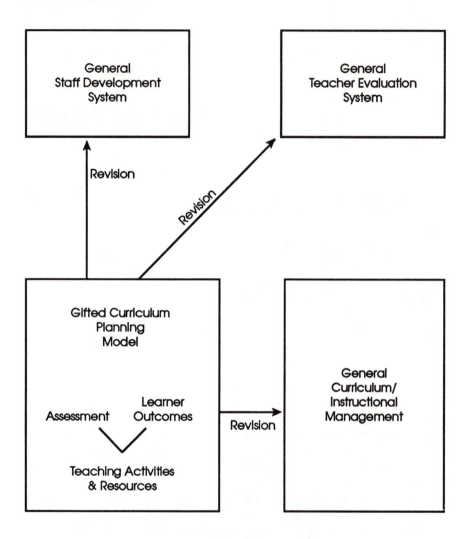

Figure 8.1
INTERACTION OF THE CURRICULUM DEVELOPMENT PROCESS
WITH EXISTING SCHOOL DISTRICT MODEL SYSTEMS

The school district must recognize and accept the *centrality* of curriculum development to its overall enterprise of schooling. One way to encourage this is to link the curriculum development process inextricably to already existing efforts in the school district, such as school improvement initiatives, testing and assessment models, teacher evaluation approaches, and accepted staff development models. In this way, curriculum issues continue to be addressed over time, and revisions based on new data can be made in written documents that have relevance to district priorities.

This attempt to institutionalize the curriculum development process for special attention to the needs of the gifted learner should also impact on how curricula are viewed and reviewed for other learners as well. In that way, too, curricula for the gifted may filter down and have an impact on the general school curricula for all learners. Effective local planning in curriculum for the gifted should be able to provide that impact.

IMPLICATIONS OF CURRICULUM PLANNING ON STAFF DEVELOPMENT

One of the first school district systems that should be affected by curriculum planning efforts is staff development, the major mechanism in schools to disseminate ideas for classroom implementation. Yet, many staff development models are haphazard, taking a shotgun approach to training in the belief that providing something for everybody is a viable avenue.

In summarizing the research on effective staff development, Wade (1985) highlighted several key findings:

- Staff development training affects increased learning in participants the most; behavior change in the classroom is less affected, and student learning is affected only to a very limited degree.
- Training that involves K-12 teachers who are selected through a process of application and review is more effective than limiting staff development to given grade levels.
- Training that is initiated and developed through the university by strong leaders is more effective than school-based training designed by potential participants.
- The most effective instructional techniques with teachers have been observation of classroom practices, micro-teaching (i.e., presenting a lesson on which a teacher receives structured feedback), video/audio feedback, and practice.

These findings should be incorporated into the processes by which staff development programs are organized for teachers at local levels. The findings are complementary to the curricular planning model described in this text, in that they provide a solid backdrop to linking teachers to effective classroom implementation.

Moving teachers of the gifted from novice to expert status requires careful understanding of the skills needed to work effectively with this population and their relative sophistication. Understanding the nature and needs of the gifted, for example, is less sophisticated than being able to make appropriate inferences about curriculum experiences at a particular point in time. Thus, a model of staff development that considers these distinctions in planning experiences for

Table 8.1
TEACHER SOPHISTICATION LEVEL AND RELATED
COMPETENCIES/SKILLS

Level	Competency/Skill
Novice	Plans curriculum experiences well
	Demonstrates understanding of the educational implications of giftedness
	Uses varied teaching strategies effectively
	Conducts group discussions well
	Provides for student extension activities outside of class
	Promotes a healthy teaching/learning climate
Intermediate	Selects questions that stimulate higher-level thinking
	Utilizes creative thinking techniques
	Utilizes problem-solving techniques
	Encourages independent thinking and open inquiry
	Understands and encourages student ideas and student-directed work
Expert	Promotes critical thinking skills in appropriate contexts
	Synthesizes student assessment data and curriculum content effectively

teachers is superior to one that does not (VanTassel-Baska, 1986). Table 8.1 summarizes the relationship of the teacher's sophistication level and the competencies and skills required to implement a curriculum effectively with gifted learners.

The content of staff development programs that would support the curriculum planning model obviously should be derived from the major features of the developed curriculum, with particular emphasis on implementation strategies for helping students reach desired outcomes. Moreover, it should provide time and opportunity for follow-up practice and feedback to participants after the planned activity has taken place (Weiss & Gallagher, 1986). So that staff development can feed curriculum planning, the two systems must be viewed as interdependent, yet the curriculum planning model must be superordinate because the overall goal of staff development is to improve student learning, the outcomes of which are identified through effective curriculum planning.

IMPLICATIONS OF CURRICULUM PLANNING
ON TEACHER EVALUATION

Just as the staff development system must feed curriculum planning, so, too, the teacher evaluation system must be interdependent with the model. Desired

Table 8.2
CRITICAL/PRODUCTIVE THINKING SKILLS

Student Outcomes	Teacher Behaviors
Students will be able to:	Teacher:
1. Predict outcomes 2. Distinguish between fact and opinion	— encourages logical reasoning — encourages syllogistic reasoning — encourages student development of inference and evaluation of argument skills — calls upon inductive and deductive reasoning
3. Form hypotheses 4. Weigh evidence	— asks students to define problems in a question form — poses interpretive, open-ended, and evaluative questions for students — encourages student development of inference and evaluation of argument skills — utilizes inductive and deductive reasoning
5. Analyze information 6. Synthesize information	— asks analytical questions — encourages student participation in discussions — provides opportunities for students to summarize data in various forms — withholds own ideas and conclusions — encourages student development of inference and evaluation of argument skills — utilizes inductive and deductive reasoning

teacher behaviors emerge out of a clear understanding of what outcomes are desired for gifted learners. Therefore, teachers should be evaluated on the presence of these behaviors. Table 8.2 presents the relationship between learner outcome and teacher behaviors in teaching critical thinking. Principals could use behavioral checklists such as this to ensure that teachers are practicing these behaviors. Even four 40-minute visits to a classroom during the year would yield important data regarding the use of critical statements. This example then might serve as a model for the development of more appropriate and targeted teacher evaluation systems in school districts.

IMPLICATIONS OF CURRICULUM PLANNING
ON CURRICULUM/INSTRUCTIONAL MANAGEMENT

The system by which a district maintains and changes its curriculum also represents a critical linkage to the curriculum planning model for the gifted. Frequently managed by a director of curriculum, or an assistant superintendent in smaller districts, this system controls the rate and nature of curriculum change and is fed by mandates from federal, state, and local boards of education. The power and control of district-level curriculum emphasis is clearly vested here. How ironic it is that this system is given such limited attention and resources in many districts, limiting its capacity to be effective. Regardless of its relative importance in a district, however, this system must be open to the sub-set of curriculum planning for the gifted so that each effort is moving in the same direction rather than operating counterproductively. The following are foremost considerations in merging these systems:

1. Membership on all district-wide curriculum committees should include a representative of the gifted curriculum planning effort, ensuring ongoing communication between the two efforts.
2. Collaborative planning of all curriculum development efforts should be undertaken by the gifted coordinator in concert with the director of curriculum and instruction and his or her staff in individual content areas.
3. The structure, format, and language of curriculum development used in planning curricula for the gifted should mirror the district-wide models. Although this issue may seem trivial, it carries enormous implications for communication to teachers, other educators, and the community concerning the relationship of gifted curricula to general curriculum practice.
4. The superordinate system of curriculum management in the district must clearly understand and accept differential learner outcomes and assessment models. Points of convergence and divergence with the basic curriculum framework should be delineated and highlighted. Thus, important distinctions can be made between the gifted effort and the general curriculum effort without viewing the gifted curriculum as a totally separate enterprise.

These considerations are central to activating a meaningful curriculum system for the gifted that is not perceived as different from the mainstream business of teachers and learners for all students in schools. Gifted education has to be accepted into these generic systems if it is to become integrated into the basic functions of local education.

CHALLENGES IN IMPLEMENTING CURRICULA

Factors impacting the process of curriculum development in many school districts and hindering the achievement of desired goals of curriculum implementation typically include:

— traditional organizational patterns along elementary and secondary lines, which inhibit curriculum integration across grade levels.
— limited communication, exchange, and cooperative planning between elementary and secondary divisions.
— limited time available for teachers at the elementary and secondary levels to work together in planning and structuring curricular experiences for gifted learners.
— lack of involvement, in the development process, of teachers who are responsible for implementing the curriculum.

Another factor, outside school district purview, that may impede curriculum development is the focus on program development rather than curriculum development. Because the emphasis has been on putting operative programs in place at all stages of development for the gifted learner, curriculum issues have been given much less consideration. What has emerged is a kind of potpourri of curriculum experiences for a given group of students identified as gifted at various grade levels. The recent national spotlight on educational reform and curricular change, coupled with a shift and refocusing at the state level from program development issues to comprehensive curriculum planning for the gifted, has caused a resurgence of interest in curriculum planning and development, and a healthy climate for change.

Still another concern is that many teachers do not utilize gifted curricula to guide instruction. Rather, they often derive course content exclusively from adopted textbooks. Some indicate that they used specific aspects of the developed curriculum to supplement the textbooks, but not on a consistent basis. Their decisions about using the written curriculum typically reflected compromises they had made. Many believe they are prevented from effectively utilizing skills and concepts of an ideal curriculum for gifted students by administrators, mandated texts and tests, or subtle community pressures.

Another issue revolves around the commitment of time necessary to develop effective curricula. Sufficient time has to be scheduled for curriculum work during the school day rather than at the end of the teaching day. Further, time has to be provided during non-student attendance periods so that major writing, revisions, and recommendations might take place. The concentration of time available during the summer months makes it ideal for curriculum development work. These time segments taken in concert probably provide the most effective approach to keeping the curriculum development experience dynamic and meaningful.

Related to the time issue is the process for ensuring a team approach, one that allows for a continuous, flexible planning process and utilizes teachers and content area experts together in deciding the direction of curriculum work. Teachers selected for participation should have knowledge and experience in working with gifted learners in a variety of classroom settings, show an interest and aptitude for developing curricula, and have mastered the skills of adapting

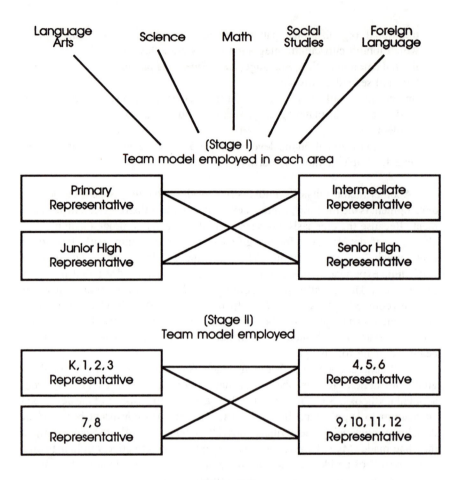

Figure 8.2
ORGANIZATION OF CURRICULUM WRITING TEAMS AT
TWO STAGES OF THE PROJECT

curricula successfully for the gifted learner. As members of the team, the teacher's role would be to provide critical pedagogical insights into the decision-making process for specific settings: what to include, what to exclude, and how to adapt and modify various learning experiences, strategies, and resources.

Teachers also would receive training in this process by consultants who would provide guidance in understanding conceptual and instructional designs of curricular models and developing appropriate and effective curricula for the gifted. Content experts would supply key ideas and concepts in designing the curricular structure in specific domains of study and share major approaches to organizing courses. Moreover, district-level curricula and gifted coordinators would provide the support and the feedback necessary to keep the curriculum work going.

The organizing structure for curriculum work clearly is a major consideration in attaining success. Team representation by content disciplines and grade-level clusters is critical because the emphasis has to be on articulating the curriculum across K-12. Curriculum writing teams may be organized to represent every grade level in each of the major disciplines. The organizing structure is depicted in Figure 8.2.

CONDITIONS CONTRIBUTING
TO SUCCESSFUL CURRICULUM DEVELOPMENT

Factors crucial to the success of broad-based curricula include the following:

1. Conducting a comprehensive *needs assessment,* to determine the actual and preferred status of the curriculum for the gifted, sets the climate for change. Understanding needs and documenting them provides a necessary starting point for examining the curriculum and implementing change. It also installs a framework for effecting shared values and mutual support for the project. The needs assessment is instrumental in formulating a set of tentative goal statements, determining the acceptability of learner performance, and translating high-priority goals into plans.
2. Keeping central office staff (curriculum directors and content area supervisors) informed of the scope of the work, actively involving them in all stages of the project, is essential. Providing opportunities for them to assist and make recommendations is crucial to the process. *Administrative support* is instrumental in institutionalizing curriculum change.
3. Assuring teachers that curriculum change does not mean throwing out all previous documents and replacing them with something totally new is also important. Teachers need to be informed that the results of a needs assessment typically indicate that *modification* can be made based on previously developed materials. In knowing this, they will be more receptive to becoming involved in the process.
4. *Involving teachers in the decision-making process* is perhaps the most crucial aspect of the process from a personnel morale perspective. Informative sessions, to convey to teachers the overall process and the conceptual design of various curricular models to be used, should be held. Teachers should be given sufficient opportunities to voice concerns, raise questions, and offer suggestions regarding the plan. This type of involvement gives teachers a stake in the adaptation and curriculum development process and inspires the acquisition of skills and knowledge needed later for curriculum implementation.

5. Marshaling staff members who are *sophisticated in the principles* of gifted education and *committed* to meeting the needs of students is valuable to the curriculum planning process. Selected teachers have to be sufficiently *grounded in their disciplines* to adapt and modify curricula for the gifted population in a given area. Many who get involved in the process come to view their involvement in curriculum development as one of their primary professional responsibilities.

6. Enlisting the support of *consultant resources* (curriculum and subject matter specialists) to assist in devising a comprehensive plan of action, supplying key ideas and concepts regarding content areas and providing expertise outside the domain of the district, strengthens the curriculum effort. Utilizing university-based content consultants on an ongoing basis well into the implementation stage is helpful. Gary Community School Corporation in Gary, Indiana, uses content specialists year round to assist teachers with the issues associated with curriculum development.

INHIBITING FACTORS AND BARRIERS

In conclusion, factors representing potential problems in the overall implementation of a large curriculum effort are delineated.

1. The emphasis on textbook adoption, state competency requirements, and state-mandated tests creates situations in which local curriculum objectives are driven by these priorities rather than by identified instructional needs of gifted students in the district. When school districts become obsessed with standardization, individuals or groups that attempt to deviate from the prescribed pattern are likely to be vulnerable. Amazingly, though, common sense prevails in many districts if educators continue to stress the importance of curricula tailored to need.

2. Not all teachers working with the gifted are equally skilled or interested in the task of curriculum development. Consequently, at some grade levels and in some content areas, more effort will be needed to prod teachers into capturing curriculum experiences on paper and then implementing a tailored version of them. Thus, adapted curricula face political hurdles in classroom translation. Just as we do not want standardized curricula for the gifted, we also do not want standardized implementation if it implies reaching a goal in exactly the same way. In translation in the classroom, there is significant room for diversity and individual preferences. What should be held constant, however, is the shared consensus on overall learner outcomes. If these are not valued by all teachers working with the gifted, faithful implementation procedures will not be possible.

3. Difficulties in scheduling time when all relevant individuals in the curriculum development process can meet, plan, and write together will be ever present. In keeping with the overall goal of "connected" curriculum, achieving this

aim is difficult if key players are missing. Still, the reality of schools is that unplanned events many times drive our planned priorities. Building and classroom emergencies, bad weather, and individual needs all influence timely implementation of a curriculum plan. The key to holding these disparate pieces together is the curriculum project manager, the individual in the school district coordinating the effort. This person must invest a significant amount of energy in pacing the entire project and ensuring that timelines are set and monitored and work is ultimately accomplished within appropriate time frames.

4. Staff turnover in a program can manifest itself in the "starting over" syndrome during a multi-year period. Each new teacher who becomes involved during subsequent years has to become oriented to prior stages of the project, resulting in much time spent in reviewing the evolution of the curriculum development process. Although change in staff can be a problem, it does reflect the reality of schools and must be addressed systematically.

Through careful planning within the district, school districts can avoid many of these problems in undertaking long-term curriculum projects. Even so, some difficulties may be inevitable in a curriculum development model driven by the consensus-building process.

SUMMARY

Curriculum development is central to schools, and it is dynamic, in a state of continual change. Implementation of the curriculum planning model should be done from a systems perspective so the effort becomes an ongoing part of school district operations. Curriculum planning has implications for staff development, in that teachers can be trained to become more sophisticated in the skills needed to work effectively with the gifted. Further, teacher evaluation should accurately reflect these behaviors. Curriculum and instructional management should be merged through collaborative planning, adherence to district-wide models, and an understanding of the distinctions between general and gifted efforts.

Potential problems may arise in a focus on traditional patterns, limited communication, scarce time, lack of teacher involvement in the development process, emphasis on program development rather than curriculum development, use of standardized materials as a basis, the need for training, and the lack of a team approach, among others. In contrast, successful curriculum development incorporates a comprehensive needs assessment, a well informed central office staff, prudent modification of existing materials, teacher involvement in the decision-making process, a committed staff, and the support of consultant resources.

QUESTIONS FOR REFLECTION

1. How can we influence existing school district initiatives to make sure that gifted education is on the list of priorities?
2. How might we develop a plan for ensuring the inclusion of curriculum development efforts for the gifted in general staff development, teacher evaluation, and curriculum management systems at the district levels?
3. What are other issues to consider in institutionalizing curricula for the gifted?

REFERENCES

VanTassel-Baska, J., et al. (1988). *Comprehensive curriculum for gifted learners*. Boston: Allyn & Bacon.

VanTassel-Baska, J. (1986). Lessons from the history of teacher inservice in Illinois: Effective staff development in the education of the gifted. *Gifted Child Quarterly, 30*(3), 124–261.

Wade, R. (1985). What makes a difference in inservice teacher education: A meta-analysis of research. *Educational Leadership, 42*(4), 48–54.

Weiss, P., & Gallagher, J. (1986). Project TARGET: A needs assessment approach to gifted education inservice. *Gifted Child Quarterly, 30*(3), 114–118.

PART TWO
Specific Considerations in Planning Curricula for Special Populations of Gifted Learners

P lanning and developing curricula for special populations of gifted learners requires additional filters for the lenses examined in Part One of
this book. These required filters must take into account developmental
discrepancies in the profiles of these learners that may call for considerable
adjustment of the curriculum landscape. These developmental discrepancies lead
us to think about special populations of gifted learners as possessing uneven
profiles, with peaks and valleys that require special accommodation in the curriculum development process. To address the strengths in curriculum areas for
these gifted learners is insufficient. We also need to develop value-added curriculum opportunities that address the relatively weaker aspects of their profiles,
some of them in noncognitive areas. Current identification and programming
practices for the gifted have not been sensitive to these uneven profiles; consequently, talent has gone unrecognized.

In the general population of gifted learners, many students are lower in
social, emotional, and physical development than in intellectual development,
and at key stages of development these differences can be profound. The 5-year-
old who is intellectually precocious but unable to control tantrums in the class-

room, and the 9-year-old math prodigy who cannot compete athletically with age-mates are both examples of children who are not equally strong in all areas of human endeavor at a given point in their development. This pattern of uneven development, even in the highly gifted, is seen as a sign of weakness, of not being fully functioning. As a consequence, the approach schools typically take is to "even out" the profile, insisting on addressing the weaker issues instead of focusing on strengths.

In special populations the nature of the uneven profile many times varies based on the defining issues associated with the condition of "specialness." And we frequently have treated these conditions as the major point of intervention rather than the child's unique talents and abilities. In disadvantaged populations we may see academic skill deficiencies and a lack of early educational nurturance as the weaker aspects of the profile. In underachievers we see the lack of academic achievement as a major profile discrepancy. In handicapped gifted learners we see a specific disability of a physical or learning nature. In the learning disabled gifted child, for example, these disabilities may take the form of behavioral problems (hyperactivity, aggression/withdrawal, frustration, lack of impulse control) resulting in or causing poor peer relations and specific learning disabilities such as memory, visual/auditory processing, and visual/motor integration.

Several issues surrounding these special populations of learners seem worth stating. One of the most obvious is our need as a field to involve other professionals who may have greater expertise in their areas of specialization than we do in understanding the uneven profile of these students. In this part of the book, I have deliberately solicited chapters from a content-based curriculum specialist, a school psychologist, and two special educators, one a "generalist" and the other an expert in learning disabilities, to help in framing the issues and suggesting feasible ways of addressing them in a learning disabled gifted student's world of home and school. My own recent work with disadvantaged gifted learners has been a collaborative effort with a colleague whose background is in social psychology and multicultural education. If we are to progress as a field in working with special populations, we must engage and collaborate more with professionals from relevant other disciplines.

A second issue relates to choices of school program delivery systems. As the need to understand both individual and group differences of gifted learners becomes greater, our resource capacity becomes more limited and we are forced to rely on existing school organizational structures to deliver curriculum services. Consequently, we are experiencing a movement to provide for gifted learners in the regular classroom, toward cooperative teaching strategies and away from pull-out programs that use a resource teacher approach. While instructional grouping and regrouping is the hallmark of effective cooperative teaching, less separate and distinct grouping of gifted learners is likely to occur under this model. This may be unfortunate, because we need more focused time with these learners to discover how to work with them most effectively. Special programs that have been effective in the past for these special populations have been self-contained (Daniels, 1983; Maker & Schiever, 1989; Whitmore, 1980). Moreover, most of the current programs funded under the Javits Act also employ a self-contained service delivery model to effect change with these special population students.

A third issue is the role of families, both nuclear and extended, in helping these special population students develop their potential. The home has always been perceived to be the most important force in the talent development process (VanTassel-Baska & Olszewski-Kubilius, 1989), but work with parents of disadvantaged learners in particular has proven difficult and elusive. New models for parenting intervention and family counseling hold promise for making inroads in this important task (Comer, 1989). Helping these families understand the importance of their role as monitors and guides for their child's educational progress is central to such an effort. A family planning model may offer a system for easy self-monitoring and follow-up on progress. The families of these special population students are even more attuned to the needs of their children than other parents of the gifted, although they may require additional resources. We know, for example, that parents of disadvantaged gifted learners in general maintain a strong belief in the values of education and the work ethic (VanTassel-Baska, 1989).

Last, the new direction in curricula for the gifted will promote new curriculum prototypes based on special population needs and profiles and more extended use of individualized plans, derived through collaborative processes and executed in group settings. This direction for curricula should cause us to rethink existing models and adapt them to nascent needs.

Part Two of this book looks at these issues in some depth. A chapter is devoted to a review of research and relevant practice with special populations of gifted learners. This is followed by a chapter on identification and nurturance of the disadvantaged gifted learner, which presents a conceptual model for program development. It also features a case study of two nationally reviewed programs for disadvantaged gifted learners and critiques them by key features. It concludes with new directions for curricula with these learners.

Chapter 11 focuses on the role of collaboration in working with handicapped gifted learners and lays out a case study. The next four chapters provide differential perspectives on this case study, which exemplifies the concept of an uneven profile. "Diane Bradford" is viewed through the lenses of four professional educators, each having a different perspective. These perspectives are merged in a culminating chapter that pulls together the multiple viewpoints into a model learning plan for Diane Bradford. The concluding chapter lays out key trends and issues for the future in the areas of curricula and instruction for the gifted.

REFERENCES

Comer, J. (1988). Educating poor minority children. *Scientific American, 259*(5), 42–48.
Daniels, P. R. (1983). *Teaching the gifted/learning disabled child*. Rockville, MD: Aspen.

Maker, J., & Schiever, S. (Ed.). (1989). *Critical issues in gifted education,* (Vol. 2). Austin, TX: Pro-Ed.

VanTassel-Baska, J. (1989). The role of the family in the success of disadvantaged gifted learners. In J. VanTassel-Baska & Olszewski (Eds.), *Patterns of influence: The home, the self, and the school* (pp. 66–80). New York: Teachers College Press.

VanTassel-Baska, J., & Olszewski-Kubilius, P. (1989). *Patterns of influence on gifted learners: The home, the self, and the school.* New York: Teachers College Press.

Whitmore, J. R. (1980). *Giftedness, conflict and underachievement.* Boston: Allyn & Bacon.

CHAPTER NINE

Special Populations
of Gifted Learners

U pon reviewing the literature on special populations of gifted learners, four central issues emerge that affect all of these populations. For various reasons, each group is prone to underachievement. Each group shows evidence of needing highly personalized services in order to effect educational success. Each group also struggles with intrapersonal issues, battles of the self, that add to the difficulty of mounting appropriately tailored educational experiences. Finally, these special populations many times represent multiple conditions, making solutions to their educational dilemmas more complex and therefore more difficult to attain.

In these special populations of gifted learners, underachievement is a common theme affecting performance differentially at various stages of life. For the handicapped gifted, the masking of high ability because of disability often limits the opportunity for high-level production in their areas of strength or serves as a psychological limitation to creative work. For the disadvantaged, lack of early and sustained nurturance sets up a pattern of underachievement, revealing itself in lowered aptitude and achievement performance. For culturally diverse groups, adherence to values of the sub-group may impede mainstream cultural expectations for achievement and assimilation and thus limit traditional educational attainment and advantage. For gifted girls, the onset of puberty and its concomitant social role expectations act as a depressant on achievement that continues well into adulthood. And for underachievers as a special population, a constellation of personality variables interacting from early ages with nonconducive environmental conditions seems to contribute to a persistent debilitating pattern.

Our systems of education are ill prepared to identify or serve these populations of gifted learners well. We are organized to serve groups, not individuals. Education's general preoccupation with accountability has led schools to define student progress through norm-referenced reporting measures while ignoring important variability within groups and individuals. When we identify children for gifted programs, we make group comparisons, while these special populations defy group norm standards. Both identification and intervention rely heavily on a sensitive, caring individual in the educational environment, who sees the ability and empowers the child, the family, and the system to activate that ability in the service of educational development. The most striking examples of success with these learners are case studies in which the role of an individual in these children's lives has made a substantial positive contribution to their growth. Individual caring that allows students to overcome or cope with disadvantage may be the more important variable that is not being measured or accounted for in school models.

Individuals who make up special populations of gifted learners are frequently engaged in "battles of the self" to a greater extent than the typical gifted population. They must psychologically handle their giftedness and their lack of it in a simultaneity mode of functioning that calls for appropriate compensatory strategies. The handicapped learn to compensate for physical or other weaknesses through coping mechanisms idiosyncratic to the individual and the nature of the handicap. The disadvantaged learn to use their deprivation of circumstances of birth as a catalyst for "catching up" while being cognizant of their limited repertoire of experiences. Culturally diverse groups internally battle a dual value system message — one that calls for sub-group loyalty and adherence to tribal, family, and cultural traditions, and the other that calls for individuation and excellence in a mainstream world. The underachieving gifted fight their own predispositions and view of self to make progress. The conflict for gifted girls is one of pursuing career fulfillment that allows for creative production and at the same time satisfying social responsibility and personal standards around home and family. Each of these special populations must find coping mechanisms that work to reduce their psychic conflict in these various dualities of circumstances.

In studying special populations of gifted learners, another commonality is the extent of overlap among the conditions and circumstances affecting the label of special populations. The most common overlap found in the literature is between the disadvantaged and the culturally diverse, especially African-Americans. This entanglement of low socioeconomic status and race raises special issues in attempting to provide appropriate educational nurturance. Another area of overlap occurs with underachievement and handicapping conditions. Undiscovered handicaps of a neurological or cognitive processing nature may yet explain a greater percentage of underachieving gifted behavior. And some overlaps are more generic. For example, a gifted girl who is African-American comes from a low-income background and exhibits a learning disability. In cases like this, a study of one special population may be insufficient to understand the phenomenology inherent in individual cases that cut across the labels we have given to these special populations of gifted individuals.

DISADVANTAGED GIFTED

The special population of learners termed "disadvantaged" tends to have two foci in the literature. One focus in on minority groups that are culturally diverse, and the other is on low socioeconomic groups that cut across ethnic/racial lines. Although these groups overlap, key features may differentiate them, and in the process render the term "disadvantaged" unsuitable and inappropriate as an umbrella designation.

Definitional Issues

A 3-year study of key demographic features of disadvantaged gifted learners in the Midwest defined "disadvantaged" in purely economic terms (VanTassel-Baska & Willis, 1988), whereas large-scale sociological studies have considered father's education and occupational status as the key variables (Jencks, 1972). More pervasive efforts within the field of gifted education have designated minority status and cultural difference as key variables in defining the term (Baldwin, 1985; Frasier, 1980; Maker & Schiever, 1989). No one definition seems to be clearly accepted by the field, for these variables can occur singly or in combination (Baldwin, 1985).

The result of this variance can be seen in the State of California omnibus definition of disadvantaged gifted, which considers all of the following diverse factors: environmental, economic, cultural, language, and social. Many minority groups object to the term "disadvantaged" because of its negative value connotation (Frasier, 1979; Tonemah, 1987). After conducting a national survey in this area, VanTassel-Baska, Patton, and Prillaman (1989) recommended the definition, "at-risk for accessing educational advantages in the larger society" as a replacement for the perceived negative term "disadvantaged."

A definitional structure for "disadvantaged gifted" linked to educational issues would seem to be salient, because students who are educationally disadvantaged have been exposed to inappropriate educational experiences in at least one of three institutional domains: the school, the family, the community. Lack of adequate resources for education is the main issue to be considered in this definition. Five key indicators associated with educational disadvantagement are (Pallas, Natriello, & McDill, 1989):

— minority racial/ethnic group identity.
— living in a poverty household.
— living in a single-parent family.
— having a poorly educated mother.
— having a non-English language background.

These variables were selected based on their correlation with poor performance in school. Indications are that 20–25% of school-age children are educationally disadvantaged according to the definition indicated; National Assessment of Educational Progress (NAEP) reading test data substantiate that as many as 35–40% of students can be so classified (see Pallas et al., 1989).

Studies on disadvantaged gifted populations based on an omnibus definition have focused on two issues related to definition:

1. The use of nontraditional measures to identify disadvantaged students (Bernal & Reyna, 1974; Bruch, 1978; Frasier, 1979; Torrance, 1971).
2. Recognition of cultural attributes and factors in deciding on identification procedures (Baldwin, 1985; Gay, 1978; Miller, 1974; Samuda, 1975; Witty, 1978).

These issues have tended to strongly emphasize minority group membership rather than socioeconomic status per se.

Minority Issues and Groups

Historically, most minority groups have been underrepresented in programs for the gifted, and much of the research on minority gifted has set out to find appropriate assessment protocols to remedy the underrepresentation. Less research has been conducted on effective intervention strategies with these populations. Maker and Schiever (1989) provide an in-depth treatment of theory, research, and practice in this area.

Research reviews suggest that traditional assessment methods, including standardized IQ tests, teacher recommendations, and parent questionnaires, are inadequate in identifying gifted minorities (Amodeo & Flores, 1981; Frasier, 1984; Masten, 1985). Problems in current identification methods include: neglect of subcultural values and abilities; middle-class mainstream bases of measurement instruments; tests standardized without sufficient numbers of minorities; lack of knowledge about or identification of culturally valued talents; and negative consequences of adverse environmental factors (Masten, 1981).

The use of traditional tests to identify gifted minority students has proved to be limiting. Reschly and Ross-Reynolds (1983) summarized areas of potential bias in the testing of all minorities, including inappropriate test content, inappropriate standarization samples, examiner and language bias, inequitable social consequences, measurement of different constructs, and differential predictive validity. Identification of gifted minorities typically has involved some combination of testing and inventories and checklists. In a study of 60 local programs serving minority students, VanTassel-Baska, Patton, and Prillaman (1989) found that the use of non-biased assessment protocols at the local level frequently included norm-referenced tests, non-traditional tests such as the Raven Progressive Matrices, and nominations from educational personnel, parents, and community. Recommendations to improve assessment protocols have focused on administering tests in the child's dialect and having children say their responses instead of write them (Masten, 1985).

Cultural norms also may hold back minority gifted students. These norms include: (a) the degree of importance placed on social acceptance; (b) a tendency to reject solitary activity; and (c) sanctions against questioning cultural values. Many minorities place the needs of the group before those of the individual and, therefore, may discourage full development of the gifted child (Amodeo & Flores, 1981). Thus, there is a need to recognize: (a) intracultural variability in respect to motivation, social organization, and ways of speaking and thinking, because these variances are based on education, income, and class status; and (b) cultural compatibility as a guide for selecting educational program elements (Tharp, 1989).

Lindstrom and VanSant (1986) have identified several issues as critical to gifted minority students:

- Low cultural expectations for achievement, manifested in little encouragement or support.
- Peer rejection, particularly for young Black men.
- Conflict generated by developing one's potential and succeeding in the "majority" culture and leaving one's own cultural community to do so.
- Lack of long-range planning.
- Career development.

Evidence of intrapersonal strengths of minority children are impressive. Theanacho (1988) summarized research related to the self-concept of adolescents from minority cultures. His analysis indicates that minorities within background and ability levels do have higher self-concepts than Whites. Prom-Jackson et al. (1987) found that "academic self-concept" was the best predictor of her minority subjects' gradepoint average, followed by "orientation to tasks."

Low Socioeconomic Status

Although low socioeconomic status (SES) is frequently entangled with cultural group membership, it seems to have a powerful influence in its own right on academic and personality development of gifted individuals. Frierson (1965) investigated the difference in characteristics of gifted students of lower SES and those from a more favorable environment. He found a trend for the gifted advantaged to show superiority in superego development (greater conscience and self-discipline). In the area of activity preferences, significant differences were obtained between the advantaged and disadvantaged gifted; the advantaged preferred reading, whereas the disadvantaged gifted favored participation in games and competitive sports. The advantaged gifted also were superior to the disadvantaged gifted on measures of creative thinking.

The influence of the home plays a crucial role in the development of students from low SES backgrounds. In an ethnographic study of successful gifted disadvantaged students, VanTassel-Baska (1989) found the role of family members, including extended family, to be a critical support structure, stressing the value of education and the work ethic and monitoring the child's education. Most educational opportunities, however, came through the mechanism of school. McIntosh and Greenlaw (1986) found that gifted students from lower SES homes have different achievement messages communicated to them than do those from upper and middle class homes. In the low SES homes, education tends to be devalued, possessing a "job" is considered more important than pursuing a "career," post-secondary education is considered unnecessary, and the focus is on the immediate present rather than on future planning.

Expectations in the homes of low SES students can be unrealistic, hampering the flow of appropriate messages between home and school. Entwisle and Hayduk (1978) found that primary-level students from working class backgrounds and schools had unrealistically high expectations for academic success when compared to students from middle class backgrounds and schools. Although both groups of parents were better predictors of their child's level of success in school than were their children, working class parents were less able to predict their child's school achievement than middle class parents. Racial differences in expectations were minimal.

Hanson and Ginsburg (1986) found that high expectations contributed positively to high achievement patterns in low SES students. They specifically found that values exert twice the influence of the effects of SES variables in determining school success. High parental expectations, peers who value education, personally high educational expectations, and fate control were all associated with increases in achievement over time.

In comparative terms, low SES has a depressing effect on standardized test scores, even among the most able. VanTassel-Baska and Willis (1988) found that gifted disadvantaged students, as defined by low income, consistently scored significantly lower on all sections of the Scholastic Aptitude Test (SAT) than more advantaged learners. This difference held up within each minority group, as well as for Caucasians, lending credence to the idea that score levels are affected negatively by low SES.

A study commissioned by the Secretary of Education cited the following statistical conditions in our schools as indicative of the need to address the issue of disadvantaged gifted learners more specifically (Alamprese & Erlanger, 1988):

1. Whereas students from low-income backgrounds comprise 20 percent of the student population, they make up only 4 percent of those students who perform at the highest levels on standardized tests (those who score at the 95th percentile or above);

2. High school seniors from disadvantaged families (in which the mother did not complete high school) are less than half as likely to have participated in gifted and talented programs as more advantaged seniors; and

3. Disadvantaged students are far less likely to be enrolled in academic programs that can prepare them for college and are about half as likely to take coursework in advanced math and science than more advantaged students. Only 2 percent of high school seniors from poor families take calculus, whereas approximately 7 percent of those from more advantaged backgrounds do. (p. v)

Intervention Issues

Whether we are talking about minority students or poor White students from rural areas, one factor remains common to each group: They reside outside the mainstream networks that provide access to educational advantage. This knowledge is crucial to converting high aspirations into creative, productive achievement at various stages of development. The role of key interventions is critical to this conversion process.

At their best, in-school programs have provided rigorous coursework comparable to what advantaged learners in the best school settings would receive. Other school programs have set out to remediate skill deficits or offer programs in nonacademic areas, such as the performing arts. A national survey identified only 60 programs for the disadvantaged gifted at the local level across the United States, although directors of gifted programs named more than 100 districts thought to be providing service (VanTassel-Baska, Patton, & Prillaman, 1989). Most of these programs were not differentiating service delivery for the disadvantaged gifted, even though they did include them in programs for the gifted.

Because differential interventions for disadvantaged gifted learners have been limited thus far, we should seek to understand what seems promising in this area for the future, given a greater emphasis on this special population at the federal level. Perhaps the most important ideas about intervention for this population are related to timing. Early intervention has been found to be influential in reducing later academic problems for disadvantaged students (Ramey, Yeates, & Short, 1984; Seitz, Rosenbaum, & Apfel, 1985).

Moreover, school context variables seem to be vital considerations for all disadvantaged learners. Effective school models, in particular, are a good source for addressing appropriate interventions with the disadvantaged. Research on school and classroom environment is extensive, much of it centered on schools with sizable populations of lower SES students (Lezotte & Bancroft, 1985; Mann, 1985; Maskowitz & Hayman, 1976; Ornstein, 1983; West, 1985).

Although school quality issues have been examined extensively, the specifics of what impacts differentially on learning at the classroom level for disadvantaged learners are less clear-cut. Several researchers have focused on group rather than individual models of learning as more facilitative for minority group students.

Slavin and Oickle (1981) found a greater increase in Black students' academic performance in cooperative learning groups. Hale-Benson (1986) advocated peer tutoring, and Holliday (1985) emphasized enhanced teacher-student interactions. Dunham and Russo (1983) recommended the use of mentors, community involvement, and early counseling to help broaden ideas on future career roles for disadvantaged learners. The literature on disadvantaged gifted has tended to emphasize the following intervention strategies:

1. Attention to strengths in nonacademic areas, particularly in creativity and psychomotor domains (Torrance, 1977; Hilliard, 1976; Bruch, 1975).
2. Creation of programs that address noncognitive skills and enhance motivation (McClelland, 1978; Moore, 1978).

UNDERACHIEVERS

Underachievement among the gifted has plagued educators for the last 70 years. Why do able children fail to utilize their high-level abilities in productive ways? What can parents and educators do to curb this condition? How might the ability of these learners be channeled productively to enhance their own sense of self? These questions are as open to debate today as they were in Terman's day. A sizable amount of research has been conducted on this topic, and we have reason to speculate that unrealized potential among the gifted has a high incidence. About half of the gifted children who score in the top 5 percent of intellectual ability on individualized IQ tests have been reported to not match their ability with comparable school achievement (Gallagher, 1975; Gowan, 1955; Laycock, 1979; Perkins, 1969; Pringle, 1970; Raph, Goldberg, & Passow, 1966; Terman & Oden, 1947; Wolfe, 1954).

Gifted underachievers, as compared to achievers, manifest certain patterns of behavior: social immaturity, emotional problems, antisocial behavior, and low self-concept. Studies have further indicated that this is primarily a male phenomenon. Also, families of underachievers are more likely to be unstable, lower income, single-parented, and offer fewer social/educational opportunities (Bricklin & Bricklin, 1967; Colangelo, 1979; Hecht, 1975; Newman, Dember, & Krug, 1973; Pringle, 1970; Raph, Goldberg, & Passow, 1966; Saurenman & Michael, 1980; Wellington & Wellington, 1965; Whitmore, 1980).

Several studies have compared gifted students who achieve and those who do not achieve on personality measures. Davis and Connell (1985) reported that high IQ, achieving fourth through sixth graders were higher on internal control and lower on control by powerful others compared to low-achieving students of equal ability. Kanoy, Johnson, and Kandy (1980) compared high- and low-achieving academically talented fourth graders. The high achievers had higher scores on intellectual self-concept and on a measure of internal locus of control, compared to the low achievers. Ringness (1967) compared high-IQ eighth grade achievers and nonachievers. Low achievers were lower on achievement motivation and higher on affiliation motivation than the high-achieving, talented students. Davids and Sidman (1962) compared high- and low-achieving gifted high school students on the Adjective Check List. High achievers were higher in self-control than low-achieving groups. These authors also found that high achievers were higher than the low achievers in self-assurance, socialization, maturity, achievement potential, and intellectual efficiency. In a more recent study (Laffoon, Jenkins-Friedman, & Tollefson, 1989), high-achieving gifted learners attributed success and failure to effort, whereas underachievers attributed success to ability and failure to luck, fate, or other people.

Colangelo and Dettman (1983) reviewed research on the importance of home environment and family relations on achievement. Some of these studies indicate that the underachiever frequently experiences parental rejection and hostility, whereas achievers have accepting and affectionate parents. Parental expectations and pressure to achieve also have been cited frequently as causes for underachievement. When parents gave their children support, encouragement, and independence, however, the children seemed to have appropriate levels of achievement. These parental factors included high levels of involvement with the child at home, greater parental trust and approval in contrast to a restrictive and severe attitude, and a family morale that fostered positive attitudes toward teachers, school, and intellectual activities. In contrast, low self-esteem in relation to the family was seen as a cause of underachievement.

Some of the adjustment problems and underachievement displayed by the bright underachiever may stem from the school environment itself (Pirozzo, 1981). French and Garden's (1968) study pointed out that the school setting rather than the students was the problem. These researchers reported that bright male dropouts were more uninhibited than male non-dropouts, placed much more importance in being able to be an individual, and thus fought strong pressures toward conformity within the school. Richards and Bear (1986) concluded that extreme underachievers at every grade level in their study displayed the most negative academic attitudes of any group. Gallagher, Greenman, Karnes, and King (1960) emphasized that the school and the teachers, in their attempts to deal with these nonconforming and angry children, are likely to take more strict and repressive measures, which will turn the children even more against them.

In the past, two major strategies have been applied to alleviate or reduce the problems of underachieving gifted and talented children (Gallagher, 1975, 1979). The first strategy entails personal counseling based upon the research findings indicating that these students have a low self-image and feelings of inferiority. The second strategy involves changes in the educational environment and programming. This approach has attempted to enhance the student's self-concept through better school performance. Homogeneous grouping is the most common educational modification schools have employed to deal with underachieving gifted children.

According to Whitmore (1980), the Cupertino project for underachieving students at the elementary level showed positive results after three years of full-time grouping, diagnostic prescriptive approaches to basic skills, and counseling, mentoring, and tutorial strategies for about 60% of the students. She concluded that effective interventions for these learners must be intensive and long-term.

Another strategy the literature advocates to help underachievers is attribution retraining that promotes an internal locus of control in students, especially regarding failure situations (Diener & Dweck, 1978). Through self-monitoring, these students can improve their persistence, goal-setting behavior, and positive self-talk (Covington & Omelich, 1979; Ellis, 1985).

The results of several studies strongly suggest that underachievement becomes a life pattern for the gifted. McCall and Evahn (1987) compared underachievers and achievers 13 years after high school. Underachievers pursued further schooling and took jobs consistent with their grades, not with their abilities. Further, underachievers had a substantially lower likelihood of completing four years of college and a greater likelihood of divorce than did non-underachieving students. Some underachievers ultimately did catch up to their abilities — those who, as high school students, had high educational and occupational experiences, who had high self-esteem and perceived competence, who participated in activities (especially females), and whose parents were well educated. But serious underachievers of medium to high mental ability did not catch up. They attained very little relative to other groups. Students from less educated families were less likely to achieve levels commensurate with their ability than students from better educated families.

The literature on underachievement presents a well documented pattern of the behavioral characteristics of underachievers, especially when compared to high achievers. These students exhibit negative attitudes toward school and academic learning, tend to have poor self-concepts, have a preference for non-productive use of leisure time, and lack the ability to persevere with tasks or exhibit goal-directed behavior. What is less clear from the literature is how parents and teachers might effectively combat these debilitating characteristics when they surface. No one intervention strategy is likely to be successful but, rather, an approach that combines early identification and sustained academic stimulation and challenge and small-group counseling as a part of the total school program. Parenting models that reinforce productive behavior and provide a collaborative linkage to school efforts also seem important to employ as early as possible.

GIFTED GIRLS

The special population of gifted girls forces us to consider and understand the discrepancy between high-level ability and early achievement and depressed levels of achievement from adolescence onward. While the debate around giftedness in girls has centered in recent years on mathematical ability differences between males and females, the larger issue of unrealized potential, particularly among adult gifted women, has received less attention. Both gender research and research on gifted women have continued to highlight this problem.

There have been more perceptions of intellectual differences based on gender than have been borne out in the literature in recent years, even in the field of mathematics. The relationship between mathematics, science, and spatial ability has been assessed by Linn and Petersen (1985), who examined the nature, magnitude, and age of first appearance of gender differences in these three domains. After an extensive analysis, they concluded that no consistent pattern of gender differences exists either between or within these ability areas. Indeed, independent of the issue of gender, mathematics, science, and spatial abilities are themselves shown not to be unitary ability domains.

Earlier reviews of studies comparing male and female performance on intellectual tasks found gender differences in verbal behavior (Maccoby & Jacklin, 1974; Sherman, 1971), but current research does not (see Hyde & Linn, 1988, for a review). In their comparison of verbal-ability scores of girls and boys, Hyde and Linn (1988) found that the differences between the sexes has been reduced across the last decades. Similar decreases in gender differences over the last two decades have been shown in a variety of other intellectual abilities (Feingold, 1988; Rosenthal & Ruben, 1982).

In summary, tests of intellectual abilities have differentiated girls and boys less and less over the last decades. The only exception to this trend is at the highest end of the mathematics-ability continuum, where the ratio of boys outscoring girls has remained constant over the years (Feingold, 1988).

Research over the past several decades has consistently demonstrated that females receive higher grades than males throughout elementary school, high school, and college (Achenbach, 1970; Coleman, 1961; and Davis, 1964). Reis (1981) found that the products completed by males and females across elementary grade levels do not differ significantly in quality and that equivalent numbers of males and females initiate advanced-level work when given the opportunity. But Fitzpatrick (1978) found a significant downward trend in school achievement for girls from grade 6 onward. And Callahan (1980) noted that, in spite of approximately equal numbers of male and female gifted children, an overwhelming number of adults identified as gifted are men.

Arnold and Denny (1985) reported on a longitudinal study of male and female high school valedictorians and salutatorians. They discovered women's estimates of their intelligence lowering between high school and their sophomore year in college as compared to their male counterparts. These women also had lower career aspirations and less ambitious goals as sophomores than when they had graduated from high school.

Fear of success may cause some females to believe that they may be rejected by their peers or appear undesirable to the opposite sex if they are too competent or successful (Horner, 1972; Lavach & Lanier, 1975). Although more current research suggests that fear of success can be eliminated with age and experience (Birnbaum, 1975; Hoffman, 1977), preliminary findings in a study of high school valedictorians found that female students who had done well in high school lose confidence in their ability after a few years of college (Arnold & Denny, 1985).

Other research on gender differences has revealed related areas of concern for gifted girls. Dweck (1986) noted a tendency toward low expectancies, avoidance of challenge, ability attribution for failure, and debilitation under failure as characteristics of bright girls when compared to boys. Dweck (1986) also reported that measures of children's actual competence do not strongly predict their confidence in future attainment. Thus, gender differences in motivational and personality patterns emerge as central issues to consider in explaining achievement patterns.

Attitudes of teachers in the school environment also are cause for concern. Sadker and Sadker (1985) found that boys vocally dominate the classroom and that boys get more attention and encouragement than do girls. Their research also found that teachers behaved differently when boys or girls called out in class without raising their hands. When boys answered without being called on, teachers accepted their answers; the same behavior from girls resulted in negative responses about raising their hands before speaking. Teachers called on boys more often and praised them more often. High-achieving girls received the least attention. Some evidence suggests that girls are treated differently in classrooms in college as well as in elementary and secondary school (Schmidt, 1982).

Studies have consistently reported more positive self-concepts and higher levels of self-esteem among career-oriented women. Also, greater self-esteem is associated with stronger career orientation among adolescents. Self-esteem is strongly related to achievement motivation in college-age females. And high levels of self-esteem are characteristic of women in male-oriented professions. Probably of even greater importance is that academic self-concept consistently has been shown to influence academic success, career choice, and test performance (Eccles, 1987).

Although there is evidence of ability and achievement gaps narrowing between girls and boys in most areas of school learning, the tendency for gifted girls to do less well than gifted boys on mathematical aptitude tests remains. Findings also tend to coalesce around other issues for gifted girls and women: (a) that teachers differentially reward girls and boys for assertive behaviors, with gifted girls being least rewarded, (b) that neither past evidence of competence nor achievement is a good predictor of future achievement in gifted girls during or after adolescence, and (c) that higher education and a strong career orientation are accompanied by higher self-concept and greater life satisfaction in gifted women.

THE HANDICAPPED GIFTED

Gifted individuals who have learning disabilities and those who have physical disabilities in one or several areas comprise another group subsumed under the rubric of a special population. These students have perhaps the most discrepant pattern of all of the sub-groups discussed in this chapter, for they portray real disabilities in functioning. Their profile is atypical in respect to strengths, when compared to our classic conceptions of giftedness, and it forces us to entertain a conception of subnormal functioning in the gifted, a condition not readily acceptable in the conceptual framework of understanding giftedness.

Learning Disabilities

Individuals with learning disabilities as a categorical group are represented by children with diverse problems. Academic disabilities may be found in reading, writing, arithmetic, and spelling. Developmental disabilities include attention, perceptual memory, concept formation, and problem solving (Kirk & Chalfant, 1984). Moreover, children with learning disabilities typically have behavioral dysfunctions as well in the areas of peer interaction, frustration tolerance, and aggressive or withdrawal tendencies.

Although many gifted children who do not perform up to classroom expectation levels are labeled "underachievers," research suggests that these children should be tested for learning disabilities (Hansford, Whitmore, Kraynak, & Wingenback, 1987; Silverman, 1989). Rosner and Seymour (1983) contend that teachers "have been unable to conceptualize the essence" of a gifted learning disabled child. In fact, teachers reading the same vignette about a gifted child (alternately nonlabeled or labeled, or labeled as learning disabled or physically handicapped) believed that nonlabeled and physically handicapped students should be placed in a gifted program to a greater degree than students with learning disabilities (Minner et al., 1987). The definitions of both giftedness and learning disabilities have been cited as impeding identification of children as gifted learning disabled. Although many school systems rely on IQ test cutoff scores ranging from 120–140, methods of identifying the gifted learning disabled population have also included WISC-R sub-test scatter, discrepancy in WISC-R Performance and Verbal scores, and discrepancy in intelligence and achievement scores.

Research has been conducted using the WISC-R to identify the unique characteristics of gifted children with learning disabilities, but no clear pattern has yet emerged (Barton & Starnes, 1989). Schiff, Kaufman, and Kaufman (1981) found that verbal performance discrepancies were greater for the learning disabled students with superior ability than learning disabled students with average ability, as were higher verbal than performance scores, and wide sub-test scatter. Maker and Udall (1983) found wide sub-test scatter and significantly higher performance than verbal scores with the lowest sub-tests, including digit span, information, block design and coding. Larger scale studies have found significant percentages of learners who manifest both WISC-R sub-scale patterns (Fox, Brody, & Tobin, 1983).

Based on clients seeking assessment at the Gifted Child Development Center, Denver, Colorado, Silverman (1989) reported that approximately one-sixth of the children assessed for giftedness at the Center were gifted learning disabled. Their giftedness was evidenced in their high scores on vocabulary, similarities, and block design, whereas the disabilities were observed in the large discrepancies between their weaknesses and strengths. Even though these children may make intuitive leaps and excel at reasoning, their weaknesses in the sequential skills may be manifested as difficulties in rote memorization, phonics, and performance under timed conditions. Many of these students also have been identified as having auditory sequential processing impairments.

Based on their review of the literature, Suter and Wolf (1987) presented some generalizations regarding identification of the gifted learning disabled population:

1. A multidimensional approach to identification is necessary to determine areas of strengths and weaknesses.
2. The WISC-R is helpful in identifying strengths and weaknesses, as well as overall performance.
3. Academic testing is necessary to determine the discrepancy between potential and performance.
4. Important information can be obtained from parents and teachers about activities that may not be revealed on standardized tests.
5. Evaluators should spend time interviewing and assessing the quality of children's responses for signs of giftedness.

After analyses of the files at the Temple University Reading Clinic, Fox, Brody, and Tobin (1983) concluded that (a) learning disabled/gifted children exist in our schools, and that (b) the vast majority are unrecognized as such because their disability is not severe enough for their performance to be noticeably below grade-level expectations on standardized tests or in normal classroom functioning. Their analysis of data for the gifted and comparison groups suggested no definitive profile on the WISC-R that could be used for quick screening, although a significant discrepancy between Similarities and Digit Span did appear frequently in the gifted groups. They further suggest that the most promising avenue of research is for teachers to use an informal reading inventory for quick screening, with emphasis on the discrepancy between listening comprehension and instructional level, even if the child is reading at grade level.

The literature has suggested several differentiated approaches to take with gifted children who have learning disabilities, including separate class grouping (Daniels, 1983), counseling and adaptive behavior programs (Wolf & Gygi, 1981), technological aids (Tobin & Schiffman, 1983), and the teaching of compensation strategies (Suter & Wolf, 1987). Moreover, most writers urge the use of strategies appropriate for all gifted learners. Adaptations for school and home use to enhance learning for the gifted learning disabled include (Hansford et al., 1987; Silverman, 1989; Suter & Wolf, 1987):

1. Use visuals and hands on experiences.
2. Provide a quiet place for work.
3. Take a sight approach to reading rather than phonics.
4. Use a word processor with a program to check spelling.
5. Promote visualization as a memory aid.
6. Tape-record lectures instead of requiring note taking.
7. Concentrate on the child's strengths, especially to compensate for weaknesses.
8. Move students to advanced concepts after age 9, even if basic skills are not totally internalized.
9. Provide conceptual organizers for all information bases to be taught.
10. Bolster self-esteem through positive reinforcement, attention, and praise.

For adaptations in the home, Sah and Borland (1989) examined the effects of a structured time table of the subjects' homes after school on home and school behavior and academic performance. The gifted children with learning disabilities were found to have deficits in organizational skills. After parent training and interventions, positive changes were observed in all areas, including decreases in "problem behaviors," improved grades, and increases in homework submission. Dykstra (1990) also found executive processing problems in the learning disabled gifted to be their most problematic issue, calling for attention to learning strategies that may enhance this weak area of their profile.

Understandably, gifted children with learning disabilities also have been found to have lower self-concepts than typical gifted children. Waldron, Saphire, and Rosenblum (1987) found that teachers perceived gifted learning disabled children as quieter and more pensive than more typical gifted children in their study; moreover, teachers perceived the gifted learning disabled as more asocial and less popular. In the same study, gifted learning disabled students scored lower than typical gifted learners on all self-concept factors; and the lowest factor rating was on their own feelings of intelligence and school status. The most positive personal factor rating for gifted students with learning disabilities was their perception of their behavior. Self-ratings also revealed more anxiety and personal dissatisfaction among the gifted/learning disabled group than the typical gifted group.

One study suggests the importance of emphasizing the giftedness aspect of learning disabled gifted children's profiles. Nielsen and Mortorff-Allen (1989) compared various levels of special education service received by gifted learning disabled students, including self-contained classes, a combination of learning disabled resource and a gifted pull-out program, learning disabled service only, and gifted programming only. Students receiving either a combination of both gifted and learning disabled service or only gifted service reported higher self-concepts than did students receiving intense or exclusive learning disabled service.

Studies of children with learning disabilities also indicate that they are viewed as different (Hallahan and Bryan, 1981) and that they do seem to act sufficiently differently — such that even naive observers can see the learning disabled child as distinct from the norm (Bryan & Bryan, 1978). Physical and behavioral manifestations of learning dysfunction seem to put these children at even greater risk for adequate social adjustment.

An area frequently overlooked by the learning disability field is the psychological adjustment and reaction of the children to their dual status — being at the upper limits of one critical intellectual area and at the lower limits of another. Krippner (1968) observed that a tendency exists among talented youngsters with learning disabilities to show greater adjustment difficulty. He categorized this difficulty in the areas of social immaturities, psychopathic tendencies, neurotic tendencies, psychotic tendencies, and unfavorable educational experiences.

Physical Handicaps

Little research has been done on gifted individuals with physical handicaps except of a retrospective nature on eminent individuals (Goertzel & Goertzel, 1962) or a case study perspective (Whitmore & Maker, 1985). Maker et al. (1978) profiled successful scientists with physical handicaps in an effort to understand how they perceived and attributed their success. She found that these individuals manifested persistence, self-confidence, and strength/force of character to a great extent and that they attributed their success primarily to ability, although they did learn specific strategies to enlist the help of others to facilitate their success.

Over the last 15 years Karnes (1979) pioneered the identification and programming of preschool children, with physical handicaps, through the use of multiple talent screening checklists and other multidimensional techniques that supplement traditional identification methods and measures. Evaluation data from the Retrieval and Acceleration of Promising Young Handicapped and Talented (RAPYHT) project suggest that: (a) young handicapped gifted children can be identified; (b) effects of early educational experiences tend to be positive both in the realm of achievement patterns and in self-concept and its development; (c) parental involvement and approval of the program was high; and (d) program participation seemed to bolster RAPYHT children's opportunities for a mainstreamed education (Karnes & Johnson, 1987).

ASSESSMENT NEEDS

Much of the past research emphasis for special populations of the gifted has been on identification measures, particularly finding the right test to use in locating them. We already have spent too much time attempting to reinvent the testing wheel and would be better served by supplementing our best testing models with other data sources that would enhance our understanding of a particular child in a particular social context for the specific purpose of intervention. Culturally normed checklists, behavioral characteristics in specific domains, and parent, peer, and teacher nominations in tandem with standardized tests might serve us well if they were used for diagnostic information in planning a program of study.

The emphasis in assessment has to shift from testing in its narrow function of labeling to its more useful role in providing instructional data for curriculum intervention and be seen as a part of the information bank necessary to work with special populations of gifted learners in programs. But we still need to work out an assessment protocol that schools can actually employ to find these learners both efficiently and effectively.

EFFECTIVE INTERVENTIONS

As we begin to examine effective interventions, several directions seem promising:

1. *Separate instructional opportunities for students with the same developmental profile.* Data across special populations suggest the importance for within-group instructional time that allows for interaction based on similar conditions whether it be gender, social background, or handicapping conditions.
2. *The use of technology, especially microcomputers, to aid in transmission of learning for many special population learners.* Although new technology has been used most predominantly with handicapped gifted learners, it holds promise for targeted use with other learners who evidence discrepant learning patterns and can profit from compensatory intervention.
3. *Small-group and individual counseling, mentorships, and internships for special population learners.* These interventions all constitute individual attention to affective as well as cognitive issues of development.
4. *A focus on the arts as a therapeutic intervention as well as a creative and expressive outlet.* Through the arts, the dissynchronies of one's experience can be reduced and absorbed into a higher pattern of integration. Thus, the arts can enhance higher-level functioning.
5. *Use of materials rich in ideas and imagination coupled with emphasis on higher-level skills.* Both self-concept and motivation are in jeopardy if prolonged use of compensatory strategies and basic level materials are maintained in the educational process of these learners. Challenging content with attention to ideas and creative opportunities is essential to combat further discrepant performance.

COLLABORATION

As we review where we are in our understanding and appropriate treatment of students who are characterized as "special populations," the field of gifted education stands at an important juncture in shaping appropriate responses to the needs these students present. Though it is clear that identification protocols must be liberalized and value-added interventions must be structured, it is less clear how we might proceed to forge linkages with general and special educators to carry out the needed tasks. Our greatest challenge in providing service to these learners will be in our efforts to reach out to other educators in collaborative ways. Only in this way can we deal realistically with the complexity of these students' profiles.

SUMMARY

Understanding and acceptance of giftedness in individuals whose profiles display individual abilities and disabilities is an important overall consideration in identifying and serving the gifted handicapped population. Major approaches to identification include tailoring the protocol to the handicapping condition, using multidimensional procedures, and soliciting nominations from various individual sources. Programming should allow for opportunities comparable to nonhandicapped populations but with special considerations for personalized services, technology aids, and sensitivity to the nature and extent of the handicap in selecting modes of learning.

Special sub-groups include the disadvantaged gifted, underachievers, gifted girls, and gifted children with handicaps. Each of these sub-groups has its unique set of needs, and each child within each sub-group also represents the diversity present.

Educators have grappled with the definition of "disadvantaged," and lack of resources in the school, family, and community is key. Minority groups tend to have been underrepresented in programs for the gifted, because of their cultural and language differences, which do not serve them well in many tests standardized on a nonminority population. Low socioeconomic status also tends to impede gifted potential because of unrealistic expectations in the home.

The dynamics of underachievers, another sub-group of the handicapped gifted, has eluded educators for years. Underachievement has been correlated, with some consistency, with social immaturity, emotional problems, antisocial behavior, and low self-concept. Therefore, intervention should focus on these areas, including counseling and programs designed to elevate self-concept through better school performance.

The sub-group of gifted girls warrants a special designation because these girls show discrepancy with their gifted male counterparts in achievement. Though ability levels are largely the same, achievement becomes more disparate as time goes on.

Finally, the most discrepant pattern of the special gifted populations is found in the gifted with learning disabilities and those with physical handicaps.

In dealing with the duality of their condition, schools have a major challenge. Identification of their "hidden" giftedness requires concentrated efforts in assessment and specific adaptations in the learning environment.

QUESTIONS FOR REFLECTION

1. How might schools organize to focus on individual rather than group needs of learners?
2. What mechanisms might be tried to enhance relationships between parents of gifted learners and schools?
3. If "uneven development" is the norm among gifted special populations, how can this concept be translated into appropriate expectations at home and at school?
4. What strategies might enhance the development of gifted girls over the critical ages 10–17?
5. How might we as a field undertake action research to try out and share successful techniques in working with special populations of gifted learners?

REFERENCES

Achenbach, T. (1970). Standardization of a research instrument for identifying associative responding in children. *Developmental Psychology, 1,* 283–291.

Alamprese, J. A., & Erlanger, W. J. (1988). *No gift wasted: Effective strategies for educating highly able, disadvantaged students in mathematics and science* (p. v). Washington, DC: Cosmos Corporation for the U.S. Department of Education.

Amodeo, L. B., & Flores, L. J. (1981). *Parental involvement in the identification of gifted Mexican American children.* Paper presented at Council for Exceptional Children National Conference for the Exceptional Bilingual Child, Phoenix.

Arnold, K., & Denny, T. (1985). *The lives of academic achievers: The career aspirations of male and female high school valedictorians and salutatorians.* Paper presented at annual meeting of American Educational Research Association, Chicago.

Baldwin, A. Y. (1985). Programs for the gifted and talented: Issues concerning minority populations. In F. D. Horowitz & M. O'Brien (Eds.), *The gifted and talented: Developmental perspectives* (pp. 223–249). Washington, DC: American Psychological Association.

Barton, J. M., & Starnes, W. T. (1989). Identifying distinguishing characteristics of gifted and talented/learning disabled students. *Roeper Review, 12*(1), 23–29.

Bernal, E. M., & Reyna, J. (1974). *Analysis of giftedness in Mexican-American children and design of a prototype instrument* (Report for Southwest Educational Development Lab, Austin, TX). Washington, DC: Dept. of Health, Education & Welfare, Office for Gifted and Talented.

Birnbaum, J. A. (1975). Life patterns and self-esteem in gifted family-oriented and career-committed women. In M. T. S. Mednick, S. S. Tangri, & L. W. Hoffman (Eds.), *Women and achievement* (pp. 396–419). New York: John Wiley.

Bricklin, B., & Bricklin, P. (1967). *Bright child, poor grades.* New York: Delacourt Press.

Bruch, C. B. (1975). Assessment of creativity in culturally different gifted children. *Gifted Child Quarterly, 19*(2), 164–174.

Bruch, C. B. (1978). Recent insights on the culturally different gifted. *Gifted Child Quarterly, 22*(3), 374–393.

Bryan, T., & Bryan, J. (1978). *Understanding learning disabilities* (2nd ed.). Sherman Oaks, CA: Alfred Publishing Co.

Callahan, C. (1980). The gifted child: An anomaly? *Roeper Review, 2*(3), 16–20.

Colangelo, N. (1979). Myths and stereotypes of gifted students: Awareness for the classroom teacher. In N. Colangelo, C. C. Foxley, & D. Dustin (Eds.), *Multicultural nonsexist education* (pp. 458–464). Dubuque, IA: Kendall/Hunt.

Colangelo, N., & Dettman, D. F. (1983). A review of research on parents and families of gifted children. *Exceptional Children, 50*(1), 20–27.

Coleman, J. (1961). *The adolescent society*. New York: Free Press.

Covington, M., & Omelich, C. (1979). Effort: The double-edged sword in school achievement. *Journal of Educational Psychology, 71*(2), 169–182.

Daniels, P. R. (1983). *Teaching the gifted/learning disabled child*. Rockville, MD: Aspen.

Davids, A., & Sidman, J. (1962). A pilot study — impulsivity, time orientation, and delayed gratification in future scientists and in underachieving high school students. *Exceptional Children, 29* (4), 170–174.

Davis, H. P., & Connell, J. P. (1985). The effect of aptitude and achievement status on the self-system. *Gifted Child Quarterly, 29*(3), 131–136.

Davis, J., (1964). *Great aspirations: The school plans of America's college seniors*. Chicago: Aldine.

Diener, C., & Dweck, C. (1978). An analysis of learner helplessness: Continuous changes in performance, strategy, and achievement cognitions following failure. *Journal of Personality & Social Psychology, 35*(5), 451–462.

Dunham, G., & Russo, T. (1983). Career education for the disadvantaged gifted: Some thoughts for educators. *Roeper Review, 5*(3), 26–28.

Dweck, C. (1986). Motivational processes affecting learning. *American Psychologist, 41*(10), 1040–1048.

Dykstra, L. (1990). Keynote address on learning disabilities. Project Director's Meeting for the Department of Education, Washington, DC.

Eccles, J. S. (1987). Gender roles and women's achievement-related decisions. *Psychology of Women Quarterly, 7*(2), 135–137.

Ellis, A. (1985). *Overcoming resistance: Rational-emotive therapy with difficult clients*. New York: Springer.

Entwisle, D. R., & Hayduk, L. A. (1978). *Too great expectations*. Baltimore: Johns Hopkins University Press.

Feingold, A. (1988). Cognitive gender differences are disappearing. *American Psychologist, 43*, 95–103.

Fitzpatrick, J. L. (1978). Academic underachievement, other-direction, and attitudes toward women's roles in bright adolescent females. *Journal of Educational Psychology, 27*, 44–62.

Fox, L., Brody, L., & Tobin, D. (1983). *Learning-disabled/gifted children: Identification and programming*. Baltimore: University Park Press.

Frasier, M. M. (1979). Rethinking the issue regarding the culturally disadvantaged gifted. *Exceptional Children, 45*(7), 538–542.

Frasier, M. M. (1980). Programming for the culturally diverse. In J. Jordan & J. Grossi, *An administrator's handbook on designing programs for the gifted and talented*. Reston, VA: Council for Exceptional Children.

Frasier, M. (1984). *Increasing minority representation in programs for the gifted and characteristics of the home environment of potentially gifted minority children* (Commissioned paper, contained in EC 162812). ERIC Clearinghouse on the Handicapped and Gifted.

French, J. L., & Garden, B.W. (1968). Characteristics of high mental ability school dropouts. *Vocational Guidance Quarterly, 16*(3), 162–168.

Frierson, E. (1965). Upper and lower status gifted children: A study of differences. *Exceptional Children, 32*(2), 83–90.

Gallagher, J. J. (1975). *Teaching the gifted child*. Boston: Allyn & Bacon.

Gallagher, J. J. (1979). Issues in education for the gifted. In A. H. Passow (Ed.), *The gifted and the talented: Their education and development* (pp. 28–44). Chicago: University of Chicago Press.

Gallagher, J. J., Greenman, M., Karnes, M., & King, A. (1960). Individual classroom adjustments for gifted children in elementary schools. *Exceptional Children, 26*, 409–422.

Gay, J. (1978). A proposed plan for identifying black gifted children. *Gifted Child Quarterly, 22*(3), 353–360.

Goertzel, V., & Goertzel, M. (1962). *Cradles of eminence*. Boston: Little, Brown.

Gowan, J. C. (1955). The under-achieving gifted child. A problem for everyone. *Exceptional Children, 21*, 247–249.

Hale-Benson, J. E. (1986). *Black children: Their roots, culture and learning styles* (2nd ed). Baltimore: Johns Hopkins University.

Hallahan, D. P., & Bryan, T. H. (1981). Learning disabilities. In J. M. Kauffman & D. P. Hallahan (Eds.), *Handbook of special education*. Englewood Cliffs, NJ: Prentice Hall.

Hansford, S. J., Whitmore, J. R., Kraynak, A. R., & Wingenbach, N. G. (1987). *Intellectually gifted learning disabled students: A special study*. Reston, VA: ERIC Clearing House on Handicapped and Gifted Children.

Hanson, S. L., & Ginsburg, A. (1986). *Gaining ground: Values and educational success among disadvantaged students*. Washington, DC: U.S. Dept. of Education.

Hecht, K. A. (1975). Teacher ratings of potential dropouts and academically gifted children: Are they related? *Journal of Teacher Education, 26,* 172–175.

Hilliard, A. (1976). *Alternative to IQ testing: An approach to the identification of the gifted in minority children* (Report No. 75175). San Francisco: San Francisco State University.

Hoffman, L. W. (1977). Fear of success in 1965 and 1974: A follow-up study. *Journal of Consulting & Clinical Psychology, 45,* 310–321.

Holliday, B. G. (1985). Towards a model of teacher-child transactional processes affecting black children's academic achievement. In M. B. Spencer, G. K. Brookins, & W. R. Allen (Eds.), *Beginnings: The social and affective development of black children* (pp. 117–131). Hillsdale, NJ: Lawrence Erlbaum Associates.

Horner, M. S. (1972). Toward an understanding of achievement related conflicts in women. *Journal of Social Issues, 28,* 157–175.

Jencks, C. (1972). *Inequality*. New York: Basic Books.

Kanoy, R. C., Johnson, B. N., & Kanoy, K. W. (1980). Locus of control and self-concept in achieving and underachieving bright elementary students. *Psychology in the Schools, 17*(1), 395–399.

Karnes, M. (1979). Young handicapped children can be gifted and talented. *Journal for the Education of the Gifted, 6,* 157–172.

Karnes, M., & Johnson, L. (1987). An imperative: Programs for the young gifted/talented. *Journal for the Education of the Gifted, 10*(3), 195–213.

Kirk, S. A., & Chalfant, J. C. (1984). *Academic and developmental learning disabilities*. Denver: Love Publishing.

Krippner, S. (1968). Etiological factors in reading disabilities of the academically talented, in comparison to pupils of average and slow learning ability. *Journal of Educational Research, 61,* 275–279.

Laffoon, K., Jenkins-Friedman, R., & Tollefson, N. (1989). Causal attributes of underachieving gifted, achieving gifted, and nongifted students. *Journal for the Education of the Gifted, 13*(1), 4–21.

Lavach, J. F., & Lanier, H. B. (1975). The motive to avoid success in 7th, 8th, 9th, and 10th grade high-achieving girls. *Journal of Educational Research, 68,* 216–218.

Laycock, F. (1979). *Gifted children*. Glenview, IL: Scott Foresman.

Lezotte, L. W., & Bancroft, B. A. (1985). School improvement based on effective schools research: A promising approach for economically disadvantaged and minority students. *Journal of Negro Education, 54*(3), 301–311.

Lindstrom, R. R., & VanSant, S. (1986). Special issues in working with gifted minority adolescents. *Journal of Counseling & Development, 64,* 583–586.

Linn, M. C., & Petersen, A. C. (1985). Emergence and characterization of sex differences in spatial ability: A meta-analysis. *Child Development, 56,* 1479–1498.

Maccoby, E. E., & Jacklin, C. N. (1974). *The psychology of sex differences*. Stanford, CA: Stanford University Press.

Maker, C. J., Redden, M., Tonelson, S., & Howell, R. (1978). *The self perceptions of successful handicapped scientists*. Albuquerque: University of New Mexico, Department of Special Education.

Maker, C. J., & Schiever, S.(Ed.) (1989). *Critical issues in gifted education* (Vol. 2). Austin, TX: Pro-Ed.

180   *Specific Considerations*

Maker, C.J., & Udall, A. (1983). A pilot program for elementary-age learning disabled gifted students. In L. Fox, L. Brody, & D. Tobin (Eds.), *Learning disabled gifted children: Identification and programming* (pp. 223–242). Baltimore: University Park Press.

Mann, D. (1985). Effective schools for children of the poor. *Education Digest, 51,* 24–25.

Maskowitz, G., & Hayman, J. T. (1976). Success strategies of inner city teachers: A year long study. *Journal of Educational Research, 69,* 283–289.

Masten, W. G. (1981). *Approaches to identification of gifted minority students* (Paper for U.S. Department of Education, National Institute of Education). Educational Resources Information Center (ED 234578).

Masten, W. G. (1985). Identification of gifted minority students: Past research, future directions. *Roeper Review, 8*(2), 83–85.

McCall, R. B., & Evahn, C. (1987). *The adult educational and occupational status of chronic high school underachievers.* Paper presented at the annual meeting of American Educational Research Association, Washington, DC.

McClelland, D. C. (1978). Managing motivation to expand human freedom. *American Psychologist, 33,* 201–210.

McIntosh, M. E., & Greenlaw, M. J. (1986). Fostering the post-secondary aspirations of gifted urban minority students. *Roeper Review, 9*(2), 104–107.

Miller, L. (1974). *The testing of black students: A symposium.* Englewood Cliffs, NJ: Prentice Hall.

Minner, S. (1987). Referral and placement recommendations of teachers toward gifted handicapped children. *Roeper Review, 9*(4), 247–249.

Moore, B. (1978). Career education for disadvantaged gifted high school students. *Gifted Child Quarterly, 22*(3), 332–337.

Newman, J., Dember, C., & Krug, O. (1973). He can but he won't. *Psychoanalytic Study of the Child, 28,* 83–129.

Nielsen, M. E., & Mortoff-Allen, S. (1989). The effects of special education service on the self-concept and school attitude of learning disabled/gifted students. *Roeper Review, 12*(1), 29–36.

Ornstein, A. C. (1983). Educating disadvantaged learners. *Educational Forum, 47*(2), 225–247.

Pallas, A. M., Natriello, G., & McDill, E. L. (1989). The changing nature of the disadvantaged population: Current dimensions and future trends. *Educational Researcher, 18*(5), 16–22.

Perkins, H. V. (1969). *Human development and learning.* Belmont, CA: Wadsworth Publishing.

Pirozzo, R. (1981). Curriculum modifications for gifted and talented children. *Journal of the Association of Independent Schools of Queensland, 2*(2), 56–63.

Pringle, M. L. (1970). *Able misfits.* London: Longman Group Ltd.

Prom-Jackson, S., Johnson, S. T., & Wallace, M. B. (1987). Home environment, talented minority youth, and school achievement. *Journal of Negro Education, 56*(1), 111–121.

Ramey, C. T., Yeates, K. O., & Short, E. J. (1984). The plasticity of intellectual development: Insights from preventive intervention. *Child Development, 55,* 1913–1925.

Raph, J. B., Goldberg, M. L., & Passow, A. H. (1966). *Bright underachievers.* New York: Teachers College Press.

Reis, S. (1981). *An analysis of the productivity of gifted students participating in programs using revolving door identification model.* Unpublished doctoral dissertation, University of Connecticut, Storrs.

Reschly, D. J., & Ross-Reynolds, J. (1983). An investigation of WISC-R item bias with four sociocultural groups. *Journal of Consulting & Clinical Psychology, 51*(1), 144–146.

Richards, H. C., & Bear, G. G. (1986). Attitudes toward school subjects of academically unpredictable elementary school children. Paper presented at the American Educational Research Association, Chicago, IL.

Ringness, T. A. (1967). *Mental health in the schools.* New York: Random House.

Rosenthal, R., & Rubin, D. B. (1982). Further meta-analytic procedures for assessing cognitive gender differences. *Journal of Educational Psychology, 74,* 708–712.

Rosner, S. L., & Seymour, J. (1983). The gifted child with a learning disability: Clinical evidence. In L. H. Fox, L. Brody, & D. Tobin (Eds.), *Learning-disabled gifted children: Identification and programming* (pp. 77–97). Baltimore: University Park Press.

Sadker, M., & Sadker, D. (1985). Sexism in the schoolroom of the '80s. *Psychology Today, 19*(3), 54–57.

Sah, A., & Borland, J. H. (1989). The effects of a structured home plan on the home and school behaviors of gifted learning-disabled students with deficits in organizational skills. *Roeper Review, 12*(1), 54–57.

Samuda, R. J. (1975). *Psychological testing of American minorities: Issues and consequences.* New York: Dodd, Mead.

Saurenman, D., & Michael, W. (1980). Differential placement of high-achieving and low-achieving gifted pupils in grades 4, 5, & 6 on measures of field dependence-field dependence, creativity, and self-concept. *Gifted Child Quarterly, 24,* 81–85.

Schiff, M. M., Kaufman, A. S., & Kaufman, N. L. (1981). Scatter analysis of WISC-R profiles for learning-disabled children with superior intelligence. *Journal of Learning Disabilities, 14,* 400–404.

Schmidt, P. J. (1982). Sexist schooling. *Working Woman, 7*(10), 101–102.

Seitz, V., Rosenbaum, L. K., & Apfel, N. H. (1985). Effects of family support intervention: A ten year follow-up. *Child Development, 56,* 376–391.

Sherman, J. A. (1971). *On the psychology of women.* Springfield, IL: Charles C Thomas.

Silverman, L. K. (1989). Invisible gifts, invisible handicaps. *Roeper Review, 12*(1), 37–42.

Slavin, R. E., & Oickle, E. (1981). Effects of cooperative learning teams on student achievement and race relations: Treatment by race interactions. *Sociology of Education, 54,* 174–180.

Suter, D. P., & Wolf, J. S. (1987). Issues in the identification and programming of the gifted/learning-disabled child. *Journal for the Education of the Gifted, 10*(3), 227–238.

Terman, L. M., & Oden, M. (1947). *Genetic studies of genius — IV. The gifted child grows up.* Stanford, CA: Stanford University Press.

Tharp, R. G. (1989). Psychocultural variables and constants: Effects on teaching and learning in schools. *American Psychologist, 44,* 349–359.

Theanacho, S. O. (1988). Minority self-concept: A research review. *Journal of Instructional Psychology, 15*(11), pp. 3–11.

Tobin, D., & Schiffman, G. B. (1983). Computer technology for learning-disabled/gifted students. In L. Fox, L. Brody, & D. Tobin (Eds.), *Learning-disabled gifted children: Identification and programming* (pp. 195–206). Baltimore: University Park Press.

Tonemah, S. (1987). Assessing American Indian gifted and talented students' abilities. *Journal for the Education of the Gifted, 10*(3), 181–194.

Torrance, E. P. (1971). Are the Torrance Tests of Creative Thinking biased against or in favor of disadvantaged groups? *Gifted Child Quarterly, 15,* 75–80.

Torrance, E. P. (1977). *Discovery and nurturance of giftedness in the culturally different.* Reston, VA: Council for Exceptional Children.

VanTassel-Baska, J. (1989). The role of the family in the success of disadvantaged gifted learners. In J. VanTassel-Baska & P. Olszewski (Eds.), *Patterns of influence: The home, the self, and the school* (pp. 66–80). New York: Teachers College Press.

VanTassel-Baska, J., Patton, J., & Prillaman, D. (1989). Disadvantaged gifted learners at-risk for educational attention. In *Focus on Exceptional Children, 22*(3), 1–16. Denver: Love Publishing.

VanTassel-Baska, J., & Willis, G. (1988). A three year study of the effects of low income on SAT scores among the academically able. *Gifted Child Quarterly, 31,* 169–173.

Waldron, K. A., Saphire, D. G., & Rosenblum, S. A. (1987). Learning disabilities and giftedness: Identification based on self-concept, behavior, and academic patterns. *Journal of Learning Disabilities, 20,* 422–428.

Wellington, C., & Wellington, J. (1965). *The underachiever: Challenges and guidelines.* Chicago: Rand McNally.

West, C. (1985). Effects of school climate and school social structure on student academic achievement in selected urban elementary schools. *Journal of Negro Education, 54*(3), 451–461.

Whitmore, J. R. (1980). *Giftedness: Conflict and underachievement.* Boston: Allyn & Bacon.

Whitmore, J. R., & Maker, C. J. (1985). *Intellectual giftedness in disabled persons.* Baltimore: Aspen.

Witty, E. P. (1978). Equal educational opportunity for gifted minority children. *Gifted Child Quarterly, 22*(3), 344–352.

Wolfe, J., & Gygi, J. (1981). Learning disabled and gifted: Success or failure? *Journal for the Education of the Gifted, 4,* 199–206.

Wolfe, D. L. (1954). *America's resources of specialized talent.* New York: Harper & Row.

CHAPTER TEN

Identifying and Nurturing Disadvantaged Gifted Students

F or decades sociological studies have cited the different life development paths taken by individuals based on socioeconomic status (SES). Disadvantaged individuals born into the triangulation of low-income homes, low educational level of parents, and low occupational status of the father have rarely risen above the SES level of their parents (Jencks, 1972; Sennett & Cobb, 1972). Many educators of the gifted have expressed concern for the representation of minorities and low socioeconomic learners in programs for the gifted (Baldwin, 1989; Frasier, 1989; Maker & Schiever, 1989; Richert, 1982). Moreover, studies have shown the gap between advantaged and disadvantaged populations in accessing educational advantage (VanTassel-Baska & Willis, 1988).

Though it can be argued that all disadvantaged children and families need assistance, the need is particularly compelling for highly promising learners within this group. Their unique gifts and talents are likely to be overlooked if, because of low socioeconomic status, cultural differences, or handicapping conditions, they do not manifest the behaviors traditionally associated with giftedness. These individuals are typically excluded from or underrepresented in gifted programs because of (a) fewer environmental opportunities that enhance intellectual achievement (Gallagher, 1985; Kitano & Kirby, 1986); (b) the exclusive use of standardized tests, which reflect middle-class, majority values and do not reflect exceptional abilities, experiences, cultural styles, and values of minority students (Kitano & Kirby, 1986; Davis & Rimm, 1985); and (c) the impact of sensory, motor, language, learning, or emotional disorders on performance as assessed through traditional measures (Fox, Brody, & Tobin, 1983; Maker & Schiever, 1989).

CONCEPTUAL FRAMEWORK

Based on a thorough review of the literature on disadvantaged gifted, a conceptual framework was developed that specified three components critical in developing effective programs for disadvantaged populations of gifted learners: (a) program features that influence the development and operation of exemplary gifted programs; (b) interventions found successful in programs for the disadvantaged, and (c) student outcomes that result from the implementation of program features and school classroom practices (VanTassel-Baska, Patton, & Prillaman, 1989).

Table 10.1 portrays this conceptual framework. On the left side is a list of exemplary features of gifted programs (Cox, Daniels, & Boston, 1985; VanTassel-Baska, 1989). The ways these features would affect school/classroom practices, derived from a literature review of interventions with culturally diverse/low-income learners, are listed in the second column. Program goals for gifted exemplary programs for disadvantaged learners have been cast into student outcomes, listed in the third column. This framework portrays key assumptions concerning the relationships among the program features, the classroom/school practices that are implemented, and the student outcomes the practices produce.

Key Elements

Moreover, specialized programs for gifted learners are shaped in a larger social context. The key elements associated with this larger context of learning are (a) the family support system, (b) the planned change system, and (c) the quality of schooling. The family system conducive to talent development transmits value messages and provides key support and nurturance. Effective schools influence current school management practices. And the synthesis of planned change issues must be present to effect change in school contexts. These elements represent home and school support systems that provide a backdrop to the framework described. Specifically, they encompass the following elements:

1. The family support system
   - Valuing of education
   - Strong work ethic
   - Monitoring child's progress
   - Involvement with the learning process
   - Providing encouragement and incentive

Table 10.1
CONCEPTUAL FRAMEWORK FOR STUDY
OF DISADVANTAGED GIFTED PROGRAMS

General Program Level Provisions Essential for Exemplary Gifted Programs	Facilitative Classroom Level Interventions with Disadvantaged Learners	Student Level Outcomes for Disadvantaged Gifted Learners
Program has a stated philosophy and goals	Focus on hands-on, expressive creative activities in classrooms	Evidence of progressive development of school-based skills at high levels
Identification practices are multicriterial, employing both traditional and nontraditional approaches and measures	Focus on personalized learning experiences including mentorships, tutorials, internships, counseling programs	Evidence of motivation for learning; persistence on school tasks
Program addresses needs of identified population	Focus on active, cooperative learning experiences	Use of effective metacognitive strategies ("problem-solving about learning" tasks)
Program requires establishment of desired student outcomes	Focus on development of metacognitive strategies (goal-setting, organizing, time management)	Evidence of goal-directed behavior in regard to future education and career
Evaluation data translate into program improvement on a regular basis	Focus on the use of community resources such as universities, parents, volunteers	
Program provides for systematic staff training	Focus on early intervention activities at K-2 level	
Parent and community education and involvement comprise an ongoing part of the program		
Program is comprehensive and articulated across a substantial portion of schooling years		

2. The quality of schooling (effective schools)
   - Cooperative learning
   - Peer tutoring
   - Coaching models
   - High principal/teacher expectations for student performance
   - Parental involvement

3. The planned change system
   - Collaborative planning
   - Shared governance
   - School climate
   - Empowerment of teachers and other staff
   - Staff development

Rating Scale for Programs

Recognizing the correspondence of the three aspects of the conceptual model, we can develop a scale to rate programs for these learners. The following set of indicator questions can guide self-evaluation of effective opportunities in programs for these learners. Each question is to be rated according to the following criteria: 3 = Evidence of indicator is high; 2 = Evidence of indicator is present; 1 = No evidence of indicator.

General Program Questions

_____   Is the relationship of the philosophy and goals of the program consonant with the desired student outcomes?

_____   Are the policies and procedures for identifying disadvantaged gifted learners consonant with current best practices?

_____   Are the needs of this population assessed on a regular basis?

_____   Does the district have appropriate training activities for this population?

_____   Are well articulated options for disadvantaged gifted learners in evidence across K-12?

_____   Are evaluation data on programs for disadvantaged gifted used to improve the program annually?

Classroom Observation Questions

_____   Are creative thinking activities present in the classroom?

_____   Are manipulatives used?

_____   Is student-centered learning utilized?

_____   Are personalized learning experiences used formally or informally in the program (e.g., mentorships/internships; considerable use of individualization based on student need)?

_____   Are metacognitive strategies used within the program?

_____   Is the community sufficiently involved with the program?

_____   Does the program contain an early intervention component?

Student Outcome Questions

_____   What is the evidence that students are performing/achieving appropriately in their academic work?

_____   What is the evidence that appropriate academic behaviors are being developed?

_____ What is the evidence that students are managing the learning process well (e.g., deadlines, homework)?

_____ What is the evidence that these students are engaged in appropriate planning for future course-taking, college and careers?

IDENTIFICATION

One of the aspects of programs for disadvantaged gifted learners that has received much attention over the past 20 years is identification. There has been a belief system prevalent among gifted educators that finding or creating the right test would assist us greatly in finding these learners. After 20 years of searching, we are forced to admit that neither the problem nor the solution resides in finding the magic testing tool but, rather, in the intelligent use of information we can access.

Two school districts, among many others, have struggled with these issues for over a decade. Their practices for identifying disadvantaged gifted learners are delineated here to provide an understanding of the complexity of the issue at the local level. Chicago Public Schools in Illinois and Hampton City Schools in Virginia offer an interesting pairing of school districts for comparison regarding identification of disadvantaged gifted learners. The identification systems in these two districts share similar features:

1. Both districts are conscious of the importance of including more minority students in gifted programs and have instituted an identification model sensitive to this need.
2. Both districts have a high percentage of minority and low-income students within their district population of students; Hampton approaches 50 percent and Chicago 85 percent.
3. As a goal, both districts see representative numbers of minority children in the gifted program similar to the school district as a whole.
4. Both districts utilize extensive testing and involve school psychologists heavily to carry out assessment procedures.

Each of these districts, however, has considered the issue of identification in different ways and with different results. An overview of each program follows.

Chicago Study: Early Identification for Regional Gifted Centers

The Chicago gifted program represents a multidimensional approach to serving gifted children, with more than 597 programs serving approximately 23,000 students ranging from kindergarten to college course work. Six full-time coordinators and 12 pupil personnel staff members assist local schools in developing these programs through inservice training and information sharing relative to identification, administrative arrangements, curriculum, and evaluation. A central office with six regional field offices provides a distribution of services that include program development, individual testing, and family counseling.

One of the most comprehensive approaches to gifted programming is represented in the six gifted center elementary schools that are part of each of these regions. Admission to the centers is based on a nomination procedure initiated by the parents or classroom teachers, who then are asked to complete a checklist of "gifted" characteristics for the child. Staff conducts testing in April of the kindergarten year, under the supervision of the regional psychologist. Approximately 200 applicants are selected by region, and the highest scoring students are admitted to the first grade program the following September.

The 431,000 students of the Chicago Schools are identified by census figures into ethnic categories: 60% Black, 23% Hispanic, and 13% White. The remaining 4% are identified as Asian, Pacific Islander, or Native American. The ethnic housing patterns of the city have resulted in racially isolated schools, a problem of many large cities. Court sanctions have ordered desegregation of the schools, which has led to large-scale busing of students to reduce these disparities. This desegregation process has become a permanent part of providing programs for the gifted as well, and a general guideline of 65% minority and 35% majority culture students is the rule. Although this does not correspond equally to prevalence in the school population, it does attempt to follow the direction of population trends. The Chicago gifted program in its evolving form has been operating for 18 years.

The philosophy and goals of the program are encapsulated in the following statements:

- Providing for the unique abilities of gifted students by offering a full-day, challenging curriculum in homogeneous settings leading to a maximum enhancement of their potential.
- Providing training and assistance to staff in developing curriculum and experiences appropriate to the needs of these children.
- Providing services and assistance to families regarding educational options for their children.
- Articulating progress K-12 through the gifted program options suitable to the unique aptitudes and interests of a given child.

Identification Protocol

Children who have displayed academic or outstanding reasoning skills in kindergarten are the first source of nominees for each of the regional centers. Publication of child-find procedures with a checklist of gifted characteristics appears in the general bulletin in February of the school year. Home school kindergarten teachers are asked to fill out a checklist for each nominee, to be forwarded to the regional office. Parents who think their child meets the gifted criteria are also encouraged to apply even though they may not be teacher-nominated. The first grade selection program is the major entry point for these centers, but transfers and attrition do allow for openings in the later grades. The measures used have included three sub-tests of the Peabody Individual Achievement Test (PIAT) and the Raven Coloured Progressive Matrices. Raw scores for these measures are transformed into standard scores for comparisons and to rank the students on an overall composite score.

Annual Regional Testing is supervised by one of the six offices each year on a rotating basis, with the responsibility for staff training and the logistics of data gathering carried out by each office. Children are invited to a testing center in their region for a 30-minute evaluation with a single tester. During the testing, information is given to the parents, and questions are answered about the history and goals of the program. This testing includes:

— the Raven Coloured Progressive Matrices.
— the Mathematics sub-test of the PIAT.
— the Reading Recognition sub-test of the PIAT and, if the raw score for this section is better than 25, the Reading Comprehension sub-test of the PIAT.
— the General Information sub-test of the PIAT.

The protocol for the PIAT Reading Comprehension sub-test is altered in that the child is asked to read aloud. In this way, a check of decoding skills is possible so a decision can be made as to the most reliable measure of reading ability which is then selected for reporting. Only one of the reading scores will be included in the final aggregation, so the final constructs are nonverbal, math, reading, and general information measures, each to be given equal weighting.

The choice of this group of test measures resulted from evaluation studies in 1979 and 1980 conducted in one of the centers. Stepwise regression analysis showed significant correlation with the Stanford-Binet, L-M for General Information, Math, Raven, and Reading, in that order. This battery also was adopted for the kindergarten selection process of the Chicago Classical schools in 1987. To keep testing procedure secure, however, Chicago alternates procedures annually or on a 2-year cycle using alternative test forms. Consequently, the Chicago test battery encompasses various test groupings; Woodcock-Johnson (brief scale and broad reasoning clusters) or the PIAT Raven Battery described, or Cognitive Abilities Test (CogAt) (verbal) and Ravens CPM, or CogAt (verbal and nonverbal), or CogAt (verbal) and Matrix Analogies Test (MAT) or Otis Lennon School Abilities Test (OLSAT) (has verbal and nonverbal). These combinations of standardized tests tap into key constraints deemed important to program success: student reasoning, problem solving, vocabulary, verbal comprehension, nonverbal reasoning, and quantitative concept skills.

Students are ranked in descending order by score on racial-ethnic lists pre-set by a court consent decree including White, Black, Hispanic, Asian, and Native American. A baseline for success in the program determines how many students are placed on each list. The baseline is derived by past experience in evaluating student success at the six centers, and no students that fall below the baseline are included on the lists.

Students are placed into the centers starting with the highest scoring students on any list, and placement continues until all students on a list are placed or the racial-ethnic quota on any list is filled. Placements are verified by parents and by transportation officials before the end of the school year.

Program Intervention

Experienced teachers with superior ratings are encouraged to apply for staff positions and then are specially selected from interviews with the principal's committee. Inservice training or additional planning time are provided to the staff personnel through resources of the regional office.

The centers offer subjects in much greater depth than the regular elementary school, and include more subjects, such as foreign language, formal library science, philosophy (in some), computer lab work, and two years of laboratory science. One goal of the program at some centers is to compress the traditional 8 years of schooling into 6 years to allow entry to the Magnet High School program that begins at grade 7 with a curriculum usually offered to 9th graders. This compression of curriculum sometimes allows for advanced placement course-work before the senior year or enables the student's early entrance into college coursework through cooperating universities.

Students who do not adapt to the rigor of the program are given tutorial help or counseling to determine the nature of the difficulty. In some instances, students or families have opted to return to their local school for a variety of reasons, a common one being the bus travel time involved for students.

The self-contained gifted centers compress the general curriculum and offer enrichment through cooperation with educational departments of many Chicago museums and other "package" options that have been a part of gifted programs for many years. Some examples are: Introductory Physical Science, Man: A Course of Study (MACOS), Philosophy for Children, and Junior Great Books. The Gifted "Museology" program, a highly successful option for gifted children, has led to links with educational departments of the Museum of Science and Industry, Field Museum, Shedd Aquarium, Newberry Library, Chicago Academy of Sciences, Art Institute, and other selected museums. This linkage has helped provide field trips and special one-day a week programs for the students from 7th through 12th grades.

The identification process is built into the gifted program proposals through the use of staff for record screening, training, and testing procedures. Although the time allotted for the screening does take away from other professional pursuits, it keeps the entire staff focused on the needs of each incoming group of students and provides interactive meetings for ongoing discussion of the major issues of identification and evaluation. Staff time in conducting and testing incurs the major cost of this procedure while score results are processed through the central office, department of research and evaluation.

Evaluation data indicate the efficacy of the identification measures in two respects:

1. When viewed against the Stanford-Binet L-M, the testing measures are highly correlated, demonstrating their utility for measuring intellectual ability in a shorter time frame and, in the case of the Raven's and the MAT, a different format.
2. When the measures have been viewed with respect to program success, ranges for each sub-test have been documented, identifying necessary and sufficient entry-level aptitudes for program success.

Hampton Case Study: PROJECT LEAP

Hampton is a school district in southeastern Virginia with 20,000 students, of which about 47% are Black. The district serves approximately 6% of its population in a gifted program that begins at third grade and utilizes a one-day a week center-based program experience in addition to some enrichment in the regular classroom.

PROJECT LEAP is an assessment program designed to identify minority Black children at the second and third grade levels who may be overlooked by traditional testing procedures used in the district to identify gifted students. Children are screened for the project at their home school and then transported to special sessions at Hampton University during a school semester. These special sessions provide key activities for the students in all academic areas, using the basic Structure of Intellect (SOI) Model as a framework. Teachers trained in working with gifted learners evaluate the level of responsiveness to these activities on the part of LEAP students, and additional testing is also conducted. Based on careful assessment procedures over 18 weeks, LEAP students are recommended for appropriate placement, either in the gifted program or another year of LEAP activities in the home school setting or regular classroom.

PROJECT LEAP serves approximately 500 students annually, beginning with a few kindergarten children, 120 first graders, 240 second graders, and 120 third graders. About a third of the children who participate in PROJECT LEAP are recommended for the gifted program. Specific data on numbers of minority students served in PROJECT LEAP and subsequently identified for the gifted program are being analyzed. The program has been in existence for 5 years.

The program philosophy and goals for PROJECT LEAP are:

- Effecting a more cooperative effort in gifted and talented assessment between Hampton University and Hampton City Schools.
- Exploring a new model for gifted and talented identification and instruction that provides staff development opportunities for school administrators and teachers.
- Generating a data-base to validate alternative instruments and procedures in gifted identification.

- Training student aides and student teachers in assessment and differentiated instruction.
- Providing resource personnel and professional materials tailored to the needs of the classroom teacher for follow-up and reinforcement of higher-level thinking skills.

Identification Protocol

Although some attention is given to early assessment of kindergarten and first grade children of promise through the services of an itinerant teacher in a given school, the focus of the assessment model is at second grade. All second grade students are administered the Ravens Coloured Progressive Matrices. Students who score above the 90th percentile, based on local norms, are recommended for program consideration. Students who would be identified for the gifted program based on their Cognitive Abilities Test scores from first grade are dropped from the list of eligible students. The remaining students (approximately 210 each year) are invited to participate in a series of five assessment sessions at Hampton University over a semester. In any given semester there is an attempt to preserve equal representation from the 24 elementary schools in Hampton as well as representative minority participation based on the demographics of each elementary school.

Groups of 15 PROJECT LEAP students attend a 2½-hour session every two weeks during a semester at Hampton University. The purpose of these sessions is to conduct an in-depth assessment of each student's potential for success in the district's gifted program by exposing students to higher-level thinking activities and then evaluating their capacity to handle them effectively. Additional testing is done on each student, including the traditional battery used in the gifted program. Assessment tools the program employs to come up with a global recommendation after a semester of observation and testing are:

— Sub-scales of the Renzulli-Hartman (Creativity, Motivation, Learning), completed on each child after the third session of activities by the graduate assistant assigned to the program from Hampton University.
— Anecdotal log, completed on each child by the LEAP teacher after each session of activities. A checkmark for low, medium, or high performance is recorded each time for science, math, language arts, and creative problem-solving activities. Additional comments are noted.
— Student journals, completed after all five sessions, based on student writing samples produced during the LEAP program experiences. Criteria judged include sentence length, variety of ideas, use of words, and others.
— Human figure drawing, completed after the fourth session by a psychologist.
— Cattell Culture Fair Test, administered after the last session of third grade for second-year LEAP students.
— Slosson, administered by a psychologist after the five sessions.
— Peabody Individual Achievement Test (PIAT), administered by a psychologist after the five sessions.

Based on these assessment procedures, second grade LEAP students are recommended for one of the following placements:

1. Referral to the gifted program.
2. Referral for a second year of LEAP activities.
3. Referral to the regular classroom.

Second-year LEAP students are reassessed at their home school site by an itinerant LEAP teacher, who recommends either placement in the gifted program at the end of the third grade or reassignment to the regular classroom.

Program Intervention

LEAP uses an experiential approach to the identification and assessment of gifted and talented primary students by exposing students to differential educational experiences designed to expand problem-solving abilities and creative thinking. Multiple disciplines are integrated in encouraging the development of productive, abstract, and higher-level thinking skills.

Observation of PROJECT LEAP activities in both second and third grade revealed a heavy emphasis on higher-level thinking in the context of traditional content domains. These activities were hands-on and required students to make predictions, to deduce, and to problem-solve in small groups and individually. Activities changed about every 20 minutes. Each session contained activities in science, mathematics, language arts, and creative problem solving, and, in the second grade session, journal writing activities. The following sample activities provide insight into the nature and extent of each LEAP session.

Grade Two — Session Three

I.   General Introductory Activities

II. *Content Area:*   Science and Mathematics
     Objective: To develop the ability to generate relations between
                       figural items, relations which must be arrived at
                       uniquely and organized constructively.
     Activity: "Marble Roll" — generating mathematical data to be
                       recorded in a consistent manner.

III. *Content Area:*   Creative Problem Solving and Mathematics
     Objective: To develop the ability to deduce meaningful information
                       implicit in given information.
     Activity: "Magic Squares" — Using deductive reasoning to
                       determine the method and mathematical operations used
                       in the "number trick."

IV. *Content Area:*   Language Arts
    Objective: To develop the ability to judge which objects or ideas could best be transformed or redefined to meet new requirements.
    Activity: Creative Application — Sponge Stories

V. *Content Area:*   Language Arts
    Activity: "Reflective Writing" — Journal Entries

VI.   Structured Assessment Activity (Human Figure Drawings)

One of the interesting features of this program is the collaborative involvement of a school system and a university in its conceptualization, planning, and implementation. Hampton University provides the site for the program, a well equipped classroom in its laboratory school, with an observation room adjacent for visitors to view the program in action. The university makes available a graduate assistant. Faculty members are encouraged to use the program as a demonstration or clinical observation site. The school district administers the program and employs the teachers and psychologists who work with LEAP students. The district also pays for the bus transportation to Hampton University.

Benefits of the collaborative effort are perceived to be mutually reinforcing. The university provides a consultant to the project, who becomes an important resource link to the school district by sharing up-to-date research on teaching and learning, assisting in teacher placements, serving on committees, and generally establishing positive interpersonal relationships and enhancing attitudes about university involvement. The program has proved to be a good public relations effort for both parties, with prevalent media coverage over the years of operation. And having young students on campus at Hampton presents aspiration models for African-American students and multicultural appreciation for Caucasian students.

The LEAP program staff meets twice a year with the gifted staff to review potential candidates for the gifted program in the district. All data are shared, and each student is discussed in the context of these meetings. A major concern is the potential for a student's success in the more traditional structure of the gifted program, which relies heavily on verbal strengths. Annually, approximately 20% of these students are recommended for placement in the gifted program.

The identification project will be judged successful if it increasingly identifies minority students who will succeed in the Hampton Gifted Program. Data are currently being analyzed to ascertain trend lines over a 5-year period.

Case Study Commentary

Interesting distinctions between the Chicago and Hampton assessment models are summarized in Table 10.2. One of the first lies in the emphasis in Hampton

Table 10.2
CONTRASTING MODELS
OF DISADVANTAGED GIFTED ASSESSMENT

Hampton Model	Chicago Model
Emphasis: Curriculum assessment (performance on classroom-based activities)	*Emphasis:* Multiple tests including nontraditional and recommendations from parents and teachers
Instrumentation: Multiple and wide-ranging measures; Ravens used for screening	*Instrumentation:* A combination of high quality standardized measures for selection
Selection Process: Selection committee approach; no established quotas	*Selection Process:* Rank ordering of standard scores with minority quota considerations
Level: Focused at second grade	*Level:* Focused at end of kindergarten
Evaluation: Process approach; limited evaluation data of effectiveness in respect to major goal	*Evaluation:* Effectiveness judged in respect to program success
Follow-Up Program Model: Pull-out gifted program experience one day a week	*Follow-Up Program Model:* Full-time self-contained gifted center placement
Curriculum Focus: Thinking skills, research, affective development	*Curriculum Focus:* Comprehensive academic areas with specialized options in key areas

on classroom-based activities over a series of eight sessions. These activities, loosely based on the Structure of Intellect (SOI) model, include activity modules in language, arts, math, science, and creative problem solving. Emphasis is placed on thinking skills, and students are carefully assessed on each lesson. Chicago's emphasis is based on a more traditional assessment model, emphasizing a combination of tests and recommendations.

Although both sites use the Ravens, the PIAT, and the Cognitive Abilities Test in common, other instrumentation differs. Hampton employs many more assessment measures, including student writing samples. Moreover, the length of time for assessment is much greater in Hampton, extending over an entire semester. Chicago is perhaps more typical of other school districts, limiting to one day of student time the number of measures used and the time frame for assessment.

The selection process in Hampton involves a selection committee made up of the assessment team from LEAP and the gifted program staff. No quotas are set for inclusion of minority students in selection decisions. Judgment on readiness for the program is the major consideration. In Chicago, the selection process is based on a rank order for the top program slots; minority group students typically fill the top slots.

The Chicago program focuses on younger ages, identifying students who are finishing kindergarten for a full-time program at first grade. In contrast, Hampton offers its most intensive testing at second grade as a prelude to a center-based pull-out program at third grade. Thus, grade-level differences exist between the two models, although both activate identification early in the primary years.

The approach to evaluation differs significantly between the two districts. Chicago consistently has attempted to validate its procedures against both the standard psychometric instrument for intelligence (Stanford-Binet) and against the standard of success in the program. Hampton, however, has chosen to emphasize the equity of the assessment process. Current efforts in Hampton call for analyzing patterns to include more minority children in the gifted program as a result of the extended assessment model.

Finally, a difference exists between the two districts in respect to the program into which students will go once they have been identified. In Chicago, that program is an intensive all-day accelerated and enriched experience continuing for 8 years. By contrast, Hampton's program provides one-day-a-week enrichment in a center-based model over 4 years. The curriculum for Chicago's program is comprehensive, articulated, and integrated with all major content areas. The Hampton curriculum emphasizes critical and creative thinking skills, affective development, and independent research.

Each of the two programs attempts to address, at a local level and in a sociopolitical context, the issue of more minority and low-income participation in gifted programs. Questions that remain unanswered, however, are the following:

1. *Is the extra time and expense for assessment in Hampton warranted from the standpoint of minority/low-income inclusion in gifted programs?* Hampton deliberately includes only those children not selected at grade 2 for the gifted program in PROJECT LEAP. These minority students would have been overlooked in the more traditional assessment model. But how many children so identified constitute the worth of the protocol? Hampton itself has not identified a criterion level and therefore cannot judge this issue.

2. *Does the Chicago assessment program overlook promising students in its more efficient approach to identification?* Although the Chicago evaluation data on identification support the instrumentation used for the nature of the program administered, they do not allow for false negatives (students who would be capable of meeting program standards if they had the opportunity).

3. *How much more successful could the Hampton model be if the follow-up gifted program were to tap into the same behaviors identified through semester-long activities?* At present, the Hampton gifted program activities do not have substantial overlap with the LEAP activities. Consequently, the efficacy of the curriculum-based assessment (CBA) model cannot be sufficiently determined.

4. *Should elaborate assessment procedures be followed if no specialized program for minority/low-income students ensues — only a "typical" gifted program?* Each district "finds" minority/low-income students in its assessment protocol. Yet, neither district deliberately tailors its curriculum to respond to minority or low-income concerns or issues. Thus, even if students are identified through a broader net, how successfully can they negotiate a mainstream gifted program without additional support services?

CURRICULUM APPROACHES

Because most of the emphasis in disadvantaged gifted programs has been on identification, in an attempt to address equity issues and include a more diverse group of learners, curriculum efforts have been limited. Much of what we know about curriculum approaches for disadvantaged gifted learners is derived either from educational paradigms used with minority children in general or from mainstream gifted strategies. Current work, however, is attempting to forge new connections to effect more powerful curriculum interventions for these learners. Within these efforts, several perspectives are emerging for consideration by curriculum developers.

Anderson (1980) views current curriculum efforts for minority groups as reflecting Anglo-European concepts of cognitive functioning, learning, and achievement and failing to identify the cognitive assets and learning preferences of individual cultural groups. He finds that the narrow White male perspective of most American educational settings does not affirm the cognitive/learning styles and devalues the cultures of ethnic populations, and that the greater the acculturation gap between a cultural group and the school, the greater is the likelihood that the group will not succeed. Because different cultures produce different learning styles, modes of perception, and cognitive behaviors, Anderson sees the need for altering the belief systems of educators to understand and respond to non-Western perceptions. Based on his ideas, the curriculum implications in Table 10.3 might be appropriate for working with culturally diverse gifted learners. Some of the ideas have salience for curriculum content, others for instructional approaches.

A more Afro-centric view is taken in the Portland Public Schools curriculum project and resultant materials. Starting with a set of baseline essays written by African-American educators (Hilliard et al, 1988), the project has spawned curriculum units for use in classroom settings (Leonard & Barader, 1988). Unlike other materials that take a multicultural perspective, these curricula are grounded

Table 10.3
CURRICULUM IMPLICATIONS IN FOCUSING ON
NON-WESTERN WORLD VIEW

Non-Western World View	Curriculum/Instructional Implications
Emphasizing group cooperation Being socially oriented Valuing group achievement	Share self through tutorial and community assistance Employ cooperative learning Use dyadic instruction Initiate group projects
Valuing harmony with nature	Study ecology Use interdisciplinary units on nature Teach spiritual philosophy
Believing that time is relative	Allow freedom of movement in the classroom Provide flexible time frames for activities
Accepting affective expression	Use role playing and psychodrama Provide time to discuss feelings Use inquiry-based teaching
Having an extended family model	Provide role models from literature Select materials that portray extended family concept

Preferring holistic thinking	Incorporate interdisciplinary concepts
	    and themes
	Utilize analogical reasoning and
	    associative thinking
	Teach and use synthesis activities

Believing that religion permeates culture	Study religions of the world Study philosophy and values of several cultures
Accepting world views of culture	Use multicultural materials in teaching and learning Teach multiple perspectives of the world

in only one perspective — that of Africa as the center of civilization. This material may be useful in tandem with other materials that present other cultural perspectives if it is adapted for use with gifted learners.

A recent approach to enhancing the education of minority students has been to focus on better interactions between parents and school staff. Comer (1988) cites 5-year gains for minority achievement in a project conducted by Yale's Child Study Center, which stressed psychosocial development in students through increasing trust and cooperation within school staff and between staff and parents. This goal was accomplished successfully by involving parents in school governance and social events and creating teams of specialists who worked cooperatively to solve problems of individual students.

Another project, through Northwestern University, focused directly on gifted disadvantaged students in the city of Chicago (Scott, 1987). It emphasized family empowerment by providing seminars for junior high students and their parents regarding college choices, how to obtain scholarships, and academic planning. The second and third years of the program were directed toward student mentorships and internships.

A College of William and Mary program and curriculum, entitled Libraries Link Learning (Boyce, Bailey, & VanTassel-Baska, 1990), was designed to serve at-risk gifted primary students in the language arts, of which multicultural literature is a central aspect of the program. Each session features a different book whose characters represent the diverse cultural backgrounds of African Americans, Hispanic Americans, Native Americans, and Asian Americans. The appendix to this chapter contains the overview of eight sessions in the program and a core lesson plan developed from one session. The literature chosen for the program reflects key criteria for selecting books for the intellectually gifted (Baskin & Harris, 1980), affective criteria (Halsted, 1987), and criteria for appropriate multicultural literature (Hernandez, 1989). Classroom activities were structured to address discussions utilizing higher-level thinking skills and the writing process. Extension activities were developed as a link to the family as well as a reinforcement for each lesson.

Other curricular directions and new curricula currently are being developed through several federally funded projects in gifted education. The next few years should yield additional ideas for curriculum and instructional practice with disadvantaged gifted learners.

SUMMARY

The need to identify disadvantaged gifted students is acute, as their unique gifts are likely to be overlooked. Three program components are critical: features that influence the development and operation of exemplary gifted programs, successful interventions, and desired student outcomes. Key ingredients are the family support system, the planned change system, and the quality of schooling.

Two early identification programs are the Chicago Gifted Program, Early Identification for Regional Gifted Centers; and PROJECT LEAP, a collaborative assessment program between Hampton (Virginia) City Schools and Hampton University. These have similarities and dissimilarities, pointing up the need to tailor each program for the environment in which it resides.

Curriculum approaches have to reach out into community, family, and cultural settings, in addition to traditional methods used with gifted students. Materials and resources often draw upon ethnic cultural heritage.

As we examine how to identify and nurture disadvantaged gifted learners, we have to be concerned with several variables simultaneously: social context, program model, classroom opportunities, and outcome expectations. Identification, of course has to be tied to effective curricula and instruction. The central issue surrounding interventions for these learners is the nature of the tailoring process to be used in developing curricula and how curricula fits with existing curricula for the gifted. To effect the type of tailoring needed, we need to find ways of blending various cultural perspectives that have personalized approaches with active learning in various modalities. Moreover, we must recognize that individual school districts, based on their own contextual issues, will necessarily carry out such curriculum plans in very different ways.

QUESTIONS FOR REFLECTION

1. How might schools systematically identify their at-risk students when they enter, and actively seek to find talent within that group?
2. What ties might we make with social agencies on behalf of the at-risk poor?
3. What aspects of family background contribute to at-risk status for gifted learners?
4. What are the advantages and disadvantages of serving at-risk gifted learners in totally self-contained settings?

REFERENCES

Anderson, J. (1980). Cognitive style and multicultural populations. *Journal of Teacher Education,* January-February, pp. 1–9.

Baldwin, A. (1989). The purpose of education for gifted black students. In J. Maker, *Critical issues in gifted education.* Austin, TX: Pro-Ed.

Baskin, B., & Hargis, K. (1980). *Books for the gifted child.* New York: Bowker and Co.

Boyce, L., Bailey, J., & VanTassel-Baska, J. (1990). *Libraries link learning resource guide.* Williamsburg, VA: College of William and Mary, Center for Gifted Education.

Comer, J. (1988). Educating poor minority children. *Scientific American, 259*(5), 42–48.

Cox, J., Daniels, N., & Boston, B. (1985). *Educating able learners.* Austin: University of Texas Press.

Davis, G., & Rimm, S. (1985). *Education of the gifted and talented.* Englewood Cliffs, NJ: Prentice Hall.

Fox, L., Brody, L., & Tobin, D. (1983). *Learning-disabled gifted children.* Baltimore: University Park Press.

Frasier, M. (1989). Identification of gifted black students: Developing new perspectives. In J. Maker, *Critical issues in gifted education*. Austin, TX: Pro-Ed.

Gallagher, J. (1985). *Teaching the gifted* (3rd ed.). Boston: Allyn & Bacon.

Halsted, J. (1988). *Guiding gifted readers from preschool to high school*. Columbus, OH: Ohio Psychology Publishing Co.

Hernandez, H. (1989). *Multicultural education*. Columbus, OH: Merrill Publishing.

Hilliard, A., et al. (1988). *Afro-American baseline essays*. Portland, OR: Portland Public Schools.

Jencks, C. (1972). *Inequality*. New York: Basic Books.

Kitano, M., & Kirby, D. (1986). *Gifted education*. Boston: Little, Brown.

Leonard, C., & Barader, M. (1988). *African-American lesson plan (K-5)*. Portland, OR: Portland Public Schools.

Maker, C. J., & Schiever, S. (1989). *Critical issues in gifted education: Vol. 2. Defensible programs for cultural and ethnic minorities*. Austin, TX: Pro-Ed.

Richert, S. (1982). *National report on identification: Assessment and recommendation for comprehensive identification of gifted and talented youth*. Sewell, NJ: Educational Improvement Center-South.

Scott, J. (1987). *New horizons project*. Evanston, IL: Northwestern University, Center for Talent Development.

Sennett, R., & Cobb, J. (1972). *The hidden injuries of class*. New York: Random House.

VanTassel-Baska, J. (1989). A comprehensive model of gifted program development. In J. Feldhusen, J. VanTassel-Baska, & K. Seeley, *Excellence in educating the gifted*. Denver: Love Publishing.

VanTassel-Baska, J., Patton, J., & Prillaman, D. (1989). A status report on the disadvantaged gifted learner: At risk for educational attention. *Focus on Exceptional Children, 22*(4), 1–16.

VanTassel-Baska, J., & Willis, G. (1988). A three year study of the effects of income on academically able students. *Gifted Child Quarterly, 31*(4), 169–173.

Libraries Link Learning (LLL)
Sample 8: Session Program

Session	Literature	Writing	Bookmaking
1	Students will respond to *I'm in Charge of Celebrations*	Students will brainstorm topic lists of special things that have happened to them; things they know a lot about; things they care a lot about.	*Parent Training* Parents will be invited to hear an overview of the LLL program.
2	Students will respond to *Bringing the Rain to Kapiti Plain*	Students will share their written work and respond to other authors.	*About the Author* Students will write their own autobiographical paragraph.
3	Students will respond to *Owl Moon*	Students will conference with facilitators, responding to questions about their writing	*Publishing Process* Students will view a video about book publishing and examine bookmaking materials.

4	Students will respond to *Grandpa's Face*	During individual conference sessions, students will revise their stories in order to add more details, clarify the story, or create better story structure.	*Book Covers* Students will examine different book cover types and make individual book covers.
5	Students will respond to *Mufaro's Beautiful Daughter*	Students will choose a work to publish.	*Endpapers* Students will tape book covers together and glue endpapers onto inside bookcovers.
6	Students will respond to *Ming Lo Moves the Mountain*	During individual conferences, students will edit their stories.	*Dedication Pages* Students will write their own book dedication.
7	Students will respond to *Anno's Journey*	Students will illustrate their stories.	*Signatures/ Illustrations* Students will sew their book signatures, illustrate them, and glue them into their book covers.
8	Student author readings of published books		*Public Presentation* Students will present their bound books to their parents.

Source: Excerpted from *LLL Resource Guide,* Center for Gifted Education, College of William and Mary. Alexandria, Virginia.

Session #2

I. Literature Objectives
  - The children will demonstrate critical thinking about literature.
  - The children will show evidence of originality in written or oral responses.

Literature Activities

1. Read *Bringing the Rain to Kapiti Plain* by Verna Aardema. After the story, spend a few minutes asking guided questions such as:
   What do you like about this book?
   What caused the grass to turn brown?
   What are some of the other things that happened as a result of no rain?
   What important qualities did Ki-pat have?
   Pretend you are Ki-pat. What makes your job hard?
   What if the cows had died? How might the story have been different?
   In your opinion, what is the best part of the story? Why?
2. Divide the group in half and have a different activity for each group:
   (a) Have felt cut-outs ready, which represent different parts of the story. Children can retell the story using a felt board to show the story sequence.
   (b) Have Cray-pas or waterpaints available. Have children look at the story illustrations and ask, "How has the illustrator used color to help tell the story? How has the illustrator used shape to help tell the story?"
   Have the children choose a scene from the story and change the color or shape. How might that change the story?

II. Writing Objectives
  - The children will choose an idea from their topic lists and compose a story about the idea.
  - The children will respond to individual conference questions about their writing.
  - The children will share their stories with each other and respond to the shared stories.

Writing Activities

1. Have children pick up their writing folders and continue working on their stories from last week. If they have not yet started composing a story, they get a blank draft book, choose one of their topic ideas, and begin to write about it.

2. Facilitators circulate and individually conference with children, asking:
   What are you writing about today?
   Can you read me what you wrote?
   Can you tell me more about _____?
   I don't understand why you wrote _____. Can you give me
   more information to help me understand that?
   What is going to happen next?
3. After 15–20 minutes of free-writing and conferencing time, gather children into a sharing circle.
4. Ask for a volunteer author to read his/her story. Have the rest of the children listen for what they liked about the story and what they would like
   to know more about.
5. After the author shares his/her story, let the author ask the others what they
   liked about the story and then what they would like to know more about.
   (Two/three authors may be able to share per session.)

III. Bookmaking Objectives
   ▪ The students will learn that books often have information about the author
     and will write their own autobiographical paragraphs for their books.

Bookmaking Activities
1. Read some illustrative "About the Author" pieces from a selection of
   children's books.
2. Have the children write a paragraph about themselves, which can be saved
   in their writing folder to be used when their book is published.
3. Take a Polaroid picture of each child, to be used with the "About the
   Author" paragraphs.

Materials/Resources
Bringing the Rain to Kapiti Plain by Verna Aardema (New York: Dial, 1981).
Felt board and felt pieces of story (can be made from cutting illustrations from
   paperback or discarded book).
Cray-pas or waterpaints and drawing paper.
Individual writing folders with topic idea lists.
Blank writing booklets.
Pencils/crayons.
Poster with sharing questions:
   What did you like about my story?
   What in my story would you like to know more about?
Polaroid camera/film.
Sample "About the Author" sections from a selection of books.

Products
Interpretive story illustration.
Draft compositions.
An "About the Author" piece for their own book.

Take-Home Extension Activities

Today we read *Bringing the Rain to Kapiti Plain,* an African folktale retold by
Verna Aardema. You may want to reread *Bringing the Rain to Kapiti Plain* and
compare it to *This Is The House That Jack Built* by using this chart:

ALIKE	DIFFERENT

You also may enjoy reading other African folktales retold by Verna Aardema:

Tales from the Story Hat: African Folktales (New York: Coward-McCann, 1960).
Who's in Rabbit's House? (New York: Dial, 1977).
Why Mosquitoes Buzz in People's Ears (New York: Dial, 1975).

CHAPTER ELEVEN

Serving the Learning Disabled Gifted Student Through Collaboration

T he need for collaboration among educators representing different perspectives in educational settings has been demonstrated by the preceding chapters focusing on special populations. In studying the literature on learning disabled (LD) gifted, the way most school systems define and identify gifted students clearly must change if we are to recognize strengths and weaknesses in respect to intellectual and other areas of functioning. This change is essential to allow educators to find and serve disabled gifted children. With this population, we must address the concept of real disabilities juxtaposed with high-level capacities in key areas. Thus, we must go beyond a global IQ score in finding and serving these gifted learners.

Ample evidence (Karnes & Johnson, 1987; Suter & Wolf, 1987; Fox, Brody, & Tobin, 1983) suggests that appropriate interventions have to be: (a) carefully tailored to individual needs, and (b) sensitive to the education of the whole student. Consequently, a model of collaboration among professionals with differing perspectives on a student's needs and across institutions that can provide relevant resources is needed to bring meaningful programs and services to them.

Reasons to promote a collaboration model to facilitate service to these learners are several:

1. Learning disabled gifted learners currently receive little or no "integrated" service. Where school programs exist, they tend to be fragmented, with treatment of LD problems in isolation of treatment of giftedness.
2. The educational needs of these learners require atypical responses beyond the traditional classroom and school. Accommodation to strengths and deficit areas requires educational teaming and careful planning. Parents' role in planning and implementing a program is critical.
3. Personalized education carries with it a heavy resource commitment that may be beyond the capability of most schools to provide. The involvement of tutors and mentors is recommended, because these learners require the use of extensive community resources.
4. Gifted programs in general have little funding; therefore, funding for specialized groups of learners must be sought beyond the limited gifted budget at local and state levels. Collaborative delivery systems allow us to tap into broad-based resources, including special education.
5. Finally, as a field, we know little about successful interventions with this population from either a research or a practical perspective. We have to consult with appropriate specialists in handicapping conditions, school psychologists, and others who are knowledgeable about these learners in ways that we are not (VanTassel-Baska, 1991).

All of these factors are important to consider in developing meaningful interventions and a workable delivery system for learning disabled gifted learners.

THE CONCEPT OF LEARNING DISABLED GIFTED

A discrepant pattern of abilities is one way we might conceptualize a learning disabled gifted child. As one type of learning disabled gifted child, Dykstra (1990) perceives a child who has a strong academic deficiency in one area, typically reading or mathematics, and yet strong intellectual functioning. These children frequently are resourceful enough to compensate over time for their skill deficiency and do quite well in most settings, even high-powered academic ones. The more prevalent type of learning disabled gifted child, however, has high intellectual functioning but also has a specific academic deficit coupled with an executive processing deficit that may manifest itself in poor organization, study habits, etc. According to Dykstra, these students are the most at-risk for academic failure.

Moreover, the learning disabled gifted child often demonstrates an uneven pattern of behavior. Manifestations take the form of aggression, or withdrawal, frustration, and lack of impulse control. These characteristics either cause or exacerbate poor peer relations, which in turn feed the negative behavior. Typical intellectual strengths of gifted learning disabled children include their ability to engage in abstract reasoning (especially in oral communication), their strong problem-solving abilities, and creative strengths. Specific deficits often include

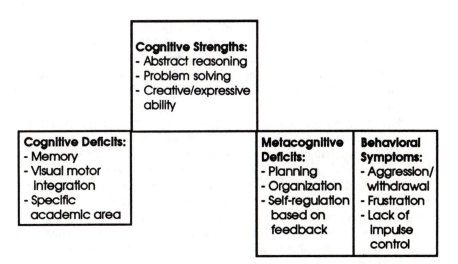

Figure 11.1
PROFILE OF LEARNING DISABLED GIFTED LEARNERS

poor memory skills and difficulty with visual-motor integration and visual/auditory processing (see Figure 11.1 for a profile).

A specific case study is presented here to highlight some of the most salient aspects of a learning disabled gifted child's profile. The authors of the following chapters and I used this case study to formulate a curriculum plan for Diane Bradford, in Chapter 16.

THE CASE OF DIANE BRADFORD

Diane was born June 14, 1980, is 9 years old, and is currently in the fourth grade. She lives with her biological parents in a large metropolitan area in the eastern United States and has a sister who is 5 years older. Her Caucasian parents are both professionally employed. Her father earned a bachelor's degree in political science and a law degree, and currently holds a prominent governmental position. Diane's mother has a bachelor's degree in education and has worked part-time as a teacher, model and clothing representative until this year, when she took a full-time position as admissions director of a private secondary school. The family is active in athletic, volunteer, church, and political organizations.

Diane was selected for child-study for several reasons. She manifests a variety of behaviors, sometimes charming, sometimes difficult, and, based on certain classification schemes, might qualify for both gifted and special education programs.

As a young child, Diane was characterized by her mother as fitful in sleep patterns, intense, and exhibiting high energy levels. She showed early signs of physical agility and precocious motor development. Health problems centered on ear infections (otitis media) and allergies. Diane was also characterized by her mother as a defiant child at home and an aggressive, easily frustrated child at school.

Because of her frustration with schoolwork and the perceived discrepancy between her ability and performance in the classroom, Diane was referred for special education testing. In the classroom Diane showed difficulty with reading, handwriting, and organization skills, such as following directions.

The special education report qualified Diane for special education services as a learning disabled student, with an IEP program that addressed visual-motor integration problems, remedial reading, reduction of workload in the classroom, and peer support. She meets weekly with a learning disabilities specialist and a speech therapist. Beginning in third grade, Diane began taking Ritalin daily and, as a result, "attentional and emotional concerns appear to have been greatly alleviated by the therapy" (IEP, p. 2).

Diane has not been referred to the gifted program, partially due to the difficulty she has experienced with schoolwork and partially due to an IQ-based cut-off score for gifted programs at a level beyond her tested functioning. On a WISC-R, her performance score was 105 and her verbal score was 124, yielding a combined IQ score of 118, and placing her at the 88th percentile on the test. Such a disparity between performance and verbal scores could suggest a learning disability; yet it also reflects a strength in verbal areas not discerned from the global IQ score. In Diane's school division, students must score at 140 or above on a global IQ measure to receive gifted services.

Strong abilities are demonstrated, however, in several areas. Outside the classroom she is actively involved in sports activities in which she competes at a high level of achievement. She has had exemplary performances within her age group on a local swim team and has competed as a third grader at an international swimming competition. In addition, Diane holds a local record in running on a recreational track team.

Diane exhibits social and leadership strengths as well. When teachers felt that certain competencies had been achieved after instruction with the special educator and that it was no longer necessary to leave her regular classroom, Diane insisted on continuing with the class so she could perform the leading role in a play that was in progress. Somehow, through finesse and persuasion, Diane managed to continue leaving the regular class to continue her role in special education for reasons that appear to be socially motivated. Diane's experience in a social studies simulation in the regular classroom provided further insights into her social capabilities. As "store manager," Diane quickly mastered her responsibilities as a link in the exchange of goods and services and performed admirably in this complex role.

Diane shows some evidence of low self-esteem, indicating to her parents that she thinks of herself as "stupid" and that other students don't like her. Her older sister was identified for the gifted program several years ago and evidences more classic "gifted behaviors," such as high test performance, early literacy development, and ease in mastering school subjects. The presence of a highly successful and achieving sibling may also affect Diane's self-perception. Yet, social-emotional assessment from observations, interview, and projective data does not reveal any serious emotional concerns.

There are indications that Diane tends to possess very high self-expectations and ambitions but may not always possess the internal resources to meet those goals. A sense of frustration and disappointment may result when goals are not attained, and this may further impact upon her self-esteem. She appears to derive a great deal of satisfaction from her athletic endeavors, and this seems to give her a sense of accomplishment. Overall, Diane appears to enjoy school but is aware of her difficulties in the classroom. Even so, she seems to maintain her motivation for academic success in the face of obstacles.

Although she possesses advanced aptitude in verbal reasoning and problem solving, Diane's perceptual organization and visual problem-solving skills are, in contrast, significantly weaker. A mild functional deficit in her visual-motor integration skills and weaknesses in her visual memory were also substantiated by her test performance. Academically, these deficits seem to interfere with skill acquisition in the areas of reading and written language. Achievement levels in these areas, though near her current grade-level placement, are significantly discrepant in comparison to her measured ability level. Diane sometimes appears to be unable to meet her very high self-expectations, which results in frustration and disappointment.

In educational terms, Diane would likely be diagnosed as gifted learning disabled based on the behaviors she demonstrates in various settings. Yet, as is the case with most special populations of gifted learners — those with handicaps, cultural diversity, low income — educational contexts have trouble accommodating the discrepancy pattern of functioning they represent. This pattern is characterized by some easily identifiable variables that cut across those populations, including peak and valley profile of behavior, underachievement, problems in normalized social environments, and atypical family dynamics, many times exacerbated by the child's behavior.

Diane's case was undertaken by a group of educators each representing a different perspective for meeting learners' special needs. Included were a general educator with an emphasis in social studies education, a special educator with a broad perspective on curriculum issues, a learning disabilities specialist, and a school psychologist. These individuals met with me over a 6-month period to discuss the case of Diane Bradford and to consider it in light of current thinking in general curricula, special education curricula, and school psychology. Chapters 12, 14, and 15 of this book represent the culmination of that effort. These chapters explore the perspectives represented within the group and provide a commentary on Diane Bradford consistent with each perspective.

Before presenting these commentaries, it is instructive to consider various approaches to collaboration that may help inform the provision of services to learning disabled gifted students like Diane Bradford. Just as our educational group had to collaborate over time to make meaning of the information we had about Diane, so, too, must other educators struggle with "boundary breaking" to deal effectively with special population problems and issues.

WHAT DO WE MEAN BY COLLABORATION?

In an educational sense, collaboration means a coming together to focus on a specific problem or issue. It can take place at several levels, and the most successful examples of collaboration often do.

Idol (1989) has defined collaboration as "an interactive process that enables people with diverse expertise to generate creative solutions to mutually defined problems. The outcome is enhanced, altered, and produces solutions that are different from those that the individual team members would produce independently." According to them, five factors underlie a successful rationale for collaboration:

1. A shared belief or goal.
2. Personal goals that can be met through collaboration.
3. A task to be done that can be accomplished *only* through collaboration.
4. An individual with skills and resources to share.
5. An individual's need for skills and/or resources.

Collaboration as Personal Interaction

The best examples of successful collaborative efforts involve individuals who choose to come together, typically pulled by a common underlying belief system or a unique blend of talents, or a combination. In medicine, Masters and Johnson shared a common value system around the need to focus on human sexual functioning as an area of medical practice. Rodgers and Hart/Hammerstein each possessed a unique talent, composing music and writing lyrics, that was enhanced through collaborative effort. In education, perhaps our most salient examples of these efforts are at the classroom level, where two individuals work together in a teaming model, called team teaching. In my 25 years in education, I have never witnessed successful team teaching when the underlying personal interaction variable was not strong. What makes collaboration work at this level of education?

1. A clear sense of each team member as to how he or she can contribute.
2. An intuitive sense of goals and objectives — what has to happen for a given child or group of children.

3. A strong sense of trust and respect for the talents of each team member.
4. A commitment to the importance of working together, of the team as greater than any individual within it.
5. Time and effort devoted to the collaborative experience so responses can reach the level of automaticity — unspoken blending of individual acts that contribute to the whole, such as recognizing the need for assistance in an area and responding without a request for assistance (forthcoming and no umbrage felt as a result of the tacit involvement).
6. A common understanding and philosophy toward teaching and learning.

Part of these necessary conditions for collaborative effort relate to values, some to attitudes, and some to skills developed over time through trial-and-error experiences. At one level, educational collaboration cannot succeed without attention to these personal issues of interaction. Natural cohesion based on similarity in gender, cultural background, and even SES can contribute substantially to collaboration. Yet successful examples abound that refute the need for this type of structuring. Of greater importance are the variables of a shared vision, a shared value system regarding work, and the time to devote to the enterprise.

A shift in the definitional structure of collaboration occurs when it is perceived in the context of consultation, a term found frequently in the special education literature. Meyers, Parsons, and Martin (1979) presented this composite definition of consultation derived from school psychology, mental health, and organizational development:

> A technique that at a minimum, always has the following six characteristics: (1) it is a helping, problem-solving process; (2) it occurs between a professional help-giver and a help-seeker who has responsibility for the welfare of another person; (3) it is a voluntary relationship; (4) the help-giver and the help-seeker share in solving the problem; (5) the goal is to help solve a current work problem of the help-seeker; and (6) the help-seeker profits from the relationship in such a way that future problems may be handled more sensitively and skillfully. (p.4)

The collaborative nature of consultation is clearly evident in the following definition offered by a team of counseling psychologists and a special educator (Brown, Wyne, Blackburn, & Powell, 1979):

> Consultation is usually a process based upon an equal relationship characterized by mutual trust and open communication, joint approaches to problem identification, the pooling of personal resources to identify and select strategies that will have some probability of solving the problem that has been identified, and shared responsibility in the implementation and evaluation of the program or strategy that has been initiated. (p. 8)

In special education, consultation models have two primary goals: (a) to provide remedial problem-solving services for presenting problems, and (b) to increase consultees' skills so they can prevent or respond more effectively to similar problems in the future (Gutkin & Curtis, 1982). Characteristics such as consultant cooperativeness, emotional stability, personal adjustment, ability to inspire confidence, facilitativeness, empathy, flexibility, warmth, and understanding have been associated with consultees' perceptions of successful consultation (Alpert, Ballantyne, & Griffiths, 1981; Dinkmeyer & Dinkmeyer, 1976; Downing, 1954; Fine, Granthan, & Wright, 1979; Schowengerdt, Fine, & Poggio, 1976; Weissenburger, Fine, & Poggio, 1982).

A number of investigators have highlighted the importance of consultant collaboration skills as a key to successful consultation (Cutler & McNeil, 1964; Schowengerdt et al., 1976). Eisendorfer and Batton (1972) and Reinking, Livesay, and Kohl (1978) used nurses' observations of colleagues serving as consultants to document that not only did the nurses prefer collaborative consultants but they also initiated more consultation contacts when consultants used collaboration in contrast to an expert mode of consultation. Yet overall, there is a paucity of research on the effects of consultation in educational settings.

Collaboration among individuals also can contribute to a higher order of knowing. As Palmer (1983) speaks of the process of consensus as integral to collaboration:

> It is important to note the creative role of conflict in this process. Individual perceptions of reality differ; to enter truth with each other and with reality means exposing those differences openly and honestly so that they can inform and reshape one another. In this kind of learning process, students are urged to speak with the courage of their convictions, but in the process, they open their convictions to correction and change. When we learn by consensus, we are no longer subject to the tyranny of either objective authoritarianism or subjective relativism. Instead, we enter into the mutuality and relatedness of reality itself, and our knowledge grows as we listen and respond to the complexities of the community of truth.

Collaboration as the Interaction of Roles

In educational settings we are also faced with the realities of working in a highly political environment, grounded in a militaristic model of organization. Each person has an assigned role to play in a school setting, and the role designation many times dictates behaviors. Common understandings of role relationships often guide educational decision making. Teacher judgment yields to expert opinion; administrative fiat displaces careful evaluative judgment; and special interest groups vie for supremacy of ideas in a climate of demands for accountability. Thus, collaboration enterprises must struggle against the easy retreat to playing one's assigned role rather than entering into collaborative endeavors with an open mind.

Successful collaborations that rely heavily in schools on a garden mixture of roles may best be seen in the transdisciplinary efforts of special education over the past 15 years. Outcomes from these multiple-role collaborations have succeeded based on the following variables:

1. Each person has taken responsibility for a dual role — job-based expertise coupled with a strong child advocacy perspective.
2. Each team member values the role of other members.
3. The transdisciplinary team has worked through the prescribed process to the point where it is no longer a definer of the interaction.
4. The child's IEP becomes a collage of the perspectives of individual team members rather than a collection of perspectives.

Another area of education in which collaborative efforts may be seen is in the replication of effective schools principles. The importance of teacher improvement, instructional leadership of the principal, and peer coaching all are innovations that require collaboration. Closer professional interaction may be developed through what Little (1982) calls the "critical practices of adaptability":

1. Teachers engage in frequent, continuous, and increasingly concrete and precise talk about teaching practices.
2. Teachers are frequently observed and provided with useful (if potentially frightening) critiques of their own teaching.
3. Teachers together plan, design, research, evaluate, and prepare teaching materials.
4. Teachers teach each other the practice of teaching.

Principals can facilitate collaboration by involving teachers in setting the agenda for faculty meetings, encouraging teachers to participate in curriculum and instructional planning, and helping faculty to coordinate their schedules so they have time for observations and feedback. The principal also can set some norms by actively seeking teachers' help and by helping them to improve. In fact, research indicates that principals in collaborative schools are more actively involved in observation and evaluation than in schools in which the teachers are more isolated in their classrooms (Scott & Smith, 1987). At a higher level, school boards can encourage collaboration by providing schools with the needed resources in time and money. This cooperation from district officials is necessary for administrators and teachers to become convinced that collaboration is a worthwhile reform.

Schlechty, Ingwerson, and Brooks (1988) envision a restructuring of schools by instituting exemplary schools so that teachers and principals can work toward common objectives and performance standards. Such a systematic induction process will help new teachers and administrators develop and maintain the beliefs, attitudes, skills, and values necessary to meet their standards for success. This leadership model evolved from shared decision making and a shared vision of student success.

Special educators have developed a collaborative model called *resource consultation* (Idol, 1989; Reisberg & Wolf, 1986). In this model, special education teachers provide two kinds of service: (a) assessment of and instruction in problem areas of the general curriculum for mildly handicapped learners who have been mainstreamed, and (b) consultation to general education teachers on special needs students. Collaboration assumes joint responsibility for implementation and evaluation of educational programs. Collaborating personnel are not serving as "experts," a notion more often associated with traditional consultation (Brown, 1977). Once training involves systematic didactic and practicum experiences in collaboration and consultation skills, collaborators can work successfully with special and regular education classroom teachers to meet the individual needs of children in the regular classroom.

A relationship may be drawn between the findings of research on expert-novice systems in education and processes for collaboration. Differences between experts and novices as they undertake the complex tasks associated with teaching and learning center on more selective use of planning time, greater use of instructional and management routines or automaticity, and greater sensitivity to differing aspects of classrooms favoring expert teachers (Berliner, 1986). This concept of expert-novice relationships has found a translation in schools in popular innovations such as peer coaching, cooperative teaching, peer evaluation, and other variations on the theme of experience wedded to noviate status as a relationship capable of enhancing results for the individuals involved.

Along the same line in gifted curricula has been the wedding of content experts with gifted educators to develop appropriate curricula based on the most sophisticated ideas currently at work in the disciplines. Thus, collaborative efforts at curriculum-making have resulted in higher quality products (see Gallagher, 1985). This sort of team concept also would have merit as we think about appropriate curricula for special populations. The expert role should be sought as we consider the parameters of any given learner profile. Expertise drawn from sociology and psychology may better inform the curriculum process than staying within the prescribed educational boundaries that are currently honored.

Developing interdisciplinary teams of individuals with different perspectives, experiences, and skills to focus on a special needs gifted student can greatly increase students' opportunities in educational settings. Cooperative teaching in special education is one model for accomplishing this (Bauwens, Hourcade, & Friend, 1989). In this model, a general classroom teacher works alongside a special education teacher to engage collaboratively in supportive learning activities for special needs students. Preliminary evaluation data indicate that a major benefit of the approach is the teachers' perception of increased learning potential on the part of these students. Thus, the use of varying types of expertise is useful in developing successful collaborative arrangements.

Collaboration Across Institutions

Just as interpersonal and intra-institutional collaboration efforts have unique issues, new sets of problems arise when we attempt to bring about collaborative efforts that span different types of institutions. Although we may be able to define a common culture that pervades elementary and secondary education in the United States, it is much more difficult to assimilate the various cultures represented by the business world, social agencies, museums and laboratories, and higher education. Much of what has been termed collaboration in these interagency contexts has been a partnership brought about through resource sharing of both a human and a material nature.

Stanford in the Schools is one project linking higher education professors with classrooms at the elementary and secondary levels for the purpose of stimulating action research and informing educational practice. Boston University's 10-year commitment to run the Chelsea Massachusetts schools represents another collaborative effort between higher education and K–12 education. Many companies have promoted an adopt-a-school model, in which businesses purchase equipment and materials for schools and provide personnel for specific needs.

An example of this model as it has been developed in gifted education has been the Argonne-Northwestern Program, which utilizes practicing scientists as mentors and teachers of gifted children. Key findings from such efforts include the following (VanTassel-Baska & Kulieke, 1987):

1. A workable modification of the program might be to provide an adult in the community who works in science, perhaps in a corporate laboratory or a university setting. The key elements seem to be: knowledge of science, the ability to translate it to able students, and a clear "passion" for the subject. Many communities have individuals such as these who could be asked to provide guidance to young students on original research projects.
2. A critical aspect of the Argonne-Northwestern program was the reality-testing regarding science that students were able to experience firsthand. They learned the real work of science — slow, methodical, incremental. Breakthroughs are based on the painstaking work of others who have preceded. A specific scientific problem can span many lifetimes and still remain unsolved. In addition, the students learned the value of social networks: how scientists work with others on similar problems, the importance of confirming and consulting with other scientists just to define the problem, let alone solve it; and the ability to communicate ideas to others in oral and written modes. As a result of seeing science up close, students usually become more interested, some in pursuing science as a career. In any case, a realistic sense of what science is and what it is not seems to have emerged out of the experience.
3. The selection of key personnel to work with students in a special science program for the gifted also seems crucial in respect to individual student progress. Perhaps the single most important characteristic of the successful teacher in this model program was the desire and ability to teach the intellectual process of science, not just the individual content field. In these instances, students mastered the scientific method at several levels — experientially as well as conceptually.

4. Another key element in personnel selection was the assignment of a college student to each class as a teaching assistant. The program participants could identify more closely with these older students as role models, and in some cases the teaching assistants become young mentors.

5. Multiple resources are needed to best serve talented science students. They stand to benefit from diverse role models such as teachers, tutors, and mentors working collaboratively with students; a curriculum/instructional delivery system that provides multiple perspectives on issues and demonstrates diverse teaching strategies to explore them; and access to multiple texts and science materials in a classroom as well as a library setting.

In special education, interagency collaboration is essential at the *client level* to ensure coordinated service delivery, at the *program level* to integrate administrative function, and at the *systems level* to ensure broad-based planning (Magreb & Elder, 1979). Moreover, current efforts are underway to extend these collaborative efforts through designing processes and procedures for planning, implementing, and evaluating interagency systems (Martinson, 1982).

Interorganizational arrangements between schools and other agencies may take the name of collaboration, cooperation, consultation, and partnership (words with slightly different denotations but often used interchangeably). These collaborative activities may empower educators with evolving understandings of alternative ways of teaching and learning, and they have the potential for long-term school improvements.

Agencies capable of participating in such an arrangement include parents, businesses, human service staffs, higher education faculty, and other educators. When a "you have/we need" approach dominates, however, as in companies' donating computers to schools, the expectations in the relationship limit the potential outcome by not evolving over time, involving only a few individuals, and reacting mainly to surface problems. Interactive partnerships, on the other hand, take time to develop and build upon foundations of trust and open communication.

The following are some of the common features of interactive partnerships (Jones & Maloy, 1988):

1. They involve new resources from parent and community groups, businesses, human service agencies, and institutions of higher education.

2. They promote sharing of information, resources, time, and talent that helps people think about better schools.

3. They seek greater utilization of community resources, rather than raising revenues for more of the same things.

4. They reduce the isolation of students, teachers, and schools through association with other powerful groups.

5. They encourage decision making and problem solving on a local level by those most affected by the outcomes.

6. They are voluntary, cooperative, and flexible.

Cooperation between colleges and schools can be beneficial in sustaining mutual learning processes. The interdependence of these two institutions may be seen in several areas: a common interest and stake in a well educated secondary student applicant pool, research sites and subjects for field-based studies, teacher preparation and internships, and the need for effectively translating theory into better instructional practices. At the same time, university control is a primary issue that must be addressed before meaningful inter-institutional collaboration can occur. Truly collaborative efforts require shared control with arrangements including: sharing of resources and personnel; jointly appointed faculty or faculty exchange programs; consortia, networks, or jointly controlled teacher centers; joint curriculum development; and collaborative research. The mutual benefits derived from these efforts are, for the schools, access to superior facilities, programs, delivery systems, climate, and training at lower cost, and, for the colleges, a direct link to a sub-system they seek to influence and access to the experience of practitioners for improving research, preservice training, and staff development (Hathaway, 1985).

In a special Carnegie report, Maeroff (1983) cited some principles that seem to underlie successful inter-institutional educational relationships:

1. Educators at both levels must agree there are common problems.
2. The traditional academic "pecking order" must be overcome.
3. Successful cooperative projects must be sharply focused.
4. Participants must get recognition and rewards.
5. Cooperative programs must center on action, not machinery.
6. The more an innovation is "owned" by those affected by its adoption, the more likely it will be accepted.
7. Innovations that are implemented without accompanying support from top administrators usually do not meet with lasting success.

Still another type of collaboration, that between education and social service agencies, seems to improve the lives of disadvantaged children (Cohen, 1989). Interventions with the greatest potential for effecting change involve comprehensive and intensive targeting of areas such as early childhood programs, tutorial and remedial help, before- and after-school care, family support, parent education, adult literacy, health and social services, and employment training. Professionals from each of these areas work as a team and establish a foundation of trust with children and families.

A COLLABORATIVE MODEL
FOR CURRICULUM DEVELOPMENT

All of the types of collaboration described in this chapter are relevant when considering effective curriculum development for special populations of gifted learners, especially the learning disabled. One-to-one consultation with these students, whether it takes the form of a tutorial, a mentorship, or a counseling

Table 11.1
LEVELS OF COLLABORATION NEEDED
FOR SPECIAL POPULATIONS OF GIFTED LEARNERS

Level	Form	Benefits
One	Collaboration as an interactive, one-to-one relationship between a student and a significant adult or older student	• Personalized treatment of issues, ideas, and experiences
Two	Collaboration as a team of school-based educators addressing a common problem	• Assessment for direct intervention purposes • Development of a tailored curriculum that responds to a student's presenting behaviors
Three	Collaboration as a link to other institutions on mutual issues of concern	• A broader array of resources for educational intervention • A better perspective on student needs

series, calls for the collaborative skills noted in the literature. At the school level, the collaborative engagement of various professionals in developing a curriculum for these learners is also a crucial provision. Last, inter-institutional collaboration with universities, businesses, and other social agencies constitutes a set of relationships to be nurtured on behalf of these learners. Table 11.1 illustrates the levels of collaboration described and the benefits to special populations of gifted learners addressed by them.

SUMMARY

Learning disabled gifted children present a dilemma in the context of current educational practice. They exhibit intellectual capacities comparable to other gifted learners but also demonstrate areas of deficient functioning that interfere with effective performance on academic tasks. Because of the discrepancies in functioning of these learners, the need for collaboration among educators, the institutions they represent, and the home are crucial for intervening successfully with them. Collaboration, when it is meaningful, can greatly enhance our understanding of special needs students and provide a rich commentary on ways to serve them as well.

Collaboration as an administrative and programming tool can be a vital enhancement in providing for learning disabled gifted learners. Special educators, gifted educators, and general educators must work together to plan a unified program, not a fragmented one. We must consider the resource power inherent in all successful educational collaborative relationships: mentorships, team teaching, resource consultation, cooperative teaching, partnerships — and systematically apply these successes to our work with the disabled gifted.

QUESTIONS FOR REFLECTION

1. What prevents our labeling any child with a learning problem as "potentially gifted?"
2. What strategies might work with learning disabled gifted children whose behavioral problems are extreme?
3. What are the impacts of cooperative teaching on teachers, students, and the administration?
4. If you were the parent of a learning disabled gifted child, how would you proceed to get assistance from the school?
5. What is the potential effectiveness of collaboration with special needs gifted students?

REFERENCES

Alpert, J. L., Ballantyne, D., & Griffiths, D. (1981). Characteristics of consultants and consultees and success in mental health consultation. *Journal of School Psychology, 19*(4), 312–322.

Bauwens, J., Hourcade, J., & Friends, M. (1989). Cooperative teaching: A model for general and special education integration. *Remedial & Special Education, 10*(2), 17–29.

Berliner, D. (1986). In pursuit of the expert pedagogue. *Educational Researcher, 15*(7), 5–13.

Brown, D., Wyne, M. D., Blackburn, J. E., & Powell, W. C. (1979). *Consultation: Strategy for improving education*. Boston: Allyn & Bacon.

Brown, V. L. (1977). "Yes, but . . . .": A reply to Phyllis Newcomer. *Journal of Special Education, 11* (2), 171–182.

Cohen, D. L. (1989). Collaboration: What works. *Education Week, 13*.

Cutler, R. L., & McNeil, E. B. (1964). *Mental health consultation in the schools: A research analysis*. Ann Arbor: University of Michigan, Department of Psychology.

Dinkmeyer, D., & Dinkmeyer, D. (1976). Contributions of Adlerian psychology to school counseling. *Psychology in the Schools, 13*, 32–38.

Downing, M. R. (1954). *A study of certain factors involved in the effective utilization of the services of educational consultants*. Unpublished doctoral dissertation, University of Virginia, Charlottesville.

Dykstra, L. (1990). Keynote address on learning disabilities. Project Director's Meeting for the Department of Education, Washington, DC.

Eisendorfer, C., & Batton, L. (1972). The mental health consultant as seen by his consultees. *Community Mental Health Journal, 8*(3), 171–177.

Fine, M. J., Grantham, V.L., & Wright, J. G. (1979). Personal variables that facilitate or impede consultation. *Psychology in the Schools, 16*, 533–539.

Fox, L., Brody, L., & Tobin, D. (1983). *Learning-disabled/gifted children: Identification and programming*. Baltimore: University Park Press.

Gallagher, J. (1985). *Teaching the gifted child*. Boston: Allyn & Bacon.

Gutkin, T. B., & Curtis, M. J. (1982). School-based consultation. In C. R. Reynolds & T. B. Gutkin (Eds.), *The handbook of school psychology* (pp. 796–828). New York: Wiley.

Hathaway, W. E. (1985). *Model of school-university collaboration: National and local perspectives on collaboratives that work*. Materials prepared for symposium presented at annual meeting of American Educational Research Association.

Idol, L. (1989). The resource/consulting teacher: An integrated model of service delivery. *Remedial & Special Education, 10*(6), 38–48.

Jones, B. L., & Maloy, R. W. (1988). *Partnerships for improving schools*. New York: Greenwood Press.

Karnes, M., & Johnson, L. (1987). An imperative: Programs for the young gifted/talented. *Journal for the Education of the Gifted, 10*(3), 195–213.

Little, J. W. (1982). Norms of collegiality and experimentation: Workplace conditions of school success. *American Educational Research Journal, 19*, 325–340.

Maeroff, G. I. (1983). *School and college: Partnerships in education*. (Special report). Princeton, NJ: Carnegie Foundation for the Advancement of Teaching.

Magreb, P., & Elder, J. (Eds.). (1979). *Planning for services to handicapped persons: Community education, health*. Baltimore: Paul Brookes.

Martinson, M. (1982). Interagency services: A new era for an old idea. *Exceptional Children, 48*(5), 389–394.

Meyers, J., Parsons, D., & Martin, R. (1979). *Mental health consultation in the schools*. San Francisco: Jossey-Bass.

Palmer, P. (1983). *To know as we are known: A spirituality of education*. San Francisco: Harper & Row.

Reinking, R. H., Livesay, G., & Kohl, M. (1978). The effects of consultation style on consultee productivity. *American Journal of Community Psychology, 6*(3), 283–290.

Reisberg, L., & Wolf, R. (1986). Developing a consulting program in special education: Implementation and interventions. *Focus on Exceptional Children, 19*(3), 1–14.

Schlechty, P. C., Ingwerson, D. W., & Brooks, T. I. (1988). Inventing professional development schools. *Educational Leadership, 28*–31.

Schowengerdt, R., Fine, J., & Poggio, J. (1976). An examination of some bases of teacher satisfaction with school psychological services. *Psychology in the Schools, 13*, 263–274.

Scott, J. J., & Smith, S. C. (1987). *Collaborative schools*. Paper prepared for ERIC Clearinghouse on Educational Management, Reston, VA.

Suter, D. P., & Wolf, J. S. (1987). Issues in the identification and programming of the gifted/learning-disabled child. *Journal for the Education of the Gifted, 10*(3), 227–238.

VanTassel-Baska, J. (1991). Serving the disabled gifted through educational collaboration. *Journal for the Education of the Gifted, 14*(3), 246–264.

VanTassel-Baska, J., & Kulieke, M. (1987). The role of community-based scientific resources on developing scientific talent: A case study. *Gifted Child Quarterly, 3*(3), 111–115.

Weissenburger, J. W., Fine, J. J., & Poggio, J. P. (1982). The relationship of selected consultant/teacher characteristics to consultation outcomes. *Journal of School Psychology, 20*(4), 263–270.

CHAPTER TWELVE

A Perspective on Curriculum Development for Gifted Learners

Gail McEachron-Hirsch

U nderstanding the relationship between general and gifted curriculum development is a necessary foundation for assessing curriculum differentiation for gifted students compared to curricula for more typical learners. The first question this chapter addresses is: What are the key elements in curriculum development that are shared by both gifted and general educators? Following this analysis is an examination of several curriculum programs based on their appropriateness for gifted or typical students and an attempt to address the second question: What are the persisting areas of debate on curriculum issues between gifted and general educators?

CURRICULUM TRADITIONS

Although the curriculum field as we know it today did not exist in the 18th and 19th centuries, we are indebted to Henry Barnard, U.S. Commissioner of Education (1867-1890), who kept American educators informed of the advances in pedagogical principles made by European reformers such as Pestallozi, Foebel, and Herbart (Gutek, 1970). The actual relationship between curriculum and instruction began to gain attention through the works of Bobbitt (1918) and Charters (1923), reaching national attention when the National Society for the Sltudy of Education (NSSE) prepared a composite statement about curriculum making in 1930. Since that time, curriculum greats such as Dewey (1938), Tyler

(1949), Taba (1962), and Bruner (1966) have shaped the foundation of curriculum development in ways that have continuous relevancy.

In more recent years, educators have attempted to strengthen the field of curriculum development by solidifying the links between exemplary curriculum applications and their theoretical precepts. In the 1970s, scholars argued that a curriculum program must be analyzed in all its stages of modification, from the highly specialized phase of development to the implementation phase, where the reality of the social context of the classroom presides (Dunkin & Biddle, 1974; Eisner & Vallance, 1974). Although a certain amount of disparity between curriculum development and classroom implementation is inevitable, the curriculum process from its beginning stages to learner outcomes continues to be splintered. In reflecting upon the 1980s, curriculum specialists recognize progress in outlining the basic foundations and domains of curriculum development, yet acknowledge that as a field of study, curriculum development continues to lack the political and economic support it relished from the federal government in the early 1970s.

The works of Miller and Seller (1985) and Ornstein and Hunkins (1988) provide a comprehensive examination of the factors that must be considered in curriculum analysis. These sources describe the foundations of curriculum trends in general education and, taken together, provide a basis for understanding curricular linkages between gifted and general educators. Examining the roots and components of curriculum development is a necessary undertaking for educators of students with exceptional needs so they can understand the frame of reference. Likewise, as general educators broaden their expertise by studying the needs of exceptional students, a strong foundation in curriculum development enables them to distinguish between curriculum that is truly differentiated for the individual needs of students from curriculum that is disguised with labels of exceptionality but is merely a different theoretical approach.

CURRICULUM POSITIONS

Miller and Seller (1985) present three curriculum positions — transmission, transaction, and transformation — to describe broad trends in the development of curriculum and instruction. An examination of these trends provides insight into the two areas of curriculum and instruction that are problematic for both gifted and general educators: curriculum *appropriateness* and curriculum *credibility*. Even though the three trends are described separately, some teachers utilize a variety of these approaches simultaneously.

Transmission

In contemporary education, the transmission position and its behaviorist manifestations have three major emphases: subject/discipline, competency-based education, and cultural transmission (Miller & Seller, 1985). Within the subject/discipline orientation is an emphasis on direct instructional techniques, the traditional lecture and recitation approach, and textbook learning. Competency-based education focuses more on objectives and assessment, often reinforcing skill development. Mastery learning, which is similar to competency-based education, places more emphasis upon instruction.

According to Ornstein and Hunkins (1988), this approach manifests behaviorist theoretical roots that emphasize conditioning behavior and altering the environment to shape desired responses from the learner. The influence of behaviorists Edward Thorndike, Ivan Pavlov, James Watson, and B. F. Skinner can be found in a variety of curricular adaptations. Ornstein and Hunkins examine the curriculum development approaches of Ralph Tyler, Hilda Taba, and Jerome Bruner, tracing certain approaches to Thorndike. For example, even though "Tyler and Taba disagreed with Thorndike's view of connections between specific stimuli and specific responses," they did support the connectionist notion that, "learning is based on 'generalizations' and the teaching of important 'principles' . . . to explain concrete phenomena" (Ornstein & Hunkins, 1988, p. 86). For Bruner, the emphasis upon learning the structure of a discipline facilitates the specific transfer of learning. One can say that the mark of a behaviorist is the tendency to be highly prescriptive and diagnostic in approach and to rely on step-by-step and structured methods of learning. Transmission applications reflect these approaches.

Transmission Applications in General and Gifted Education

The transmission orientation in elementary and secondary education has focused upon specific subjects and academic disciplines. In elementary education the emphasis is usually upon reading, writing, and mathematics, and in secondary education the emphasis is upon science, math, English, history, and foreign languages. To illustrate the direct instruction, mastery learning, and competency-based education cited, Ornstein and Hunkins (1988) present the following curriculum programs as general education applications of the transmission position: Direct Instructional Training (DISTAR); individualized education, such as Individually Prescribed Instruction (IPI) and Individually Guided Education (IGE); instructional design; Management by Objectives (MBO); and Program, Evaluation and Review Technique (PERT). Most of the programs are characterized by a careful sequencing of learning needs and behaviors.

In the field of gifted education, the transmission approach is evident when the same subject matter orientation described is presented to the student at an accelerated pace (Cox, Daniel, & Boston, 1985; Daniel & Cox, 1988; VanTassel-Baska, Feldhusen, Seeley, Wheatley, Silverman, & Foster, 1988). The approach remains the same, but the pace changes. For example, the Study of Mathematically Precocious Youth at Johns Hopkins University provided opportunities for students with high SAT-M scores to complete 2 or 3 years of high school mathematics in a 4-week summer session (VanTassel-Baska, 1988). Similar programs can be found at Purdue, Northwestern, Duke, and Denver universities, and in a number of regional contexts throughout the country (Simpson, 1983;

Stanley, 1980). Another curriculum program for gifted students that "relies heavily on stated behavioral or performance objectives with measurable outcomes that can be tested in order to determine educational progress or achievement" originates from Title IV-C gifted projects (VanTassel-Baska, 1988).

Both general and gifted educators continue to implement this most longstanding approach to curriculum development and instruction in the United States. By reviewing what the proponents and critics of the transmission position say, insight into some of the conflict between gifted and general educators can be derived. Disagreement generally arises not from whether the transmission approach is appropriate for both gifted and regular students but, rather, the extent to which the approach should be emphasized.

Proponents and Critics of the Transmission Position

The transmission position has many advocates as well as critics. Proponents say the organized subject matter orientation fosters a nation-wide scope and sequence because of the reliance on textbooks. By providing general guidelines from grade level to grade level, teachers are in a better position to avoid redundancy. Other transmission approaches — competency-based education and mastery learning — have been commended because they encourage educators to be more clear and precise in their instructional goals. In addition, the success with individualized achievement in a noncompetitive atmosphere is attributed to mastery learning.

Critics of the transmission approach to curriculum development maintain that it places too much emphasis upon behaviorally stated goals and objectives and that this trend has limited the various methods of teaching and learning. In response to criticism of too many electives and not enough accountability for vague, or not behaviorally stated goals, most states developed minimum competency standards for elementary and secondary students (Miller & Seller, 1985). Critics of this trend maintain that curricula should be planned with "reference to the developing experience of the individual pupil and to his educational needs or requirements rather than to the demands of those bodies of knowledge that are felt to be useful to society . . . ." (Blenkin & Kelly, 1983, p. 12).

This view has been strengthened by developmental psychologists who suggest that intellectual development can best be promoted through more active forms of learning. By ignoring the developmental stages of learning, it is far too easy to: place emphasis upon lower levels of learning, ignore the affective domain, oversimplify curricula in the face of cultural pluralism, and reduce subject matter to the extent that it becomes meaningless (Miller & Seller, 1985). In sum, the overarching criticism of the transmission approach to curriculum development is its emphasis upon mechanical learning, in which the student is a recipient of knowledge, rather than an emphasis upon the processes of learning appropriate for a certain stage of development.

Transaction

According to the transaction position, education is an interactive process between the student and the curriculum, which the teacher presents in such a way that developmental needs are taken into consideration. The central elements in the transaction position are: (a) an emphasis upon cognitive process orientation, (b) problem-solving skills, (c) democratic citizenship, and (d) disciplines orientation (Miller & Seller, 1985). Ornstein and Hunkins refer to these learning orientations as "cognitive developmental," which means curriculum specialists have widely recognized growth and development, especially at the elementary level, which spans three of the stages. At the secondary level the theories of Dewey (1938), Bruner (1959) and Phenix (1964) find support largely because of the emphasis upon problem solving within subject matter from the various disciplines.

To demonstrate curricular adaptations of cognitive developmental theories, Ornstein and Hunkins discuss the influence of Piaget (1948) and Dewey (1938) upon Tyler, Taba, and Bruner. For Piaget, assimilation, accommodation, and equilibration are the three cognitive processes that form the basis of growth; for Dewey the three processes are situation, interaction, and continuity. Ornstein and Hunkins suggest that Tyler's principles of learning and his methods of organizing learning (purpose, educational experiences, organization and evaluation) can be traced to Piaget's environmental theories and Dewey's educational experiences. For Taba, the notion of transforming complex concepts and subject matter and mental operations are continually deepened as they progress to a more complex form (Ornstein & Hunkins, 1988, p. 94).

Historically, the transaction position can be traced to the curriculum practices advanced by a Swiss educator, Johann Heinrich Pestalozzi, whose instructional principles began with concrete objects and ended with abstract concepts. Modern applications are evident in the disciplines orientation advanced by Schwab (1962) that began in the early 1960s. For example, the Biological Sciences Curriculum Study (BSCS) was designed to teach students skills similar to the methods of scientific investigation biologists use. Similarly, Science Research Associates developed a curriculum that placed students in investigative roles, emphasizing the work social scientists perform.

Because the cognitive developmental or cognitive process orientation emphasizes how people think and solve problems, curriculum programs also flourished in support of these principles. Attempts to break with the traditional process of transmitting information to students led to studies of thinking, including: levels of thinking (Bloom, 1956); hierarchical learning (Gagne, 1985); structure of intellect (Guilford, 1967); creative and reflective thinking (Dewey, 1938; Conant, 1951); critical thinking (Lipman, 1984; Sternberg, 1984; 1986); creative thinking (Torrance, 1965); and intuitive thinking (Bruner, 1959).

In addition to the discipline-centered and thinking skills approaches to curriculum development, cognitive developmental theorists have pursued the inquiry-discovery method. "Although Bruner went to great lengths to fuse the inquiry-discovery methods in the sciences and mathematics, Phenix (1964), Taba (1962), and Inlow (1964) claimed that the discovery method was separate from inquiry and that both methods of thinking cut across all subjects" (Ornstein & Hunkins, 1988, p. 101). Today, the terms "inquiry" and "discovery" are also used interchangeably in the teaching profession without the theoretical distinctions articulated by Bruner, Taba, and Inlow. Current usage of both terms seems to signify Bruner's idea of discovery as "learning that takes place when students are not presented with subject matter in its final form" (Ornstein & Hunkins, 1988, p. 102).

Transaction Applications in General and Gifted Education

Bruner's (1959) *The Process of Education* outlined the major disciplinary orientation that led to a number of curriculum-development projects in biology, physics, math, and social studies. His *Man: A Course of Study* (MACOS) illustrates the transaction approach well because it demonstrates an exemplary inquiry/discovery curriculum that has been successful with gifted and regular students alike. MACOS was developed by a multidisciplinary team of experts including Jerome Bruner, Danish ethnographer Knud Rasmussen, and the eminent anthropologist Irven DeVore, to address the questions: What is human about human beings? How did they get that way? How can they be made more so? The curriculum is designed to be presented in a highly structured manner but in a way that is open-ended enough to allow for a variety of interpretations. By comparing the lifestyles of herring gulls, the Pacific salmon, baboons, and the Netsilik Eskimos, students and teachers engage in discussions that ponder the existence of humankind and, in so doing, reflect upon their own perceptions of ethics and morality.

In the United States, debates surrounding MACOS reached scandalous proportions when a member of Congress condemned its open-ended quality that gave far too much rein for interpretations questioning the underlying assumptions of U.S. cultural values. The debates that were launched are outlined in detail in the 1974 and 1975 issues of *Social Education* (e.g., Conlan, 1975; Dow, 1975; Herlihy, 1974; Larkin, 1975).

The criticisms were a harbinger of what was to come in the latter half of the 1970s and 1980s as the conservative movement in education continued. *A Nation at Risk* (Commission on Excellence in Education, 1983) identifies many of the designated reforms by advocates of this movement during the 1980s. At the time of the Congressional debates on MACOS, however, educators reacted to the general political climate by removing MACOS from various social studies programs, with a few exceptions. The exceptions were in communities characterized by parents who did not perceive the examination of crosscultural contrasts raised in MACOS as a threat to their own value system.

The impact of these political battles on gifted educators followed a separate path, however. When looking for curricula appropriate for gifted students, MACOS was identified as a viable program because it has several salient components: It is interdisciplinary, open-ended, and interactive, and designed to follow an inquiry/discovery technique. As a consequence, educators of gifted students salvaged the MACOS programs that had been shelved for general educators. For general educators, it has never been made clear why MACOS is reserved for gifted students when it was removed for political reasons from regular classrooms.

This series of events raises several questions about the decision-making process surrounding curriculum selection (a topic that will be pursued later in this chapter). As a curriculum trend, however, the transaction position has received less attention in the general classroom when compared to direct instruction.

Proponents and Critics of the Transaction Position

The transaction position has been the main source of educational innovation and reform for the past 30 years. In recent years curriculum developers have attempted to synthesize the cognitive-process orientation and the disciplines orientation, thereby giving support, refinement, and expansion to various kinds of transaction approaches. As a result, educators have drawn from cognitive psychology to provide analyses of problem solving, children's thinking in specific content domains such as science (e.g., Beyer, 1979; Driver & Erickson, 1983), schemata function, conceptual change (e.g., Hewson & Hewson, 1981; Posner, 1982), and classroom interaction (Miller & Seller, 1985). Further research is needed, however, to examine how individuals process information, solve problems, and make decisions.

A major criticism of the cognitive-developmental, or transaction, orientation is the narrowness with which certain academics approach analytical problem solving. The individuals who focus on left-brain, logical, analytical problem solving and ignore right-brain, intuitive, synthetic problem solving continue to perpetuate inquiry models related to the scientific method and do not further our knowledge of how problem solving occurs in other contexts (Miller & Seller, 1985). In addition, for critics of the transaction position, deciding what knowledge is worth knowing, whether thinking skills can be taught in a generic fashion, and how to better understand the process of creative problem solving continue to be issues relevant to all educators (Resnick & Klopfer, 1989).

Transformation

The transformation position can be represented by two different ideologies: (a) the phenomenological or humanistic element, and (b) the social-change orientation. The former finds its roots in the works of Jean Jacques Rousseau, Friedrich Froebel, Leo Tolstoy, A. S. Neil, Carl Rogers, Abraham Maslow, and John Holt. The other stems from a social change position, influenced by the works of George Counts, Theodore Brameld, Jonathan Kozol, and Michael Apple.

Phenomenology, sometimes referred to as humanistic or third-force psychology, is "illustrated by the individual's awareness that he or she is an 'I' who has feelings and attitudes, who experiences stimuli, and who acts upon the environment" in a purposeful way (Ornstein & Hunkins, 1988, p. 103). Furthermore, the individual exerts some sense of control and freedom in responding to the environment. Phenomenology is influenced by existentialist philosophy, both emphasizing the study of immediate life experiences as one's reality. For phenomenologists, what one does and the extent to which one learns is closely tied to one's view of self.

Maslow's humanistic psychology (1962) stresses three major principles: "(1) centering attention on the experiencing person, and thus focusing on experience as the primary phenomenon in learning; (2) emphasizing such human qualities as choice, creativity, values and self-realization, as opposed to thinking about people in mechanistic or behavioral terms and learning in cognitive terms; and (3) showing ultimate concern for the dignity and worth of people and an interest in the psychological development and human potential of learners as individuals" (Ornstein & Hunkins, 1988, p. 105). In this view, the student is positive, purposive, active, and involved in organizing his or her life experiences. "Learning is experimental, its essence being freedom and its outcome full human potential and reform of society" (p. 105).

Rogers (1983) argued that interpersonal relationships among learners are just as important as cognitive experiences. Rogers maintains that children's perceptions, which are highly individualistic, influence their learning and behavior in class. Following Rogers' theory, the teacher's role is nondirective, that of a facilitator. In this role, the teacher helps students explore ideas about their lives, schoolwork, relations with others, and interaction with society. The curriculum is concerned with process, not products; personal needs, not subject matter; psychological meaning, not cognitive scores; and changing environmental situations, not predetermined environments. Students must have freedom to learn, not restrictive or planned activities.

Humanistic education became a dominant force in education in the 1960s and can be placed under two general categories. The first, having roots in Maslow's work, focuses on developing positive self-concept, and the second, having roots in Rogers's theory, centers on building interpersonal skills. William Purkey, Arthur Combs, and Raths, Merrill, and Simon have increased our understanding of self-concept in relation to the school environment. Purkey (1970, 1978) advances the notion that a student's self-concept does not cause the student to behave in a particular way but, instead, interacts with other classroom variables to affect how the student behaves and performs in school. Combs's (1982) theory of perceptual psychology states that in order to encourage a positive student self-concept, the teacher must have a positive view of himself or herself. Values clarification is a program developed by Raths, Harmin, and Simon (1978) to develop positive, purposeful, and consistent behavior and attitudes in students through a process of valuing. Weinstein and Fantini (1970) developed a strategy linking students' concerns to the concepts they will study.

The other area in which the transformational position has made significant contributions to the field of education is interpersonal skills. The transpersonal orientation advanced by Rudolph Steiner (1975, 1976), known as Waldorf education, focuses on reconnecting the inwardness of individuals with the universe. Central to Waldorf education is artistic activity, which involves "focusing on how form, color, and rhythm are part of the wholeness of experience" and how art, feeling, and movement are related to learning. Moore and Yamamoto (1988) have developed a series of videotapes and curriculum guides to demonstrate some of these principles.

The social-change orientation — the parallel orientation to the humanistic transformation position — focuses on the social context of schooling. Educators supporting the transformation position would argue that teachers should be at the forefront of social change. Brameld (1950), Newmann (1975), Alschuler (1980), Apple (1986), and Apple and King (1977) are some of the scholars who maintain that the schools must be an integral part of the reforms that have to take place to deal with social issues such as class and racial struggles. If not dealt with directly, these issues become ingrained in the hidden curriculum (Giroux & Purpel, 1983).

Transformation Applications in
General and Gifted Education

In general education, the classic example of the phenomenological approach to education is A. S. Neill's (1960) Summerhill school in Great Britain. Founded in 1921 and still in operation, Summerhill presents educational experiences to students when they express a desire to learn. A residential program, Summerhill began as an alternative to the typically structured public school program. As a result of what was going on in Summerhill and the British educational system, described in the Plowden Report (Central Advisory Council for Education, 1967), writers such as Paul Goodman, John Holt, Herbert Kohl, and the free-school movement in the United States began to reflect the British sentiments. In the 1960s and 1970s the open-education movement adopted programs and philosophies emphasizing child-centeredness and began to design curricula that fostered more decision making on the part of students.

According to Blenkin and Kelly (1983, p. 11) British advocates of this approach continue to refine and articulate curricular applications based on the philosophy that curriculum "must be planned and assessed in terms of its own intrinsic values and merits rather than as instrumental to the achievement of" social, economic, or vocational goals. In the United States, by contrast, conservative trends in education have stymied phenomenological curriculum development.

In gifted education, curriculum models developed by Renzulli (1977) and by Feldhusen and Kolloff (1978) reflect child-centered orientations whereby gifted students "become responsible for their own curriculum through contracts with a facilitator who assesses interest, ability, and maturity factors" (VanTassel-Baska, 1988, p. 4). Independent investigation proceeds with periodic interaction between teacher and student.

Proponents and Critics
of the Transformation Position

Proponents of the transformation position argue that the development of the child as learner is central to a curriculum view. Thus, child-centered curriculum is essential, as was promoted with the individually guided education (IGE) movement of the 1960s.

Despite the theories pioneered by Rogers and Maslow, few comprehensive programs have been developed. Instead, initial attempts to apply "humanistic" principles were questioned on the basis of invasion of privacy. For example, the well intentioned efforts of teachers during the 1970s to discuss personal concerns during "Magic Circle" time was often met with suspicion by parents who questioned the appropriateness of dealing with personal family issues in the classroom. The contemporary role of guidance counselors and elementary school counselors is one of the legitimized avenues for dealing with interpersonal issues, but questions about the extent to which a classroom teacher should venture into students' personal lives remain at the forefront as these new phenomenological curriculum strategies are developed.

ARRIVING AT ANSWERS

Returning to the original questions — What are the key elements shared by gifted and general educators? What are the persisting tensions between the two? — three broad and interrelated factors require professional attention to bring the efforts of both camps closer:

1. Conservative political and economic climate in the field of education.
2. Deficit attitudes toward educators and the educational system.
3. Pedagogical devisiveness among general, gifted, and special educators.

The first two reflect the key elements shared by gifted and general educators, and the third area represents the major source of tension between the two.

Conservative Political and Economic Climate

The Reagan administration will be remembered among educators as one that cut federal spending by 10%, leaving states and local governments to take even more responsibility for educating students. Prior to these cuts, federal expenditures for elementary and secondary education were more than $4 billion per year, expanding opportunities for lower-income families and making college almost universally accessible (Lowi & Ginsberg, 1990, pp. 710-711). During the Reagan administration the programs affecting the educational opportunities of minorities and low-income families were hit hardest by financial cutbacks while, paradoxically, the political rhetoric insisted that the United States was a "nation at risk." The very programs the Reagan administration cut served to increase the number of students who might be considered "at risk."

Both general and gifted educators were affected by the federal cutbacks. The Federal Office for the Gifted was closed in 1981, leaving the 50 states to respond without a national policy. In Florida, budgets for gifted programs reached $80 million, whereas other states offered only minimal support (Feldhusen, 1989). Following a period in the 1970s, during which the Marland Report had made significant gains for the developing field of gifted education, the 1980s brought scattered progress depending upon the efforts of individual states.

Deficit Attitudes Toward Education

For general educators the message delivered from various media surveys, Gallup Polls, falling scores on standardized tests, and documents such as *A Nation at Risk* was loud and clear: General educators were failing dismally. If ever a national policy could succeed in "blaming the victim," the Reagan administration deserves such a distinction. What it succeeded in doing was to remove an existing federal program that acknowledged the relationship between the need for resources in helping minorities and low-income families achieve higher educational levels and, at the same time, to attack the schools for not producing higher performances on standardized tests. How the scores of "at risk" students are figured into the overall averages did not seem to be a consideration. While general educators were being attacked on the national front by politicians and the media, their cohorts — gifted educators — were pursuing their goals by maintaining that "gifted youth were left to languish or go unserved in American schools. . . ." (Feldhusen, 1989).

What gifted and general educators shared was the need to respond to the shifting political messages from federal and state governments. But, while individual states supported the sentiment of gifted educators by providing economic support, thereby endorsing the notion that the needs of gifted students were not being met in the regular classrooms, the result was further condemnation of the general educator's role. Inadvertently perhaps, educational bureaucracies had sacrificed the teacher's role to enhance the student's role. When such decisions result in incongruous outcomes for the educational system as a whole, tensions are bound to emerge. The major source of tension is the underlying attitude that classroom teachers are deficient. The media constantly reinforces the deficiency attitude toward general educators. But, to a certain extent, gifted educators have maintained some distance from these assaults because they share the position of the media and political rhetoric of the 1980s by pointing out the inadequacies of general education.

The divisiveness between gifted and general educators is exacerbated somewhat by the funding mechanisms through which federal, state, and private grants are awarded. Funds set aside for specific groups and projects — international education, public policy, law-focused education, free enterprise, science and mathematics, literacy, at-risk gifted — tend to drive educational program development, not the other way around. Rather than focusing on long-range curriculum development, with goals and objectives that meet the needs of all students in a given state or school district, and a master plan for reaching these goals, educators take a reactionary stance, responding to the latest funding fad. Needless to say, curriculum development takes place in a haphazard and splintered fashion, with specialized forces competing with each other rather than working together. This trend has characterized the relationships among special, general, and gifted educations ever since passage of The Education for All Handicapped Children Act (Public Law 94-142) in 1975, and it continues to affect relationships among newer roles such as elementary guidance counselors as well as longstanding relationships with school psychologists and vocational educators.

Divisiveness Within Education Itself

Curriculum development is a key vantage point from which to bring the specialized roles together. Overall program and curriculum development is crucial for redefining the role of educators as proactive and informed rather than as deficient professionals and maintaining a reactionary posture. One lesson to be learned from the 1970s, when curriculum development reached a hiatus, is that exemplary curricula can be created when interdisciplinary collaboration is supported with financial resources and incentives. The hardest lesson that was learned, however, was that without an overall plan for program development and institutionalized commitment, progress is short-lived and determined by external criteria. Nowhere is this more evident than in the pedagogical divisiveness among general, gifted, and special educators.

During the curriculum development regression of the 1980s, general educators responded by reviving the traditional instructional strategy — or transmission approach. During this period the instructional principles extrapolated from Madelyn Hunter's curricular efforts easily lent themselves to behaviorally stated goals and objectives and accountability for teachers and students (e.g., anticipatory set, objectives, instructional input, modeling, guided practice, independent practice), so much so that teachers refer to having "Hunterized" their curriculum, even though such translations may not have been intended.

As teachers in regular classrooms were retreating from the curriculum innovations characterized by process and inquiry in the 1960s (transaction approaches), gifted programs were developing throughout the United States. Because they were intended to be somewhat innovative as a developing field, they did not experience the constraints that teachers in regular classrooms felt. Hence, many of the innovations that were beginning to develop in the area of general curriculum in the 1960s were expanded upon, repackaged or relabeled, and utilized by gifted educators during the 1970s and 1980s. To general educators, some of what gifted educators call "gifted curriculum" or "enrichment" is typically the transaction position.

From a curriculum and instruction standpoint, the basis for these differing programs is not the result of a match between the curriculum and the gifted characteristics of the students but, rather, on the basis that the curriculum is *different* from a methodological, theoretical, or topical standpoint. Decisions about the appropriateness of curricula that are made on such grounds only serve to confuse curriculum development issues. General educators argue that varied instructional strategies from both approaches are appropriate for students in regular classrooms, but unless gifted educators can demonstrate through field-tested situations that their curriculum is *inappropriate* for students in regular classrooms, their rationale for making it separate and distinct is not credible.

Additional divisiveness is sported when general educators are accused of teaching to the masses as opposed to meeting the needs of individual students. Although inconsistencies are present among school districts in the policies for matching curricula to students who are above or below grade level, the issue is not whether general educators are capable of meeting the individual needs of students but, instead, what the overall plan for a given school district allows. Some school districts encourage a match between individual ability and achievement levels with instructional groupings; others advocate heterogeneous grouping for all instruction. Summarily dismissing all general education as instructing the masses without concern for the individual is unfair, just as summarily dismissing all gifted programs as being merely methodologically different is unfair.

The challenge for professionals who are interested in meeting the needs of all students lies in integrated, long-range curriculum planning. Collaboration among special, gifted, and general educators, along with administrators, counselors, and school psychologists, is necessary to ensure that individual needs of students are not compartmentalized. Flexible grouping and flexible pacing are prerequisites for these programs to be effective. Reinstating the importance of curriculum development and collaboration would foster more comprehensive teaching approaches. No longer should innovations in curriculum and instruction be limited to special sub-groups within the teaching profession. Curriculum planning that is coordinated in an equitable fashion should be designed to maximize resources across the spectrum of student need.

As it is now, special, gifted, and general educators may be duplicating each others' efforts or making superficial changes without truly differentiating curricula. Research in curriculum development and evaluation should be pursued so that curriculum programs can be field-tested with a variety of populations. In this way, the necessary documentation can be made to support the differentiated curriculum and instruction that will emerge. Being able to articulate the match between a particular curriculum and a particular kind of student will add credibility to the rationale for grouping or separating students for instructional purposes.

Curricula then can be targeted appropriately rather than merely in response to externally imposed criteria.

INTEGRATING CURRICULUM APPROACHES:
THE CASE OF DIANE BRADFORD

Selecting curricula for students with a variety of needs is the challenge that educators face when presented with a myriad of curricular options. The case example of Diane Bradford can be used to demonstrate how one general educator would envision the interrelationships among the three curricular trends of transmission, transaction and transformation. To do so, one must look at Diane's unique and sometimes polarized strengths, weaknesses, and interests, both inside and outside the school environment.

What immediatley comes to mind is the probability that Diane's learning disabilities and placement in special education classes are masking her athletic and expressive strengths. Even though she was initially reluctant to go to "special" classes, Diane has since not only developed a liking for these classes but also has made efforts to continue in them beyond the time necessary to correct specified disabilities.

Upon further examination of the instructional strategies operating in both contexts, a pattern of attraction and aversion emerges. It is not what is going on in the regular classroom, in general, that brings about negative responses from Diane. Rather, depending upon what is going on and what teaching mode is used, Diane selectively opts in or out of the situation. When timed spelling and math tests, English skills lessons, or reading comprehension exercises are in progress, Diane becomes restless and frustrated. As she stated in a videotaped interview, she has to concentrate really hard, and when she gets home, she needs to run around and blow off steam. These frustrations are directly related to her difficulties with sensory motor integration. Problems that require speed, usually in a competitive context, and interpretations from reading stories or following directions are especially taxing because of learning disabilities.

On the other hand, when students are performing dramatizations or simulating real life experiences, whether in a special education or a regular classroom, Diane becomes totally absorbed. Her creativity bursts upon the scene as she either develops her star role as "princess" or perfects her role as "entrepreneur" in the marketplace. When describing these performances, Diane becomes animated and, beyond that, incredibly articulate in recalling the lines of characters in the play, as well as the interdependence and dynamics of the diversified roles in the economics simulation. Other creative talents were evident in Diane's artwork and creative story development. In these contexts, Diane's energy seemed to be focused and intense in a positive manner, unlike the bottled-up frustration stemming from the exercises described earlier.

After school, Diane swims for an hour in a neighborhood swimming program. Although she complains about the set structure of this activity, Diane expresses a sense of "heightened energy and relaxation" once this hour of exercise is over. In addition to swimming, Diane goes horseback riding on alternating days. She speaks fondly of this time, a situation that allows for open-ended riding as opposed to structured skill building and competition.

The transmission, transaction, and transformation positions are useful in analyzing recommended curricular strategies for Diane's particular strengths and weaknesses. Clearly, if left to her own choosing entirely, Diane would probably decide to function in some form of the transactional mode best described by Dewey, in which the classroom is set up as a microcosm of the larger society, along the lines of the marketplace simulation. Also, the interactive nature in which Diane acted out the role of a princess, based on a story read during her speech class, reflects opportunities for creative problem solving given specific subject matter — in this instance, a story appropriate to a 9-year old's developmental interests.

Application of the transmission position was evident in the manner skills lessons were presented. In the regular classroom, when the skills lessons were taught in a way that required listening, reading, and following directions in a setting where peers were all on the same task at the same time and completing it much more quickly, Diane's frustration level increased. When the same skills lessons were presented in an atmosphere where speed was not a criterion and help was available when needed, however, Diane was able to function much more successfully without anxiety. In this comparison, the transmission mode was made more appropriate by altering logistical and rate expectations.

The transformation position is more difficult to ascertain as a deliberate curriculum pattern, but its philosophy is evident in some of Diane's behaviors. Recalling that phenomenology emphasizes that what one does and the extent to which one learns are closely tied to one's view of self, Diane revealed purposive behavior with these motivations in operation. For example, her desire to stay in speech class so that she could function at an appropriate level and thus avoid frustration clearly indicates an awareness of herself and her own capabilities. By self-selecting to stay in speech, even after she had mastered the specific objectives, Diane is revealing her desire and need to participate in expressive opportunities that result in intrinsic and social rewards. The importance of one's self-esteem, as it is affected by failure and success in school, is an area given greater attention by the transformation position.

As a general educator participating in a transdisciplinary team, I would recommend a curriculum tailored to Diane's needs that crosses all three curriculum positions. A curriculum offering flexible scheduling would best facilitate Diane's versatile needs. Diane will continue to require help with reading, writing, and listening skills. Although some of these skills can be presented in a non-hurried, self-paced (e.g., computer) atmosphere, or where a teacher might be conducting direct instruction, additional opportunities in story development and dramatization are necessary to provide a creative balance. For science and social studies, Diane would best be placed with a teacher who emphasizes transactional approaches such as the project method, hands-on experiences, and simulations. Given Diane's high energy level, an active role would be desirable for many of the science and social studies lessons.

Diane's athletic, creative problem solving, and expressive abilities should be recognized and encouraged by her special education, regular classroom, and physical education teachers. Further, Diane should be allowed to interact with children who have similar energy levels and creative problem-solving strengths. These opportunities would allow her to collaborate with peers rather than merely "taking charge of them." The need to be sensitive to Diane's difficulty with reading comprehension, writing skills, following written directions, and organizational skills should be brought to the attention of all teachers who work with her. One area in which Diane could begin to exercise more growth is in self-management. Many children who tend to have mood swings and an intense range of moods benefit from self-regulating behavior, which enables them to have more control over their moods and behavior, as opposed to seeing their life and actions as merely reacting to adult expectations.

SUMMARY

The three basic curriculum approaches can be categorized as transmission, transaction, and transformation. Within the transmission position, which has behaviorist theoretical roots, there are three major emphases: subject/discipline, competency-based education, and cultural transmission. The former centers on direct instructional techniques, traditional lecture and recitation, and textbook learning. The transmission orientation focuses upon teaching and learning specific subjects and academic disciplines. It is sometimes characterized by individualized approaches. According to the transaction position, education is an interactive process between the student, teacher, and curriculum, taking developmental needs into account. The central elements include: cognitive process, problem-solving, democratic citizenship, and inquiry within the discipline's orientation. Transformation encompasses two different ideologies: phenomenology, or humanism, and social change. Proponents see the child-centered curriculum as essential, especially the effects of curricular decisions upon self-esteem. Opponents, sometimes parents, see it as an invasion of privacy.

By integrating the transmission, transaction, and transformation approaches, curriculum developers can organize curriculum so that it responds to individual student needs. Gifted, general, and special educators can make significant contributions to the field of curriculum development through collaboration on the assessment of such needs. Although the changing political and economic climates seem to signify dramatic and sometimes divisive effects upon our educational system, the primary educational goals should stay at the forefront. As educators, we need to create and maintain the bridges within our profession, or we, too, will be mere passengers on the pendulum.

REFERENCES

Alschular, A. (1980). *School discipline: A socially literate solution*. New York: McGraw-Hill.
Apple, M. (1986). *Teachers and texts*. Boston: Routledge and Kegan Paul.
Apple, M., & King, N. (1977). What do schools teach? In R. H. Weller (Ed.), *Humanistic education*. Berkeley, CA: McCutchan.
Beyer, B. (1979). *Practical strategies for the teaching of thinking*. Boston: Allyn & Bacon.
Blenkin, G. M., & Kelly, A. V. (Eds.) (1983). *The primary curriculum in action*. New York: Harper & Row.
Bloom, B. S. (1956). *Taxonomy of educational objectives: Handbook I. Cognitive domain*. New York: Longman.
Bobbitt, F. (1918). *The curriculum*. Boston: Houghton Mifflin.
Brameld, T. (1950). *Ends and means in education*. New York: Harper & Row.
Brameld, T. (1950). *Patterns of educational psychology*. New York: World.
Bruner, J. (1959). *The process of education*. Cambridge, MA: Harvard University Press.
Bruner, J. (1966). *Toward a theory of instruction*. Cambridge, MA: Harvard University Press.
Central Advisory Council for Education. (1967). *Children and their primary schools (The Plowden Report)*. London: HMSO.
Charters, W. (1923). *Curriculum construction*. New York: Macmillan.
Combs, A. (1982). *A personal approach to teaching*. Boston: Allyn & Bacon.
Commission on Excellence in Education. (1983). *A nation at risk*. Washington, DC: U.S. Government Printing Office.
Conant, J. B. (1951). *Science and common sense*. New Haven, CT: Yale University Press.
Conlan, J. (1975, Oct.). MACOS: The push for a uniform national curriculum. *Social Education,* 388–392.
Cox, J., Daniel, N., & Boston, B. O. (1985). *Educating able learners*. Austin, TX: University of Texas Press.
Daniel, N., & Cox, J. (1988). *Flexible pacing for able learners*. Reston, VA: Council for Exceptional Children.
Dewey, J. (1938). *Experience and education*. New York: Macmillan.
Dow, P. (1975, Oct.). MACOS revisited: A commentary on the most frequently asked questions about "Man: A Course of Study." *Social Education,* 388–389, 393–396.
Driver, R., & Erickson, G. (1983). Theories-in-action: Some theoretical and empirical issues in the study of students' conceptual framework. *Studies in Science Education, 10,* 37–60.
Dunkin, M. J., & Biddle, B. J. (1974). *The study of teaching*. New York: Holt, Rinehart & Winston.
Eisner, E. W., & Vallance, E. (Eds.) (1974). *Conflicting conceptions of curriculum*. Berkeley: McCutchan Publishing.
Feldhusen, J., VanTassel-Baska, J., & Seeley, K. (1989). *Excellence in educating the gifted*. Denver: Love Publishing.
Feldhusen, J., & Kolloff, M. (1978). A three stage model for gifted education. *Gifted Child Today, 1,* 53–58.
Gagne, R. M. (1985). *The conditions of learning* (4th ed.). New York: Holt, Rinehart.
Giroux, H., & Purpel, D. (1983). *The hidden curriculum*. Berkeley, CA: McCutchen.
Guilford, J. (1967). *The nature of human intelligence*. New York: McGraw-Hill.
Gutek, G. (1970). *An historical introduction to American education*. New York: Thomas Crowell.
Herlihy, J. (1974, May). Man: A course of study: An exemplar of the new social studies. *Social Education,* 442–443, 455.
Hewson, M., & Hewson, P. (1981). *Effect of instruction using students' prior knowledge and conceptual change strategies on science learning*. Paper presented to meeting of the National Association for Research and Science Teaching (NARST), Ellenville, NY.
Inlow, G. (1964). *Maturity in high school teaching*. Englewood Cliffs, NJ: Prentice Hall.
Larkin, B. (1975, Nov./Dec.). News of our profession. *Social Education,* 445–450.

Lipman, M. (1984, September). The cultivation of reasoning through philosophy. *Educational Leadership,* pp. 51–56.

Lowi, T., & Ginsberg, B. (1990). *America's government.* New York: Norton.

Maslow, A. (1962). *Toward a psychology of being.* New York: Van Nostrand Reinhold.

Miller, J. P., & Seller, W. (1985). *Curriculum perspectives and practice.* New York: Longman.

Moore, C., & Yamamoto, K. (1988). *Beyond words: Movement observation and analysis.* New York: Gordon & Breach Science Publishers.

Neill, A. (1960). *Summerhill: A radical approach to child rearing.* New York: Hart.

Newmann, F. (1975). *Education for citizen action: Challenge for secondary curriculum.* Berkeley, CA: McCutchan.

Ornstein, A. C., & Hunkins, F. P. (1988). *Curriculum: Foundations, principles, and issues.* Englewood Cliffs, NJ: Prentice Hall.

Phenix, P. (1964). *Realms of meaning.* New York: McGraw-Hill.

Piaget, J. (1948). *Judgment and reasoning in the child.* New York: Harcourt Brace.

Posner, G. (1982). A cognitive science conception of curriculum and instruction. *Journal of Curriculum Studies, 14,* 343–351.

Purkey, W. (1970). *Self-concept and school achievement.* Englewood Cliffs, NJ: Prentice Hall.

Purkey, W. (1978). *Inviting school success: A self concept approach to teaching and learning.* Belmont, CA: Wadsworth.

Raths, L., Harmin, M., & Simon, S. (1978). *Values and teaching* (2nd ed.). Columbus, OH: Merrill.

Resnick, L., & Klopfer, L. (Eds.). (1989). Toward the thinking curriculum: An overview. *Toward the thinking curriculum: Current cognitive research* (1989 Yearbook of the Association for Supervision and Curriculum Development). Washington, DC: ASCD.

Renzulli, J. (1977). *The enrichment triad.* Wethersfield, CT: Creative Learning Press.

Rogers, C. (1983). *Freedom to learn for the 1980's* (2nd ed.). Columbus, OH: Merrill.

Schwab, G. (1962, July). The concept of the structure of a discipline. *Educational Record,* pp. 197–205.

Simpson, N. (1983). *Evaluation of Midwest Talent Search Summer program. Final report.* Evanston, IL: Northwestern University.

Stanley, J. (1980). On educating the gifted. *Educational Researcher, 9,* 8–12.

Steiner, R. (1975). *Education of the child in the light of anthroposophy.* London: Anthroposophic Press.

Steiner, R. (1976). *Practical advice to teachers.* London: Rudolph Steiner Press.

Sternberg, R. (1984, September). How can we teach intelligence? *Educational Leadership,* pp. 38–48.

Sternberg, R. (1986). Intelligence, wisdom, and creativity. *Educational Psychologist,* Summer, pp. 175–190.

Taba, H. (1962). *Curriculum development: Theory and practice.* New York: Harcourt Brace.

Torrance, E. P. (1965). *Rewarding creative behavior.* Englewood Cliffs, NJ: Prentice Hall.

Tyler, R. (1949). *Basic principles of curriculum and instruction.* Chicago: University of Chicago Press.

VanTassel-Baska, J. (1988). The ineffectiveness of the pull-out model in gifted education: A minority perspective. *Journal for the Education of the Gifted, 10*(4), 255–264.

VanTassel-Baska, J., Feldhusen, J., Seeley, K., Wheatley,G., Silverman, L., & Foster, W. (1988). *Comprehensive curriculum for gifted learners.* Boston: Allyn & Bacon.

Weinstein, G., & Fantini, M. D. (1970). *Toward humanistic education: A curriculum affect.* New York: Praeger.

CHAPTER THIRTEEN

Curricula for Exceptional Children: A Special Education Perspective

Virginia Laycock

A s the field of special education has evolved over the latter half of this century, it has focused attention on a number of issues vital to the education of exceptional learners. At times, however, concerns such as advocacy, eligibility, placement, legislation, and litigation have overshadowed other concerns critical to effective service delivery. In particular, insufficient attention has been given to curriculum, the actual content of special education programs (Laycock & Korinek, 1989; Meyen, 1988). Whereas the primary legacy of the 1970s is legal assurance of the educational rights of individuals with disabilities, the 1980s may be remembered as a decade of struggling to define the meaning of "appropriate" education for these learners. This search for quality as a step beyond compliance is now being directed to curricular issues.

These developments within the field of special education have relevance for gifted education. Although special education has concerned itself primarily with the needs of those with disabilities — learning disabilities, behavior disorders, mental retardation, physical, sensory, or health impairments — its overall commitment to education of exceptional learners extends to the gifted and talented as well. In the face of realities of public policy, funding resources, and organizational-administrative structures, the relationship between special and gifted education has been strained at times.

In particular, enactment of the Education for All Handicapped Children Act (PL 94–142) in 1975 charted a distinct course for special education. This act assured free, appropriate public education to all handicapped children, but it did not mandate comparable services for the gifted. Although some states have legislation for the gifted modeled after PL 94–142, no federal mandate impacts on gifted education in the same way that PL 94–142 and its subsequent amendments have shaped the field of special education.

Beyond the impact of the law, as both fields have matured, they have achieved more separate identities. Yet, both special and gifted education continue to have in common the imperative to differentiate school curriculum for those with special learning needs. Sharing perspectives on educating students with disabilities and giftedness may enrich the knowledge base in both professions.

CONCEPTS OF CURRICULA
FOR EXCEPTIONAL LEARNERS

Several terms have been used rather interchangeably in special education to refer to the education provided to students with disabilities. Curriculum itself has seldom been differentiated clearly from related aspects of programming, such as service delivery settings or instructional methods. Some have questioned whether there is such a thing as "special education curriculum" or whether it represents merely adaptations of the general or basal curriculum. Indeed, PL 94–142 defined special education as " . . specially designed instruction at no cost to parents to meet the unique needs of a handicapped child" (*Federal Register,* 1977). The law is silent on the issue of curriculum, focusing instead on instructional accommodations.

Curriculum itself has been defined as a structured series of intended learning outcomes (Johnson, 1968). At least four different types of curricula may be operative in any structured learning situation. Hoover (1987) has described three of them: (a) the *explicit curriculum,* the formal, stated curriculum that teachers and students are expected to follow; (b) the *hidden curriculum,* the curriculum the teacher interprets and implements in the classroom; and (c) *absent curriculum,* that which educators choose not to teach in the school and classroom. Gifted educators have referred to the explicit and hidden curriculum as the "intended" and "delivered" curriculum. They also have acknowledged the *received curriculum* as that internalized by students (VanTassel-Baska et al., 1988).

For many students with mild disabilities, the explicit or intended curriculum for general education is in fact appropriate. The way in which that curriculum is delivered is what determines how effectively it is received. To meet the special needs of these learners, a variety of instructional modifications may be necessary in both general and special education settings.

In certain areas of concern for students with mild disabilities, however, the schools offer no explicit curriculum. For example, students may be expected to acquire adequate personal-social skills, study skills, career preparation skills, and so forth on their own. Because these students tend to be poor incidental learners, they frequently need to be taught these types of skills directly. Curricular needs thus begin to differ when what is absent in the general curriculum has to be defined as an explicit curriculum for students with specific disabilities. For students with moderate to severe disabilities, the explicit curriculum of general education is even less appropriate. Radical adjustments in delivery would not be sufficient, because these individuals need more functional than academic content to maximize their independence in present and future environments.

I believe that a distinct special education curriculum is justifiable for certain students in certain curricular areas. The explicit curriculum for general education must be acknowledged as the standard, however; and educators must recognize the extent to which any departures from this standard curriculum may restrict, maintain, or expand students' options for successful functioning in more integrated settings.

THE IEP APPROACH TO CURRICULAR PLANNING

A hallmark of special education since its inception has been its emphasis on individualized education programs (IEPs) for students. By the mid-1970s, a number of alternative models were being used to guide program planning, implementation, and evaluation efforts. Although these models differed in their terminology, basic practices for systematic (McCormack et al., 1976; Snell, 1978), directive (Haring & Schiefelbusch, 1976; Stephens, 1977), programmed (Tawney et al., 1979), clinical (Lerner, 1976; Smith, 1974), prescriptive (Charles, 1976; Mercer, 1979; Moran, 1975; Peter, 1965), and precision (Bijou, Lindsley, & Haughton, 1972) teaching were highly similar. Furthermore, many states already had passed legislation to mandate documentation of individualized plans for students receiving special education services (Hayes & Higgins, 1978). This commitment to individualization was affirmed, and practices were made more consistent nationally when PL 94–142 mandated the development of a written individualized education program for every student receiving special education services.

The U.S. Department of Education (1981) has characterized the IEP as a communication vehicle between parents and school personnel; a written commitment of resources for special education and related services; a management tool for ensuring provision of specified services; a compliance/monitoring document for local, state, and federal agencies; and an evaluation device for determining student progress. From a curricular vantage-point, most educators view the IEP as essentially a management system for planning and monitoring the special education curriculum. To some, however, IEPs constitute the curriculum of special education. In any case, both the required processes for developing IEPs and the specific components included have greatly influenced curricular efforts in special education.

Several of the major provisions of PL 94–142 with particular relevance are summarized here to provide a context for understanding the IEP:

1. *Nondiscriminatory assessment.* Each student must receive a comprehensive individual evaluation before placement in a special education program. Tests and other evaluation procedures must be validated for the purposes used, and administered by trained personnel in the student's native language. No single measure should serve as the sole criterion for determining an appropriate program.
2. *Multidisciplinary involvement.* The comprehensive evaluation is to be conducted by a team of specialists, and the following individuals are to participate in developing the IEP: an administrative representative, the student's teacher, one or both of the student's parents, the student when appropriate, other individuals at the request of parents or public agency, and a member of the evaluation team if the student has been evaluated for the first time. Parent involvement is strongly emphasized.
3. *Least restrictive environment.* To the maximum extent possible, students with disabilities are to be educated with their nonhandicapped peers. A full continuum of services should be available, ranging from support services for instruction in the regular classroom to instruction in special classes, schools, hospitals, and institutions.

Components of the IEP

As specified in PL 94–142, the written IEP must contain:

1. A statement of the child's present level of educational performance, including academic achievement, social adaptation, prevocational and vocational skills, and self-help skills;
2. A statement of annual goals that describes the educational performance to be achieved by the end of the year under the child's IEP;
3. A statement of short-term instructional objectives, which must be measurable intermediate steps between the present level of educational performance and the annual goals;
4. A statement of specific educational services needed by the child (determined without regard to the availability of those services) including a description of:

a. All special education and related services needed to meet the unique needs of the child, including the type of physical education program in which the child will participate, and

b. any special instructional media and materials needed;

5. The date when those services will begin and the length of time the services will be given;

6. A description of the extent to which the child will participate in the regular program;

7. A justification for the type of educational placement the child will have;

8. A list of the individuals responsible for implementation of the IEP;

9. Objective criteria, evaluation procedures and schedules for determining, on at least an annual basis, whether the short-term instructional objectives are being achieved. (Section 121a, 225)

A written IEP encompassing all of the above components has been required since 1978 for every school-aged student receiving special education and related services. In Amendments to the Education of the Handicapped Act, PL 99–457 required that by 1991 states not already doing so had to begin developing IEPs and providing services to children with disabilities between ages 3 and 5.

PL 99–457 also created a counterpart of the IEP entitled an individualized family service plan (IFSP), to document early intervention services for infants and toddlers and their families. Although the basic components of the IFSP are similar to those of the IEP, a number of significant differences exist. The IFSP takes a family-centered approach, includes any services other than strictly medical services needed by the child or the family, demands coordination of interagency services, requires designation of a case manager, and specifies steps to support the transition from early intervention to school programs (Turnbull & Strickland, 1990). Although this chapter focuses on curricular needs of school-aged children, the expanded scope of the individualized plans for infants and toddlers who qualify for services should be recognized.

The sections of the IEP dealing with annual goals and short-term objectives specify the intended outcomes (i.e., the curricular content) of the student's program. Establishing these curricular priorities is one of the most difficult challenges for the team. Deciding what is most important for a given student at a particular point in time requires careful consideration of a number of factors, including the nature and severity of learner needs, learning history, age or grade level, critical needs in present environments, critical needs in the next less restrictive environment, and logical sequencing within each curricular area (Laycock, 1982). In practice, special education teachers frequently assume major responsibilities for writing goals and objectives and may refer to criterion-referenced tests, curriculum guides, and IEP decision-support systems or objective banks for assistance.

The IEP Approach in Gifted Education

Although conceived initially in the context of special education, the concept of the individualized education program has been extended to gifted and talented learners as well. As a system for curricular planning, it offers a structure to ensure that personalized programs are developed and revised annually with input from parents, teachers, related service personnel, and students themselves, where appropriate. The content of the document includes descriptions of current functioning, reasonable expectations for achievement over the coming year, and specific strategies for evaluation.

Several authors have discussed applications of the IEP approach to gifted education (Renzulli & Smith, 1988; Whitmore, 1985). The processes for development and the components to be included in the IEP for gifted education are nearly identical to the IEP for special education. The obvious difference is the definition of student needs and the goals, objectives, and services chosen to meet those needs. Whereas a special education IEP primarily targets performance deficits for intervention, the gifted education IEP primarily addresses areas of individual strength through advanced programming.

Because the IEP approach has become such a dominant model for exceptional learners, it has been adopted in many programs for the gifted. IEPs have been mandated for gifted education in 12 states, and 10 states have guaranteed due process procedural safeguards similar to those in PL 94–142 (Houseman, 1987; Karnes & Marquardt, 1988).

A 1988 Pennsylvania Supreme Court decision on gifted education (Centennial School District *v.* Department of Education) may have established a precedent for a court's recognition of individualized educational planning for the gifted. The court held that the school district's group enrichment program was not sufficient to provide an appropriate, individualized program for the gifted student. The school district must formulate an IEP and provide an appropriate program for the individual student, rather than relying on a general enrichment program as gifted education. This ruling, binding in Pennsylvania, is being hailed as a landmark decision likely to influence services, especially in the other 24 states with gifted education mandates (Karnes & Marquardt, 1988). Legally as well as educationally, the concept of individualized programming is being applied in gifted education.

Relationship of the IEP to Instruction

Because the IEP addresses all major components of an educational program for an entire year in most cases, curricular elements of the plan are somewhat broad-based and general in scope. In a sense, the IEP functions as a master plan or educational blueprint, giving direction to the more specific curricular and instructional programming that then must take place.

Figure 13.1 presents a general model for diagnostic-prescriptive teaching that is highly consistent with the IEP process (Laycock, 1982). The figure

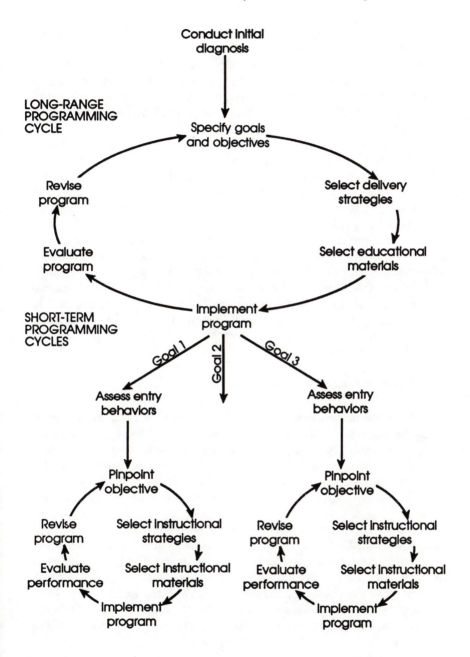

Figure 13.1
DIAGNOSTIC PRESCRIPTIVE TEACHING MODEL

illustrates the relationship between long- and short-term planning, as it shows the same sequence of seven basic steps being repeated at different levels of specificity. The student's needs are carefully identified (step 1) to guide selection of appropriate objectives, instructional strategies, and materials (steps 2, 3, and 4). The program is then implemented as planned (step 5). The remaining steps involve evaluation of program effectiveness (step 6) and revision of the program as necessary (step 7).

The large oval at the top represents the long-range programming cycle corresponding to development, implementation, and evaluation of the annual IEP. The second tier of the diagram presents a series of shorter-term programming cycles occurring during the implementation phase of the IEP. As illustrated, each long-range goal is addressed through its own carefully designed program. At times, several different goals may be clustered to be addressed through an integrated curricular program. These minicycles are roughly analogous to instructional units. Even a third tier could be added to the diagram to illustrate further refinement of the process for daily lesson planning, delivery, and evaluation.

Through this systematic diagnostic-prescriptive process, the defined curriculum is translated into specific instructional experiences for the learner. The *intended* curriculum documented in the IEP, unit, and lesson plans becomes the curriculum *delivered* to the student to permit evaluation of what has been learned, the *internalized curriculum.*

The Diagnostic-Prescriptive Approach in Gifted Education

The diagnostic-prescriptive approach in special education has its counterpart in gifted education. For the gifted, the diagnostic prescriptive approach is most relevant for modification of core curricular content. The point of entree for both models is pretesting to determine an individual's level of functioning in reference to defined scope and sequence. Not only is the instructional program individually paced, but the curricular content is also restructured to promote effective mastery learning.

In special education, this is likely to mean paring down objectives to essential outcomes and breaking up these objectives into smaller steps through task analysis for a slower instructional pace overall. In contrast, the diagnostic-prescriptive approach for gifted education should allow for fast-paced, compressed, economized versions of the regular curriculum (VanTassel-Baska, 1986). Thus, though the general processes are highly similar, the diagnostic-prescriptive approaches yield nearly opposite curricular accommodations to meet the unique needs of students with disabilities and the gifted.

Limitations of the IEP Approach to Curriculum

The IEP and related diagnostic prescriptive processes described are essential for special education, not only to ensure compliance with federal mandates but, more important, to promote tailoring of educational programs to individual student needs. The IEP has become a necessary component of curricular planning in special education, but it is not sufficient. In fact, its powerful emphasis on individualization may have left many special educators without a more comprehensive framework for conceptualizing curriculum (Laycock & Korinek, 1989). The absence of curricular bases to provide direction to special education programs has created a void that often results in haphazard decision making (Goldstein, 1986).

Teachers frequently derive their objectives from the results of testing without recognizing that the very choice of assessment instruments already constitutes a decision about curricular priorities. Team members measure student performance only in the areas perceived as most relevant, or perhaps in the areas for which assessment devices are most familiar and available. Furthermore, many of the standardized tests used to drive IEP decision making are technically inadequate for disabled students and inappropriate for the purposes of planning curricula and instruction as well (Ysseldyke & Algozzine, 1983).

In addition, the sheer magnitude of the IEP may discourage sufficient attention to its curricular components. Decisions regarding placement (where the program is to be delivered) frequently take precedence over decisions regarding goals and objectives (what constitutes the program). The many details of service delivery to be spelled out in the IEP may detract from its most essential curricular function — specification of the program's intended learning outcomes.

Finally, a singular focus on the annual IEP may easily result in skewed and disjointed programming over time. From year to year, programs may address academic, social, behavioral, career-vocational, and other needs in haphazard fashion. The lack of cohesion and continuity may actually increase the restrictiveness of educational programming by limiting students' options and failing to equip them with necessary skills to negotiate the demands of less restrictive settings. For the IEP to function effectively as a curricular tool, it must be referenced to a more comprehensive conceptual model that incorporates a full range of curricular options for special education, accommodates changing priorities for individual students over time, and promotes systematic movement toward less restrictive curricula (Laycock & Korinek, 1989).

CONCEPTUAL FRAMEWORKS
FOR CURRICULAR PLANNING

In response to the need for a more comprehensive framework to assist educators in programming for students with disabilities, several models have been developed in recent years. These models have advanced understanding of the range of available program and curricular options, particularly for learners with mild disabilities (Deshler, Schumaker, Lenz, & Ellis, 1984; Polloway, Patton, Epstein, & Smith, 1989; Zigmond, Sansone, Miller, Donahoe, & Kohnke, 1986).

A model proposed by Laycock and Korinek (1989) specifically highlights the relationship of curriculum to other critical aspects of educational programming. The concentric circles in Figure 13.2 depict a series of distinct but interrelated areas for decision making when educators attempt to develop least restrictive educational programs. Consideration moves from the major influences that shape curricula to alternative curricular options and content areas to instructional methods and settings for service delivery. This progression corresponds to the logical and intended sequence of steps for developing individual student IEPs. As a comprehensive guide, the model delineates a menu of options in each category that may then be selected and tailored to individual student needs.

Placement of examples on Figure 13.2 schematically represents typical interrelationships among components and the need for appropriate matching of curricular, instructional, and service delivery options in response to changing priorities for educational programs.

Components of the Model

A brief overview of the specific components of the model follows.

Sources of Influence

Curriculum development efforts require judgments to include and exclude certain content. The knowledge bases and value systems that influence these curricular decisions form the backdrop or grounding for the model. These sources of influence, the primary origins of teachable content, include: (a) student needs and interests, (b) academic disciplines and organized subject matter, and (c) societal values and ecological demands. Although all three sources must be taken into account, their relative importance varies with individual students. Priorities for any individual also may shift over time.

Curricular Options

The outer band of the model shows a range of curricular options emanating from the three primary sources of influence. Placement on Figure 13.2 is intended to suggest the relative strength of the influences that have shaped that curricular option. The standard curriculum, for example, has been placed near academic subjects as a source of influence because that curriculum is driven primarily by the structure of the disciplinary subject matter. Other major curricular options are positioned around the band as follows: parallel alternate curriculum, remedial basic skills, thematic units, affective education, social-behavioral skills, career-vocational education, and learning strategies. Each of these curricular options for special education is described later in the chapter.

Curricular Content

The second band specifies the nature of curricular content or the intended learning outcomes. Eleven curricular content areas are presented as particularly relevant for students with special needs: academic subjects, basic skills, high-interest current issues, intrapersonal skills, leisure-recreational skills, behavioral

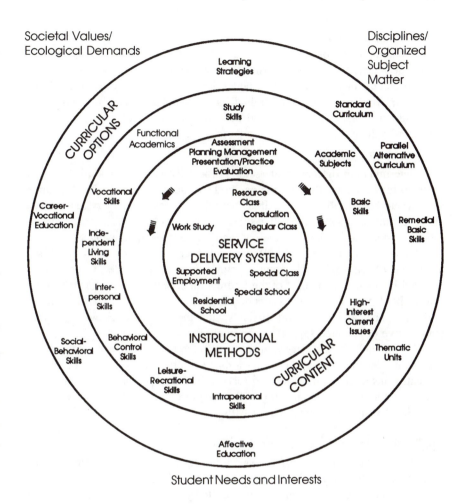

Societal Values/
Ecological Demands

Disciplines/
Organized
Subject
Matter

Learning
Strategies

CURRICULAR OPTIONS

Study
Skills

Standard
Curriculum

Functional
Academics

Assessment
Planning Management
Presentation/Practice
Evaluation

Academic
Subjects

Parallel
Alternative
Curriculum

Vocational
Skills

Career-
Vocational
Education

Inde-
pendent
Living
Skills

Inter-
personal
Skills

Resource
Class

Consulation

Work Study   Regular Class

SERVICE
DELIVERY SYSTEMS

Supported   Special Class
Employment

Special School

Residential
School

Basic
Skills

Remedial
Basic
Skills

High-
Interest
Current
Issues

Social-
Behavioral
Skills

Behavioral
Control
Skills

INSTRUCTIONAL
METHODS

Leisure-
Recreational
Skills

Intrapersonal
Skills

CURRICULAR
CONTENT

Thematic
Units

Affective
Education

Student Needs and Interests

Figure 13.2
COMPONENTS OF THE CONCEPTUAL MODEL

Source: Adapted from "Toward Least Restrictive Curriculum for Behaviorally Disordered Adolescents" by V. K. Laycock and L. Korinek in *Programming for Adolescents with Behavioral Disorders* (Vol. 4), edited by S. L. Braaten, R. B. Rutherford, Jr., T. F. Reilly, and S. A. Di Gang, 1989, Reston, VA: Council for Children with Behavior Disorders.

control skills, interpersonal skills, independent living skills, vocational skills, functional academics, and study skills. Again, these are located on the model to suggest linkages with sources of influence and curricular options. The lack of one-to-one correspondence can be confusing; some curricular programs address multiple content areas and, conversely, some content areas are included in multiple curricular programs.

Instructional Methods

The components of the model discussed thus far have dealt with the explicit or intended curriculum. The next band deals with instructional methods to deliver the curriculum. Positioning on the model depicts the sequence of instructional decisions. Alignment with surrounding bands is not an issue, as assessment, planning, presentation, practice, and management strategies are central to all curricular content areas.

Service Delivery Systems

Determination of appropriate settings for delivery of curricula is the final decision for educational programming. In the center of Figure 13.2 is the range of alternatives typically included in a continuum or cascade of services: regular class, regular class with consultative support, resource class, special class, special school, residential school, work study, and supported employment.

Laycock and Korinek (1989) provide several examples to illustrate the usefulness of this model. The standard curriculum, for example, would be represented by a slice or segment of the figure with organized subject matter at the rim as the driving influence, academic subjects as curricular content, a variety of instructional and evaluation methods, and the regular class with possibly consultative or resource support as the likely service delivery modes.

This model offers a context or frame of reference for educators engaged in curriculum development by depicting a range of options and linking curricular content to instructional methods and service delivery systems. The macro view stimulates more effective planning at the program level, and ultimately, at the micro level with the development of IEPs.

Applications in Gifted Education

Because the model described was designed to conceptualize curricula for students with disabilities, it represents a special education perspective. Many aspects of the model, however, are relevant for gifted education. The schematic itself reflects a sequence for decision making that is useful in gifted as well as special education. The sources of influence are operable on curricula for all learners, although, as noted, their relative impact may vary depending upon defined priorities. The specific curricular options, curricular content, instructional methods, and service delivery systems described for special education have their counterparts in gifted education. To focus directly on curriculum, only the curricular analogs will be explored in more detail.

Remedial Basic Skills and the Concept Mastery Model

The curricular alternative most frequently employed in special education is remedial basic skills (Deshler et al., 1984). Based on the assumption that proficiency in the tool subject areas is essential for further learning, the intent of this approach is to identify and correct specific deficits in reading, language arts, and mathematics. The approach is highly individualized as students progress at their own rates through defined sequences of skills. An analog in gifted education is the *content mastery model* (VanTassel-Baska, 1986).

Both of these curricular approaches represent departures from the standard curriculum through combined efforts to restructure the subject matter and adjust the pacing. These models obviously differ from one another in the direction of curricular modifications. A remedial approach involves deceleration of the curriculum through more fine-grained analysis of component skills to accommodate delayed development of students with disabilities. The content mastery approach, on the other hand, involves *acceleration* of the curriculum by compressing content into larger increments to accommodate the advanced abilities of gifted learners.

Parallel Alternative Curricula and Compacted Curricula

Although the remedial basic skills model is the dominant approach in special education for elementary students, a parallel alternative curriculum is often preferred for meeting the needs of adolescents with mild disabilities in the content areas. This approach emphasizes instructional accommodations to promote mastery of essential objectives from the standard curriculum in English, mathematics, science, social studies, and other content areas. Because the curricular content remains intact, students earn appropriate credits toward graduation. Students with special needs are typically grouped for instruction that incorporates alternative delivery and evaluation strategies (Hartwell, Wiseman, & VanReusen, 1979).

The counterpart of this approach for gifted learners is the *compacted curriculum*. Academic content is delivered to students in more homogeneous groups through modified instructional procedures tailored to their unique learning characteristics. Again, although the basic premise may be the same for parallel alternative and compacted curricula, the specific instructional modifications are quite different for handicapped and gifted learners.

Thematic Units

In both special and gifted education, thematic units are popular curricular options. Typically, interdisciplinary content is organized around issues or themes of special interest to the learners. The students themselves take an active role in shaping the course of study through cooperative and independent activities. Community resources may be used extensively.

Beyond these common characteristics of a unit approach, thematic units function quite differently in special and gifted education. For learners with disabilities, the unit provides a vehicle for addressing basic skill development (e.g., reading, written expression, mathematics) in a more meaningful and functional context. The actual content or subject matter of the unit may be a secondary consideration. Units also provide important motivational tools to capture or maintain interest, and even attendance.

Thematic units serve different purposes in gifted education. More complex topics and issues are chosen to encourage an epistemological orientation. Desired outcomes include heightened perceptions and insights as well as aesthetic appreciation of the nature, structure, and power of knowledge.

Learning Strategies and Process/Research Approach

One of the most recent curricular developments in special education is the *learning strategies approach*. Based largely upon the work of Donald Deshler and his associates at the University of Kansas, the learning strategies approach emphasizes principles, rules, and techniques that enable students to learn, solve problems, and complete tasks independently (Deshler & Shumaker, 1986; Ellis & Lenz, 1987). Although specific curricular content varies with academic subject matter, environmental demands, and student abilities, strategies have been developed in areas such as note taking, paragraph writing, test taking, error monitoring, comprehension, mnemonics, and self-questioning, as well as in some areas of social functioning. Additional executive strategies have been defined to help students apply higher-order organizational and learning skills.

The emphasis on generic problem identification and problem solving makes the learning strategies approach similar in many respects to the *process/research model* in gifted education. Through both approaches, students develop more effective strategies or processes for acquiring, organizing, retaining, and expressing information. A major difference is in the level of sophistication of the learning strategies versus the research approach. Whereas learning strategies are intended to empower students to cope with the demands of an educational setting and to become more effective lifelong learners, the intent of the research approach for gifted learners is to prepare them to produce knowledge. The latter is far less structured and directive. The gifted curriculum is organized to promote not only investigatory skills but also appreciation of the scientific inquiry process and creativity in its pursuit.

Social Skills, Affective Education, and Leadership Development

For students with emotional/behavioral disorders, affective development and interpersonal functioning have been primary areas of concern. In recent years, special educators have recognized that these are critical needs of nearly all children and adolescents with disabling conditions. Developing social competence has thus become a major curricular priority in special education. The majority of programs emphasize basic communication skills and problem solving or negotiation. Effective programs include training both in specific skills and in situations, to promote generalization and maintenance in natural environments (Korinek, 1989; Schumaker, Pederson, Hazel, & Meyen, 1983).

The emphasis so far in special education has been on coping and survival (Robinson, Braxdale, & Colson, 1985; Silverman, Zigmond, & Sansone, 1981). The curriculum has focused on identified skill deficits of the population of special needs students. Although some gifted students do have difficulty in personal-social adjustment, their needs are more likely to be addressed through counseling than an explicit curricular program. Curricular goals for the gifted in the affective domain have generally encouraged self-understanding, inner consistency, ethical standards, and appreciation of one's own uniqueness and responsibility to society (Maker, 1986; Passow, 1986). Interpersonal skills have been emphasized in the area of leadership development.

Career/Vocational Education and Arts Curriculum

In the early 1970s, career education became a curricular thrust in both general and special education. Broadly defined, it emphasizes the totality of experience through which one learns about and prepares to engage in work (Hoyt, 1975). In special education, the concept of "life-centered education" (Kokaska & Brolin, 1985) has prevailed. Although vocational skills are included, the curriculum encompasses functional academics, intra- and interpersonal skills, leisure-recreational skills, and independent living skills as well. Career education is conceived as a K–12 curriculum. In the elementary years, key concepts are infused into the curriculum; career and specific vocational education become more explicit curricular foci in secondary schools. For learners with more severe disabilities, the entire school curriculum has a strong functional emphasis to prepare individuals for maximum independence in home, school, work, and community environments.

Career education has a less explicit role in gifted education. Career awareness and exploration may be infused into the curriculum, and more focused preparation addressed through internships and mentorships. One facet of the life-centered approach that has been emphasized for the gifted and talented is the arts curriculum. The visual arts, music, drama, and dance may be woven into the core curriculum or represent disciplines in their own right. Magnet schools in the arts provide one option for talented students to pursue the arts more comprehensively. Overall, curriculum in the arts varies greatly, and talented students often rely on private instruction to be sufficiently challenged (Seeley, 1988).

SUMMARY

Characterization of current practices has to acknowledge the role of the individualized education program, as this federal mandate has become the standard curriculum planning approach in special education. One comprehensive IEP model emphasizes the range of curricular options appropriate for different learners at different points in their school careers. Although no federal mandate comparable to PL 94–142 has driven practice in gifted education, special and gifted education share many common orientations. The IEP approach for the gifted, required by law in 12 states, has offered a rubric for individualized programming for the gifted.

The major curricular options in special education have counterparts or analogs in gifted education. In many instances, the ways in which the standard curriculum can be modified or extended for exceptional learners are highly similar. The major difference in programming for handicapped and gifted students stems from the specific purposes for differentiating the curriculum. Handicapped learners need curricula that address their weak areas in order to maximize their participation in mainstream society; gifted learners need curricula that challenge their strengths in order to manipulate potential. This distinction is central to our understanding of the divergence of curriculum development efforts of the two fields.

REFERENCES

Bijou, S. W., Lindsley, O. R., & Haughton, E. (Eds.). (1972). *Let's try doing something else kind of thing: Behavioral principles and the exceptional child.* Reston, VA: Council for Exceptional Children.

Charles, C. M. (1976). *Individualizing instruction.* St. Louis: C. V. Mosby.

Deshler, D. D., Shumaker, J. B., Lenz, B. K., & Ellis, E. S. (1984). Academic and cognitive interventions for LD adolescents: Part 2. *Journal of Learning Disabilities, 17*(3), 170–187.

Deshler, D. D., & Schumaker, J. B. (1986). Learning strategies: An instructional alternative for low-achieving adolescents. *Exceptional Children, 52,* 583–590.

Ellis, E. S., & Lenz, B. K. (1987). A component analysis of effective learning strategies for LD students. *Learning Disabilities Focus, 2*(2), 94–107.

Federal Register. (1977, August). (Vol. 42, pp. 42474–42515). Washington, DC: U.S. Government Printing Office.

Goldstein, M. T. (1986). Curriculum: The keystone for special education planning. *Teaching Exceptional Children, 18*(3), 220–223.

Haring, N. G., & Schiefelbusch, R. L. (1976). *Teaching special children.* New York: McGraw-Hill.

Hartwell, J. D., Wiseman, D. E., & Van Reusen, A. V. (1979). Modifying course content for mildly handicapped students at the secondary level. *Teaching Exceptional Children, 12,* 28–32.

Hayes, J., & Higgins, S. (1978). Issues regarding the IEP: Teachers on the front line. *Exceptional Children, 44*(4), 267–273.

Hoover, J. J. (1987). Preparing special educators for mainstreaming: An emphasis upon curriculum. *Teacher Education & Special Education, 10*(2), 58–64.

Houseman, W. (1987). *State of the states gifted and talented education report.* Topeka: Kansas State Department of Education, Council of State Directors of Programs for the Gifted.

Hoyt, K. B. (1975). *An introduction to career education: A policy paper of the U.S. Office of Education.* Washington, DC: U.S. Office of Education.

Johnson, M., Jr. (1968). Definitions and models in curriculum theory. In E. C. Short & G. D. Marconnit (Eds.), *Contemporary thought on public school curriculum* (pp. 42–50). Dubuque, IA: Wm. C. Brown.

Karnes, F. A., & Marquardt, R. G. (1988). The Pennsylvania Supreme Court decision on gifted education. *Gifted Child Quarterly, 32*(4), 360–361.

Kokaska, C. J., & Brolin, D. E. (1985). *Career education for handicapped individuals* (3rd ed.). Columbus, OH: Merrill.

Korinek, L. (1989, September). *Social skills programs for behaviorally disordered students.* Paper presented at Council for Children with Behavior Disorders Conference, Charlotte, NC.

Laycock, V. K. (1982). Basic educational practices. In J. G. Greer, R. M. Anderson, & S. J. Odle (Eds.), *Strategies for helping severely and multiply handicapped citizens* (pp. 43–76). Baltimore: University Park Press.

Laycock, V. K., & Korinek, L. A. (1989). Toward least restrictive curriculum for behaviorally disordered adolescents. In S. L. Braaten, R. B. Rutherford, Jr., T. F. Reilly, & S. A. DiGamgi

(Eds.), *Programming for adolescents with behavioral disorders* (Vol. 4, pp. 11–25). Reston, VA: Council for Children with Behavior Disorders.

Lerner, J. L. (1976). *Children with learning disabilities* (2nd ed.). Boston: Houghton Mifflin.

Maker, C. J. (1986). Developing scope and sequence in curriculum. *Gifted Child Quarterly, 30*(4), 151–157.

McCormack, J. E., et al. (1976). *Systematic instruction for the severely handicapped: Teaching sequences.* Medford, MA: Massachusetts Center for Program Development and Evaluation.

Mercer, C. D. (1979). *Children and adolescents with learning disabilities.* Columbus, OH: Charles E. Merrill.

Meyen, E. L. (1988). Current instructional practices. In E. L. Meyen & T. M. Skrtic (Eds.), *Exceptional children and youth: An introduction* (pp. 49–79). Denver: Love Publishing.

Meyen, E. L. (1981). *Developing instructional units* (3rd ed.). Dubuque, IA: Wm. C. Brown.

Moran, M. R. (1975). Nine steps to the diagnostic prescriptive process in the classroom. *Focus on Exceptional Children, 6*(9), 1–14.

Passow, A. H. (1986). Curriculum for the gifted and talented at the secondary level. *Gifted Child Quarterly, 30*(4), 186–191.

Peter, J. L. (1965). *Prescriptive teaching.* New York: McGraw-Hill.

Polloway, E. A., Patton, J. R., Epstein, M. H., & Smith, T. E. D. (1989). Comprehensive curriculum for students with mild handicaps. *Focus on Exceptional Children, 21*(8), 1–12.

Public Law 94–142. (1975). 94th Congress, S.6. Education for All Handicapped Children Act of 1975, November 29, 1975.

Public Law 99–457. (1986). 94th Congress, S.2294. Education of the Handicapped Act Amendments of 1986., October 8, 1986.

Renzulli, J. S., & Smith, L. H. (1988). A practical model for designing individual education programs (IEPs) for gifted and talented students. *Gifted Child Today, 11*(1), 34–40.

Robinson, S. M., Braxdale, C. T., & Colson, S. E. (1985). Preparing dysfunctional learners to enter junior high school: A transitional curriculum. *Focus on Exceptional Children, 16*(4), 1–12.

Schumaker, J. B., Pederson, C. S., Hazel, J. S., & Meyen, E. L. (1983). Social skills curricula for mildly handicapped adolescents: A review. *Focus on Exceptional Children, 16*(4), 1–16.

Seeley, K. (1988). Arts curriculum for the gifted. In J. VanTassel-Baska, J. Feldhusen, K., Seeley, G. Wheatley, L. Silverman, & W. Foster (Eds.), *Comprehensive curriculum for gifted learners* (pp. 300–313). Boston: Allyn & Bacon.

Silverman, R., Zigmond, N., & Sansone, J. (1981). Teaching coping skills to adolescents with learning problems. *Focus on Exceptional Children, 18*(6), 1–20.

Smith, R. M. (1974). *Clinical teaching: Methods of instruction for the retarded.* New York: McGraw-Hill.

Snell, M. E. (Ed.). (1978). *Systematic instruction of the moderately and severely handicapped.* Columbus, OH: Merrill.

Stephens, T. M. (1977). *Teaching skills to children with learning and behavior disorders.* Columbus, OH: Merrill.

Tawney, J. W., et al. (1979). *Programmed environments curriculum: A curriculum handbook for teaching basic skills to severely handicapped persons.* Columbus, OH: Merrill.

Turnbull, A. P., & Strickland, B. B. (1990). *Developing and implementing individualized education programs* (3rd ed). Columbus, OH: Merrill.

U.S. Department of Education (1981). *Assistance to states for educating handicapped children: Interpretation of the individualized education program (IEP).* Washington, DC: U.S. Government Printing Office.

VanTassel-Baska, J. (1986). Effective curriculum and instructional models for talented students. *Gifted Child Quarterly, 30*(4), 164–169.

VanTassel-Baska, J., Feldhusen, J., Seeley, K., Wheatley, G., Silverman, L., & Foster, W. (1988). *Comprehensive curriculum for gifted learners.* Boston: Allyn & Bacon.

Whitmore, J. R. (1985). *Developing individualized education programs (IEPs) for the gifted and talented*. Reston, VA: ERIC Clearinghouse on Handicapped and Gifted Children.

Ysseldyke, J. E., & Algozzine, B. (1983). On making psychoeducation decisions. *Journal of Psychoeducational Assessment, 1*(2), 187–195.

Zigmond, N., Sansone, J., Miller, S. E., Donahoe, K. A., & Kohnke, R. (1986). *Teaching learning disabled students at the secondary level*. Reston, VA: Council for Exceptional Children.

CHAPTER FOURTEEN

Gifted Children with Specific Learning Disabilities

Lori Korinek

O nly in the past decade has it been widely acknowledged that giftedness and specific learning disabilities (LD) could coexist within the same learner. The field, however, is far from translating this recognition into systematic identification and programming for students with gifts and talents as well as learning disabilities. Probably no two educational terms are more fraught with controversy or more difficult to operationally define in a way that garners appropriate services for the students involved than the terms "gifted" and "learning disabled." In this chapter the term "gifted learning disabled" will be used to refer succinctly to students who demonstrate characteristics of both categories. The intent is that the child be the primary focus and characteristics associating him or her with any label or category be considered only in terms of their helpfulness in securing needed services for the student.

Some may question the necessity of programming for students who, in the general school program, may show few of the positive behaviors, such as leadership and communication skills, typically associated with gifted individuals. Nor do many of the gifted learning disabled manifest the obvious inability to perform near grade level as LD youngsters typically do; their disabilities may be more subtle. But the arguments for identifying and serving gifted learning disabled students are numerous and compelling. The longer the delay in providing appropriate instruction, the greater is the difficulty in helping the child overcome problems and achieve his or her potential. Failure to identify and serve these students who typically require assistance to develop their gifts results in tremendous individual and social losses, compared to the considerable benefits to them and society to be realized by nurturing their talents (Daniels, 1983; Marland, 1972; Williams, 1988). Student motivation and attitudes toward school and continued learning deteriorate when their unique educational needs are not being met. Failure to address these needs also puts students at risk for low self-esteem, which may lead to negative behaviors and further decrease their opportunities for an appropriate educational program — a challenging curriculum in areas of strength coupled with assistance for their specific learning disabilities (Tannenbaum & Baldwin, 1983). Students with learning disabilities also have a legal right to a free appropriate public education under the Education for All Handicapped Children Act of 1975 (PL 94–142). For the gifted child with learning disabilities, "appropriate" means a program that attends to areas of strength as well as weakness, allowing the child to benefit from his or her education.

CHARACTERISTICS OF GIFTED CHILDREN WITH LEARNING DISABILITIES

The task of characterizing, identifying, and serving gifted children with learning disabilities is complex and inexact at best (Fox & Brody, 1983; Silverman, 1989; Tannenbaum & Baldwin, 1983; Vaughn, 1989; Waldron, Saphire, & Rosenblum, 1987; Whitmore & Maker, 1985). Issues and concerns related to the gifted population in general also apply to gifted learning disabled students. Matters are further complicated by problems inherent in the field of learning disabilities, including all of the major aspects of program development: assessment, identification, intervention, and service delivery.

The most widely quoted federal definition of learning disabilities in PL 94–142 sets forth the following criteria for a specific learning disability: (a) average or above average intellectual potential; (b) a disorder in the basic psychological processes (attention, perception, and processing of information); (c) significant discrepancy between potential and actual performance in one or more areas including oral expression, written expression, basic reading skills, listening comprehension, reading comprehension, mathematical calculation, and mathematical reasoning; and (d) learning problems not due primarily to a visual, motor, or hearing handicap; mental retardation; emotional disturbance; or environmental, cultural, or economic deprivation. The child may have severe problems in one or more areas, mild problems across several areas, or other combinations of specific disabilities and severity levels.

Discrepancy formulas are frequently used to determine the presence of a severe discrepancy between intellectual ability and achievement or between task performance and academic areas, but there is little agreement on which formula is best or how severe the discrepancy has to be for an individual to qualify for services. The task of operationally defining LD in terms of specific requirements for services falls upon the local school districts. Here, multidisciplinary teams determine if an individual has a specific learning disability in relation to the federal criteria and locally determined cut-off scores on assessment measures. As with gifted students, the resulting group of individuals identified as LD is extremely heterogeneous, requiring many variations in programming to meet unique educational needs. Obviously, even more diversity is introduced when a child shows both giftedness and learning disabilities.

Ironically, students who are both gifted and LD are often overlooked for services in either category because of the masking effect of one condition upon the other. The LD may contribute to depressed scores on standardized tests typically used to identify gifted students for special programs. On the other hand, the creativity and compensating abilities may enable the gifted LD student (with great effort) to achieve at or near grade level, masking his or her need for specialized services in specific areas of weakness. Frequently the exceptionality is discovered only when the child's disability (more typically) or giftedness is extreme enough to warrant referral for additional assessment to determine eligibility for special programs. Rosner and Seymour (1983) contend that *unless* the child is performing remarkably above or below grade level, referral is unlikely. In other cases, social, emotional, or personality problems trigger more in-depth assessment likely to uncover traits associated with exceptionality (Senf, 1983).

Given the many possible manifestations of specific learning disabilities and giftedness, complicated by the interaction of the two conditions, no single set of characteristics typifies all or even most gifted LD individuals. The literature offers many characteristics based upon case studies, personal reports, school and clinical observations, and a relatively small body of descriptive research with these students. Tannenbaum and Baldwin (1983) use the term "paradoxical" to describe gifted learning disabled students who defy stereotypes of either exceptionality.

Academic Characteristics

Depending upon the nature and severity of their learning disabilities and their strengths, gifted LD students may or may not demonstrate specific characteristics associated with either separate category. They may display exceptional reasoning, analytic abilities, and comprehension of complex concepts, relationships and principles, but may have difficulty with basic skills such as phonetically decoding words, spelling, and recalling simple math facts. A child with weak visual memory and extreme reading difficulties may use exceptional reasoning ability to spell phonetically, memorize information presented auditorally, and rely on context clues to understand text (Weill, 1987). Another child may clearly excel in areas such as math, science, art, music, business, or electronics, but appear to have limited capabilities in other academic subjects. The gifted LD child may do well in class discussions but perform poorly on tests of achievement. He or she may fail easier test items and pass higher-level ones, or perform better on complex tasks than simpler ones (Tannenbaum & Baldwin, 1983).

A sophisticated sense of humor and well developed vocabulary are common in these children, yet some may have difficulty interpreting humorous remarks and social cues/nuances that negatively affect their personal interactions. The gifted LD child may have a wide variety of interests or intense interest and concentration/perseverance in a particular area yet be highly distractible and impulsive in other academic tasks (Daniels, 1983; Fox, 1983; Gunderson, Maesch, & Rees, 1987; Silverman, 1989; Vaughn, 1989; Whitmore & Maker, 1985).

Unevenness — in academic growth, in demonstrated areas of competence, and in interests — seems to be the hallmark of the gifted LD child. Unfortunately, teachers and others often interpret this unevenness as evidence that the child is not truly gifted (Silverman, 1989). Observers may focus upon the child's weaknesses or identified learning disabilities to the exclusion of his or her strengths. This results in lack of attention to areas of potential and underreferral of these children for gifted programs.

Psychosocial Characteristics

The psychosocial characteristics manifested by a child with gifts and specific learning disabilities often seem to reflect attempts at reconciling areas of strength, interest, and understanding with difficulties encountered in subjects or skills affected by the learning disabilities. In some instances, students with great potential in leadership and interpersonal skills use their social skills to compensate for or distract attention from weaker areas. On the other hand, perceptual, processing, memory, or motor problems may result in poor listening and concentration, slow reactions or extreme levels of activity, poor organization and study skills, and difficulty adapting to new situations and environmental demands. These students may feel perplexed, frustrated, or anxious because of their difficulty with tasks that are apparently easy for peers. Continued difficulty over time, failure to live up to their own typically high expectations of themselves, and lack of success in the curriculum may lead to decreased self-esteem, passivity, defensiveness, and negativity (Udall, 1985).

Gifted LD children also may employ defense mechanisms such as denial, withdrawal, and attention seeking (Weill, 1987) or intellectualization, demonstrated by their becoming extremely knowledgable about specific subjects or trivia experts (Rosner & Seymour, 1983). Or behavior patterns may be more overtly negative and include expressions of boredom, intense criticism of the school program and personnel, diversion of discussions to topics of greater interest, creative avoidance of difficult tasks, or outright refusal to perform in weak areas. These characteristics further distract teachers' and others' attention from seeing and dealing with the child's areas of strengths and recognizing the behavior for what it is rather than attending to the behavior in its "presenting" form. Rather than being identified as gifted, the gifted LD child often is seen as disruptive, uncooperative, inattentive, disorganized, and antisocial (Bryan & McGrady, 1972).

Socially, gifted LD children may have difficulty identifying with and relating to either general class or learning disabled peers. Their peers typically fail to demonstrate similar interests and understanding in areas of strength, yet readily master skills that present great difficulty for the gifted LD student. When participating in programs for the gifted, this individual also may have problems relating to other students whose gifts and talents are not affected by disabilities. Fragile self-concepts and sometimes overtly negative behavior patterns may impair the gifted LD child's social relationships and add to the cycle of frustration most of these children experience unless they receive appropriate identification and intervention.

IDENTIFICATION OF GIFTED CHILDREN WITH LEARNING DISABILITIES

Difficulties in identifying gifted LD individuals are well documented in the literature (e.g., Daniels, 1983; Maker, 1977; Senf, 1983; Tannenbaum & Baldwin, 1983; Waldron, Saphire, & Rosenblum, 1987). Because of the complex interactions of giftedness and LD within any child and the wide variety of characteristics that may manifest this dual exceptionality, identification of gifted LD individuals requires the use of multiple measures of potential and performance. Eligibility for services under the category of learning disabilities requires completion of medical, psychological, educational, and social/cultural assessments by qualified personnel. Measures typically include standardized intelligence and aptitude tests and various indicators of academic achievement. Eligibility committees rely on data from these assessments, and observation, to determine if the child is eligible for special education because of his or her learning disabilities.

In addition to standardized assessments used to identify learning disabilities, other measures that can add valuable data about the child's unique pattern of strengths and weaknesses include curriculum-based measures, teacher recommendations or checklists, measures of creativity, student products, and information from parents, peers, and the students themselves. These may indicate giftedness as well as LD. In the case of a gifted child with milder disabilities, these less traditional procedures and observations may initially alert educators to the child's strengths and follow-up assessments might reveal the presence of the specific learning disabilities. Pendarvis and Grossi (1980) stress the importance of nontraditional approaches and modifications of existing instruments to assess potential and present achievement of gifted LD individuals, yet few specific procedures have been developed for this purpose. Various assessment measures that can be used in the identification process are described next.

Observation

Recommendations of teachers, counselors, reading specialists, gifted specialists, or other educational personnel who have observed the child's performance in various learning situations and environments constitute one important source for identifying students with gifts as well as LD. The child's chances of being referred for more in-depth assessment for specialized programming is dependent not only upon the degree of exceptionality but also upon the opportunities to demonstrate and develop potential that the student has been exposed to in his or her educational program.

Because of the typically depressing effect of the LD on areas of strength, many potentially gifted LD youngsters are overlooked because they are functioning at or near grade level despite functioning far below their capabilities (Gunderson et al., 1987). Rarely do gifted LD students demonstrate characteristics such as efficient study skills and excellence in completing school assignments quickly and accurately — characteristics that tend to get more typically gifted students referred for special programming. In many cases, clinicians depend on parents, teachers, or administrators to refer the child (Tannenbaum & Baldwin, 1983; Whitmore & Maker, 1985).

Karnes, Shwedel, and Lewis (1983) recommend extended observation and provision of stimulating experiences related to areas of giftedness (intelligence, academics, creativity, visual and performing arts, leadership, and psychomotor skills) for students with disabilities suspected of having special gifts/talents. This is necessary because some children may need time and opportunities to exhibit their potential in areas to which they have not been exposed. Tannenbaum and Baldwin (1983) point out that, at this stage, assessment is primarily of potential in areas of strength rather than well developed gifts and talents.

Programs that expose large numbers of children to enrichment experiences and opportunities to develop and demonstrate their skills in areas not typically included in the standard educational program provide a vehicle for observing characteristics of giftedness that otherwise may not surface (e.g., Baum, 1988; Baum, Emerick, Herman, & Dixon, 1989). Vaughn (1989), Silverman (1989), and others call for a liberal criteria for inclusion into enrichment opportunities and programs. Classroom teachers should be given training and assistance in how to provide experiences to cultivate children's gifts/talents, and to recognize behaviors and outcomes indicative of giftedness in children, particularly those who have disabilities (Gunderson et al., 1987; Kranz, 1981; Tannenbaum & Baldwin, 1983; Vaughn, 1989). Checklists such as those developed by Silverman (1989), Whitmore (1980), and Udall and Maker (1983) may be helpful in guiding and documenting observations in these contexts.

Formal Measures of Ability and Achievement

Gifted LD students tend to do poorly on group-administered achievement and intelligence tests because their learning disabilities interfere (Gunderson et al., 1987; Vaughn, 1989). Individually administered measures of achievement and ability (e.g., the Wechsler Intelligence Scale for Children – Revised [WISC-R] and Woodcock-Johnson Psychoeducational Battery) typically render more representative and helpful information about specific strengths, weaknesses, and areas of potential than do the group-administered tests typically used for screening purposes. But even individualized tests may not be designed or validated for special populations and, therefore, may discriminate against gifted children with learning disabilities. To help minimize this effect, reporting of verbal, performance, and sub-test scores indicating particular areas of strength and weakness as well as overall scores on these standardized tests is recommended. The quality of the child's responses and how he or she approaches the tasks presented also should be noted and shared with the eligibility and planning teams (Tannenbaum & Baldwin, 1983).

Investigators agree that, although discrepancies are apparent on individualized intelligence tests such as the WISC-R, no single profile reliably identifies the gifted LD child (Barton & Starnes, 1989; Fox & Brody, 1983). Various studies have found varying patterns of WISC-R sub-scale scores in groups of learners identified as gifted and LD. Possible patterns that have been noted include: (a) scattered scores in either or both Verbal and Performance scales, usually with a wide range between the child's high and low scores; (b) a Verbal score from 15 to 40 points higher than the Performance score for children with perceptual motor difficulties but strong language abilities, or (c) a Performance score 10 to 30 points higher than the Verbal score for children with reading and verbal expression problems (Clements & Peters, 1967). A difference of 15 points between Verbal and Performance scores is significant at the .01 level. Although it is an insufficient condition to diagnose a child as gifted LD, if the child's Verbal or Performance score greatly exceeds the other so that one falls in the superior range, giftedness with learning disabilities should be considered (Fox & Brody, 1983).

In terms of performance on specific sub-tests, Silverman (1989) studied profiles of more than 200 children identified as gifted LD and found a pattern of high scores on the Vocabulary, Similarities, and Block Design sub-tests and on the abstract verbal and spatial reasoning portions of standardized intelligence scales, with much lower scores on Digit Span, Coding, and Arithmetic, which require sequencing ability. Udall and Maker (1983) found wide sub-test scatter and significantly higher Performance than Verbal scores, with the lowest sub-test scores on Digit Span, Information, Block Design, and Coding. These findings are similar to those of Schiff, Kaufman, and Kaufman (1981) and Fox (1983), who also found that sub-test scatter of the gifted/disabled group was significantly greater than that of comparison groups.

In the identification of LD, achievement scores are also required to document discrepancy from the child's potential as typically measured by an intelligence test. Scores of gifted LD students on standardized achievement tests, however, may be depressed by perceptual and processing difficulties inherent in the learning disabilities. Students with reading disabilities are at a great disadvantage because of the timed nature of these tests and the presentation of items in written form. Low scores on standardized achievement tests also may reflect inadequate learning stemming from inadequate teaching or a mismatch between the test and the curriculum used with the student. Further, the overall scores of these tests do not reflect the types of items answered correctly. In light of these considerations, some experts recommend a test of abstract reasoning, such as the Raven's Progressive Matrices, to help identify high-ability learners who perform poorly on verbal measures as a result of their LD (Fox & Brody, 1983; Steeves, 1982).

As with intelligence tests, individualized achievement tests generally yield more representative performance than do group measures and are more likely to identify students who would qualify for special services. Unfortunately, given the resources needed for individual testing and the general lack of funding for gifted and talented programs, public schools are likely to continue relying on teacher recommendations and scores on group tests of intelligence and achievement to identify gifted students, unless their disabilities are severe enough to warrant assessment for special education (Fox & Brody, 1983).

Curriculum-Based Measures

Considering the gifted learning disabled child's potential difficulties with standardized tests and the often questionable match between the test items and the curricular experiences to which the child has been exposed, more curriculum-based measures (CBM) should be included in any diagnostic battery attempting to identify the presence of giftedness or learning disabilities, or both. Curriculum-based tests may be commercially produced or teacher-made, may be normed for any given area or population, but must be directly linked to the local school curriculum (Blankenship, 1985; Deno & Fuchs, 1987; Marston, Deno, & Mirkin, 1984).

Items test the tasks and concepts the student encounters in whatever curriculum is used as the foundation for the child's education. For example, key concepts and skills from the various content areas such as science, social studies, or math could be tested to assess the child's actual performance in given disciplines. Curriculum-based assessment (CBA) of basic skills the child is expected to master or study skills and social behaviors necessary for succeeding in school should also be sampled. If potential is being assessed for special programs in the performing arts, specific opportunities to develop/demonstrate talents in music, drama, dance, or art may comprise the assessment in that area.

Well designed curriculum-based measures add valuable information regarding a student's potential and abilities in specific disciplines or areas of talent that comprise the local curriculum upon which students' educational experiences are based. Information gleaned from CBAs may also be used for instructional grouping, peer tutoring, and cooperative learning projects that may be vehicles to address the needs of the gifted LD child in the classroom.

Ecological Assessment

Ecological assessment is another type of assessment particularly critical to the gifted student with specific learning disabilities whose disabilities and gifts may not be as obvious as those of a child demonstrating characteristics of just one of these conditions. This type of measurement provides information regarding the educational environments within which the child is expected to function, helps to identify problem areas, and pinpoints potential areas for modification to meet student needs and enhance performance. Class expectations, rules, structure, teaching and response modes, the nature of interactions of different teachers and support personnel with the child, the nature of the child's interactions with his or her peers, and resources available for enrichment within various programs, classes, and extracurricular opportunities are some of the areas that ecological assessments may sample.

Curriculum-based measures may be formated as checklists, questionnaires, or observation schedules to be completed by teachers and other personnel involved with the child or with programs from which the child may benefit. They may be locally developed and tailored to existing programs and personnel. Commercial instruments such as The Instructional Environment Scale (TIES, Ysseldyke & Christenson, 1987), the Systematic Approach for Adapting the Learning Environment (SAALE model, Wood, 1988), and various checklists such as those developed by Mercer and Mercer (1989), Wiener (1986), Silverman, Zigmond, and Sansone (1981), Hoover (1988), and Robinson, Braxdale, and Colson (1985) also may be used or adapted to collect the information needed to find the best match between individual students and learning situations. Table 14.1 lists the areas assessed by various measures.

In addition to the above-mentioned measures, student products (e.g., artwork, writing samples, stories, performances, inventions) can be used to document performance and potential. Parent reports, peer reports, and even self-nominations also may be valuable sources of information in identifying the gifted child with learning disabilities.

Table 14.1
CONTENT AREAS OF ECOLOGICAL ASSESSMENTS

Assessment Measure	Areas Assessed
TIES (Ysseldyke & Christenson, 1987)	Classroom environment, teacher expectations, cognitive emphasis, motivational strategies, relevant practice, academic engaged time, feedback, adaptive instruction, progress evaluation, instructional planning, student understanding
SAALE (Wood, 1988)	Social/emotional/behavioral environment, physical environment, instructional environment including teaching, media, content, evaluation techniques
Mercer & Mercer (1989)	Learner expectancies, teacher expectancies, peer expectancies, parental expectancies, physical properties, instructional arrangements, instructional techniques, materials, learning style preferences, student responses, teacher feedback
Wiener (1986)	Classroom demands and evaluation procedures, questions on essay/project/report writing, test preparation and test taking, note taking, gaining information from text
Silverman, Zigmond, & Sansone (1981)	Study skills including using the text, note taking, homework, test taking, listening, bringing materials, following directions; academics including reading, math, writing; behaviors including punctuality, in seat, attending, peer interactions
Hoover (1988)	Reading rate, listening, note taking/outlining, report writing, oral presentations, graphic aids, test taking, library usage, reference/dictionary usage, time management, self-management
Robinson, Braxdale, & Colson (1985)	Listening, self-management, record keeping, reading content for comprehension, test taking, interactive learning

Tests of Creativity

Tests of creativity, though somewhat controversial and not thoroughly researched with gifted LD individuals, may provide valuable information on learning, thinking, and problem-solving abilities not assessed by typical aptitude and achievement tests. These tests do not depend as heavily on reading or spelling proficiency as do most commonly used standardized tests. Two of these measures, which have been used in attempts to identify disadvantaged gifted students, are the Torrance Tests of Creative Thinking (Torrance, 1977) and the Structure of the Intellect Learning Assessment (Meeker, 1966).

CURRICULUM FOR GIFTED LEARNERS
WITH LEARNING DISABILITIES

In determining an appropriate curriculum for gifted LD learners, the primary consideration should be the individual's unique needs. But determination of these needs, and the best way to meet them, does not occur in a vacuum. Decision making must take into account the contexts in which the student finds himself or herself that drive expectations for success and influence the development and selection of curricular options. Thus, the student's needs are considered in relation to organized subject matter or the content of the various disciplines, as well as environmental or societal considerations that influence curricula. The relative importance of student needs and interests, academic subject matter, and ecological demands varies for different learners at different points in their educational careers. Factors that influence educational priorities at any given time include parent, general class, and special education variables, as well as student variables such as age, grade, years remaining in school, achievement, motivation, and social/behavioral competence (Polloway, Patton, Epstein, & Smith, 1989).

If all these influences are not considered, the student's overall curriculum may be fragmented and fail to prepare him or her to be successful in school and life situations. Development in areas of strength also may be impeded if the child is not systematically afforded the experiences that equip him or her for continued learning and success in a variety of environments.

Taking into account the student's needs, interests, organized subject matter, and environmental demands, curricular options that may be considered for the gifted LD learner include:

1. The standard curriculum offered in general education.
2. Remedial basic skills for areas of weakness.
3. Advanced curriculum in areas of strength.
4. Learning strategies to provide the student efficient and effective approaches to learning.
5. Social-behavioral skills and affective education for relating to peers and dealing with the emotional aspects of being both LD and gifted.
6. Career-vocational education to focus the student's preparation on post-school as well as in-school success.
7. Thematic units.
8. Special projects related to the student's interests and talents.

If the student is determined to be eligible for special education under the category of learning disabilities, the individualized education plan (IEP) team, composed of the special educator, resource personnel involved with the child, the school administrator, the child's parents, and the child himself or herself when possible, determines annual goals and short-term objectives that form the basis of programming for the child's special education. These goals and objectives address actual curricular content — knowledge, skills, and attitudes or intended learning outcomes included in the various curricular options selected as appropriate for meeting the child's learning needs.

At present, only the goals and objectives related to the child's learning disabilities are legally mandated for the IEP. Best practice, however, demands that the general educator and the gifted specialist be highly involved in developing the overall program for the LD child who is also gifted. Without dialogue and planning, the student's program may be redundant, lack integration, fail to address critical needs and skills, and overlook areas of strength and interest that should be nurtured in the child.

Because IEP goals and objectives for the LD child are based on present educational levels and address the student's disabilities documented by assessment, and because gifted services are seldom mandated, particularly for those of questionable eligibility, a danger exists that the LD gifted child's program will be overly focused on disabilities to the exclusion of strengths. Each curricular option with its corresponding content must be carefully considered for inclusion in the gifted LD child's educational program, with the overall goals of remediating or compensating for areas of weakness associated with the LD, while ensuring the child opportunities for continued growth in areas of demonstrated or potential giftedness. Thus, a blend of goal statements that address strengths as well as weaknesses is recommended for the LD gifted student.

INSTRUCTIONAL METHODOLOGY AND
SERVICE DELIVERY SETTINGS

Once curricular options and content have been determined (the *what* of curriculum), the planning team should direct attention to the instructional methods best suited to convey the selected content (the *how* of curricular planning) and the setting(s) in which programming will be implemented (the *where*). Some commonly mentioned suggestions from the literature (e.g., Baum, 1988; Daniels, 1983; Fox, Brody, & Tobin, 1983; Gallagher, 1983; Silverman, 1989; Vaughn, 1989; Whitmore & Maker, 1985) on accommodations and methods for working with gifted LD learners include:

1. Provision of high-interest, challenging topics to motivate students and nurture strengths.
2. Provision of opportunities to increase self-awareness, self-esteem, and self-management.
3. Active learning and student participation in decision making.

4. Multisensory approaches to instruction and avoidance of repetitive drill-and-practice activities.

If an individual child is determined to have learning disabilities with suspected or demonstrated giftedness, information collected and recommendations of the interdisciplinary eligibility team can be helpful in deciding upon instructional methods. Input from the general class teacher, the special education teacher, and the gifted education specialist is essential for collaboratively planning how to incorporate teaching techniques best suited to the child's learning style into instruction throughout the school day. The gifted specialist can contribute ideas and resources for providing the child with experiences that nurture his or her areas of strength, as well as guide the pacing and level of presentation in the general curriculum. The reading specialist, counselor, psychologist, or other resource persons may be called upon for input relating to their specific areas of expertise relevant to student needs.

The special educator certified to teach students with learning disabilities can help the others working with the child to understand the nature of the child's specific disabilities and how they influence learning and performance in academic and nonacademic tasks. Working closely with the general and gifted educators as well as the parents, the special educator can suggest modifications in modes of instruction, student responses, content and evaluation of assignments, and other accommodations that can be managed within the general or the gifted programs. The special educator also typically works directly with the student to develop learning strategies, study skills, social-behavioral skills, and compensating behaviors to minimize the negative effects of the LD and maximize the child's learning in the designated curriculum.

In deciding upon the nature and extent of collaboration among the various professionals involved with the gifted LD child, the principal manager of the child's program has to be selected. Even though the special educator is responsible for monitoring the IEP goals and objectives related to the child's disability, he or she may not be the person with whom the child spends the most time. The general educator or the gifted program coordinator may be a more logical choice to oversee the child's total program, with clear communication and involvement of all concerned.

The specific ways in which the special, general, and gifted educators collaborate and the setting for service delivery may vary with different children and in different school systems. The range of settings includes the general classroom with consultation, resource assistance, full-time class placement for gifted or learning disabilities with consultation/collaboration, center-based programs, honors/accelerated classes, special education classes, regional centers, and residential programs. Appropriate education for the gifted LD student may be a combination of services provided within these settings.

In programs structured on a more consultative model (e.g., Idol, 1989; West & Idol, 1987), the gifted LD child remains in his or her main classroom with specialists acting as consultants to the teacher in that class. The primary classroom teacher would then carry out the child's instruction under the guidance/consultation of the LD and gifted specialist.

In other cases, the child remains in the main classroom for the majority of instruction and sees the LD or gifted specialist, or both, in the resource room for short periods to work on certain skills or projects. This pull-out model, though popular, may present problems in the child's generalization of skills from one classroom to another, integration of the child's total program, and limitations in the numbers of students whose needs can be served.

Team teaching in the context of the general education or gifted education programs may be an even more desirable service delivery alternative (Bauwens, Hourcade, & Friend, 1989). Co-teaching may involve both the special educator and the general or gifted educator cooperatively planning and implementing lessons for all groups of students in the general or gifted classroom. Another variation of teaming may involve one teacher presenting the lesson and the special educator teaching complementary skills such as learning strategies, study skills, or research skills to help students with disabilities remember and master the content presented in the lesson. The special educator also may design special practice activities to help students reach proficiency on skills related to the lesson. In these arrangements, other students besides those officially labeled as exceptional may profit from both teachers' expertise. The teachers also have firsthand knowledge of the curriculum their partner presents. In addition, co-teaching enhances the possibilities for generalization of the skills learned, as well as integration of all facets of the student's educational program.

To date, not enough research has been done to define the optimal program and setting for gifted LD children. Given their varied characteristics, options from the full continuum of service delivery systems are likely to be used by local school systems. The most appropriate setting for any individual child is the one most supportive of implementation of the curriculum options, content, and methodology decided upon by the programming team.

APPLICATIONS OF THE CURRICULUM MODEL FOR DIANE BRADFORD

Diane is a learner who exemplifies the unevenness and paradoxical characteristics typical of the gifted child with learning disabilities. She demonstrates strong verbal reasoning, knowledge, and interest in a wide variety of topics, excellent auditory memory of information she finds useful or meaningful, a flair for dramatic activities, and exceptional athletic skills in the areas of track (running), swimming, and horseback riding. She holds several records for her age group in running, despite little practice.

Diane's interpersonal and leadership skills surface in her ability to gain reinforcement from many of the adults and peers in her environment. For example, she persuaded her teachers to allow her continued participation in speech services, to play the leading role in the speech class play, after being officially discharged. She enjoys organizing class parties and developed her own neighborhood social "club" to put on plays, write stories, make and sell items, and engage in other projects under her leadership. Diane, of course, is club president.

Despite her facility for oral language and verbal reasoning, her visual processing difficulties and perceptual-motor difficulties negatively affect her performance in reading and writing language. Relatively low-level tasks requiring visual-fine motor coordination and visual memory, such as handwriting, copying from the board, spelling, and other assignments requiring spatial or temporal organization, are laborious for Diane. She often has difficulty interpreting and following directions, is easily distracted from basic skills assignments, demonstrates impulsivity and a high degree of activity during the school day, and is often frustrated with her inability to perform what seem like simple tasks for her grade level. Timed tasks such as exams, spelling tests, and standardized assessments appear to intensify her frustration. Though she enjoys organizing social activities for her peers, her organizational skills in relation to academic tasks and study skills are problematic and interfere with successful school performance.

Her parents report that Diane shows extreme sensitivity, low self-esteem, lack of self-control, and low frustration tolerance. They described several episodes during which Diane began to excessively argue, cry, and demand an unusual amount of attention and consolation over relatively minor incidents. On occasion she has been verbally and physically aggressive toward her classmates, but this behavior has diminished with age.

Diane's Assessment Profile

In second grade, Diane was referred for a comprehensive evaluation to determine eligibility for special education based upon her observed academic performance and behavioral characteristics. She demonstrated significant discrepancies between her Verbal (124) and Performance (105) scores on the WISC-R, between sub-areas of the Woodcock-Johnson Psychoeducational Battery (e.g., 98–100 on the Reading, Writing, and Skills areas versus 117 and 120 on the Math and Knowledge sub-tests), and between her actual achievement in academic subjects and her expected performance based upon her full-scale WISC-R score of $118 = 5$. Although the interdisciplinary team determined her to be eligible for special education services under the category of specific learning disabilities, she has not been earmarked for services or enrichment activities in her areas of strength. Diane typifies the child whose learning disabilities may be masking her gifts/talents and depressing her performance and achievement, yet whose gifts allow her to creatively compensate for her difficulties and perform near grade level in academic subjects.

Given Diane's academic performance and assessment profile, the failure to be identified as gifted is not surprising. Despite recognition that multiple measures are necessary to identify children with gifts and talents in a variety of areas, the vast majority of schools still rely upon cut-off scores on standardized tests and teacher referrals as eligibility requirements for gifted programs. The fact that Diane's greatest strengths (in athletics and drama) might not correspond to programs already in place for gifted students in her school may have further decreased her chances of being identified as gifted.

Proposed Curriculum for Diane

Using Diane's profile to exemplify the curricular process proposed in this and the previous chapter, the general education curriculum seems appropriate in most academic subjects, judging from test scores, input from team members, and teacher reports. Modifications or adaptations in instruction and response modes could be necessary, but the basic curricular content would be acceptable for most subjects if it were carefully sequenced and were to provide stimulation in higher-level thinking as well as basic skills. It is critical that Diane attain a level of functioning that enables her to successfully negotiate her school environment and basic understandings of the disciplines, particularly those in which she demonstrates potential.

In the area of language arts, Diane would benefit from activities designed to enhance visual memory and visual-motor coordination in tasks such as handwriting, copying, and spelling. Word attack skills could also be improved to help Diane read for information from high-interest materials that may be above her present reading grade level but commensurate with her level of understanding. Whole word approaches, context clues, and meaning-based syllabic strategies would be advisable. Less restrictive media (e.g., films, videos, discussions, presentations, talking books) might also be considered for areas of interest in which Diane's understanding and auditory reception exceed her ability to read from text. Alternative response modes (e.g., allowing her to tape-record or make oral or pictorial reports) and alternative grading in advanced classes related to her interest/strength areas and in which her capacity to learn the concepts exceeds her ability to express her learning in more traditional forms also provide ways to reasonably challenge Diane in areas of potential.

This combination of remediation, compensation, and accommodation balances her educational program between attending to her deficits and nurturing her strengths. If her areas of interest are used only for remediation of weak skills, she may develop negative associations between these areas and her disability, quickly losing interest and motivation. The goal is to prevent frustration and to maintain interest and growth in important areas of study.

Diane also could benefit from programming and practice in "school survival skills" (Silverman, Zigmond, & Sansone, 1981) — academic and interactional behaviors necessary for dealing successfully with the school environment. These skills allow the child to negotiate the "hidden" or implicit school curriculum mastered by successful learners. Among these survival skills, Silverman et al. (1981), Robinson et al. (1985), and others include self-management, behavioral control, social/adaptive skills, and study skills.

Learning strategies, or rules/guidelines for making, implementing, and evaluating decisions about the best way to solve problems and approach educational tasks independently (Deshler & Schumaker, 1986; Schumaker, Deshler, Alley, & Warner, 1983) also enhance the student's success and allow greater independence in learning. Many students with learning disabilities have limited repertoires of strategies. Although gifted LD students may have developed more strategies than most of their LD counterparts, the strategies they use may not be the most efficient or effective for the task demands they face. They may not be consciously aware of how they approach learning situations or of alternative strategies at their disposal. Nor may they be aware of how to develop new strategies suited to their learning style and preferences. Gifted LD students are likely to benefit from training in learning strategies and encouragement to develop their own strategies for new situations.

Survival skills and learning strategies that could be logically integrated into Diane's educational program include:

— study skills and learning strategies related to decoding, test taking, and mnemonics.
— organizational strategies including time and materials management.
— research skills for completing assignments and investigating areas of interest.
— social skills for working cooperatively with others, including opportunities to channel her leadership skills.
— behavioral self-control and self-management.

More specifically, *learning strategies* of particular use to Diane may include comprehension strategies such as story mapping or semantic mapping (a visual representation or "wheel" of key story or text elements) (Idol, 1987; Jones, Pierce, & Hunter, 1989; Rooney, 1988; Schewel, 1989; Walton & Hoblitt, 1989). Other strategies involving prediction, checking, questioning, and summarizing techniques (Palinscar & Brown, 1984; Paris & Oka, 1989) may also prove useful. These strategies help the learner to understand and remember higher-level reading selections and isolate essential information related to areas of interest. A decoding strategy for individual words found in text is DISSECT, a word identification strategy that employs lists of prefixes and suffixes and applies rules for decoding multisyllabic words that may be in a student's vocabulary but present difficulty when encountered in print (Lenz, Schumaker, Deshler, & Beals, 1984). Test-taking strategies such as SCORER (Carman & Adams, 1972), PIRATES (Hughes, Schumaker, Deshler, & Mercer, 1988), and those described in Ritter and Idol-Maestas (1986) may help to maximize Diane's performance on timed/untimed tests and reduce her anxiety and frustration in test situations.

Given Diane's problems with visual memory of factual material, mnemonics such as pegword, keyword (Mastropieri, Scruggs, & Levin, 1985; Pressley, Levin, & Delaney, 1982), or other visualization strategies and the FIRST strategy for making and memorizing lists (Nagel, Schumaker, & Deshler, 1986) may enhance memory and demonstration of learning in areas of difficulty. Alternative multisensory approaches to spelling (Graham & Miller, 1983) may be advisable if the typical study-test approach proves to be an overwhelming problem for Diane. It also would be worthwhile for her to learn to use word processing and spelling check programs along with spelling dictionaries to compensate for her handwriting and spelling difficulties. This would be particularly helpful in areas of special interest that do not focus primarily on spelling and handwriting as objectives.

Time management techniques for Diane include working with a schedule or assignment book, and listing and allotting time to required activities during a class period, day, evening, and eventually week or longer. This may help her organize her time to ensure assignment completion and relieve some of the frustration she may feel trying to juggle her schoolwork and extracurricular activities. Visual representations of her scheduled activities also may enhance her awareness of necessary tasks and allow her some autonomy in deciding when to do each task.

Self-management is an important area for Diane to develop, given what has been described as her poor impulse control and distractibility. She also demonstrates a desire to control her environment and expresses resentment at adults' attempts to give her direction. Yet she seems to perform better in a rather structured situation. The goal of self-management training would be to make Diane more aware of her behavior, its antecedents, and consequences, and gradually assume more responsibility for controlling her own behavior. A strategy such as IPLAN (VanReusen, Bos, Schumaker, & Deshler, 1987), in which the student learns to systematically analyze his or her own strengths, weaknesses, and preferences and convey this information to educators responsible for program planning, may be helpful in developing self-control. Allowing Diane more input into her educational program may contribute to her motivation, goal-setting capabilities, and sense of responsibility for her own learning. This strategy also may help Diane to develop a greater awareness of and confidence in her strengths, while dealing realistically with her areas of weakness.

Cognitive behavior modification techniques (Meichenbaum, 1977; 1980), which involve self-instruction or self-talk through tasks and situations, and self-monitoring/evaluation of behavior could also be employed in efforts to increase Diane's self-management. After having the desired response or learning process modeled using self-talk, and being coached through the behaviors using self-instruction, the student learns to talk himself or herself through the responses appropriate to the situation. Self-recording (Hallahan, Lloyd, & Stoller, 1982) and self-reward of behavior may accompany this procedure until the behavior is well established. These techniques could be applied to academic problem solving, assignment completion, impulse control, and direction following. Self-instruction also may be helpful in relaxation exercises designed to decrease tension and anxiety in situations that cause Diane to become upset and require more intense external direction and control. Her increasing ability to control her own actions and respond constructively to tense situations would gradually give Diane more of that sense of control for which she has indicated a need.

As with all gifted LD children, Diane's educational program must address areas of potential or demonstrated giftedness or talent. Athletics represent Diane's primary area of demonstrated strength, with potential in leadership and drama. She has access to experiences in running, swimming, and horseback riding by virtue of her parents' advocacy and ability to support her activities in these areas. Not all children who show potential in given areas are as fortunate.

At issue in cases similar to Diane's is the school's definition of the child's curriculum. In most public schools across the country, activities related to athletics and drama (Diane's areas of strength), if available at all, are considered extracurricular rather than an important part of the school curriculum. The child's participation is often contingent upon a number of variables including performance in basic subjects, availability of transportation, and parental perferences or participation, none of which may relate directly to the child's potential or demonstrated strengths. For the disabled gifted child with talents in nonacademic areas, programs generally regarded as extracurricular should be viewed as an integral part of the educational curriculum. An appropriate education for these children is one that addresses their strengths as well as their weaknesses. Extracurricular programs provide a vehicle to develop their particular talents and provide them with necessary experiences to enhance their self-esteem and sense of competence.

Opportunities for leaderships also should be incorporated into Diane's school experiences to capitalize on her strengths in this area and to appropriately channel her desire to be in control of the situation. Organizing class projects, participating in school groups and organizations, and playing various leadership roles in the classroom may be vehicles to further develop Diane's leadership talents.

Other fertile areas for programming for Diane based on her potential strengths include drama, dance, and other "bridges" between the cognitive and motor domains. If the school does not have organized opportunities in these areas, community groups, local libraries, private organizations or individuals, mentorship programs, and institutes of higher education may be resources for providing experiences to develop and maintain interest and foster growth in areas of potential.

Because most of Diane's school day was spent in the mainstream class, the general education teacher may be in the best position to identify academic tasks and behavioral expectations with which she has the most difficulty. Her teacher also may have valuable insights into activities and topics of greatest interest to Diane and those in which she showed particular aptitude or ability. For example, Diane's general class teacher noted her difficulties comprehending written directions and texts, expressing herself in writing, testing under timed conditions, and performing routine drill-and-practice exercises. In contrast, she excelled in her role as store manager in a social studies class simulation of community interdependence, after expressing frustration with her previous role as banker and convincing the teacher to change her assignment. Similarly, the teacher noted Diane's strong preference for other active learning projects and hands-on activities in the classroom, for story telling and artwork requiring creativity, and for opportunities in which she can take a leading role in developing dramatizations or simulating real-life experiences.

Working collaboratively, the general, special, and gifted educators could implement these curricular suggestions and instructional adaptations to address Diane's strengths and help to overcome her limitations. In addition, cooperative learning structures and peer tutoring situations such as those described by Jenkins and Jenkins (1985), Johnson and Johnson (1986), Slavin (1983), and Kagan (1985) would allow Diane structured opportunities to interact with her peers, assume different roles as a part of a group working toward a common goal, and receive support from her peers in areas of weakness (e.g., spelling, written expression, reading directions, research) so that she could concentrate upon learning the concepts and skills for which the cooperative activities were designed. She, in turn, could contribute her creative ideas, planning expertise, presentation skills, and other strengths that may not be highlighted in other types of classroom assignments.

SUMMARY

Diane's case study has been used to illustrate the challenges of identification, the conglomeration of contradictory characteristics, and the many possibilities for curriculum development and implementation for but one profile of a gifted child with learning disabilities. With other types of gifted LD children, the characteristics and curriculum may look very different.

The process of curricular decision making, however, remains the same. Team decisions, taking into consideration curricular influences, available curricular options and specific content, instructional methodology best suited to implementing the program, and, finally, the most supportive setting for programming, move toward development of an appropriate education for any given child. As factors in the decision-making process change, the curriculum must be adjusted accordingly. This dynamic, flexible, yet structured approach to curricular planning and development provides a vehicle to translate philosophical commitment to serving children with exceptionalities into workable programs to meet their diverse educational needs.

REFERENCES

Barton, J. M., & Starnes, W. T. (1989). Identifying distinguishing characteristics of gifted and talented/learning disabled students. *Roeper Review, 12*(1), 23–29.

Baum, S. (1988). An enrichment program for gifted learning disabled students. *Gifted Child Quarterly, 32,* 226–230.

Baum, S., Emerick, L. J., Herman, G. N., & Dixon, J. (1989). Identification, programs, and enrichment strategies for gifted learning disabled youth. *Roeper Review, 12*(1), 48–53.

Bauwens, J., Hourcade, J. J., & Friend, M. (1989). Cooperative teaching: A model for general and special education integration. *Remedial & Special Education, 10*(2), 17–22.

Blankenship, C. S. (1985). Using curriculum-based assessment data to make instructional decisions. *Exceptional Children, 52*(3), 233–238.

Bryan, T., & McGrady, H. J. (1972). Use of a teacher rating scale. *Journal of Learning Disabilities, 5,* 199–206.

Carman, R. A., & Adams, W. R. (1972). *Student skills: A student's guide for survival.* New York: John Wiley & Sons.

Clements, S., & Peters, J. (1967). Minimal brain dysfunction in the school-age child. In Frierson & Barbe (Eds.), *Educating children with learning disabilities: Selected readings.* New York: Appleton-Century-Crofts.

Daniels, P. R. (1983). *Teaching the gifted/learning disabled child.* Rockville, MD: Aspen.

Daniels, P. R. (1983). Teaching the learning-disabled/gifted child. In L. H. Fox, L. Brody, & D. Tobin (Eds.), *Learning-disabled/gifted children: Identification and programming* (pp. 153–169). Baltimore: University Park Press.

Deno, S. L., & Fuchs, L. S. (1987). Developing curriculum-based measurement systems for data-based special education problem solving. *Focus on Exceptional Children, 18*(8), 1–16.

Deshler, D. D., & Schumaker, J. B. (1986). Learning strategies: An instructional alternative for low-achieving adolescents. *Exceptional Children, 52*(6), 583–590.

Education for All Handicapped Children Act of 1975, 10 U.S.C. section 1401-1461.

Fox, L. H. (1983). Gifted students with reading problems: An empirical study. In L. H. Fox, L. Brody, & D. Tobin (Eds.), *Learning-disabled/gifted children: Identification and programming* (pp. 117–139). Baltimore: University Park Press.

Fox, L. H., & Brody, L. (1983). Models for identifying giftedness: Issues related to the learning-disabled child. In L. H. Fox, L. Brody, & D. Tobin (Eds.), *Learning-disabled/gifted children: Identification and programming* (pp. 101–116). Baltimore: University Park Press.

Fox, L. H., Brody, L., & Tobin, D. (Eds.). (1983). *Learning-disabled/gifted children: Identification and programming.* Baltimore: University Park Press.

Gallagher, J. J. (1983). The adaptation of gifted programming for learning-disabled students. In L. H. Fox, L. Brody, & D. Tobin (Eds.), *Learning-disabled/gifted children: Identification and programming* (pp. 171–181). Baltimore: University Park Press.

Graham, S., & Miller, R. (1983). Spelling research and practice: A unified approach. In E. L. Meyen, G. A. Vergason, & R. J. Whelan (Eds.), *Promising practices for exceptional children: Curriculum implications* (pp. 245–271). Denver: Love Publishing.

Gunderson, C. W., Maesch, C., & Rees, J. W. (1987). The gifted/learning disabled student. *Gifted Child Quarterly, 31*(4), 158–160.

Hallahan, D. P., Lloyd, J. W., & Stoller, L. (1982). *Improving attention with self-monitoring: A manual for teachers.* Charlottesville, VA: University of Virginia Learning Disabilities Research Institute.

Hoover, J. J. (1988). *Teaching handicapped students study skills* (2nd ed.). Lindale, TX: Hamilton.

Hughes, C., Schumaker, J. B., Deshler, D. D., & Mercer, C. D. (1988). *The test-taking strategy instructor's manual*. Lawrence, KS: The University of Kansas.

Idol, L. (1987). Group story mapping: A comprehension strategy for both skilled and unskilled readers. *Journal of Learning Disabilities, 20,* 196–205.

Idol, L. (1989). The resource/consulting teacher: An integrated model for service delivery. *Remedial & Special Education, 10*(6), 38–48.

Jenkins, J., & Jenkins, L. (1985). Peer tutoring in elementary and secondary programs. *Focus on Exceptional Children, 17*(6), 1–12.

Johnson, D. W., & Johnson, R. T. (1986). Mainstreaming and cooperative learning strategies. *Exceptional Children, 52*(6), 553–561.

Jones, B. F., Pierce, J., & Hunter, B. (1989). Teaching students to construct graphic representations. *Educational Leadership, 46*(4), 20–25.

Kagan, S. (1985). Dimensions of cooperative classroom structures. In R. Slavin, S. Sharan, S. Kagan, R. Hertz-Lazarowitz, C. Webb, & R. Schmuck (Eds.), *Learning to cooperate, cooperating to learn* (pp. 437–462). New York: Plenum Press.

Karnes, M., Shwedel, A. M., & Lewis, G. F. (1983). Long-term effects of early programming for the gifted/talented handicapped. *Journal for the Education of the Gifted, 6*(4), 266–278.

Kranz, B. (1981). *Kranz talent identification instrument.* Moorhead, MN: Moorhead State College.

Lenz, B. K., Schumaker, J. B., Deshler, D., & Beals, V. L. (1984). *The word identification strategy.* Lawrence: University of Kansas.

Maker, C. J. (1977). *Providing programs for the gifted handicapped.* Reston, VA: Council for Exceptional Children.

Marland, S. P. (1972). Education of the gifted and talented, Volume I. *Report to the Congress of the United States by the U.S. Commissioner of Education.* Washington, DC: Government Printing Office.

Marston, D., Deno, S., & Mirkin, P. (1984). Curriculum-based measurement: An alternative to traditional screening, referral, and identification. *Journal of Special Education, 18*(2), 109–117.

Mastropieri, M. A., Scruggs, T. E., & Levin, J. R. (1985). Memory and strategy instruction with learning disabled adolescents. *Journal of Learning Disabilities, 18,* 94–100.

Meeker, M. N. (1966). The structure of the intellect: Its interpretation and uses. Columbus, OH: Merrill.

Meichenbaum, D. H. (1977). *Cognitive behavior modification: An integrative approach.* New York: Plenum.

Meichenbaum, D. (1980). Cognitive behavior modification with exceptional children: A promise yet unfulfilled. *Exceptional Education Quarterly, 1*(1), 83–88.

Mercer, C. D., & Mercer, A. R. (1989). *Teaching students with learning problems* (3rd ed.). Columbus: Merrill.

Nagel, D. R., Schumaker, J. B., & Deshler, D. D. (1986). *The first-letter mnemonic strategy.* Lawrence, KS: Excel Enterprises.

Palinscar, A. S., & Brown, A. L. (1984). Reciprocal teaching of comprehension-fostering and comprehension-monitoring activities. *Cognition & Instruction, 1*(2), 117–175.

Paris, S. G., & Oka, E. R. (1989). Strategies for comprehending text and coping with reading difficulties. *Learning Disability Quarterly, 12*(1), 32–42.

Pendarvis, E., & Grossi, J. (1980). Designing and operating programs for the gifted and talented handicapped. In J. B. Jordan & J. A. Grossi (Eds.), *An administrator's handbook on designing programs for the gifted and talented* (pp. 66–88). Reston, VA: Council for Exceptional Children.

Polloway, E. A., Patton, J. R., Epstein, M. H., & Smith, T. E. C. (1989). Comprehensive curriculum for students with mild handicaps. *Focus on Exceptional Children, 21*(8), 1–12.

Pressley, M., Levin, J., & Delaney, H. D. (1982). The mnemonic keyword method. *Review of Educational Research, 52,* 61–92.

Ritter, S., & Idol-Maestas, L. (1986). Teaching middle school students to use a test-taking strategy. *Journal of Educational Research, 79*(6), 350–357.

Robinson, S. M., Braxdale, C. T., & Colson, S. E. (1985). Preparing dysfunctional learners to enter junior high school: A transitional curriculum. *Focus on Exceptional Children, 18*(4), 1–12.

Rooney, K. (1988). *Independent strategies for efficient study*. Richmond, VA: J. R. Enterprises.

Rosner, S. L., & Seymour, J. (1983). The gifted child with a learning disability: Clinical evidence. In L. H. Fox, L. Brody, & D. Tobin (Eds.), *Learning-disabled/gifted children: Identification and programming* (pp. 77–97). Baltimore: University Park Press.

Schewel, R. (1989). Semantic mapping: A study skills strategy. *Academic therapy, 24*(4), 439–448.

Schiff, M. M., Kaufman, A. S., & Kaufman, N. L. (1981). Scatter analysis of WISC-R profiles for learning disabled children with superior intelligence. *Journal of Learning Disabilities, 14*, 400–404.

Schumaker, J. B., Deshler, D. D., Alley, G. R., & Warner, M. M. (1983). Toward the development of an intervention model for learning disabled adolescents. *Exceptional Education Quarterly, 4*(1), 45–84.

Senf, G. M. (1983). The nature and identification of learning disabilities and their relationship to the gifted child. In L. H. Fox, L. Brody, & D. Tobin, (Eds.), *Learning-disabled/gifted children: Identification and programming* (pp. 37–49). Baltimore: University Park Press.

Silverman, L. K. (1989). Invisible gifts, invisible handicaps. *Roeper Review, 12*(1), 37–42.

Silverman, R., Zigmond, N., & Sansone, J. (1981). Teaching coping skills to adolescents with learning problems. *Focus on Exceptional Children, 18*(6), 1–20.

Slavin, R. E. (1983). *Cooperative learning*. New York: Langman.

Steeves, K. J. (1982). *Memory as a factor in the computational efficiency of dyslexic children with high abstract reasoning ability*. Unpublished doctoral dissertation, Johns Hopkins University, Baltimore.

Tannenbaum, A. J., & Baldwin, L. J. (1983). Giftedness and learning disability: A paradoxical combination. In L. H. Fox, L. Brody, & D. Tobin (Eds.), *Learning-disabled/gifted children: Identification and programming* (pp. 11–36). Baltimore: University Park Press.

Torrance, E. P. (1966). *Torrance tests of creative thinking*. Bensenville, IL: Scholastic Testing Service.

Udall, A. (1985). Chapter reaction to intellectually gifted persons with specific LD. In J. R. Whitmore & C. J. Maker, *Intellectual giftedness in disabled persons* (pp. 207–209). Rockville, MD: Aspen.

Udall, A. J., & Maker, C. J. (1983). A pilot program for elementary-age learning-disabled/gifted students. In L. H. Fox, L. Brody, & D. Tobin (Eds.), *Learning-disabled/gifted children: Identification and programming* (pp. 223–242). Baltimore: University Park Press.

Van Reusen, A. K., Bos, C. S., Schumaker, J. B., & Deshler, D. D. (1987). *The education planning strategy*. Lawrence, KS: EXCELLenterprises.

Vaughn, S. (1989). Gifted learning disabilities: Is it such a bright idea? *Learning Disabilities Focus, 4*(2), 123–128.

Waldron, K. A., Saphire, D. G., & Rosenblum, S. A. (1987). Learning disabilities and giftedness: Identification based on self-concept, behavior, and academic patterns. *Journal of Learning Disabilities, 20*(7), 422–427.

Walton, S., & Hoblitt, R. (1989). Using story frames in the content-area classes. *Social Studies, 80*, 103–106.

Weill, M. P. (1987). Gifted/learning disabled students: Their potential may be buried treasure. *Clearing House, 60*, 341–343.

West, J. F., & Idol, L. (1987). School consultation (Part 1): An interdisciplinary perspective on theory, models, and research. *Journal of Learning Disabilities, 20*(7), 388–408.

Whitmore, J. R. (1980). *Giftedness, conflict, and underachievement*. Boston: Allyn & Bacon.

Whitmore, J. R., & Maker, C. J. (1985). *Intellectual giftedness in disabled persons*. Rockville, MD: Aspen.

Wiener, J. (1986). Alternatives in the assessment of the learning disabled adolescent: A learning strategies approach. *Learning Disabilities Focus, 1*(2), 97–107.

Williams, K. (1988). The learning-disabled gifted: An unmet challenge. *Gifted Child Today,* (May/June), pp. 17–18.

Wood, J. W. (1988). *SAALE model-systematic approach for adapting the learning environment.* Richmond, VA: Project TRAIN, Virginia Commonwealth University.

Ysseldyke, J. E., & Christianson, S. L. (1987). Evaluating students' instructional environments. *Remedial & Special Education, 8*(3), 17–24.

CHAPTER FIFTEEN

Bridging Family and School: A School Psychologist Perspective

Agnes Donovan

C hildren with exceptional intellectual abilities and talents are a source of great joy and a challenge to their parents and teachers. School and family share the responsibility for recognizing signs of gifted potential, and for developing plans for appropriate local educational programs to meet the special learning and instructional needs of gifted students (Rogers, 1986).

Families can make unique contributions to the development of gifted potential in their children linked with the practice of psychologists in schools. Traditionally school psychologists have contributed to the educational process a knowledge of individual learner differences and atypical development in children. A school psychologist with a systems perspective can provide a broader function in schools by applying knowledge of the atypical development of the gifted learner with an understanding of the contexts of a child's development — the family and the school.

The case of Diane Bradford, a gifted learning disabled student, introduced to readers in preceding chapters, will be considered from a family-oriented school psychologist's perspective. Diane and her family illustrate how a family can positively influence the development of a child's exceptional abilities, and her case suggests ways in which school psychologists collaborating with educators and the gifted child's family can augment the realization of exceptional potential.

FAMILY THEORY

Theoretical advances in the social sciences during the last 30 to 40 years have resulted in more sophisticated understanding of family factors associated with positive child development outcomes. Psychological research has led to models of family influence on child development that are increasingly complex and mirror more closely the realities of family life. (See Bristol and Gallagher's, 1983, discussion of the evolution of psychological research.) The models of developmental influence (the unidirectional, bidirectional and triadic models of parent-child interaction, family systems and family ecological systems models) are not mutually exclusive; actually, the later and more complex models often contain sub-parts of earlier models.

Research rooted in psychodynamic theories of child development focused exclusively on the direct influence of the mother on child socialization (Bowlby, 1969; Freud, 1963; Maccoby & Martin, 1983). Bell's classic papers (1971; Bell & Harper, 1977) reinterpreted the direction of effect in correlational studies of mother-child interaction and suggested that children shape the behavior of their parents. Serious attention began to be paid to the contribution of child characteristics to parent-child interaction and subsequent child development. Differences in child characteristics, such as the level of emotional responsivity, activity level, cognitive abilities, and verbal skills, elicit and reinforce different levels and intensities of parent involvement and caregiving. Borrowing concepts from the science of physics, family systems theory provided a coherent framework for understanding the family as an interacting unit. For example, family systems theory used the homeostatic model to explain the equilibrium-maintaining qualities of behaviors in families and suggested that the goal of family adjustment to crises or developmental change was the restoration of a functioning system.

Family ecological systems theory added a dimension to family systems theory. The new approach cast the family within a larger social context by proposing that the family is only one system within an interactive, interdependent set of systems "nested" within each other (Bronfenbrenner, 1977). Therefore, a family was viewed as a system with internal hierarchies, sub-systems and boundaries, which also interacted with, and were interdependent upon, larger systems such as the extended family, neighborhood, community, and nation.

The evolution in family theory has had a profound impact upon the kind of questions family researchers ask and the nature of family interventions psychologists and educators provide. Research on families with children who are gifted has shared in this psychological history.

GIFTEDNESS IN A CULTURAL CONTEXT

American parents and educators are noted for their inconsistent and ambivalent attitudes and reactions to the gifted. Best practices in gifted education may be caught in the cross currents of prevailing cultural attitudes. Recognizing the basis of these conflictual perspectives on gifted education is an important first step in helping parents articulate their concerns regarding gifted programs for their child. School psychologists and other educators must recognize the bases of parents' reservations and hesitancies regarding gifted education.

Several negative or erroneous attitudes toward giftedness pervade the American cultural context. The first is manifested in the often heard refrain: "Leave them alone — they'll do all right regardless." Within educational circles and among parents, this reflects the commonly held belief that gifted students are destined for success as students, and in their personal lives, with little effort by the student, his or her family, or the school. The thought that a gifted student could fail is difficult for many people to accept; they tend to perceive a gifted student's failure as wanton misuse of talent. Emerging literature is beginning to document the frequency with which specially gifted children fail to reach their potential and to identify what families and schools can do to stop the erosion of this talent (Whitmore, 1979, 1980).

Second, in some fundamental way the funding of programs for gifted students seems to run counter to the democratic ideal of equality. A disproportionate expenditure of resources on any sub-group of students requires justification and the willingness of the American people. Using the democratic ideal of equal opportunity, the 1975 Education for All Handicapped Children Act (PL 94–142) argued persuasively for a substantial and disproportionate expenditure to educate children with handicaps. Previous lack of specialized programming effectively excluded these children from the educational system. Advocates for gifted students have never claimed that exceptionally talented students have been systematically denied access to schools, but they argue that students with exceptional abilities and talents may be the most underserved population in schools (Freeman, 1979) because of the lack of specialized education services appropriate to their different learning needs.

Third, most American parents are steeped in the Judeo-Christian cultural heritage, which contends that a person's responsibility to contribute to society is proportional to the gifts and benefits he or she enjoys. In this culture, identification as an academically gifted student is likely to heighten the perception of the child's ultimate responsibility to society. Although this is reasonable, and even motivating for the gifted student, parents are often concerned about the implicit burden these high expectations place on the shoulders of their children. This concern is exacerbated when parents disagree with the gifted designation. Cornell's (1983) research suggested that nearly half of parents with children identified as gifted by schools did not share this view of their child. Conflicting perceptions of a student by educators and parents are likely to affect academic performance adversely and confuse the student. Gaining a deeper understanding of parents' perception of giftedness, encouraging greater parental involvement in the identification process, and providing informational programs that introduce parents to the current definitions of giftedness are vital factors in garnering the parental support and understanding necessary for gifted students to benefit optimally from gifted educational programs.

Fourth, efforts to understand the nature of the gifted child's learning abilities, and to identify the characteristics of educational environments and instructional approaches most conducive to realizing that exceptional potential are necessary. But the needs of gifted students are viewed as superfluous when the American educational system is burdened by many urgent problems including the chronically poor report card given United States education, large-scale illiteracy among graduates of the nation's public schools, and the impact on the public education system of unsolved social problems such as drugs, teen parenthood, and violence. Perhaps the "positive dilemma" surrounding exceptional talent loses some of its force and persuasiveness as an argument when the needs of gifted students are compared with the magnitude and urgency of the needs of other students. Special investment in the education of gifted students must be justified at a time when multiple demands are being made upon an educational system of shrinking resources.

Fifth, proponents of gifted education are prone to describe students with exceptional abilities and talents as one of the nation's most precious human and natural resources. The potential danger in objectifying these students by speaking of them as a commodity — as one would describe so much unmined gold within the nation's boundaries — is to prescribe too specifically, and in too utilitarian a way, the direction this latent talent should take. Parents may perceive their own values to be in conflict with those of educators and worry about the values that will shape the expression of their child's abilities. The conflict may be manifested at the time of identification in a reluctance deriving from a parent's natural protective function.

THE GIFTED CHILD IN THE FAMILY

Although retrospective accounts of the early childhoods of eminent adults are colorful, and they periodically reveal glimpses of the family lives of these individuals (Goertzel & Goertzel, 1972; Bloom, 1985), a systematic study of family life of gifted and creative people has not been done. Nonetheless, a recent research interest in gifted education in family influences on the development of gifted students is evident (Colangelo & Brower, 1987; Cornell, 1983; Cornell & Grossberg, 1986; Karnes, Shwedel, & Steinberg, 1984; Runco & Albert, 1986). This noteworthy development occurs at the same time that an active interest in the role of the family in children's development is a leading concern of practitioners and researchers in child development, psychology, and education.

Intelligence is thought to be distributed predictably (following a theoretically normal distribution) throughout the human community. An interesting phenomenon, however, has been brought to light by several researchers (Terman, 1925) who discovered an unexpectedly frequent number of scorers at the upper end of the IQ distribution (IQ scores that suggest giftedness). This finding parallels the higher than expected frequencies of IQ scores found at the lower end of the same IQ distribution. The incidence of exceptional intellectual capability may be somewhat less rare than one would assume, given current reliance on a theoretically normal distribution of talent.

Influence of Heredity

Parents contribute most explicitly to their child through the genetically determined traits they pass on. Some traits, such as hair color and eye color, are known to be directly and predictably inherited. For example, based on their own color, a couple can know the likelihood with which their child will have blue eyes. Parents frequently announce the recognition of their own traits in their children. Infants are scrutinized and reported to have "Mom's nose" and "Daddy's hands." At times, even hints of an earlier generation are seen in children. This recognition, no doubt, aids in folding the child into the family. Other traits, such as personality, intelligence, and athletic skill are associated with parental characteristics, but the development of these personal characteristics is also determined to some extent by the educational and social opportunities available to the child.

Like physical attributes, the heritability of intelligence has been studied extensively (see Honzik, 1957; Jensen, 1969). Studies investigating the degree to which giftedness, in particular, is genetically determined are few. Nichols (1984) studied the relationship between twins' (both identical and fraternal) scores on the National Merit Scholarship Test. He found a correlation of .87 between the scores of identical twins and a correlation of .63 between the scores of fraternal twins. On that basis he concluded that about 70% of performance on this test is related to heredity.

More recently, in testing the hypothesis that "giftedness runs in families," Silverman (1986) used standard individual assessment instruments to measure the intellectual functioning of the siblings of 50 students identified as gifted. In 84% of the sibling pairs (42 of the 50 pairs), both scored in the gifted range. Fewer than one third of the pairs of siblings had scores more than 10 IQ points apart. The study lends evidence supporting a link between measurable intelligence of gifted students and genetic similarity.

Characteristics of Parents With Gifted Children

What distinguishes the parent of a gifted child from the parent of a child without exceptional abilities? The answer for the moment is largely unknown. It is not unreasonable to assume, however, that parents who rear children noted by schools and society to be gifted and talented may share common characteristics. Fell, Dahlstrom, and Winter (1984) undertook a preliminary study of the personality characteristics of a group of 32 parents of students identified as gifted. The mothers and fathers of these children (enrolled in kindergarten through grade 6) each were administered the Sixteen Personality Factor Questionnaire.

The authors analyzed the differences between the mothers in the study group and the standardization sample of women from the general population. On 6 of the 16 factors, the mothers in the study group were significantly different from the test sample. Mothers of the gifted tended to be more intelligent, more conscientious and persistent, more independent and self-sufficient. They preferred to make their own decisions, were more self-controlled, and were more careful and calculated in their approach to life than were the women from the general population.

The researchers likewise compared the fathers of the gifted students against the test standardization sample of males. Fathers, like the mothers, tended to be more intelligent, more independent, and more self-sufficient than the men from the general population. They also were more aloof, reserved, and critical, more assertive, confident, and dominating, and more tense, driven, and anxious than men representative of the general population.

Parenting Practices Among Parents With Gifted Children

Parenting practices are more often the focus of attention than the parents themselves. Permissiveness seems to underlie the child rearing practices of parents with gifted children (Gallagher, 1975; Getzels & Jackson, 1962). Parents of gifted children tend to allow them more freedom to choose friends and make decisions, and they encourage the child's interests and activities outside of the home. Fathers of highly creative children are less apt to pressure their gifted child into conventional behavior.

A certain lack of emotional attachment was noted between the parent and the gifted child. Parents allowed their gifted children a lack of commitment to the family and social conventions.

Influence of the Family Constellation

Investigations of the relationships among family variables and giftedness reveal that a child who is gifted is most often an only child or a firstborn child with one sibling (Barbe, 1956). For children in larger families (families with three or more children), however, birth order is unrelated to giftedness. But verbal creative abilities are enhanced for children in large families with a sibling of the same sex and close in age. The research data on this issue, however, are inconsistent. Circirelli (1967) found that sibling constellation factors are related to measures of creativity, but that family size is unrelated to ability or achievement.

Gifted Child's Impact on the Family

"All labels, positive and negative, . . . mediate social perception and thus shape the relationship between self and others" (Cornell, 1983, p. 323). In what ways does the presence of a gifted child influence family life? The logic of the question implies an interrelatedness of functioning among members of a family. The proposition that a child with exceptional abilities and talents creates a "difference in the family" has just recently begun to be analyzed.

Research and clinical experience with families who have a gifted child suggest that parents often find these children a source of pride, and a positive challenge to them as parents. In most cases, parents report warm and close relationships with their gifted children. Gifted children seem to be able to elicit and receive high levels of parent involvement; and the relationship between gifted child and parent is mutually compelling and rewarding (Colangelo & Brower, 1987; Cornell, 1983). Likewise, gifted children more often positively describe relationships with their mothers than do their nongifted siblings (Ballering & Koch, 1984). Caution should be exercised to not overgeneralize from these trends to all families, for the studies reported are characterized by small sample sizes and group comparisons. The reality is that the family's experience of life with a gifted child is varied and, at times, may run counter to these positive indications.

A more troubling aspect in identifying a child for enrollment in a program for the gifted and talented, and the accompanying perception of family members that a child is gifted, emerges from studies focusing on the gifted child's siblings. Cornell's (1983) research, grounded in family systems theory, investigated a series of family interaction effects for the identification of a child as gifted. He compared three groups — gifted students, their nongifted siblings, and a control group of nongifted children (matched on age and birth order with the nongifted siblings) — on measures of personality adjustment. Nongifted siblings, the results indicated, have a profile of less healthy personality adjustment than their nongifted peers. The nongifted siblings of gifted students were more anxious and neurotic, less careful of social rules, less outgoing, more easily upset, more shy and restrained, more excitable and impatient, and more tense and frustrated than either their gifted brother or sister or their regular classroom peers.

Consistent with a family systems perspective, and knowledge from clinical practice, labeling one child in a family as gifted may have the effect of labeling the child's sibling as nongifted. These results and subsequent findings (Cornell & Grossberg, 1986) confirming personality adjustment difficulties for siblings of gifted students are sobering.

Gifted educators and school psychologists counsel parents of gifted children in strategies for meeting the gifted child's educational needs and the emotional needs of siblings with the hope of mitigating against the potential negative consequences to siblings. Children look to the world about them, their interactions with adults and peers, for information about themselves. They seek information and draw inferences from relationship experiences in the family and at school. Open family communication, balanced sensitivity to the special characteristics and contributions nongifted children make to family life, and the family's ability to value the diversity of talent and ability, whether it be intellectual, social, artistic, or athletic, helps all children to define and identify personal characteristics and develop a positive self-image.

APPLICATION OF FAMILY THEORY: DIANE BRADFORD

In prior chapters, authors representing special education, gifted and regular education perspectives have explored Diane's academic record and recommended specific educational interventions for this gifted/learning disabled student. In this section Diane's educational program will be analyzed from a systems psychological perspective and school-based and family-based interventions recommended.

Historically, psychologists have assisted in the identification of gifted students by administering individual intelligence tests. A family orientation to the practice of school psychology has much to offer gifted education. School psychologists' interest in a family systems perspective coincides with a broader emphasis in school psychology on systems intervention practices (Donovan, in press; Hannafin & Witt, 1983; Rosenthal, Ellis, & Pryzwansky, 1987; Snapp & Davidson, 1982; and Taplin, 1980). The role of the school psychologist advocated here suggests a more comprehensive plan of psychological services to gifted students and their families.

Biographical and Academic Highlights

Diane, a 9-year-old, fourth-grade student, has qualified for special education services because of her difficulties with visual-motor integration, thought to be associated with deficits demonstrated in reading, handwriting, and organizational skills. In the regular classroom Diane is a vibrant and engaged student when instructional methodology employs techniques such as simulations and role plays. But the precision required in spelling, reading, and math drills and in reading comprehension exercises create difficulty, a source of frustration and anxiety to her.

Approximately a year ago, Diane was prescribed Ritalin to address "attentional and emotional concerns," and she continues on the medication. Although Diane has not yet been referred to the gifted program, her exemplary athletic performances, as a swimmer and field and track competitor, are noteworthy. In addition, she shows clear social and leadership strengths.

At home, Diane is the younger of two daughters in the Bradford family. Diane's sister — older by 5 years and described as having an equitable, easy-going interpersonal style — is an exceptional student who participates in the gifted education program.

A Psychological Interpretation of Academic Functioning

Psychological factors evident in the report of Diane's educational experience and family life are anticipated to influence her success as a student. Diane's academic skills profile is characteristic of many gifted learning disabled students: areas of academic skill deficiency complemented by areas of exceptional intellectual capacity and high levels of academic functioning. Diane's verbal knowledge and verbal conceptual abilities are exceptional. Functioning in this area is offset, however, by below-average development of perceptual organizational skills.

Though Diane shares some characteristics in common with students who are gifted, the nature of her own peaked profile suggests significant learning difficulties unknown to the large majority of gifted students. At the same time, she expresses an intellectual acumen not frequently associated with students who have learning disabilities. Her performance in the regular education classroom is also more variable than that of the average student. By her own description, she excels at some lessons and finds others frustrating and anxiety-provoking. Students like Diane are puzzling to their teachers and parents, and their behavior is frequently misinterpreted.

The nature of Diane's intellectual functioning and academic skills development make her eligible for special education services and appropriately considered as a student with learning disabilities, a regular classroom student, and a student who is gifted. Sharing simultaneously some of the characteristics of each of these three groups of students (more often defined by their differences) is both an asset and a liability to Diane. Not surprisingly, Diane's self-concept is jeopardized.

Self-concept is a psychological construct deriving from self theory (Rogers, 1961; Maslow, 1962; and May, 1969). The degree to which a student's self-concept is positive is dependent upon both (a) the child's ability to identify positive personal characteristics and traits related to academic performance, and (b) the child's satisfaction with the results of his or her assessment. Diane's academic self-concept incorporates both positive and negative features. At school, her assessment of her own academic competence likely has been threatened by the learning disability designation at school, and within the family, her self-concept has been weakened by the identification of her sister as gifted. (See Hobbs, 1975, for an extensive discussion of the impact of labeling.) In the family, a positive, gifted label bestowed on one child results frequently in the sibling's self-labeling as nongifted.

Diane's need for medication creates a third vulnerability to the development of a secure, positive academic self-concept. Ritalin was prescribed to help control impulsivity, to improve attention to school tasks, and to modulate emotional intensity. Children who receive medication for behavioral disorders commonly perceive a loss of physiologic integrity: The body is perceived as one's enemy. Clinical practice suggests that children on medication often believe the medication makes them learn and behave better. Incorrect beliefs such as this may cause students not to claim the learning and behavioral improvements they are making by their own efforts and, thereby, to miss an opportunity for enhancing self-concept.

Challenging students with unhelpful beliefs to recognize that a pill never has been known to learn — that it is they, themselves, who have used the opportunity of a relaxed and attentive body to learn in school — is important. Invariably, students find that this correction of their understanding of the role of medication is not trivial but, instead, helpful and self-enhancing. For this reason, psychological counseling should accompany medication. Involvement of the family in counseling around issues of medication also may be indicated. In addition, close monitoring of the need for medication with a child's increasing behavioral control is recommended.

Diane's perception of her performance as a student is uneven. She speaks with enthusiasm and energy when relating her role in the reenactment of a town's commercial life. She clearly learned readily many concepts of trade and commerce from this experience-based social studies lesson. At other points in an interview, it is poignant to hear her relate the struggle with common classroom learning tasks such as spelling quizzes and reading exercises. Like many students, Diane recognizes that she is good at some schoolwork (work she reports liking) but not at other schoolwork (tasks she dislikes). Diane demonstrates no self-conscious awareness that school tasks are not necessarily objectively "easy" or "hard," and that her own specific learning abilities and weaknesses interacting with instructional approach allow her to learn more readily or less readily. A higher level of awareness of effective learning strategies would afford this child an ability to attack new learning tasks more efficiently and, ultimately, more successfully, building the basis for a stronger, more positive academic self-concept.

On the positive side, Diane's successful leadership experiences in the context of cooperative learning and athletic activities help to counteract, to some extent, the negative impacts. Social/interpersonal skillfulness contributes to her success in these areas. Diane clearly enjoys people, participates easily in group activities, and frequently emerges as a leader. She gains much satisfaction from her success with these activities, which bolsters self-concept.

Interventions: By Setting

An understanding of Diane from a psychological perspective has been built around the issue of self-concept. Recommendations for psychological and educational interventions will be described according to the setting in which they can be most effectively carried out. The psychological interventions focus on the goals of: (a) improving Diane's academic self-concept, (b) developing more effective self-management techniques, (c) reducing/eliminating drug dependency, (d) increasing self-identification of strengths, (e) employing co-curricular activities to illustrate academic skills, and (f) mobilizing the family system to facilitate Diane's personal and academic development. The recommended interventions articulate specific approaches helpful in realizing these goals.

School-based Interventions

Recommendation 1. It is evident that Diane as a student is active in organizing her learning environment. For example, Diane continued her participation in the special education program (where she held the leading role in a drama) long after official termination of special educational services. Learning activities that simulate real life and allow for a student's high level of engagement with material make new knowledge/information more accessible to Diane. At present, her choice of learning strategies is instinctive. It is recommended that a greater self-awareness of effective learning strategies be taught and their use encouraged.

Toward this goal, process-oriented cognitive interviewing (Peverly, 1990) is recommended as a strategy for the school psychologist to employ with Diane, to augment present information about Diane as a learner, available from norm-referenced tests and curriculum-based assessments, and, more important, as a way to identify the cognitive strategies she employs. Information from process-oriented cognitive interviews then would be used in academic counseling to heighten Diane's awareness of the cognitive strategies she currently employs effectively, and of others she might include. Information on the nature of the child's cognitive strategies for learning would be shared with her teachers to assist them in matching instructional methods to Diane's learning style.

Recommendation 2. It is further recommended that an awareness of the role that cognitive processes and learning strategies play in acquiring and remembering new information be employed as a springboard to help Diane explore ways to compensate for her learning inefficiencies or weaknesses. Recognizing limitations and accessing compensatory strategies may be a wiser investment of time and energy than directly improving some deficient skills. For example, encouraging the use of word processing equipment has more benefit for a 9-year-old student than continuing handwriting drills. Also, small-group sessions to discuss project development in a science or social studies activity is likely to produce more creative and productive problem solving than organizing ideas in written outline format for Diane.

Recommendation 3. At present, Diane does not adequately recognize the intellectual strengths she brings to the learning process. She labels as "easy" those activities at which she excels. And the exceptional nature of her leadership and social skills is taken for granted. An increased awareness of her learning strengths will help this child to understand why equal effort on school tasks leads to highly variable results with academic work, and to reduce the frustration and anxiety that may arise from misattributing the causes of her learning difficulties.

Therefore, it is recommended that Diane develop a greater awareness of her learning strengths. This recommendation is set apart for emphasis. In practice, however, it is inseparable from the activities suggested in recommendations #1 and #2. Realization of the goal of this recommendation will have important positive consequences on Diane's academic self-concept.

Family-based Interventions

Recommendation 1. There is evidence that high levels of parent involvement in the educational process have beneficial outcomes for gifted students' academic and personal development (Kaufman & Sexton, 1983). In school, the gifted child's program of studies is characterized by involvement with a greater number of educational professionals, programs, and activities than the nongifted child, and is even more so for a student with the dual designation of gifted/LD. Educational services for a gifted student often draw not only upon public education services but also upon community-based programs and the family's independent resources for educational and cultural opportunities. Diane is fortunate in the extent to which her parents have given her enriching co-curricular activities. Integration of these activities and program participation both in and out of school, however, requires artful patchwork.

Diane's mother, Jane, has served the function of a case manager in monitoring her daughter's education. With access to material and professional resources, this mother has actively pursued educators' recommendations. For example, during the kindergarten year Diane's teachers first recognized early indications of a learning problem in an otherwise bright young girl. Jane promptly sought the services of a child psychologist and then involved Diane in an extended program of therapeutic intervention to remediate visual-motor integration difficulties. Jane has likewise participated in the more recent school decisions to provide Diane with special education services. It is not evident, however, that Jane's involvement has extended to an understanding of the curricular content of these interventions. An even more active participatory decision-making and advocacy role in regard to the curriculum presented her daughter is recommended.

Recommendation 2. Glimpses of Diane's relationship with her family, especially her mother and father, suggest that she may have developed interpersonal relationships within the family that focus on her as a "child with problems." Her sister is undisputably perceived as a gifted student. Furthermore, the issue of drug dependency may be linked to this relational structure in the family. As an example, more than one interpretation exists of Diane's emotional intensity and reactivity. Presently, her emotional sensitivity is viewed as one of a cluster of symptoms described as attentional deficits, but it is also plausible to view emotional intensity as an indication of giftedness. Gifted children frequently have heightened emotional sensitivity as a consequence of their exceptional cognitive abilities.

Although I perceive the Bradford family to be functional and healthy, short-term structural family therapy is recommended as a way to explore family roles and their consequences for Diane's academic performance. Structural family therapy has been demonstrated to be an effective family intervention for students whose school problems have a family component. Diane would be targeted as the client, but this form of intervention is designed to help explore the dynamics of communication and relationships in the family that support less than optimal functioning of any member.

Therefore, interpersonal interactions between parents and children, and between siblings, becomes the focus of the therapeutic process. Furthermore, this family intervention has the attraction of being consistent with Diane's preferred learning style, as the method employs *in vivo* enactments and supported in-session practice of new skills and interaction patterns.

Summary

The recommendations outlined are illustrative and designed to support the instructional interventions recommended by educators. The presence of the school psychologist and parent at the curriculum-planning meetings is vital to ensure the most productive integration of educational and psychological approaches to intervention. Diane's parents closely monitor her progress and are fortunate in being able to provide her with many co-curricular activities. Parents may be the only representative at a curriculum planning meeting who have an intimate knowledge of the child's full range of educational activities, both in and out of school.

SUMMARY

Bridging the worlds of school and family is beneficial to gifted students. School psychologists with a family orientation to practice can provide insights useful to curriculum planning. School-based teams (consisting of teachers from regular, special education, and gifted programs, the school psychologist, parent, and gifted child, when appropriate) are an effective forum for curriculum planning.

Collaborative planning is likely to result in educational programming for the gifted student that is integrated and is sensitively designed to meet special student needs. This sort of collaboration mobilizes educational and family resources in realizing the full development of student talents.

REFERENCES

Barbe, W. (1956). A study of the family background of the gifted. *Journal of Educational Psychology, 47,* 302–309.

Bell, R. Q. (1971). Stimulus control of parent or caretaker behavior of offspring. *Developmental Psychology, 4,* 63–72.

Bell, R. Q., & Harper, L. V. (1977). *Child effects on adults.* Hillsdale, NJ: Lawrence Erlbaum.

Bloom, B. S. (Ed.). (1985). *Developing talent in young people.* New York: Ballantine.

Bowlby, J. (1969). *Attachment*. New York: Basic Books.

Bristol, M. M., & Gallagher, J. J. (1983, September). *Psychological research on fathers of young handicapped children: Evolution, review, and some future directions*. Paper presented at NICHHD Conferences on Research on families with retarded persons, University of North Carolina.

Bronfenbrenner, U. (1977). Toward an experimental ecology of human development. *American Psychologist, 32,* 513–531.

Circirelli, V. G. (1967). Sibling constellation, creativity, I.Q., and academic achievement. *Child Development, 38,* 481–490.

Colangelo, N., & Brower, P. (1987). Labeling gifted youngsters: Long-term impact on families. *Gifted Child Quarterly, 31*(2), 75–78.

Cornell, D. G. (1983). Gifted children: The impact of positive labeling on the family system. *American Journal of Orthopsychiatry, 53*(2), 322–335.

Cornell, D. G., & Grossberg, I. N. (1986). Siblings of children in gifted programs. *Journal for the Education of the Gifted, 9*(4), 253–264.

Donovan, A. M. (in press). Family systems intervention and school psychology: Critical analysis of research and issues in practice. In C. I. Carlson & M. J. Fine (Eds.), *Handbook of family-school problems and interventions: A systems perspective*. Orlando, FL: Grune & Stratton.

Fell, L., Dahlstrom, M. & Winter, D. (1984). Personality traits of parents of gifted children. *Psychological Reports, 54*(2), 383–387.

Freeman, J. (1979). *Gifted children: Their identification and development in a social context*. Lancaster, England: MTP Press.

Freud, S. (1963). *The sexual enlightenment of children*. New York: Collier Books.

Gallagher, J. J. (1975). *Teaching the gifted child* (2nd ed.). Boston: Allyn & Bacon.

Getzels, J., & Jackson, P. (1962). *Creativity and intelligence: Explorations with gifted students*. New York: John Wiley & Sons.

Goertzel, V., & Goertzel, M. G. (1962). *Cradles of eminence*. Boston: Little, Brown.

Hannafin, M. J., & Witt, J. C. (1983). System intervention and the school psychologist: Maximizing interplay among roles and functions. *Professional Psychology: Research and Practice, 14*(1), 128–136.

Hobbs, N. (Ed.). (1975). *The futures of children: Categories, labels and their consequences*. San Francisco: Jossey-Bass.

Honzik, M. P. (1957). Developmental studies of parent-child resemblances in intelligence. *Child Development, 28,* 215–228.

Jensen, A. R. (1969). How much can we boost IQ and scholastic achievement? *Harvard Educational Review, 39,* 1–123.

Karnes, M. B., Shwedel, A. M., & Steinberg, D. (1984). Styles of parenting among parents of young gifted children. *Roeper Review, 6*(4), 232–235.

Kaufman, F. A., & Sexton, D. (1983). Some implications for home-school linkages. *Roeper Review, 6*(1), 49–51.

Maccoby, E. E., & Martin, J. A. (1983). Socialization in the context of family: Parent-child interaction. In P. H. Mussen (Ed.), *Handbook of child psychology*. New York: John Wiley & Sons.

Maslow, A. H. (1962). *Toward a psychology of being*. Princeton, NJ: Van Nostrand.

May, R. (Ed.). (1969). *Existential psychology* (2nd ed.). New York: Random House.

Nicholls, J. (1984). Concepts of ability and achievement motivation. In R. Ames & C. Ames (Eds.), *Research on motivation in education* (pp. 39–73), Vol. 1. New York: Academic Press.

Peverly, S. T. (1990). *An overview of the potential impact of cognitive psychology on psychoeducational assessment*. Unpublished manuscript, under review.

Rogers, C. R. (1961). *On becoming a person: A therapist's view of psychotherapy*. Boston: Houghton Mifflin.

Rogers, K. B. (1986). Do the gifted think and learn differently? A review of recent research and its implications for instruction. *Journal for the Education of the Gifted, 10*(1), 17–39.

Rosenthal, S., Ellis, J., & Pryzwansky, W. (1987). *Systems theory and school psychology: Current applications in practice.* Unpublished manuscript.

Runco, M. A., & Albert, R. S. (1986). Exceptional giftedness in early adolescence and intrafamilial divergent thinking. *Journal of Youth and Adolescence, 15*(4), 335–344.

Silverman, L. (1986). Parenting young gifted children. *Journal of Children in Contemporary Society, 18*(3-4), 73–87.

Taplin, J. R. (1980). Implications of general system theory for assessment and intervention. *Professional Psychology, 11*(5), 722–727.

Terman, L. M. (Ed.). (1925). *Genetic studies of genius: Mental and physical traits of a thousand gifted children (Vol. 1).* Stanford, CA: Stanford University Press.

Whitmore, J. (1979). The etiology of underachievement in highly gifted young children. *Journal for the Education of the Gifted, 3*(1), 38–51.

Whitmore, J. (1980). *Giftedness, conflict, and underachievement.* Boston: Allyn & Bacon.

CHAPTER SIXTEEN

An Individualized Plan for Diane Bradford

T he preceding chapters have delineated perspectives on curriculum in general education, special education, learning disabilities, and a school psychologist's view of the importance of a family systems perspective in understanding the educational needs of an example child, Diane Bradford. This chapter synthesizes the major viewpoints on Diane Bradford and puts forth an individualized learning plan that might be used with her in the context of school. The various recommendations were based on the following:

- *A thorough review of test results and other written documentation of performance.* Test results were available from two full-scale psychological examinations from kindergarten and grade 2. Moreover, written communication about the case was available from school-based teams responsible for follow-up implementation of an educational plan.
- *A review of the parental perspective.* One member of the collaborative team interviewed Diane's mother and videotaped the interview. Each of the collaborators contributed to the questions asked in the interview, and each collaborator analyzed the videotape and took notes on its content.
- *A review of the student's perspective.* A videotape was recorded using Diane as an interview subject. She was asked questions prepared by the collaborators. All of the collaborators analyzed the videotape and documented issues of relevance.

- *Substantive discussions of Diane in three group meetings.* The collaborative team met to discuss Diane as a case subject over a period of 9 months. Each discussion session was approximately 6 hours long, and each meeting addressed a different facet of the data. The topic of the first session was the written reports and the mother's videotape; the second focused on the videotape of Diane herself; and the third synthesized observations and ideas to develop a curriculum plan for Diane that would cut across the various roles represented by the collaborative team.

SUGGESTED CURRICULAR INTERVENTIONS

At a school level, the analog to the work of this collaborative team would be a school-based group of educators who would take responsibility for case management. This group of educators would include, minimally, the classroom teacher, a gifted specialist, a relevant resource consultant, the school psychologist, and the student's parent(s). These individuals would ensure the implementation of a curriculum plan honoring the needs of individual learners like Diane. The specialist in giftedness would be responsible for gathering curricular suggestions from all team members and developing a curriculum plan based on the team's input. The plan would attempt to aggregate perspectives of various team members so that the resulting plan would be multidimensional and sufficiently rich to address the complexity of learning disabled gifted individuals. Table 16.1 reflects the perspectives of each member of the collaborative team in their curriculum ideas for Diane.

As one transforms this list of ideas into a set of manageable student outcomes for Diane's curriculum, it is important to look for consonance across at least two perspectives. The resulting outcome statements reflect this shared perspective. Student learner outcomes have been grouped by generic learning domains to convey an integrated focus on the student in all of her multidimensionality.

ONE-YEAR CURRICULUM PLAN

A. Cognitive
  1. The student will develop research skills sufficient to carry out self-initiated projects.

Example for Item A.1, Research Skills

I. Defining a problem (Selecting a topic)

II. Acquiring information (Collecting data)
  Card catalog
  Table of contents
  Index

Table 16.1
INTERVENTIONS FOR DIANE BRADFORD AND HER FAMILY

Discipline	Specific Intervention
General Education	Simulations Hands-on approaches Role playing (creative dramatics) Problem solving strategies Small groups (by task, role, and interest area) Instructional grouping in math; individualization in reading Avoidance of competition in basic academics Athletic program Reading to younger children as a way to build self-esteem Use of computer for skill development in math and reading Self-regulation of behavior
Special Education	Teaching specific learning strategies and study skills such as decoding (e.g., DISSECT program), test taking, and mnemonics Teaching organizational strategies (time and materials) Focus on research skills (library skills) Development of social skills (leadership/followership) Development of self-control and self-management Planning for future learning Use of alternative media/modes for instruction (video, audio, computer)
Gifted Education	Literature-based reading program (based on interest level and book selection geared to gifted population) Diagnostic-prescriptive model in basic reading skill development Cooperative learning model in mathematics, focusing on the use of: challenge problems, real-life problems (challenge of the unknown), and spatial/visualization techniques Special project approach in teaching science and social science Thematic curriculum Strong emphasis on the arts and providing aesthetic experiences in art, music, dance, dramatic interpretation, debate, and speech Emphasis on oral expression as an alternative mode Development of creative thinking and critical thinking skills Co-curricular activities such as theatre, athletics, and art programs Diane to "try out" in a program for gifted learners, based on thinking skills and project work Regular classroom placement consideration in cluster groups for most curriculum areas

Table 16.1
(CONTINUED)

Discipline	Specific Intervention
Psychological/ Family Systems View	Ways to develop more positive self-esteem Self-control and self-management techniques Coping and compensation strategies Elimination or reduction of drug dependency with counseling Recognition by family of talent areas Horseback riding interest to illustrate and emphasize organizational skills Nongifted sibling addressed as a family issue Role relationships within the family Parent assigned as case manager

Glossary
Reader's guide
Note taking
Skimming
Distinguishing between primary and secondary references
Abstracts
Checking validity of resources: author's authenticity, copyright, sources
Bibliography
Footnotes
Retrieval systems (microfiche, ERIC)
Statistical information
Pictures
Interviewing
Surveying
Observing

III. Selecting a research method
    Case history
    Historical study
    Descriptive study
    Developmental study

IV. Testing hypotheses

V. Interpreting information
    Stating a premise
    Drawing conclusions
    Making an inference

Outlining
Identifying key words, phrases, ideas, making recommendations
Summarizing

VI. Reporting information
Developing a bibliography
Writing an abstract
Writing a proposal
Developing a report, creating tables, making graphs, etc.

Source: From *Handbook on Curriculum for the Gifted* by J. VanTassel-Baska, 1986, Evanston, IL: Northwestern University Center for Talent Development.

2. The student will enhance her critical and creative thinking behaviors.

Examples for Item A.2, Critical Thinking

Definition of critical thinking: The correct assessing of statements.

Twelve Aspects of Critical Thinking

1. Grasp the meaning of a statement.
2. Judge whether ambiguity exists.
3. Judge if contradictions exist.
4. Judge if a conclusion necessarily follows.
5. Judge the specificity of a statement.
6. Judge if a statement relates to a certain principle.
7. Judge the reliability of an observation.
8. Judge if an inductive conclusion is warranted.
9. Judge if a problem has been identified.
10. Judge if a definition is adequate.
11. Judge if a statement is credible.
12. Judge if something is an assumption.

Source: "A Critical Concept of Critical Thinking" by R. H. Ennis, *Harvard Review, 32*(1), Winter 1962.

Creative Thinking Strategies

1. Fluency: the number of responses that are relevant and not repeated within the list. *How many ideas can you come up with?*
2. Flexibility: the number of shifts to other ways of looking at the question. *Can you think of another category or another way of looking at the idea?*

3. Originality: the uniqueness of a response in comparison with other of the group or a similar group. *Can you think of an idea that no one else has come up with?*
4. Elaboration: the "fleshing out" of an idea by adding descriptive details or relating it to other ideas. *Can you add to your ideas?*

Source: From *Torrance Test of Creative Thinking* by P. Torrance, 1966, Athens, GA: Personnel Press.

Creative Problem Solving

The creative process applies to problem solving:

1. Fact finding: gathering data in preparation for defining the problem. *Identify the problem by asking questions: Who? What? Where? When? Why?*

2. Problem finding: analyzing problematic areas in order to pick out and point up the problem to be attacked.
   Question: "In what ways might I . . .?"
   Gather data

3. Idea finding: idea production — thinking up, processing, and developing numerous possible leads to solutions.
   Put to other uses
   Modify
   Magnify
   Rearrange
   Combine
   Adapt
   Minimize
   Substitute
   Reverse

4. Solution finding: evaluating potential solutions against defined criteria
   Establish criteria
   Evaluate
   Verify
   Test

5. Acceptance finding: adoption — developing a plan of action and implementing the chosen solution
   Implement
   Prepare for acceptance

Source: From *Aha! Insights into Creative Behavior* by S. J. Parnes, 1975, Buffalo, NY: DOK Publisher.

3. The student will develop skills in core domains of learning through an emphasis on the following instructional techniques: diagnostic-prescriptive approaches, cooperative and instructional grouping, use of hands-on manipulations, role playing and simulations, and thematic organization of curriculum units of study.

These are emphases suggested for use with students like Diane in regular classroom settings. For teachers to work effectively with any gifted student, these approaches have to become standard practice. If they are not in place, staff development in these areas should be instituted.

B. Affective
   1. The student will develop enhanced self-esteem through opportunities to collaborate with others in projects such as tutoring younger students, working with a mentor, or organizing a school project. Development of a strong self-concept is central to an interpretation of Diane's profile. One-to-one interactions with other students or adults like herself may help her see and understand the nature of her disability but also the strength of her own abilities. Academic self-concept will be enhanced only as a result of academic or school-based success. Thus, a direct approach to such enhancement in the context of school is warranted.
   2. The student will develop the social skills of coping with individual differences and leadership.

Example for Item B.2, Affective — Social Skills

- Diane may engage in a bibliotherapy group discussing books with characters who are different from their peers and have difficulties coping with their exceptionalities. A few examples might be:
  Feelings (Aliki)
  Miss Rumphius (Cooney)
  A Wrinkle in Time (L'Engle)
  Drop Dead (Cunningham)
  A Girl Called Al (Greene)
- Diane may participate in various leadership activities and develop skills of effective group dynamics.

C. Behavioral
   1. The student will develop the metacognitive skills of planning and organization, time and materials management, and self-monitoring.

Example for Item C.1, Behavioral

The following outline of a metacognitive curriculum has been field-tested on middle school age at-risk learners.

Stating a goal: To get students to experience the planning process with an unusual yet relevant experience.

Selecting operations to perform: Reading material about explorers' search for the Nile and the kinds of planning they did in the late 19th century; deciding to have teams of students plan for a hypothetical journey into unknown Africa.

Sequencing operations: Deciding to capture interest and try to motivate by using space exploration in the future and now before introducing past undertaking; making sure students know the limitations of 19th-century explorations; preparing to have groups of students work together and then share results; intending to have groups share what they concluded and then examining how they reached those decisions.

Identifying potential obstacles: Students not knowing enough about African geography or 19th-century life. Students not working well together in groups.

Identifying ways to recover from obstacles: Questioning students about what they know and correcting any misconceptions. Changing students from one group to another more compatible one. Providing a more structured task with a set amount of money and the value and function of the people and items that can be purchased.

Predicting desired results: Students will produce unexpected answers. Students will be able to plan but may not have reflected on their planning style or planning approach.

Source: From *Metacognitive Curriculum Modules for At-Risk Gifted Learners* by G. Bass (in preparation), developed through Project Mandela, U.S. DOE grant #R206-A00165.

D. Psychomotoric
   1. The student will develop athletic talent in swimming, horseback riding, and other pursuits of interest.
      Highlighting in Diane's plan her outstanding areas of strength is important, even though implementation of these areas falls outside the purview of school responsibility. Diane is a superb athlete and should be encouraged to continue her work in these areas.
   2. The student will participate in theatre, movement, or dance opportunities available in the school or community.
      Another application of Diane's expressive talent might be in the areas

of the dramatic arts and dance. The school might be able to nurture these through co-curricular experiences, or the community through special offerings.

E. Aesthetic
  1. The student will develop performance skills in one of the following: debate, oral interpretation, speech.
     Given Diane's predeliction for oral communication, nurturing those skills in a formal structure may be important. Of the three approaches, debate may be the most intellectually challenging to her, and supplement well the cognitive areas of the plan.
  2. The student will develop an appreciation of the interrelationship of art, music, dance, and drama by creating a media arts event, utilizing all four modes of artistic expression.
     This long-term project recommendation allows Diane to be engaged as a creative producer in areas of learning that she has not explored in any depth. Thus, it allows for new learning in an integrated way that leads to her use of creative imagination to stage an event or happening.

As can be seen from the stated learner outcomes, Diane's curriculum plan will require the continued collaboration of a school-based team at the stages of implementation and follow-up. Even some of the interventions themselves will require a team effort, such as coordination of the media arts event. Yet, in the overall efforts of a team like this lies the best route for addressing the needs of special population learners. Her curriculum plan appropriately reflects those areas of specialized need, in which emphasis in curriculum implementation is differentiated based on her unique learning profile. Moreover, the collaboration process allowed educators to view Diane as the complex person she is, free of either ameliorative or pejorative labels that can taint the process of reflective educational planning.

OPERATIONAL RULES
FOR COLLABORATIVE TEAM FOLLOW-UP

Although the development and design of a collaborative curriculum plan for special needs students is time-consuming and demanding in its own way, a strong follow-up structure is essential to guarantee a faithful rendering of the components of the plan. For an effective curriculum, all elements in Diane's plan have to be implemented simultaneously. The following actions should be undertaken by a school-based team:

1. Coordination through the principal for monitoring classroom implementation. Diane's regular classroom teacher will have to be integrally involved in

implementing her plan, particularly the A, B, and E sections. Consequently, we need to know that the modifications are being done for her in the regular classroom context.

2. Coordination with Diane's mother of extracurricular activities. Some of the plan's components require a strong commitment on the part of Diane's mother. Engaging in theatre, sports, and the like calls for out-of-school time and transportation. The parent must assume major responsibility for these elements of Diane's curriculum plan.

3. Designation of the gifted specialist as educational case manager, responsible for keeping and aggregating records, setting up appropriate meetings, and initiating action on the case. Clearly, the role of gifted education in this case is central to tilting the emphasis toward developing Diane's strengths. Because Diane is a special needs case, her progress is essential and must be tracked internally by someone on the team. The gifted educator would be a good school-based manager because of the need to collaborate with the regular classroom teacher and the special education specialist on Diane's behalf.

4. Designation of the parent as the home-based case manager, responsible for maintaining careful records, assisting in implementation of the plan in key areas, and documenting Diane's responsiveness and progress. As with any case, Diane's best advocate is her mother, and thus the parent should be encouraged to continue and even intensify the nature of record keeping she has begun on her daughter. The mother is in the best position to observe and record current progress and long-term growth well beyond the limited records of any educational establishment.

5. Use of a special educator as small-group facilitator of behavioral and social components in Diane's profile. Because children with learning disabilities bring with them a profile of behavior problems that frequently exceed, in intensity of need, their learning problems, special educators may be in a unique position to focus on these troublesome behaviors with targeted interventions. Diane's case calls for a strong emphasis on self-regulation. And in this arena, the need to observe transfer effect between the special education setting, the regular classroom setting, and the gifted setting is essential.

6. An annual review and assessment of the plan's adequacy and benchmarks of progress. A meeting will be needed at the end of the year to bring together these same players to review what worked and what didn't work for Diane. Based on the data, a second-year plan might be constructed.

This process of implementation assures the necessary attention to follow-up required in all special population cases. An educator of the gifted within the schools might be responsible for up to 10 cases of individualized needs. As the process of collaboration across professional boundaries becomes more commonplace, appropriate services to students like Diane will become a reality.

SUMMARY

A curriculum plan for Diane Bradford was developed collaboratively to illustrate effective approaches for meeting the needs of a learning disabled student. Members of the team included representatives from general education, special education, gifted education, family systems psychology, Diane's mother, and Diane herself. All these perspectives were considered in developing the one-year plan.

Progress in curriculum development for learners with special needs may depend on the willingness of educators to share varying perspectives and expertise that impact on exceptional students. Moreover, there appears to be a need for considerable consultation among educators representative of these various specialty areas in order to understand strategies for blending these perspectives into a meaningful plan of action.

QUESTIONS FOR REFLECTION

1. What other interventions might be tried with Diane Bradford?
2. How might an IEP be structured so classroom teachers can easily understand and translate it?
3. What are the relative advantages and disadvantages of using a collaborative approach to IEP development?
4. What other types of individuals might be asked to participate in the IEP process?

REFERENCES

Bass, G. (in preparation). *Metacognitive curriculum modules for at-risk gifted learners*. Washington, DC: U.S. Department of Education.

Ennis, R. H. (1962). A critical concept of critical thinking. *Harvard Review, 32*(1), Winter.

Torrance, P. (1966). *Torrance test of creative thinking*. Athens, GA: Personnel Press.

Parnes, S. J. (1975). *Aha! Insights into creative behavior*. Buffalo, NY: DOK Publisher.

VanTassel-Baska, J. (1986). *Handbook on curriculum for the gifted*. Evanston, IL: Northwestern University, Center for Talent Development.

The Challenge
for the Future

W
here is curriculum and instruction for the gifted headed over the next several years? Clearly, the field of gifted education is changing. Our conceptions of intelligence, and therefore of giftedness, have changed. Our conceptions of the delivery context for serving the gifted have changed. Our population focus has changed. This shift presents a dilemma, but is also challenges us to grow and develop as a field. Perhaps the result will be a field that is responsive to the individual needs of children rather than to preordained labels; to the social context of schools and the networks that hold them together rather than the categorical approach to gifted education as a separate enterprise; and more responsive to change in general, which requires us to compromise hard positions and join forces with all educators who care about students with special needs.

If gifted education is to be meaningful for the students it wants to serve, curriculum planners for the gifted should be cognizant of the importance of maintaining a balanced perspective toward key issues. The theme for approaching and dealing with these issues revolves around *balance* — a balance that must be effected through alliances with general and special education models without diffusing efforts to maintain a distinguishable set of curriculum principles appropriate *only* for gifted learners.

One of the dangers of reaching out to the more entrenched curriculum models of general education or the specialized administrative models of special education is a loss of identity in what gifted education itself represents. If current research efforts show that the degree of exceptionality is not sufficiently great to warrant a special administrative structure and special settings for gifted learners, our claims as a field to separate program considerations becomes weakened. If, at the same time, exemplary approaches to curriculum in general education are demonstrated to be both necessary and sufficient for gifted learners, our claims to a qualitatively different set of educational experiences for the gifted are weakened. Although we as a field may have made too much of our distinctiveness and specialness, by the same token we must guard against too quickly abandoning the very principles on which the field has been grounded for the last 70 years — the basic principles of the gifted student's unique needs that call for acceleration, grouping, and enrichment in school settings.

Balance is also important in considering the needs of learners who are gifted in all cognitive areas, in comparison to those gifted only in one. How do we provide appropriate curricular experiences for specialized talents as well as provide comprehensive services to more broad-based ones? This issue is particularly worthy of our reflection at the level of developing a curriculum scope and sequence. Should the outcome expectations of secondary school for the science-prone, for example, differ from the expectations for the intellectually gifted student whose interests and aptitudes are broader? If they should, how might these differential expectations be articulated K-12? Or should specialized talent development even be a function of the public school arena?

Certainly Bloom's (1985) work on talent development would support the contention that it has not been traditionally a part of what public schools have taken on as their responsibility. Perhaps it is in the specialized areas of talent — art, music, mathematics, chess — where the school's major role may be that of broker and facilitator of talent development for students who show early promise. It is for these learners that tutorials, mentorships, and internships in the larger community might be reserved because their aptitudes and interests are more finely tuned to the need for individualized adult expert instruction.

Balance is also a theme in the domains of study to be valued in a comprehensive curriculum for gifted learners. In an earlier text, I argued for giving the affective, aesthetic, and social domains of study as much attention as the cognitive in the gifted learner's overall development (VanTassel-Baska et al., 1988). This balanced perspective on curriculum development is needed lest we limit our recognition of gifted learners' integrated needs and narrow the educational options available to them. Including the arts, for example, provides a vehicle for development of aesthetic appreciation and an expressive outlet that enhances the creative impulse. Scientists foreshadow discoveries in metaphors and visual symbols. Mathematicians strive for elegance in form. Philosophers value the symmetry of an argument. In most professional fields at high levels of creative work, the aesthetic, artistic aspects of the work come strongly into play. To ensure that curriculum for gifted learners is heavily infused with these emphases throughout their schooling seems vital.

Honoring the affective development of the gifted is integral to a comprehensive, balanced curriculum view. These students' need to understand their own exceptionality, their intensity and sensitivity of feelings, their need for coping strategies to help them deal with their own perfectionism and vulnerability all dictate the necessity of a strong affective orientation to their curriculum. These students require teachers who are sensitive to the nature of gifted students, and counseling services that can respond to their psychosocial, academic planning, and career planning needs.

Another facet of a balanced curriculum for the gifted is the area of social development, undertaken with the long view toward adult leadership. Though much of the work in leadership curriculum for the gifted has focused on political leadership (e.g., Gallagher, 1982), we should expand our thinking to embrace a concept of leadership that recognizes the other forms of leadership that gifted individuals in a society provide, including intellectual leadership in various areas and, for many gifted women, social service leadership. The skills of understanding group dynamics, the organization of complex tasks, and how to motivate others, however, are fundamental to all forms of leadership and must underlie a curriculum for the gifted.

We also need to view our purposes in constructing specialized curricula for gifted learners. We often have argued that differentiating curricula for the gifted is important to meet individual needs, yet we view the potential contribution of the gifted to society as equally important. The metaphor of the gifted as a national resource has been exploited more than once in our history as a field. In the policy arena, at least, we should keep these purposes in a healthy tension that allows for both views to be made explicit. For at a fundamental level, the gifted develop as individuals in a reciprocal relationship with their society. Thus, their creative work carries meaning beyond themselves whether it is fully intended to or not. By the same token, a society is enriched by having individuals actively engaging in self-chosen creative endeavors.

The translation of this paradox of individual and societal needs at the classroom level can be seen in the cooperative learning concept. To what extent does use of the gifted learner as a tutor/teacher/model to others in group settings become exploitation and costly to his or her own development? To what extent does prolonged independent or homogeneous group work carried out in isolation contribute to rejection by the gifted of their natural connection to other learners in the classroom? To ensure full development of the gifted learner in a social context, a healthy balance must be struck between independent and homogeneously grouped pursuits and heterogeneous group opportunities. Can we tolerate individual excellence within a social framework that honors the integrity of everyone and is hospitable to all learners? This, it seems, is the fundamental question in school classrooms today.

As curriculum planners reflect on these somewhat traditional issues, they must not reject their importance in favor of the more "trendy" questions that may be asked. If curriculum planning is to have merit, the need for a balanced perspective in the areas of general and specialized talent development, equal valuing of cognitive, affective, aesthetic, and social development of the gifted, and a concern for both individual and social contributions must be satisfied. For groups of typical gifted learners, as well as gifted learners with individual needs such as those from special populations, attention to these issues at the planning stage will be most beneficial. School districts must remember that their curriculum for the gifted, its goals and purposes, as well as its delivery systems, speaks loudly to how talent and its development is honored and nurtured in a community.

Another set of curriculum and instructional trends may be identified as the potential emphases of this field for some time to come. These trends can be characterized as the following:

- *Curriculum will be tailored to the nature of the gifted learners being identified.* As the emphasis on schooling becomes more bound up with achievement issues of underrepresented groups, gifted curricula must adapt more to the needs of special populations. This means broadening the scope of curriculum areas provided as well as focusing more sharply on appropriate levels for intervention. Greater use of the direct teaching of metacognitive skills, computer skills, and social-relational skills will be likely as deliberate content for curriculum to ensure that special needs students are well served. More emphasis will be placed on cooperative learning that emphasizes hands-on, active experimentation with various learning areas.

- *Curriculum will reflect a balance between traditional and nontraditional offerings.* As we expand the scope of our curriculum efforts for the gifted, a healthy tension between past practice, and new paradigms, will probably develop. Out of such a healthy struggle should arise a new balance in the curriculum structure, one that is responsive to the academic rationalist's cry for fundamental content knowledge in traditional domains but also an acceptance of the need for new offerings that emphasize relevancy and social-cultural relatedness. Thus, mathematics curriculum may entertain more use of hands-on manipulatives, more emphasis on practical applications and problem-solving, and the infusion of spatial visualization as a key strand to be taught at all stages of development. Multicultural curriculum that stresses the themes and concepts of a global society may become a legitimate partner in the social studies curriculum enterprise alongside traditional history and geography.

- *Curriculum will be organized so that thinking skills are embedded into all domains of study for all learners.* Whereas gifted education has enjoyed a long, productive and somewhat exclusionary relationship with thinking skills, the next phase in our curriculum growth will call for a systematic process of embedding these skills into all content areas, as well as addressing them as entities in their own right. Clearly, the general curriculum has taken that direction. What will make this effort distinctive for gifted education will be a recognition of the need for making the contextual problems in thinking for the gifted more complex and challenging. All learners will be taught the requisite higher-level thinking skills; the gifted will be taught them through more difficult problem sets, at earlier stages of development, and in more open-ended paradigms.

- *Curriculum will become more conceptually oriented and interdisciplinary in its organization.* Given the current spate of national reports from curriculum organizations as well as from policy groups, curriculum clearly is being forced to change from the inside out. New conceptual frameworks in each discipline and learning outcomes for each content area are being developed by most state departments across the country. New materials and textbooks are being developed in response to these curricular shifts. Implications of this flurry of curriculum activity include a greater emphasis on interdisciplinary ideas as an organizer for teaching and learning. Whether it is the concept of "change" in science or the whole language approach in the teaching of reading activities, evidence of this new direction in curriculum is growing. For gifted learners, it may bring relief from routinized skill development exercises and more opportunities for interaction with the world of ideas.

- *Curriculum implementation in classrooms will use more diagnostic-prescriptive approaches.* Even though many in the field of gifted education have advocated greater use of diagnostic-prescriptive approaches (Benbow & Stanley, 1983; VanTassel-Baska, Feldhusen, Seeley, Wheatley, Silverman, & Foster, 1988), the current emphasis on special populations should provide sufficient impetus to make it a more standard practice. Without careful diagnostic testing, the chances of intervening successfully with children who have uneven profiles is significantly reduced. Moreover, as heterogeneous classrooms become the norm, the gifted cannot be served adequately without some adaptation of a continuous progress/mastery learning model. This practice will likely gain favor in opening up a new role for specialists in gifted education as diagnosers of individual learning needs and developers of appropriate learning plans.

- *Cooperative teaching in the regular classroom will become the most commonplace model for delivery of special curriculum to the gifted by trained teachers of the gifted.* The emphasis on serving the gifted in the regular classroom will intensify the need for a differentiated staffing pattern to assist in delivering a more tailored plan of study, as well as assist the regular classroom teacher in learning more individualized strategies to use with gifted learners. Just as special education has benefited from this approach, so too should gifted education, if funding levels will sustain the resource needs in this area. Regular classroom teachers working side by side with trained teachers of the gifted will offer new collaborative strengths to the development of more comprehensive and better articulated curriculum experiences than typically have been available to gifted students in the past.

- *Instructional grouping and cooperative learning grouping of the gifted by interest and ability will emerge as the most viable models to provide a differen-*

tiated curriculum plan to the gifted in the regular classroom. As ability grouping at a generic level gives way to more in-class grouping strategies, gifted educators ·clearly must press strongly to maintain and expand instructional grouping in key domains of learning. Moreover, cooperative learning across ability groups must be tempered by opportunities for cooperative learning within and among gifted learners who share similar aptitudes and interests. We need to encourage more dyadic instruction and small-group problem solving among the gifted in order to highlight adequately the benefits of learning collaboratively.

CONCLUSION

Rising curriculum and instructional trends provide an interesting challenge for the future of gifted education. Can we successfully promote the individualization required to serve the diverse populations of gifted learners currently being identified? Can we mobilize other professional groups and the educators in them to become sufficiently interested in gifted learners to engage with us in collaborative problem solving? Can we sufficiently tailor curriculum experiences to address the needs of the highly gifted, as well as the learning disabled gifted, in all areas? Can schools become sufficiently flexible in curriculum demands and organizational models to accommodate the individual differences reflected in the gifted populations described in this book? The next 10 years hold the answers to these overriding questions. The needs of all gifted learners have waited long enough to hear an affirmative response.

REFERENCES

Benbow, C., & Stanley, J. (1983). *Academic precocity*. Baltimore: Johns Hopkins Press.
Bloom, B. (1985). *Developing talent in young people*. New York: Ballantine Books.
Gallagher, J. A. (1982). *Leadership curriculum units*. New York: Trillium Press.
VanTassel-Baska, J., Feldhusen, J., Seeley, K., Wheatley, G., Silverman, L., & Foster, W. (1988). *Comprehensive curriculum for gifted learners*. Boston: Allyn & Bacon.

APPENDIX
Sample Curriculum Units

The following curriculum units are based on the curriculum design model explicated in Part One of this book. They were all developed by educators working with gifted learners at various grade levels and in various content areas. They provide some concrete applications of the ideas outlined and, I hope, offer a spark of motivation to engage in the curriculum development process at an individualized level.

Tessellations Unit
Fifth Grade

Carol Cawley and Janice Mort
Hampton School Division
Hampton, Virginia

RATIONALE AND PURPOSE

This unit is designed to provide students with an opportunity to develop basic geometric concepts in a mode that incorporates their creative talents. It is designed to convey the spirit of adventure and fun in the use and application of mathematics. The unit takes an interdisciplinary approach as it reveals the mathematical underpinning of the Escher-type art.

NATURE OF DIFFERENTIATION FOR GIFTED LEARNERS

Recognizing that gifted students have different needs from the average learner, this unit is designed to expose the students to advanced geometric concepts as well as to raise their appreciation of math concepts as found in works of art. Throughout the unit, the students are challenged by activities that incorporate the higher reasoning skills of analysis, synthesis, and evaluation. Students will create meaningful, aesthetically pleasing products as they weave an understanding of the relationship tessellations play in the reality of our daily lives. Opportunities are provided for short-term to long-range independent study projects. The unit follows an interdisciplinary approach recognizing tessellations as observed in nature, art, and architecture.

CONTENT

A. Major Concepts
  1. Regular Tessellations
     a. Triangles
     b. Quadrilaterals
     c. Hexagons
  2. Semiregular Tessellations
  3. Escher Tessellations
  4. Transformations
     a. Translation
     b. Rotation
     c. Reflection
  5. Tessellations
     a. Translational
     b. Rotational
     c. Reflectional
  6. Escher-type Tessellations

B. Extended Activities
  1. Symmetry
     a. Translational
     b. Rotational
     c. Reflectional
  2. Tessellations in Nature
  3. Fibonacci Numbered Plants
  4. Nonpolygonal Space-Filling Patterns
  5. Crystallography

PREREQUISITES

Students will need conceptual understanding of geometric angles, lines, line segments, and polygons (triangle, quadrilateral, pentagon, hexagon, septagon, octagon, nonagon, and decagon). Success in the production of tessellation products is greatly enhanced by the development of fine-motor skills.

OBJECTIVES

1. To recognize the relationship between art and math through exploring tessellations.
2. To nurture cooperative learning skills in students.
3. To analyze tessellation patterns as they are found in real-life situations.
4. To evaluate art work through convergent as well as divergent thinking.
5. To extend and further develop students' understandings and appreciations of symmetry.

SAMPLE ACTIVITY 1: REGULAR TESSELLATION

A. Teacher-Directed

Provide cut-outs of triangles, squares, pentagons, hexagons, septagons, octagons, nonagons and decagons. Briefly discuss characteristics of each shape with students. Tell students that they will determine which of the shapes can be repeated to cover a surface to make a tessellation. (To tessellate a plane means to completely cover a surface with no gaps and no overlaps.)

B. Student-Directed

Students (entire group) will complete a chart on the chalkboard, which includes the above polygons and the number of sides each has.

Students will work individually to try to complete a tessellation for the above polygons. Each student will select a polygon and use a quantity of those pattern pieces to determine if the shape will tessellate.

Students will determine that regular triangles, squares, and hexagons will tessellate.

SAMPLE ACTIVITY 2: SEMIREGULAR TESSELLATIONS

A. Teacher-Directed

Review definition of tessellation. Provide students with pattern pieces of shapes listed in Activity 1. Ask students to try to make tessellations using more than one polygon (as many of the pattern pieces as they need). Background information: Semiregular Tessellations.

B. Student-Directed

Students will use whatever combination of pattern pieces they need to complete tessellations. Students will discover eight semiregular tessellations.

C. Extension

Challenge students to find tessellations in nature.

SAMPLE ACTIVITY 3: NUMBER DESIGNATION

A. Teacher-Directed

Tell students that tessellations are named according to the number of sides and frequency of appearance at a vertex.

B. Student-Directed

Using the regular and semiregular tessellations completed with the pattern pieces in Activities 1 and 2, students will determine the number designation for each.

SAMPLE ACTIVITY 4: COLOR PATTERNS

A. Teacher-Directed

Provide black-line copies of semiregular tessellations for students.

B. Student-Directed

Students give color patterns to the tessellations. As a class or in small groups, students compare and contrast the different color combinations given to each tessellation.

SAMPLE ACTIVITY 5: WALKING TOUR

A. Teacher-Directed

Demonstrate to students how to make a rubbing of a surface. A rubbing is a type of print made when paper is placed over a surface and the side of a crayon is "rubbed" over the surface. Provide students with newsprint and crayons.

B. Student-Directed

Students take a walking tour of the building and grounds, looking for wall, floor, sidewalk, and other surfaces that are tessellations. Students make rubbings of as many of these surfaces as they like. Students point out the number designation of the tessellation.

C. Extension

Encourage students to make rubbings of tessellations found in their own neighborhood.

SAMPLE ACTIVITY 6: COMPLETE A TESSELLATION

A. Teacher-Directed

Provide students with rulers and incomplete tessellation 3^46. Instruct students to work with a partner and find the pattern of the tessellation, then complete the tessellation.

B. Student-Directed

Students work with partners to discover the pattern of tessellation 3^46. Each student completes his or her tessellating pattern. A color pattern can also be developed.

SAMPLE ACTIVITY 7: TESSELLATING LETTERS

A. Teacher-Directed

Provide students with graph paper and scissors. Ask student to select any letter of the alphabet and shade in the selected letter on the piece of graph paper. Shade in full blocks or half blocks along the diagonal.

B. Student-Directed

Students cut out the letters and use the graph paper to attempt to create a tessellation of each letter. Students trace around the pattern, then reposition it. The class makes a chart of which letters will tessellate and which will not.

C. Extension

Other shapes can be made and tested. Isometric dot paper can be used also. Example: Make a concave quadrilateral on isometric dot paper.

SAMPLE ACTIVITY 8: MAGAZINE COLLAGE

A. Teacher-Directed

Provide students with old magazines, scissors, glue, and construction paper. Have students look through magazines for examples of tessellations.

B. Student-Directed

Students may work individually or in small groups. Students use the examples of tessellations cut from the magazines to make a collage. The number of samples collected will determine if each individual makes a collage or if these are made by small groups.

C. Extension

Students may design wallpaper that is a tessellation.

SAMPLE ACTIVITY 9: THE ART OF M. C. ESCHER

A. Teacher-Directed

Obtain several examples of Escher or Escher-type tessellations (Abrams, 1981).

Give students background information on Escher. Escher was inspired by geometric figures used by the Moors to make the space-filling patterns that decorate the Alhambra. He added a new twist by making drawings of animals, people, angels, devils, and other interesting things, which he fits together to fill a plane (Escher, 1972).

Art works by Escher that may be of special interest are: *Reptiles, Metamorphosis III, Sky and Water, Regular Division of the Plane III, Day and Night, Circle Limit IV (Heaven and Hell), Circle Limit III, Smaller and Smaller,* and *Fish.*

B. Student-Directed

Sample Questions for Students

1. Most of these art works were created 30 years ago. Which ones look like they were done in your lifetime? Why?
2. What did you notice about the painting only after you had looked at it a while?
3. Compare or contrast selected art works.
4. How do you see yourself in this painting?
5. If you could commission a painting by M. C. Escher, what would you want it to be like?

SAMPLE ACTIVITY 10: TRANSFORMATIONS

A. Teacher-Directed

Demonstrate to students the three transformations that will cause the shape of a polygon to change but the area to remain constant: translations, rotations, and reflections.

B. Student-Directed

Students may select one of the above techniques to alter a polygon (square, triangle, or hexagon). The square is the easiest for beginners.

C. Extension

Select slides from the slide collection, *Geometry in Our World* (Engelhardt, 1987), of art works that are tessellated surfaces. Have students decide what original shape was used and then explain how it was changed to make the tessellated shape.

SAMPLE ACTIVITY 11: USE YOUR "ARTIST'S EYE"

A. Teacher-Directed

Review the transformation techniques given in Activity 10. Provide grid paper, scissors, glue, construction paper for cutting shapes (two or more colors), construction paper or tag to serve as a background, and marking pens.

B. Student-Directed

Students may use the shapes they made in Activity 10, or they may devise new ones. Then, using imagination (their "Artist's Eye") and marking or drawing pens, each student turns his or her shape into an Escher-type "thing." The original shape is used as a pattern to trace and cut out duplicates. After each piece is given the same artistic treatment, fit the pieces together on a background and glue in place. A color pattern may also be incorporated. When completed, each student has an Escher-type work of art.

SAMPLE ACTIVITY 12: TRANSLATIONAL, ROTATIONAL, AND REFLECTIONAL SYMMETRY (EXTENSION)

A. Teacher-Directed

Talk with students briefly about symmetry (Walch, 1970, pp. 57–65). Review transformation techniques. Additional reference: Rebl & Rebl, 1986, p. 11.

B. Student-Directed

Students develop patterns showing translational, rotational, and/or reflectional symmetry.

SAMPLE ACTIVITY 13: TESSELLATIONS IN NATURE (EXTENSION)

A. Teacher-Directed

Discuss examples of tessellations that are found in nature. Examples: animals or their homes that have tessellated designs or structure (giraffe, alligator, turtle, oyster); sea star shows rotational symmetry; reflectional symmetry — human being. Reference: Rebl & Rebl, 1986, pp. 11, 40.

B. Student-Directed

Students make a list or poster showing examples of tessellations (including tessellations of symmetry) found in nature. An album of sketches or of photographs would also be an appropriate product.

SAMPLE ACTIVITY 14: FIBONACCI NUMBERED PLANTS (EXTENSION)

A. Teacher-Directed

Write the following pattern on the chalkboard: 1, 1, 2, 3, 5, 8, 13, ____, ____, ____, . . . Ask students to figure out the Fibonacci pattern. (The last number written, added to the one before it, gives the next number in the series. Example: $13 + 8 = 21$; the next number is 21.) Reference: Rebl & Rebl, 1986, pp. 2, 22.

B. Student-Directed

Independent or small-group activities for students:

1. Investigate the origin and use of Fibonacci numbers.
2. Make a display of different plants whose leaves contain different numbers of points. Can you use your display to illustrate the occurrence of Fibonacci numbers in nature?

SAMPLE ACTIVITY 15: NONPOLYGONAL SPACE-FILLING PATTERNS (EXTENSION)

A. Teacher-Directed

Discuss space-filling patterns that are not regular polygons. Reference: Pappus, 1972, pp. 99–101.

B. Student-Directed

Independent or small-group activities for students:

1. Investigate the 17 types of space-filling patterns that are not regular polygons (see above reference).
2. Create a space-filling pattern.
3. Find examples of these patterns in architecture.

SAMPLE ACTIVITY 16: CRYSTALLOGRAPHY (EXTENSION)

A. Teacher-Directed

Assist students in finding information about crystallography (the science governing the forms, structures, and shapes that make up crystals or compose tessellations) (Escher, 1972, pp. 102–104).

B. Student-Directed

Independent study activity:

1. Investigate crystallography and how its rules govern making a tessellation.

MAJOR INSTRUCTIONAL STRATEGIES

In a conscious effort to make learned geometric skills applicable to real life situations, this unit takes a problem-solving approach in math. The idiosyncratic nature of gifted students is satisfied through numerous inquiry activities and independent study work. To encourage the development of cooperative learning skills, students are clustered in flexible small groups. As students are guided in analysis and evaluation of man-made tessellations, a variety of open-ended style questions are used to nurture the divergent as well as convergent thinking of the students.

EVALUATION PROCEDURES

A skills inventory and pretest is utilized to establish if students have the geometric conceptual understanding necessary for creating tessellations.

Lower thought processes, higher thought processes, student opportunity for involvement in class discussion, classroom climate, and student opinions are measured via the Class Activities Questionnaire (CAQ) by Renzulli (1975). An evaluation scale for visual arts and a pupil self-evaluation are also used.

TEACHER BIBLIOGRAPHY

Betts, G. T., & Neihart, M. (1966). Implementing self-directed learning models for the gifted and talented. *Gifted Child Quarterly, 30* (Fall), 174–177.

Cotleur, S. (1977). Stained glass tessellation posters. Palo Alto, CA: Creative Publications.

Doherty, E. J. S., & Evans, L. C. (1987). *How to develop your own curriculum units.* East Windsor Hill, CT: Synergetics.

Engelhardt, J. (Ed.). (1987). *Geometry in our world.* Washington, DC: National Council of Teachers of Mathematics.

Epley, T. M. (1982). *Models for thinking.* Ventura, CA: Ventura County Superintendent of Schools Office.

Escher, M. C. (1972). Space-filling drawings borrowed from nature. In I. Adler (Ed.), *Readings in mathematics.* Lexington, MA: Ginn & Co.

Fennell, F., Reys, B. J., Reys, R. E., & Webb, A. W. (1987). *Mathematics unlimited.* New York: Holt, Rinehart & Winston.

Geis, D. (Ed.). (1983). *M. C. Escher — 29 master prints.* New York: Harry N. Abrams.

Geometry and Visualization. (1977). Palo Alto, CA: Creative Publications.

Hartung, M. L., & Walch, R. (1970). *Geometry for elementary teachers.* Atlanta, GA: Scott, Foresman.

Have I Got a Problem for You. (1982). Pleasantville, NY: Sunburst Communications.

Jacobs, H. H., & Borland, J. H. (1986). The interdisciplinary concept model: Theory and practice. *Gifted Child Quarterly, 30,* (Fall), 159–163.

Maker, J. C. (1982). *Curriculum development for the gifted.* Rockville, MD: Aspen Systems.

Oliva, R. A. (1976). *The great international math on keys book.* Texas Instruments.

Pappus. (1972). On the sagacity of bees in building their cells. In I. Adler (Ed.), *Readings in mathematics* Lexington, MA: Ginn & Co.

Ranucci, E. R., & Teeters, J. L. *Creating Escher-type drawings.* Palo Alto, CA: Creative Publications.

Rebl, R., & Rebl, P. (1986). *Math in nature.* East Windsor Hill, CT: Synergetics.

Renzulli, J. S. (1975). *A guidebook for evaluating programs for the gifted and talented.* Ventura, CA: Office of the Ventura County Superintendent of Schools.

Schattschneider, D., & Walker, W. (1977). *M. C. Escher kaleidocycles.* New York: Ballantine Books.

Seeley, K. (1988). Arts curriculum for the gifted. In J. VanTassel-Baska (Ed.), *Comprehensive curriculum for gifted learners,* (pp. 300–310). Boston: Allyn & Bacon.

Stein, E. I. (1972). *Fundamentals of mathematics.* Boston: Allyn & Bacon.

Tessellations: The geometry of patterns. Palo Alto, CA: Creative Publications.

"Tessellations: Patterns in Geometry," *Student Math Notes.* September, 1985.

VanTassel-Baska, J. (1988). Curriculum design issues in developing a curriculum for the gifted. *Comprehensive curriculum for gifted learners* (pp. 53–76). Boston: Allyn & Bacon.

VanTassel-Baska, J. (1986). Effective curriculum and instructional models for talented students. *Gifted Child Quarterly, 30,* 164–169.

Wheatley, G. (1988). Mathematics curriculum for the gifted. In J. VanTassel-Baska (Ed.), *Comprehensive curriculum for gifted learners* (pp. 252–264). Boston: Allyn & Bacon.

STUDENT BIBLIOGRAPHY

Adler, I. (1968). *The giant golden book of mathematics*. New York: Golden Press.

Allington, R. (1979). *Shapes*. Raintree.

Fennell, F., Reys, B. J., Reys, R. E., & Webb, Q. W. (1987). *Mathematics unlimited*. New York: Holt, Rinehart & Winston.

Highland, E. H. (1961). *The how and why wonder book of mathematics*. Wonder Books.

Marvelous Machines
Fifth Grade

Barbara Vaccarelli
Alexandria City School Division
Alexandria, Virginia

RATIONALE

The primary purpose of this unit is:

1. To provide additional enriching material to the basal reading program, that explores creative problem solving and inventive thinking for the talented and gifted learner.
2. To develop creative writing skills in the gifted learner by providing challenging writing opportunities.
3. To encourage the gifted learner to recognize and analyze the elements of inventiveness as used in different literary themes.
4. To encourage creative thinking that is appropriate for stimulating the gifted learner.
5. To introduce students to "great" inventors that could provide appropriate role models for talented individuals.
6. To foster independent learning.
7. To encourage the development of cooperation and interaction among talented and gifted students.
8. To introduce students to the joy and excitement of discovery.

CONTEXT

This unit will be used with academically talented students in the language arts area. This unit will be taught in addition to the D.C. Heath, level 5, *Rare as Hens' Teeth*, Unit 1 basal reader. The class meets five days a week for three 45-minute periods. The periods are divided into: a directed reading group, a language arts group, and an extension group. The unit will use large-group and small-group discussions and activities. The students will be required to do both independent and group projects.

DIFFERENTIATION

This unit attempts to differentiate the curriculum in many ways. By focusing the theme on inventioneering, the emphasis will be placed on creativity and thinking. The theme of inventioneering runs throughout the basal text. Inventiveness requires the students to expand their curiosity; to broaden their skills; and to think in new and unique ways.

Students will be encouraged to develop the skills of flexibility, fluency, originality, and elaboration in order to explore new ideas, unique solutions, and creative patterns and possibilities.

The unit will also attempt to guide the learner to create original work both in written and project form. Opportunities for sharing and evaluating creative ideas, independent research, and group projects will be provided.

The unit will encourage students to expand their knowledge of science fiction by exploring different authors and common elements. The students will examine new terms; learn new techniques; and share ideas designed to foster inventioneering.

Students will be asked to use the inventive process, the SCAMPER method, and other techniques to develop creative problem solving. Students will develop their inventing skills by: brainstorming, attributing, associating, synthesizing, random wording, visualizing, role playing, and questioning.

The material in the basal text will be compressed. Activities on inventing will be combined with the skills presented in the basal to provide challenging activities appropriate for gifted learners. Students will use the concepts of inventiveness to analyze the characters, plots, and settings of the stories presented in the basal. The stories will be analyzed in greater depth according to a theme focus, reorganized around inventiveness.

Finally, the unit will address realistic and ethical issues faced by inventors (past, present, future). Students will examine needs, problems, and solutions created by inventions. This will allow gifted learners to evaluate their own skills and the role they may play in shaping society.

CONTENT OUTLINE (Time — 2 months)

 I. "What IS IT?" by Jay Williams and Raymond Abrashkin
 (excerpt from *Danny Dunn, Invisible Boy*).
 A. *Focus:* How have machines affected your life?
 B. Students will be introduced to the concept of inventions, past, present and future.
 C. Students will experiment with the SCAMPER method for inventing new ideas.

 II. "Back to the Middle Ages" by Gery Greer and Bob Ruddick
 (excerpt from *Max and Me and the Time Machine*)
 A. *Focus:* Is time travel possible?

    B. Students will be introduced to the elements of science fiction.

    C. Students will explore ideas for original inventions.

III. "Huffer and Cuffer" by Jack Prelutsky
     "Oona and Cuchulain" by James Riodan

    A. *Focus:* How important are size and strength in solving problems?

    B. Students will be introduced to the saying, "Necessity is the mother of invention." Inventions are created from need.

    C. Students will explore the ideas of minifying, magnifying, and adapting inventions for altered uses.

IV. "Looking into the Invisible" by Tom Schiele
     "The Microscope" (a poem) by Maxine Kumin

    A. *Focus:* What effect has the microscope (and other inventions) had on your life?

    B. Students will be introduced to the lives of inventors and their impact on society.

    C. Students will explore the technique of narrative poetry.

V. "Arrietty's Encounter" by Mary Norton
    (excerpt from *The Borrowers*)
    "Small, Smaller" (a poem) by Russell Hoban

    A. *Focus:* How does inventive thinking help the characters in the story?

    B. Students will be introduced to the concept of finding new uses for objects.

    C. Students will explore the idea of seeing objects from different points of view.

    D. Students will examine the elements of modern fantasy.

PREREQUISITES

Students should be reading one year above grade level. It is helpful (but not necessary) if students have a basic understanding of scientific principles. Students should possess the ability to visualize and generate ideas.

SPECIFIC COURSE OBJECTIVES

The overriding goal is for students to understand and develop creative thinking skills.

1. Inventions are created by unique individuals with original ideas and qualities: Students will research and explore the line of famous inventors. Through independent reading and group projects, students will analyze the attributes of a creative thinker.

2. Inventions have an impact on society: Students will research an invention and the way it has changed (or will change) everyday life. Through independent work, group projects, and discussions, students will evaluate the effect of inventions on their lives.
3. Creative and unique products are produced by using an inventive process: Students will create their own inventions by developing their skills for creative thinking.
4. Creative problem solving and thinking are often used as a theme in literature: Students will identify inventive ideas in different forms of literature.

ACTIVITIES FOR INDEPENDENT LEARNERS

1. Redesign a machine of today to show how it might look in the year 2010.
2. Develop an idea sheet for a story about being invisible. List five characters, five events, five settings that you could use in your story.
3. Describe your own trip with ISIT. Where would you like to go being invisible?
4. Design a time line of your life. Use the five senses to isolate special events.
5. Write the next chapter to *Back to the Middle Ages*. If you were Max or Steve, what would you do next?
6. Design a trademark for your invention.
7. Suppose you were part of a human machine. Add a repetitive movement to the human machine.
8. Design a piece of a Super Machine. Connect it to another piece to create one huge machine.
9. Select a science fiction book to read.
10. Create a time capsule about your book. Select a shape that represents your book. Select items from your book that have significance to be placed inside. Develop a series of opening instructions.
11. Research and write about the life of a famous inventor. Include a narrative poem and/or example of one of his inventions.
12. Pretend you are one of the famous inventors you have been introduced to. Let your partner interview you. Dress appropriately to be videotaped.
13. Think BIG! Draw a picture of an item, magnifying it 100 times.
14. Describe your day in a Borrower's adventure. Be inventive!
15. Create a board game about a Borrower's adventure.
16. Redesign five pictures of vegetables to create a new item.
17. Research the microscope.
18. Write a news story about the day an invention was created. Use a headline and give facts.
19. List three machines (inventions) that are most important to you. Why? How would you change them? What did it look like in 1889? 1989? 2089?
20. Think of new uses for a potato. Draw them.
21. Complete an unfinished invention.
22. Improve a pair of shoes.

ACTIVITIES FOR GROUP LEARNING AND DISCUSSIONS

1. Discuss quote on page 1, D. C. Heath:
   "In one day, three hundred inventors take their inventions to the U.S. Patent Office; 180 of them are granted a patent. Fewer than three of them ever make any money from their invention."
2. List advantages and disadvantages of "invisibility" machines. What might your group do with these machines? Is there a need for them? Could they be abused?
3. Discuss Shel Silverstein's "The Homework Machine," *A Light in the Attic* (New York: Harper, 1981). Evaluate the positive and negative aspects of this machine.
4. Discuss the SCAMPER technique.
5. Practice scampering with an item from the "junk" box.
6. Identify the elements of Science Fiction. Create five titles for a science fiction book.
7. Brainstorm a list of acronyms. Create your own original one.
8. Create a "How To" manual for one of the inventions we studied. Add a diagram.
9. Discuss the importance of goal setting and prioritizing (a) for inventors and (b) for students. Develop a planning time line for your invention project.
10. How might time travel change your life? What problems might you run into?
11. If you could travel in time, to what period would you go?
12. Create a class super machine.
13. Create a human machine.
14. With your group, research six inventors, their invention, patent, need, effect on society.
15. Create a class trademark.
16. Describe the attributes of your group's inventor. List character traits that made him/her successful.
17. Select an item from the "junk" box. Discuss with your group how a Borrower might use it.
18. List the effects of the microscope on your lives.
19. Look up examples of how the characters in Unit One were either creative or inventive in solving their problems.
20. Discuss the elements of Modern Fantasy. Create your own modern fantasy.
21. Discuss how inventions have been modified to cope with size.

MAJOR INSTRUCTIONAL STRATEGIES EMPLOYED

I. To develop problem-solving skills, students increase their abilities in fluency, flexibility, elaboration, and originality by:

— listing   — eliminating/substituting
— brainstorming   — adapting/combining/changing
— debating   — putting to other uses

- interviewing
- illustrating
- writing
- discussing
- making speeches
- role playing
- modifying/maximizing/ minifying

- extending
- enlarging
- adding on
- designing
- inventing
- redesigning
- forcing relationships

II. To develop inquiry skills, students learned by:

- researching
- discussing
- comparing and contrasting
- analyzing
- describing
- observing
- sharing

III. The student uses group approaches through:

- small-group projects
- working in pairs
- large-group discussion
- large-group projects

IV. Questioning techniques include:

- class discussions
- student-made questions
- interviews

EXTENSION IDEAS

This unit can be extended by:

- encouraging all the students to create a new invention by placing the same conditions on them. Example: Create a new eating utensil for spaghetti.
- brainstorming ideas for new uses of more items.
- combining items.
- taking apart an invention.
- inviting an inventor to speak to the class.
- having students explore redesigning and improving.
- entering a national invention contest.
- inviting a patent attorney to speak to the class.
- introducing "Rube Goldberg."
- holding an Invention Fair!

The Unexpected
Eighth Grade

Nancy Howard
Alexandria City School Division
Alexandria, Virginia

RATIONALE

> *Our impressions of human life are picked up one by one, and remain for most of us loose and disorganized. But we constantly find things in literature that suddenly coordinate and bring into focus a great many impressions.*

> Northrup Frye
> *The Educated Imagination*

Literature is a way for adolescents to compare their feelings and opinions with those of other people. In this unit, characters find themselves in unexpected predicaments where something different happens from what the characters and the readers expect. Since many facets of the unexpected are presented, students should perceive new, rich concepts about living. Each selection is part of a whole, throwing a new and different light on the central idea.

Writing about and responding to these concepts in a literature log enables students to connect personal experiences to the literature and to internalize the subject matter. In the logs, students have opportunities to raise questions about their readings, to which they receive regular feedback from the teacher and other students in ensuing discussions. The students become active participants in these discussions, raising questions and challenging each other.

As students think, write, and talk about what they read, they become more mature and thoughtful readers. Therefore, the focus is this connection between reading, writing, and oral communication.

DIFFERENTIATION

The literature content is based on a variety of genres of advanced literature organized around a central theme, "The Unexpected." The content differentiation is minimal since I use a text, *Perception,* in which the literature has already been thematically organized. Although I have made additions to existing content to further increase the depth of study, the majority of differentiation for gifted learners lies in process and product modification. The processes focus on critical and creative thinking, group problem solving, and open-ended questions which encourage divergent thinking. The student products, both written and oral, are original syntheses of the literature and/or outgrowths of it. The Unexpected theme in literature has been further expanded to relate to the use of the unexpected element in contemporary art.

CONTENT OUTLINE

A. Introduction to the Unexpected
   1. Free writing
   2. Small-group sharing
   3. Large-group sharing
   4. Discussion

B. Short Stories
   1. Assigned readings
   2. Writing: literature logs
   3. Discussion
   4. Oral reading/dramatization
   5. Writing: essay elaboration
       a. Small-group/partner writing
       b. Peer revision/editing
       c. Large-group sharing

C. Ballads
   1. Readings: assigned ballads/small group
   2. Group problem solving/planning presentations
   3. Oral/dramatic interpretations

D. Modern Art and the Unexpected Element
   1. Inquiry: open-ended individual reactions to contemporary paintings
   2. Small/large group sharing
   3. Research on the artists
   4. Oral reports on artists/paintings
   5. Lecture/slide presentation by a guest speaker: surrealism, the unexpected in art

E. Contemporary Poetry
   1. Assigned reading
   2. Literature log
   3. Oral reading/discussion/analysis
   4. Figurative language
   5. Reading/analysis: student samples of contemporary poetry/imagery

6. Writing poetry using figurative language
7. Small groups/peer response for first drafts
8. Surrealistic illustrations for poetry
9. Small group/large group sharing: final draft poems and surrealistic illustrations

F. Novella, *Our Exploits at West Poley,* Thomas Hardy
1. Discussion
2. Quizzes

G. Final Essays: The Unexpected
1. Peer response and editing
2. Small/large group sharing final drafts

OBJECTIVES

1. Through reading, writing, oral presentations, and discussion, students will develop and practice higher-level thinking skills as they interpret, analyze, and evaluate a piece of literature.
2. Students will use and master the writing process.
3. Students will demonstrate mastery of the forms employed in writing about their ideas (e.g., poetry, freewrites, and essays).
4. Students will use figurative language in their writing.
5. Students will understand that artists as well as writers utilize the element of the unexpected.

SAMPLE ACTIVITIES

Introduction: The Unexpected

Freewrites . . . Sharing: Small Group/Large Group . . . Clustering . . . Predicting

Assigned homework:

1. Think about something unexpected that has happened to you. Write an account of this happening.
2. Then write a second paragraph telling how you felt about the event at the time it happened and how you feel now, looking back at it. Have your feelings about it changed?

In class the following day:

Share your unexpected event with your group. Read it aloud and discuss. Share some of the unexpected accounts with the whole class.

Whole class follow up/discussion:

Can the events be grouped according to the kind of reactions or situations? What can we expect from the unexpected?

THE LITERATURE LOG

This first quarter, instead of answering questions to the literature selections in *Perception,* we will keep a Literature Log. You will need a separate folder for the log.

1. Format of the Literature Log
   a. One to two pages of thoughtful response to the assigned selection.
   b. Each entry is due the day following the reading assignment. It is to be written prior to coming to class and before any class discussions are held about the piece of literature. These logs you have written will serve as a springboard for discussion about the work.
   c. Each entry should be labeled with the date and the title of the work.
   d. The entry should be written in blue or black ink. Pencil is not acceptable. (You may use your word processor if you choose to do so.)

2. Content of the Literature Log
   Each log entry will have three parts:
   a. What was your reaction about what you read? In a paragraph, verbalize your emotional response in specific terms and attempt to explain it. Write about how you felt when you finished the story. Were you confused? If so, explain why. Were you sad? happy? satisfied? left hanging? etc.
   b. Make associations with what you have read. These should come from your experience. You may have had a similar experience or may have felt the same emotions as the characters. Write about these associations and explain how they fit the story.
   c. Find a most significant word or words, a passage, a feature, or phrasing, and write it down. Explain its beauty or significance.

   Or

   If you are confused about some feature or aspect of the story, write down what confuses you and discuss why.

3. Evaluation of the Literature Log
   Literature logs will be checked and read by me each time an assignment is due. The grade will be based on the amount of thinking your log reflects. There is not just one answer; I'm looking for individual reactions.

4. The literature logs will also be used for freewrites about literature during class.

DISCUSSION QUESTIONS: "MARS IS HEAVEN"

- Man tries to find solutions to puzzling situations.
- When confronted with an emotional situation, man loses power to reason as he is flooded with feelings.

1. How did the Martians use the unexpected to their advantage?
   How did the Martians create Green Bluff, Illinois?
   Why did they create Green Bluff?
2. How did the astronauts react to the unexpected situation they found?
3. Why did the astronauts abandon their ship?
4. What would have happened if Captain Black had figured out the Martians' plan earlier?
5. What did you think about the Martians' attitude toward the astronauts? Were they justified in doing what they did?
6. How did you feel when you finished reading the story?
7. What kinds of associations could you make with the story?
8. Were you confused by anything? What questions do you have about the story?
9. What is unexpected in this story?
10. Can you make any generalizations about the way people react to the unexpected from this story?

DISCUSSION QUESTIONS: "I DON'T SEE GEORGE ANYMORE,"
Philip Oakes

- Reacting to the unexpected without thinking through the consequences of the actions can create difficult situations.

1. Why did the boys shoot at the cat?
2. Why did they kill the cat instead of taking it to a vet?
3. What would you have done if you had been there?
4. Why did George sell his most prized possession, the air gun?
5. How did you feel when you finished reading the story?
6. Could you associate with the characters or the situation? How?
7. Were you confused by anything?
8. What did you consider to be the most significant passages in the story?
9. Can you make any generalizations about the way people react to the unexpected after having read this story?
10. Was there any similarity to "Mars is Heaven" as far as the unexpected goes?

DISCUSSION QUESTIONS: "ONCE UPON A TIME"
(A modern fairy tale), Nicholassa Mohr

People sometimes ignore an unpleasant unexpected event that doesn't involve them directly because it seems easier to forget it instead of getting involved.

After oral reading and an impromptu dramatization in class with a narrator, three little girls, and a dead gang leader lying on the floor, the following questions will be discussed:

1. Did the girls realize that Frankie Chino was dead?
2. Why didn't the three girls tell anyone about the incident?

3. The title is "Once upon a Time." What kind of story has this beginning?
4. What usually follows these words?
5. How does the beginning of this story differ?
6. If Mohr wrote this as a modern fairy tale, what might the message she is making about society?
7. What other elements of the story are like a fairy tale?
8. Is this story similar in any way to others we have read in this unit?
9. What generalizations might Mohr be making about humankind in this story?

ESSAY ELABORATION: "I DON'T SEE GEORGE ANYMORE"

Students are given a copy of an essay. (It is actually a first-draft essay written by a student several years ago. They do not know that it is only a first draft.)

I have a copy on the overhead projector. We read it together. Then I ask for comments (hoping that someone will realize that it is flat and empty even though it may sound good). Many students, at first glance, say that it is good. If no one comments on the lack of specific detail, I begin asking questions: Why were the boys shooting sparrows? Why did they not feel guilty about killing them? Soon, most students have questions, too. I write the questions on the overhead transparency; the students write them on their copies.

When we finish, I explain that this was only a first draft, and their job now is to rewrite it, making it rich with details so the reader gets a clear picture of the reasons why a shared sense of guilt caused the demise of the boys' friendship.

The writing and revision are done in pairs. Students choose their own partners so they can collaborate more easily.

The next day, the partners' draft is given to another pair of partners to critique. Is everything clear? Is there a need for further elaboration? (And, is the sentence structure correct? How about spelling, etc.?)

The pairs of partners have a conference and discuss the drafts. Then a final draft is written. They share these final drafts with the whole class, and students comment on the content.

I then share my former student's final draft with my students. They are amazed at the changes she made.

Why do I do this? It's a beginning lesson in the process of writing and the need for revision. From the beginning of the year, I emphasize the need for specific details in writing. The writer needs to show us instead of just tell us what happened. The activity begins this emphasis on vivid details in writing and the need for peer feedback.

GROUP PROBLEM SOLVING: BALLADS

Each group of three to five students is given a different ballad:
   "The Eriking," Goethe
   "The Ghost That Jim Saw," Bret Harte
   "The Two Sisters," Anonymous Medieval Ballad

"The Sisters," Anonymous Appalachian version of the medieval ballad
"Old Christmas," Roy Helton
"Lord Randal," Anonymous Medieval Ballad

Directions to each group:

1. Read the poem aloud several times.
2. Who is speaking in the poem?
3. Outline the plot. Sequence the events simply.
4. Write in several sentences a summary of what happens in the poem. (This will be an introduction to your dramatic presentation.)
5. Plan as a group how you will act out the poem, who will get what parts, and what props or costumes you might need.
6. Practice staging the poem several times.
7. Perform your poem — your dramatic presentation — to the class.

After a poem has been presented, discuss with the class the element of the unexpected that occurs in the poem.

INQUIRY: MODERN ART

Each student is given a different postcard-sized reproduction of a painting; the title and the artist have been purposely deleted. Students respond individually to the following questions and write their responses in their logs.

1. Look at your picture and list what you see.
2. What ideas are conveyed?
3. What feelings does the painting evoke in you?
4. List what is unexpected.
5. Identify with something and tell why.
6. Write an overall reaction to the picture: a poem, a paragraph, etc.

Share your picture and your response with someone else in the class, who will share his or hers with you. Share some responses with the entire class.

Debriefing: Each student is given the title of the work and the name of the artist. Does the title of the work give you more understanding of the painting?

Homework: Look up the artist in reference materials and make notes on his life. Try to find another painting by the artist. Either photocopy the painting or bring in the book. Organize a brief report for the class on some interesting facts you learned about the artist.

CONTEMPORARY POETRY: IMAGERY

Students are assigned to read contemporary poetry that uses the unexpected. The following is assigned for log response:

> In "Your Poem, Man . . . ," what does Edward Lueders say a poem should do? How should one go about writing a poem, according to Lueders?

Choose a poem from the remaining poems assigned and show how it does exactly what Lueders says a poem should do.

In class the following day, we read orally and discuss the message in Lueders' poem. We then continue reading orally the other poems that were assigned, and students comment on how the poems fit Lueders' "recipe."

We discuss similes and metaphors that appeared in the poems. I give out the handout on figurative language to do for homework.

The next day we discuss the handout on figurative language and brainstorm other examples of the terms listed. (Expanding creative thinking is my goal here.)

We also read more poetry (some written by former students) that combines unexpected elements. We discuss how the images become clearer because of the juxtapositioning of two unlike yet similar things.

The assignment: Write a poem using any of these as models. Illustrate it in a surrealistic or unexpected manner.

We go through the peer response editing for clarity of expression and seeing if it makes sense to the reader. Some poems are shared with the whole group. Final drafts are written and shared again.

OUR EXPLOITS AT WEST POLEY
(An adolescent novel), Thomas Hardy

There are multiple unexpected elements in this culminating work:

- Characters react differently to the unexpected.
- The situations that develop produce a series of unexpected results, enmeshing the two young boys in more and more difficulties.

Students are assigned to read two chapters each day for homework. (There are only six chapters.) They are told there will be a comprehension quiz on the assigned reading the next day in class. Since the novel is a classic and more difficult to read than contemporary fiction, I quiz them to insist on close reading; otherwise, they miss so much of the detail.

After each quiz, we discuss the assigned reading. I focus on several main points and ask the same questions each day so they will gain an overall impression of the work.

- What do you know about the characters?
- Granted that this story was written set in another period, how real are the people and their reactions to what has occurred?
- Do you know any people like these characters?
- What unexpected elements have occurred?
- Did anything surprise you?

FINAL ESSAYS: SUMMING UP THE UNEXPECTED

Choose one of the following questions. Develop it into a three- to five-paragraph essay (first paragraph, introduction; second, the body; third, the conclusion). Use vivid details from the literature texts to show the reader the point you are making.

1. How did a character in one of the novels you have read for your outside reading journals react to an unexpected event(s)? Compare his or her reaction to the reactions of one or more of the characters we read about in the Perception unit.
2. How did an unexpected event affect the life of a character in one of the novels you read for your outside reading journals? Compare this unexpected event to one that happened in the literature unit in Perception.
3. Compare an unexpected event in your life to that of a character in one of the selections we read in the Perception unit. How were your reactions to the unexpected similar?
4. How do people react to the unexpected events in their lives? Using the literature text and your outside reading journals, give examples of the different ways people react to the unexpected.
5. Discuss the similarities between the way surrealistic artists and contemporary poets use the unexpected. Give specific examples of poems and painters/paintings.

Choose one of the following and develop it into an essay similar to the one we wrote together on "I Don't See George Anymore." Make sure you have a thesis statement, which includes the title and the author as well as the point you are discussing about the story. Include many specific details that show what you are trying to prove. End your essay with a strong concluding statement that brings your thesis back into focus.

1. Discuss how the unexpected element of emotion overpowered the astronauts' ability to reason and think clearly in Ray Bradbury's short story, "Mars is Heaven."
2. Discuss how stumbling upon the unexpected can make people run away from it or ignore it, as was pointed out in Nicholassa Mohr's short story, "Once upon a Time."

3. Discuss how meddling with what is not understood can lead to unexpected and even disastrous consequences, as Thomas Hardy points out in *Our Exploits at West Poley.*

MATERIALS AND RESOURCES

Student Resources

I. Short Stories
"Mars is Heaven," Ray Bradbury
"The Necklace," Guy de Maupassant
"A Nice Old Fashioned Romance with Love Lyrics and Everything," William Saroyan
"I Don't See George Anymore," Phillip Oakes
"Once upon a Time," Nicholassa Mohr

II. Ballads
"The Eriking," Goethe
"The Ghost That Jim Saw," Bret Harte
"The Two Sisters," Anonymous Medieval Ballad
"The Sisters," Anonymous Appalachian Version
"Old Christmas," Roy Helton
"Lord Randall," Anonymous Medieval Ballad

III. Contemporary Poetry
"Your Poem, Man," Edward Lueders
"The Bicycle," Jerzy Harasymowicz
"The Toaster," William Jay Smith
"Who Has Seen the Wind," Bob Kaufman
"The Garden Hose," Beatrice Janosco
"Apartment House," Gerald Rattery
"Southbound on the Freeway," May Swenson
"Daffodils," May Swenson
"Steam Shovel," Charles Malam
"Sale Today," Phyllis McGinley
"Dreams," Langston Hughes
"Unfolding Bud," Naoshi Koriyama
"Fueled," Marcie Hans
Selected student prize winning poetry
- "Orchestra of Colors," Ha Quach
- "My Poem," Helen French
- "Minorities," Katy Hayden

IV. Novella
Our Exploits at West Poley, Thomas Hardy

V. The Unexpected in Modern Art
   Woman with Fan, 1915, Alexander Archipenko
   Cardboard Series: Cardboard Door, Robert Rauschenberg
   Improvisation 31: Sea Battle, Wassily Kandinsky
   Sentinal I, David Smith
   Untitled (Medici Prince), Joseph Cornell
   Jarama II, Frank Stella
   The Blank Signature, Rene Magritte
   The Man in the Bowler Hat, Rene Magritte
   Portrait of Valentine, Roland Penrose
   Hector and Andromache, Georgio de Chirico
   The Hat Makes the Man, Max Ernst
   The Persistence of Memory, Salvador Dali
   Head of Woman, Joan Miro
   New York City IV, Richard Lindner
   Sleep, Salvador Dali
   Sky Garden, Robert Rauschenberg
   Four Hours of Summer, Yves Tanguy
   Mae West, Salvador Dali
   Perpetual Motion, Rene Magritte
   Untitled, Mark Rothko
   Liberation, Ben Shahn
   Les Masques, Alexander Calder
   The Conquest of the Air, Roger de la Fresnaye
   Fear, Yves Tanguy
   My Thoughts/My Ideas, Larry Walker
   Hide and Seek, Pavel Tohnelitchew
   The Subway, George Tooker
   Hopscotch, Robert Vickrey

EVALUATION PROCEDURES

Composition Evaluation

These are the guidelines we use in evaluating student compositions. Separate grades are given for content and mechanics. Periodically, students use the form for self-evaluation and in peer editing.

Review Scale:	Content	Mechanics
	65–70 = A	27–30 = A
	60–64 = B	23–26 = B
	55–59 = C	19–22 = C
	49–54 = D	15–18 = D

Content

		Excellent				Poor
1.	The paper addresses the question (key concepts).	5	4	3	2	1
2.	The introduction identifies the main points to be covered	5	4	3	2	1
3.	Each paragraph supports the point made, with examples.	5	4	3	2	1
4.	Each paragraph supports the point made, by logical development	5	4	3	2	1
5.	Each point is developed adequately. (Student uses specific examples from the text and other works to analyze, synthesize, and evaluate ideas. Student makes associations and connections.)	5	4	3	2	1
6.	Good thesis statement.	5	4	3	2	1
7.	Clear plan of attack.	5	4	3	2	1
8.	Each paragraph makes only one point.	5	4	3	2	1
9.	Orderly progression of ideas (usually from most important to least important).	5	4	3	2	1
10.	Smooth transitions from point to point.	5	4	3	2	1
11.	No filler phrases or sentences used to increase length of paper.	5	4	3	2	1
12.	The paper shows creative thinking, challenges assumptions, and offers alternative solutions.	5	4	3	2	1
13.	The paper shows extension of ideas to other areas/ disciplines.	5	4	3	2	1
14.	The conclusion sums up points made.	5	4	3	2	1

Mechanics

		Excellent				Poor
1.	No punctuation errors.	5	4	3	2	1
2.	No agreement errors (subject-verb/pronoun-antecedent).	5	4	3	2	1
3.	No spelling errors.	5	4	3	2	1
4.	Same tense used consistently.	5	4	3	2	1
5.	Checked for correct diction and usage.	5	4	3	2	1
6.	Writer has avoided the ubiquitous "you" and the elusive "they."	5	4	3	2	1

Discussion Evaluation

Review Scale: 32–35 = A
                  28–31 = B
                  24–27 = C
                  20–23 = D

Group Problem-Solving Evaluation

Review Scale: 19–20 = A
17–18 = B
14–16 = C
11–13 = D

Participation:

1. Clearly states comments that contribute to the solution to
the problem and show particular insight.   5 4 3 2 1
2. Attentive to speaker; often nods, smiles, or paraphrases
comments to clarify or check understanding.   5 4 3 2 1

Facilitation:

1. Encourages others to participate often and with particular
tact and skill.   5 4 3 2 1
2. Particularly skilled at facilitating problem solving (e.g.,
defining problem, establishing criteria) and at structuring
discussion (focusing, summarizing, and/or clarifying).   5 4 3 2 1

Oral Presentation Evaluation

Review Scale: 19–20 = A
17–18 = B
14–16 = C
11–13 = D

Content:

	Excellent	Poor
1. Student addresses key concepts.	5 4 3 2 1	
2. Student uses specific examples from the text and other works to analyze, synthesize, and evaluate ideas.	5 4 3 2 1	
3. Student uses specific examples from the text and other sources to make associations and connections.	5 4 3 2 1	
4. Student shows creative thinking, challenges assumptions, and offers alternative solutions.		
5. Student extends ideas discussed to other areas/disciplines.	5 4 3 2 1	

Participation:

	Excellent	Poor
1. Student contributes relevant, well-stated comments that show unusual insight; does not state ideas as absolutes.	5 4 3 2 1	
2. Student is attentive; often paraphrases comments to clarify or check understanding of concepts.	5 4 3 2 1	

Interpretation:

	Excellent				Poor

1. Interpretation was plausible and exceptionally insightful; independently developed.   5 4 3 2 1

Delivery:

1. Pronunciation correct, enunciation clear, fluency better than expected.   5 4 3 2 1
2. Rate, volume, pitch, tone, and inflection exceptionally effective in conveying meaning or mood.   5 4 3 2 1
3. Facial expressions, body movements, and eye contact exceptionally effective in conveying mood or meaning.   5 4 3 2 1

Exponential and Logarithmic Functions
High School

Jill Lane
Graduate Student
College of William and Mary

The primary purpose of this unit is to acquaint high school students with exponential and logarithmic functions and to emphasize to students the importance that these two types of functions have in the real world. The unit goals and activities reflect these purposes with instructional focus on the concepts and skills surrounding exponential and logarithmic functions as well as heavy emphasis on applications involving them.

RATIONALE

First, a unit on exponential and logarithmic functions is a part of advanced mathematics curricula. The topic is generally treated as part of an algebra II or analysis course. Thus, one reason for teaching a unit on exponential and logarithmic functions is its existence in the high school curricula. Second, and more important, exponential and logarithmic functions have a broad range of applications. Varied topics including interest rates, annuities, pH level, growth and decay, light and sound intensity, and queuing are all related to exponential and logarithmic functions. These applications provide motivation and background for this unit. Also, as the list above indicates, regardless of a gifted student's career choice, he or she is likely to use and therefore need background knowledge of exponential and logarithmic functions. Last, an understanding of exponential and logarithmic functions, especially e and natural logs, is essential to understanding higher math courses such as calculus, differential equations, and analysis.

The rationale for teaching a unit on exponential and logarithmic functions is threefold: (1) exponential and logarithmic functions are a part of the existing high school mathematics curriculum, (2) the varied applications of exponential and logarithmic functions make knowledge of these functions pertinent to gifted high school students, and (3) understanding exponential and logarithmic functions is necessary to understanding later mathematics courses.

CONTEXT AND LEARNER CHARACTERISTICS

This unit would most likely be taught as part of a second-year algebra or analysis course. Gifted students taking these courses will probably be high school freshmen or sophomores. Gifted students enrolled in these classes are likely to be intelligent, fairly well motivated, and interested in mathematics. Some may already be considering career choices. Last, the students are capable of and enjoy both group work and project work.

CONTENT OUTLINE

I. Exponential Functions
  A. Types of exponents
    1. positive, integral exponents
    2. zero, negative integral exponents
    3. rational exponents
    4. irrational exponents
  B. Operations with exponents
    1. laws of exponents
    2. exponential equations
    3. exponential functions
    4. graphs of exponential functions
  C. Applications of exponential functions

II. Composition and Inverses of Functions
  A. Composition of Functions
  B. Inverse Functions
    1. one-to-one functions
    2. onto functions

III. Logarithmic Functions
  A. Types of logarithms
    1. various bases
    2. common logarithms
    3. natural logarithms
  B. Operations with Logarithmic Functions
    1. exponential to logarithmic form
    2. laws of logarithms
    3. computations with logarithms
    4. logarithmic equations
    5. graphs of logarithmic functions
  C. Applications of Logarithmic Functions

OBJECTIVES

Gifted students will be able to:

1. Solve problems involving exponential functions or expressions.
2. Find composition or inverse of polynomial, exponential, or logarithmic functions.
3. Solve problems involving logarithmic functions or expressions.
4. Apply logarithmic and exponential functions to real world situations.
5. Evaluate the usefulness of exponential and logarithmic functions.

PREREQUISITES

It is expected that students will have completed algebra, geometry, and possibly second-year algebra before beginning the study of exponential and logarithmic functions. Familiarity with the concepts of functions, inverses, and exponents is necessary for attacking the unit. Also, students should be able to multiply, divide, add, and subtract exponential expressions, graph polynomial functions, and manipulate variables in order to begin the unit. Also, a familiarity with creative problem solving is necessary in order to complete the project at the end of the unit.

The pretest at the beginning of the unit should detect any gaps in algebraic skills. If remediation of those skills is necessary, it will take place as outlined in the beginning of the unit. For those students who are unfamiliar with creative problem solving, remediation will take one of two forms. First, if they are a part of a group whose other members are familiar with creative problem solving, they will simply learn from their fellow group members and through applying the process. If all of the group members of a project group are unacquainted with creative problem solving, they will receive a handout outlining the process plus a short after-school training session, if they desire.

POSTREQUISITES

Upon completion of the unit, students should be able to solve real world problems involving interest rates, queuing, population growth, etc. This unit prepares students for more in-depth study in those areas of finance, physics and mathematics. This unit also gives students background knowledge necessary for understanding exponential and logarithmic functions in calculus and, later, in differential equations. Also, the graphing concepts of limits, continuity, and increasing/ decreasing functions prepare students to understand both limits and graphing techniques, a large chunk of most calculus courses. The concepts of one-to-oneness and onto-ness are important for understanding higher maths: linear algebra, abstract algebra, and discrete math.

Appropriate post-requisite experiences could take many forms. In the area of pure mathematics, students could advance to calculus, then on to differential

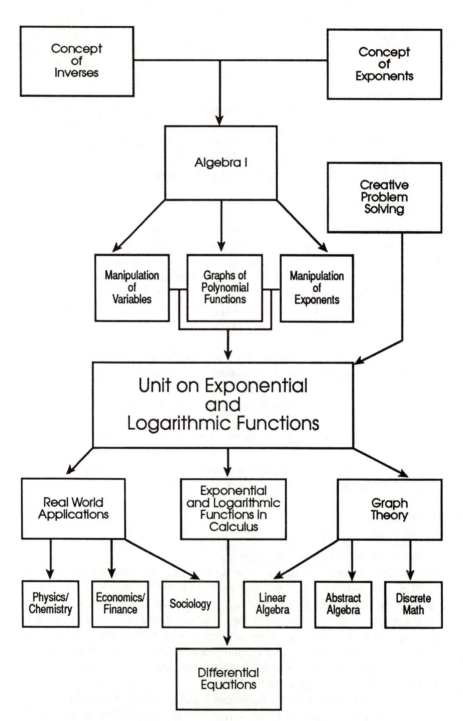

equations. In the area of applied mathematics, students might study the stock market, the banking industry, or other areas of finance. Also, students may investigate their project topic further, leading them to study population growth, radioactive decay, thermodynamics, wave physics, or queuing. As a follow-up to the projects, students might engage in a mentorship with a scientist, economist, or business person. (For more, see flow chart.)

DIFFERENTIATION

The unit on exponential and logarithmic functions will be altered in several ways to meet the needs of gifted students. The alterations in this unit incorporate bits of all three methods of curriculum adaptation for gifted learners. First, the pace of the entire unit will be accelerated in comparison to that for regular students. According to students' performance on a pretest concerning evaluation and simplification of exponential expressions, this topic will possibly be eliminated. Similarly, based on the results of a test and class participation, the topic of composition of functions will possibly be eliminated or treated only in relation to inverse functions.

In addition to the accelerated pace, gifted students will study irrational exponents, limits, mathematical uses of logarithms, and linear interpolation, topics not covered in the regular unit. Rather than being organized around specific content, the unit will be organized around the concepts of functions and inverses. There will be an independent research project incorporated into the unit. The project will concern the applications of exponential and logarithmic functions.

ACTIVITIES

1. Leading to being able to solve problems involving exponential expressions or functions:
   a. evaluate exponential expressions.
   b. simplify exponential expressions.
   c. solve exponential equations.

Students will be given a pretest (not here) to determine how many of these objectives they have already mastered. Depending on the results of the pretest, one of the following strategies will be employed:
   (1) If no more than five students score below 80% on the pretest, students will receive a sheet briefly explaining the laws of exponents for review and future study. Also, students will complete the cross-number puzzle as review and reinforcement. Those students scoring below 80% will be given extra instruction while completing the puzzle activity.
   (2) If there is a wide disparity among scores, students will be divided according to their performance on the pretest. On the day following the pretest, those who achieved 80% or better will complete the puzzle activity. Those with lower scores will receive direct teacher instruction. The next day, those who scored 80% or better will serve as tutors to

their classmates as they complete the puzzle activity. Again, all students will receive a sheet synthesizing operations with exponents.

(3) If more than half of the class scores below 80% on the pretest, the entire class will receive direct teacher instruction. Depending on the results of the pretest, some of the objectives may be covered in greater depth. Following direct instruction over the material, students will complete the puzzle activity.

d. define and describe exponential functions.

e. evaluate expressions involving irrational exponents.

This section will begin with the following activity: I will give one student a message. He or she will tell two others. Each of those two will tell two others, etc. Students will then be asked to visually illustrate the process. They might come up with something like this:

Students will then be asked to represent the number of people who "know" at each level. Thus:

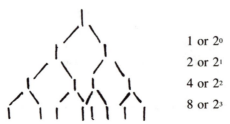

1 or 2^0

2 or 2^1

4 or 2^2

8 or 2^3

The second column most clearly gets at exponential functions. If a student arrives at this representation, I will begin the discussion of exponential functions from there. If not, I will lead students to this representation, then to a discussion of exponential functions. The discussion will begin with $Y = 2^x$ and lead students to generate other examples: 3^x, $1/2^x$, -2^x, etc. Students will then be asked to look at an overhead graph of $y = 2^x$ and list characteristics of the graph. (In order to list characteristics, students will be in self-formed groups of two or three and brainstorm possibilities.)

Using the list of brainstormed characteristics, I will discuss that 2^x is an increasing, continuous function. To get at the concept of continuity, I will first note that there are no breaks nor gaps in the graph. Second, I will explore continuity from the concept of limits. Students will be asked to find $2^{\sqrt{2}}$ using the graph. Students will be asked to approximate the value using increasingly larger graphs (enabling them to see and approximate better). It will be noted then that even our best approximation was still an approximation, but that it was better each time. Thus, students were finding the *limit:*

$$\lim_{x \to \sqrt{2}} 2^x$$

A discussion of right and left limits will follow, leading to a definition of continuity, as when right and left limits are the same. Students will then be asked to do a few practice problems involving approximating irrational powers.

f. sketch the graph of an exponential function.

From the previous lesson, students should have some background knowledge. Students will be divided into groups of two or three. The strategy for meeting this objective will be twofold, involving both computer and pencil-and-paper graphing. One group of students will work at the computer, graphing functions such as $1/2^x$, $1/3^x$, 3^x, -2^x, etc. The others will work on a worksheet involving pencil-and-paper graphs. Groups will move to the computer on a rotating basis.

Regardless of the mode of graphing, students will be asked to hypothesize (before graphing) about the shape of the graph, whether it is increasing or decreasing, continuous or non-continuous, then correct their hypotheses after graphing.

At the end of the graphing exercise, students will generalize about the graphs of exponential functions: they always pass through $(0,1)$; positive whole bases are always increasing and continuous; the larger the positive whole base, the faster it rises after $(0,1)$, falls before $(0,1)$; positive fractional bases are always decreasing and continuous; negative bases are non-continuous and therefore neither increasing nor decreasing.

g. define and apply e^x.

This section will begin with the following problem: What is the best way to invest $5000 for two years?

(1) 10% compounded annually?
(2) 9⅞% compounded monthly?
(3) 9¾% compounded continuously?

Students should already be familiar with the formula

$A = P(1 + r/n)^n$ where

A = final amt
P = principal
r = rate
n = number of time periods compounded

If so, they will be allowed to complete parts (1) and (2). If not, I will introduce and explain the formula, then allow students to complete parts (1) and (2). Looking at (3) should cause students to question how one writes "n" as continuous compounding. Given the previous discussion on limits, students might guess that what is really needed is:

$$\lim_{n \to \infty}$$

This should provide an introduction for a teacher-led discussion of e^x, which is in fact needed to complete part (3). The teacher will define e^x as

$\lim_{x \to 0} (1 + x)^{1/x}$

look at succeeding terms in the series, and discuss the approximation of e^x = 2.7183. The teacher will then introduce the formula for continuous compounding:

$A = Pe^{rt}$ A = final amt
P = principal
r = rate
t = time in years

Students should complete the problem by solving part (3) and making the appropriate comparisons. The teacher will then further discuss e^x as an important irrational base, giving students a handout on e^x, discussing other applications of e^x, and asking students to hypothesize, then graph e^x.

Also, the "Money In The Bank" exercise will begin with this lesson. Students will be told that they must invest it in one of three banks, each paying different interest rates, each having different withdrawal penalties. Following investment in a particular bank, students will draw from a "grab bag" containing "add money" and "withdraw money" occurrences (e.g., winning the lottery, or car breakdown). Students will be required to keep their balance and record it on posters in the room. The student having the most money at the end of the unit will win a prize determined by student suggestions.

Following this lesson, students will have an optional review day (students will vote on whether to have or not have a review) and quiz. If the students opt for review, they will participate in "Pass the Card." Students will be divided into groups of five, each group having a calculator and mimeographed sheet numbered 1-6. There will be a group competition; each person must solve one of the six problems on the sheet (consisting of various problems from the chapter) and write down the answer, then pass the sheet and calculator to the next person. The first group to finish all the problems correctly will be the winner.

2. Leading to finding composition or inverse of exponential, polynomial or logarithmic functions:
a. determine the composition of two polynomial functions.

It is expected that most gifted students will have mastered this objective. It will be measured as part of the pretest at the beginning of the unit. Procedure will be the same as that at the beginning of the unit.

b. determine inverses of exponential, polynomial, or logarithmic functions.

This objective will be attacked in two ways: first for polynomial functions, then for exponential functions.

Students will be asked first what they know about mathematical inverses. Discussion should center on additive inverses (what one adds to get zero back) and multiplicative inverses (what one multiplies by to get 1 back). It will then be noted that in both cases, the person is adding or multiplying to get the *identity*. In functional inverses, then, the student should be composing two functions to get the *identity*. This should lead to the question: "What is the identity in functional notation?" With a little discussional leading, students should arrive at the idea that "x" is the functional identity. Students will then be asked to hypothesize what the inverse of $y = 2x$ is. Students will be allowed to spend a few moments hypothesizing. A discussion of possible solutions and problem-solving strategies will follow. Students will be asked to complete a few examples: $3x(1/3 \ x)$, $4x(1/4 \ x)$, etc. Following this and a formal definition of inverse functions and method of finding inverses, students will graph both $2x$ and $1/2 \ x$ on the same axes. Students will notice (or be directed to notice) that the ordered pairs of inverse functions are reverses of each other and that the graphs of the two functions are symmetric with respect to the line $y = x$.

The next question posed to students will be: Do all functions have inverses, or, in better language, are the inverses of all functions themselves? Students will be divided into groups and asked to find the inverse of $y = x^2$ and to determine whether the inverse of $y = x^2$ is or is not a function. Again, students will be allowed time for problem-solving followed by a discussion of solutions and problem-solving strategies. This discussion will serve as introduction to the horizontal line test and one-one functions. One-one-ness will be discussed using a marriage analogy. Also, the teacher will discuss onto-ness of functions. Students will then complete several practice problems focusing on inverses of functions, one-one-ness, and onto-ness.

Using exponential functions, students will be led in a calculator discovery of logarithms. First, as a motivating problem, students will be asked the following: Suppose you were told if you invested $2000 in bank B, in one year, you would have $2075.00 at continuously compounded interest. What is the interest rate? Based on previous work, students should be able to arrive at the equation $2075 = 2000e^{r(1)}$. The question then becomes, "How do we get to 'r'?" or "What is the inverse of e^x?" The teacher will then lead students in a calculator discovery of logarithms. By using 10^x and log x (for various powers of x), students should discover that 10^x and log x are inverses. Also, if the calculator is equipped to do so, students will repeat the activity with e^x and ln x. The teacher will follow with definition of $\log_b y = x$ as $b^x = y$. Students should now be able to solve the interest problem. At the close of the lesson, the teacher will emphasize, through the use of problems and repeated statements, that exponential and logarithmic functions are inverses.

3. Leading to being able to solve problems involving logarithmic functions or expressions:
   a. evaluate logarithmic expressions and graph logarithmic functions.

Achievement of this objective should follow from the previous lesson. The teacher will do a few example problems, using the definition of logarithm, and allow students to complete practice problems. Graphing will be treated the same as graphing exponential functions.

b. simplify logarithmic expressions.
c. prove the laws of logarithms.

Students will receive a sheet summarizing the laws of logarithms and giving proofs for two of the three. In addition, the teacher will prove one of the laws of logarithms for the class. The third will be left for students to complete. Students will work examples involving these laws of logarithms.

d. evaluate common or natural logs.

Students will learn to evaluate these types of logarithms using both calculators and logarithmic tables. Using calculators should not be difficult and should take only a few moments of class time. Students will then spend a few moments table-reading, just enough to ascertain that everyone understands how the table works. The teacher will then introduce linear interpolation by asking students to find log 1.273 (a value not on the table). The teacher will then discuss linear interpolation using the concept of slope. Students will be given a few practice problems. Finally, the teacher will instruct students in writing logarithms in standard form.

e. solve and apply logarithmic equations.

As introduction to this lesson, students will be asked to find $\log_5 22$. They should arrive at a problem quickly. Direct teacher instruction concerning change of base will follow.

Also, as part of this lesson, students will be instructed in using logarithms to evaluate mathematical expressions (e.g., $\sqrt{4352}$) using the laws of logarithms and change of base technique. Students will be introduced to the antilog function and asked to determine its relationship to the log function. (*Note:* They are inverses.) Students will be challenged to solve several difficult problems by using logarithms. The first half of chapter test will follow this lesson before test, review day, playing "Jeopardy."

4. Leading to applying exponential and logarithmic functions to real world problems.
   a. solve "real life" problems.

Students will divide into groups of three or four. They will then choose a folder containing information regarding a particular application of exponential or logarithmic functions. Included in each folder will be information explaining the real-world application, a list of project options, and a list of problems involving the application. The topics addressed by the folders will include:

interest rates/annuities, population growth, carbon dating, earthquake measurement, sound measurement, pH level, law of cooling, aging rates, and
queuing.

Each group will complete a project based on one of the options as well
as the problems in the folder. Then, each group will present its project and
explain to the class the application and the problems surrounding that application. After the class presentations, students will complete a worksheet
involving all of the application problems. It is expected that the project will
take longer than 5 hours classtime, 7 hours in class and out of class combined.

5. Leading to being able to evaluate the usefulness of exponential and logarithmic
functions.
a. evaluate the usefulness.

Students will participate in a whole class discussion centering on the usefulness
of exponents and logarithms, the original uses of logarithms, and the awkward-
ness (sometimes) of dealing with exponents and logarithms.

EVALUATION

Check Homework.   Student will copy a given problem from the homework.
This problem will be graded for accuracy. Each problem
is worth 12.5 points. Eight of these added together will
count as one quiz grade.

Quiz.   Mid-chapter. Counts as one-half of a chapter test.

Chapter Test.   Will be given in two parts. The first part, focusing on
problems other than application, will count 80 points. The
second part, consisting solely of application problems,
will count 20 points.

Project.   Will be evaluated by both the group members themselves
and the teacher. The group self-evaluation will account
for 40 points and will be arrived at using the following
checklist (1 is the lowest; 3 is the highest).

All group members participated	1 2 3
Class time was well used	1 2 3
Group completed the project	1 2 3
Group completed the problems	1 2 3

What grade do you think you deserve?

A   B   C   D   F

Each "1" will be worth 10 pts., each "2" is worth 6.5
points, each "3" is worth 4 points. In the final question, an

"A" is worth 8 points, a "B" 7 pts., a "C" 6 points, a "D" 5 points and an "F" 4 points.

Each student will complete an evaluation form; the group grade will be found by averaging individual scores.

Teacher evaluation will account for 60 points (30 pts. project, 30 pts. class presentation) and will employ the following checklist:

Project

Completeness, clarity of project	1 2 3
Project based on approved option	1 2 3
Illustrates use of exponential or logarithmic function	1 2 3
Completion of assigned problems	1 2 3

Overall grade: A   B   C   D   F
(1 = 6 pts., 2 = 4 pts., 3 = 2 pts.
A = 6 pts., B = 5 pts., C = 4 pts., D = 3 pts.,
F = 2 pts.)

Class Presentation

Correctness of class presentation	1 2 3
Completeness of class presentation	1 2 3

Time Line: A Scientist's History of the World
Fourth to Sixth Grades

Beverly Sher
Science Teacher, Saturday Enrichment Program
College of William and Mary

I. Curriculum Course Description
   A. Title of unit: Time line: A Scientist's History of the World
   B. Grade levels: 4–6
   C. Rationale and Purpose:

   This course has been designed to provide students with a variety of hands-on scientific experiences in the context of the history of the planet Earth. Each session focuses on a different time period in the planet's history. Experiments from different areas of science that are directly relevant to events occurring during that time period are included in each session, as is teacher-directed discussion of the scientific importance of events of the time period. Students also are encouraged to relate the events of the time period under study to events occurring in the present. The purpose of the course is to help the student develop an understanding of the interrelationships of different scientific disciplines and their relevance to the world around him or her.

II. Nature of Differentiation for Gifted Learners
   A. How has the unit been accelerated, compressed, or reorganized to accommodate gifted learner needs?

   The unit includes a great deal of material that the students would not ordinarily encounter until much later in their scientific educations. Although students are not expected to retain every detail of the material presented, it should stimulate their curiosity, challenge them, and encourage them to learn more on their own.

   B. How has this unit focused on higher level process skills?

   The laboratory portions of the course require the student to use the scientific method and critical thinking skills to study a variety of scientific phenomena. In-class discussions require the students to assess the relevance of different scientific phenomena to events of the past as well as processes occurring on the planet Earth at present; they are thus required to judge information, make inferences, make predictions, and so on.

C. How has the unit engaged learners in meaningful product development?

Several of the laboratory activities result in a permanent product (for example, model meteorite craters, recovered fossils, and records of human tracks). Even though other laboratory activities create no lasting product, setting up an experiment, letting it run, and recording the results constitute product development. It's a little like performance art.

D. How has the unit addressed key themes and ideas and related them to several domains of inquiry?

The unit focuses on two major processes: biological evolution and geologic change. A variety of scientific disciplines are called upon to explain the mechanisms underlying these processes.

III. Content Outline

    A. Major content topics to be addressed in eight 2½-hour sessions:

        1. Geological change

            a. Weathering.

            b. Processes of rock layer formation.

            c. Vulcanism.

            d. Plate tectonics.

        2. Biological change

            a. Chemical evolution and the origin of life.

            b. Biological evolution.

    B. Organizational structure and order

Each session has two foci, one a specific period in the Earth's history, and the other a specific scientific topic relevant to that time period. These are:

1. Session I:	Time period: 5 Bya - 3.5 Bya	
	Scientific topic: geologic change	
2. Session II:	Time period: 3.5 Bya	
	Scientific topic: the chemistry of life; chemical evolution	
3. Session III:	Time period: 3.5 Bya - 1 Bya	
	Scientific topic: early life forms; microbiology	
4. Session IV:	Time period: 1 Bya - 500 Mya	
	Scientific topic: life in the early oceans	
5. Session V:	Time period: 420 Mya - 200 Mya	
	Scientific topic: adaptation to life on land; ecology	

6. Session VI: Time period: 65 Mya
                               Scientific topic: dinosaur evolution and extinction

7. Session VII: Time period: 65 Mya - 5 Mya
                               Scientific topic: mammalian evolution

8. Session VIII: Time period: 5 Mya - present
                               Scientific topic: human evolution; human impact on planet Earth

IV. Prerequisites

No special knowledge is required; however, students with a good scientific background (e.g., sixth graders) probably will get more out of it than children who have had little exposure to science.

V. Objectives
1. Students will demonstrate an understanding of the processes and time scale of geologic change.
2. Students will demonstrate an understanding of the processes and time scale of biological evolution.
3. Students will demonstrate an understanding of the scientific method.

VI. Sample Activities
A. Session 1: Formation and prebiotic history of planet Earth.
1. Class discussion and demonstration: time scales
a. Human history: Get children to supply events happening 1, 10, 100, 1,000, 2,000, 10,000 years ago; teacher can fill in the gaps.
b. Biological time scale: do in lifetimes.
(1) E. coli: 30 minutes
(2) Butterflies: weeks to months
(3) Mouse: 1–2 years
(4) Cat: 10–20 years
(5) Human: around 100 years
(6) Galapagos tortoise: up to 150 years
(7) Redwood tree: up to 1,000 years
(8) Bristlecone pine: 5,000 years
c. Geological time scale
(1) 1 Mya: Great Ice Age (mammoths, Cro-Magnon man)
(2) 10 Mya: first hominids
(3) 65 Mya: dinosaur extinctions
(4) 400 Mya: first life on land
(5) 1 Bya: multicellular life
(6) 3.5 Bya: life begins
(7) 4.5 Bya: Earth coalescing into a planet
(8) 12-18 Bya: Big Bang

d. To better illustrate the geologic time scale, build a time line with the kids. Use a large ball of string to represent time. Fasten it securely to a lamp post and pace backward in time (I found steps of 50 million years convenient), attaching labels to significant time points with tape. Remind the kids of how little time human beings have really been around compared to the lifetime of the planet.

2. Major events in formation of the planet
   a. Planetary accretion and the role of gravity
      (1) Gravity is a weak force between little things but a strong force between big things; the bigger something is, the harder it pulls on other things. This can be easily demonstrated: Two books don't move closer together, but the earth pulls a book to the floor quite nicely.
      (2) Briefly outline the history of Earth's formation.
   b. Meteoric impacts
      (1) Meteors as a source of water, carbon dioxide, and nitrogen for Earth's atmosphere.
      (2) Experiment: Modeling impact craters
         Before class, melt paraffin and pour it carefully into plastic plates, one per student, to a depth of ¼"–½". Allow it to harden. Collect a supply of gravel. In class, take the kids outside and space them about 6–8' apart. Have them throw gravel at the paraffin until the surface of each student's plate is heavily cratered. Bring them back inside; discuss their results.
      (3) Why does Earth lack evidence of the heavy meteor bombardment that Moon still has? Answer: Earth has an atmosphere and liquid water on its surface and thus undergoes weathering. This neatly introduces the next topic . . .
   c. Gradual geologic change: rock formation and breakdown
      (1) How do rocks break down?
         To help answer this, take the kids outside. Point out frost damage in rocks or bricks; erosion caused by wind or water; chemical damage caused by pollution and oxidation.
      (2) How do rocks form?
         First, list the three different types of rock (igneous, metamorphic, sedimentary). Pass around samples of each type. Next, start some crystals growing (many books are available with recipes for crystals, some of which take only an hour or so to work). This experiment can be designed to illustrate the effects of environmental conditions (for example, ambient temperature, presence or absence of convection currents, presence or absence of chemical impurities) on the formation of rocks.

    d. Large-scale geology

       (1) Discuss the formation of the current planetary structure (nickel-iron core, mantle, crust).

       (2) Talk about plate movements and their consequences: moving continents, earthquakes, volcanoes (the kids will have heard most of this before).

       (3) Finish off with a videotape that illustrates the effects of continental drift (we used the first tape in David Attenborough's *Living Planet* series).

B. Session II: Chemical evolution and the origin of life

  1. Basic chemistry

    To understand anything meaningful about the origin of life, the kids have to know a bit of chemistry first.

    a. Everything is made of atoms.

       (1) How big are they?

Object	Size
human	1–2 meters
little finger	a few centimeters (10^{-2} m.)
bacteria	a few microns (10^{-6} m.)
atoms	Angstroms (10^{-10} meters)
atomic nucleus	(10^{-12} meters)

       (You may have to explain scientific notation to them, but the kids who haven't seen it before catch on fast.)

       (2) What do they look like?
Basically they look like little billiard balls. Pass around a STEM picture or two (for example, one of the pictures of gallium arsenide crystals from the February 1990 issue of *Scientific American*).

       (3) How many different kinds are there?
Give each kid a copy of the periodic table. Most of them will have seen it before. Mention that there are probably even more kinds than are listed but that we just haven't been able to make them (or observe them in nature) yet. Also mention that only a few elements are really important for life: carbon, oxygen, nitrogen, phosphorous, sulfur, hydrogen, sodium, and potassium; most of the rest are needed in only small amounts, if at all.

       (4) Atoms combine to form molecules.
Talk about the different ways in which atoms can combine to form molecules.

          (i) covalent bonding: Use water as a sample structure; mention valence; discuss the energy needed to break covalent bonds. (Light a match to demonstrate.)

          (ii) ionic bonding: NaCl. Dissolve some salt in water to demonstrate the breakage of ionic bonds.

        (iii)   hydrogen bonding: ordered structure in water and ice. Mention that hydrogen bonds constantly break and re-form in liquid water.

        (iv)   if there's extra time, you could give the kids a list of valence rules for C, O, N, and H and some molecular models, and ask them to come up with structures of familiar things such as carbon dioxide, ammonia, ethanol, and benzene.

   b. Macroscopic chemistry: Chemical properties of substances

      (1) List a few; for example: color, state at room temperature, boiling point, freezing point, reactivity with other chemicals (for example, oxidation); mention the two that are most important for biology: acid-base behavior and hydrophobicity.

      (2) Miscibility with water (hydrophobicity/hydrophilicity) Demonstrate this as follows:

          — Have the kids mix cooking oil with water (hydrophobicity).

          — Have the kids mix rubbing alcohol with water (hydrophilicity).

          — Have the kids add some soap to the oil/water mixture. What happens? Mention that soap is an amphipathic molecule, one part of which is hydrophobic and the other, hydrophilic; ask them how this mixture might look at the molecular level.

      (3) Acid-base chemistry

          — Talk briefly about the pH scale (i.e., numbers 0–14, with 0 being the most acidic and 14 the most basic).

          — Pass out the acid/base chemistry lab worksheet; after the kids read it, have them do the lab.

2. Chemical evolution

   a. What happened 3.5 Bya, and how do we know?

      (1) Composition of the early atmosphere.

      (2) Urey-Miller experiment.

      (3) Chemical fossils (terpene worksheet, if time, or handout for later fun at home).

      (4) All living organisms share the same fundamental chemistry, based on DNA, RNA, and protein. Briefly explain what DNA, RNA, and proteins are and what their functions are in the cell:

         (i) DNA: the software, encoded in units called genes.

        (ii) RNA: the floppy disk that carries the software to the part of the cell that can read it.

      (iii) Proteins: the machines that run the cell and the structural components that give it shape, motility, and so on; each protein is directly encoded by a single gene.

(Mention to the kids that the detailed chemical structures of each type of molecule are in their copies of *The Daily Planet*, if they are interested. Some of them probably will be, but not all.)

   b. Exercise: Decoding DNA

Pass out the sample gene sequence handout and have the kids translate it into a protein sequence using the genetic code dictionary in *The Daily Planet*.

C. Session III: Microorganisms
1. What is life? Get the kids to define it. Definition should include reproduction, growth, and use of external energy/nutrient sources.
2. What was first life like?
   a. Show them pictures of microfossils.
   b. Show them pictures of modern-day bacteria.
   c. Diagram the parts of a bacterial cell. Mention that the inner membrane is made of amphipathic molecules that effectively form a greasy barrier around the cell and keep the liquid phases inside the cell and outside the cell from mixing, just as the very first cellular membranes must have done.
   d. Show them yogurt under the microscope; it's solid lactobacilli.
3. Given that the DNA of the first bacterial cell only contained instructions for making more bacterial cells, how is it that Earth has other life forms today?
   a. DNA can change through a process called mutation.
   b. Although most mutations are deleterious, a few improve the organism's chance of survival — natural selection.
   c. Biological evolution occurs through a process of mutation followed by natural selection.
4. The biggest change in the first billion years or so of life on this planet: the evolution of photosynthesis.
   a. Define it; give the simplified chemical reaction (CO_2 + H_2O + light energy = O_2 + sugar or starch).
   b. Photosynthesis resulted in the first major life-induced change in the planet — namely, creation of free oxygen in the atmosphere. Discuss the oxygen crisis (well reviewed in the Sara Stein *Evolution* book). Point out that we're *not* the first organism to have changed the chemistry of Earth's atmosphere.
5. Evolution of eukaryotes-engulf and symbiose.
   a. Discuss the typical structure of a eukaryotic cell, paying particular attention to the mitochondria and chloroplasts (if any). Mention

that these organelles have their own DNA and make some of their own proteins without relying on the cell's nucleus; mention the endosymbiont hypothesis.

   b. Experiments with simple eukaryotes:

     (1) Make simple French bread dough, involving the kids in mixing, measuring, and kneading it. Have each kid place a small piece in a transparent plastic cup. Have the kids flatten the top of the dough and mark with a felt-tip pen the position of the top of the dough on the side of the cup. Have them cover the cup with a tissue and mark the position of the top of the dough every 20 minutes (designate one kid as timekeeper so everyone will remember all the time points). At the end of class, ask the kids what happened.

       — Why did the dough rise? (They will have seen fermentation in action at this point, so they should be able to answer this.)

       — How long did the dough take to collapse?

       — How big were the air bubbles in the dough when it was at its highest? When it had collapsed?

       — Why do bakers punch down dough when it has just doubled in bulk, and then allow it to rise again?

     (2) Look at yeast under the microscope.

     (3) Run yeast fermentation/gas evolution experiment. Discuss the results.

     (4) Discuss other uses for eukaryotic fermentation (making soy sauce, wine, etc.).

   c. Evolution of oxidative phosphorylation

     (1) Mention that using oxygen allows organisms to extract even more energy out of their food; that's what mitochondria are for; they are also of endosymbiont origin. Give them the simplified chemical reaction (fermentation products + oxygen = CO_2 + H_2O + energy).

     (2) Mention that you can tell when your muscles switch from oxphos to fermentation — build-up of the fermentation product lactic acid (which happens when your muscles aren't getting enough oxygen) makes them ache; resting and letting them break down the lactic acid with oxygen the blood carries to them makes the aching stop.

D. Session IV: Multicellular life; life in the oceans

  1. Discuss briefly the evolution of multicellular life (what came when and why).

  2. Discuss the first forms of life to make up macroscopic fossils; include gastropods, tube-dwelling worms, and bivalves in particular.

3. Take the kids down to the fossil bed on campus. Have them fill large Ziploc bags with fossils; take them back either to the classroom or to a flat, sunny place outdoors and have the kids clean them out as best they can (a good source of running water that won't become clogged by dirt and an assortment of tools for scraping dirt out of crevices would be useful here). Have the kids line up their cleaned finds and decide how many different types of animal life they have found; identify as many as possible (we found scallops, clams, and worm tubes). Discuss the lifestyles of these organisms and help the kids figure out what the environment in which these beds were formed must have been like. This discovery process can take up to 1½ hours.

4. Provide a selection of modern mollusks for the kids to observe. As a teacher demonstration, dissect a mussel for the kids. I tried having the kids dissect their own, but they were disgusted by the process (elementary school kids are pretty tenderhearted).

5. The second videotape in David Attenborough's Living Planet series has an excellent description of the evolution of early life forms in the sea, along with footage of modern-day mollusks in their own habitats. Play as much of this as possible at the end of the session.

E. Session V: Life comes up on land

1. Briefly discuss the first organisms to colonize the land. Some of these will be familiar to the kids; be sure to include modern-day equivalents and provide actual samples (pieces of lichen, moss, and so forth).

2. Discuss the constraints posed by a land-based lifestyle and the adaptations to these constraints that were made as life colonized the land. Have the kids supply as many of these as possible (for example, thick skins that reduced evaporation, root systems for plants, hard seeds that resist drying, and so forth).

3. Introduce the concept of the ecosystem and relationships between the organisms within it. Define the following:

   a. Predator/prey
   b. Symbiosis
      (1) Commensalism
      (2) Mutualism
      (3) Parasitism
   c. Competition

4. With the kids supplying names of organisms and their relationships to each other, describe the suburban ecosystem as completely as possible. Be sure to include humans. We diagrammed it on the board using different colors of chalk to represent the different relationships. It rapidly became a colorful, convoluted mess, which

convinced the kids of the complexity of the ecosystem and of the interdependence of the organisms within it.

5. Define the concept of niche, using a couple of the organisms from Part 4 as examples. Talk about specialist niches versus generalist niches. Point out that the human is the ultimate generalist.

6. Take the kids on a nature walk. We went through the wildflower refuge at the college. Have them list the organisms they find and think about their niches (for example, millipedes are found in decaying logs but not on the branches of trees; wolf spiders are found on the forest floor and seem to patrol their own territories; moss is found in damp shady places but not dry sunny ones). Try to help the kids appreciate the vast variety of niches and of organisms adapted to fill those niches. The longer this takes, the better.

7. If time allows at the end of the session, discuss the peculiar niche of the Monarch butterfly. This is appropriate because insects were among the first organisms to colonize the land; it is also interesting because of the specialist nature of the Monarch's niche. The videotape "Pretty Poison," while somewhat sensationalistic, does a nice job of describing the migration of the Monarchs and the increasing human threat to their existence.

F. Session VI: Dinosaur evolution and extinction

1. Discuss biological classification.
   a. Define the following: kingdom, phylum, class, order, family, genus, species.
   b. Give the kids the following mnemonic to help them remember the order: King Philip comes over for giant slugs.
   c. Go back to the species definition. A key component of this is that two animals belonging to the same species can mate and produce fertile offspring. Illustrate this with the example of mules (the result of mating a male horse and a female donkey). But how do you determine whether two fossil animals were members of the same species? Point out that Chihuahuas and St. Bernards might not be classified as belonging to the same species by an alien paleontologist looking only at their skeletons.

2. Discuss the evolution of large organisms on land. I used the book *The Dinosaur Heresies*, by Robert Bakker, extensively here, as he summarizes the major evolutionary themes quite clearly.

3. Discuss the differences between the lifestyles of warm- and cold-blooded animals. Discuss the evidence that at least some of the dinosaurs were probably warm-blooded.

4. Fossil footprints have given us a great deal of information about dinosaur lifestyles and behavior. To illustrate the kinds of information that can be obtained from footprints, do the following (quite messy) experiment:

Have the kids paper the (preferably tile) floor with large sheets of newsprint that have been securely taped down. Fill disposable aluminum baking dishes with a thin layer of somewhat dilute tempera paint. Have several colors available. Have the kids (volunteers only — two of the wildest boys in the class were too fastidious for this) take off their shoes and socks, roll up their pants legs, and carefully step into the paint. They then can try the following:

a. Walking.
b. Running.
c. Walking as a group.
d. One person following another.
e. "Funny walks" (crabwalk, walking on all fours, walking backward, and anything else they can dream up).
f. Walking while carrying a heavy object.

For each kind of walk, have them:
— Measure the length of the stride.
— Determine the angle between the long axis of the foot and the direction of motion.
— Observe which parts of the foot made contact with the surface and which didn't.
— Observe the degree of pressure made on the surface with each part of the foot.

Have them compare the different kinds of walking/running. Based only on the footprints:
— Which looked most strained?
— Which looked most efficient?
— What were the differences between the patterns of people walking in a group?
— Was it possible to tell the difference between the prints of two people who had just happened to walk over the same area and those of one person actively pursuing another?
— What kind of information about human skin texture can be obtained from a footprint? Is every footprint equally informative?

5. Discuss theories that attempt to account for the mass extinctions at the end of the Cretaceous.
   a. List what died and when.
   b. Review the evidence for the gradual decline of dinosaur diversity at the end of the Cretaceous; discuss the declining shallow seas hypothesis (covered quite well in Bakker's book).
   c. Discuss the evidence for meteoric impact and the effects the impact of a large meteor (or, more likely, meteors) would have on Earth. I found David Raup's *The Nemesis Affair* quite useful (although the periodicity effect he discusses is almost certainly

nonexistent); in addition, the Larry Niven novel *Lucifer's Hammer* and the Gregory Benford novel *Shiva Descending* have quite nice descriptions of the effects of a large meteor strike on the Earth of the present. Mention nuclear winter here as well.

G. Session VII: Mammals
  1. Discuss high points in mammalian evolution:
     a. Therapsids.
     b. Monotremes.
     c. Marsupials.
     d. Placental mammals.
     e. Primate evolution.
     f. The effect of continental plate movements on the pattern of mammalian evolution (existence of marsupials in Australia, decimation of South American marsupials once Central America formed and placental mammals moved in).
  2. Discuss mammalian features:
     a. Hair and its varied uses.
     b. Evolution/formation/function of the placenta.
     c. Milk (with emphasis on the different characteristics of milk from different species of mammals).
     d. Heavy parental time and energy investment in the young — evolutionary advantages and disadvantages.
  3. Show at least the first half of the videotape "Songs of the Whales, Signs of the Apes." Use it to make the point that our nearest relatives, the great apes, are really quite close to us in their intellectual abilities as well as in their morphology. Also bring up the point (from King and Wilson's genetic studies) that we are 99% genetically identical to chimpanzees.
  4. Discuss the ethics of human uses of animals. Ask the kids to list all the ways we use animals (including food, fur, pets, medical research). With the kids' assistance, draw up a list of guidelines for the ethical uses of animals, focusing particularly on "higher" forms. Questions to bring up include:
     a. What are the tradeoffs between animal life and human life? Is it ethical to sacrifice 100 mice to possibly save one human life? 1,000 mice? 1,000,000 mice? Would it be less ethical in these cases if we were sacrificing larger mammals (rabbits or cows, for example)?
     b. When is it ethical to use members of a threatened or endangered species (chimpanzees, for example) for medical research? For example, chimps are the only other species that can become infected with the AIDS virus. Is it ethical to use chimps in AIDS research?

   c. Is it ethical to injure animals to test substances involved in non-essential products (for example, cosmetics)? Describe the Draize test.
   d. Is it ethical to use pound animals in research? To train medical students?
   e. If you disagree with a particular way in which animals are being used, is it ethical to break the law to "rescue" the animals? Describe the actions of PETA and ALF.
 H. Session VIII: Human evolution and impact on planet Earth
   1. Discuss trends in human evolution.
     a. Physical changes.
        (1) Posture.
        (2) Height.
        (3) Cranial capacity.
     b. Cultural changes
        (1) Improving tool technology.
        (2) Use of fire.
        (3) Agriculture.
        (4) Religion.
     c. Effects on the environment
        (1) Extinction of animals such as the mammoth.
        (2) Modern anthropogenic changes (get kids to make the list — they know most of them).
   2. Discuss the human population size over time and the reasons for the current exponential growth of the population. Discuss Malthus's theories.
   3. Have the kids do the thought experiment of removing humankind from the ecosystem. Each kid should do it individually; then, after they have all handed in their versions, the class should discuss it, as there will be a wide variety of opinions on the subject.
   4. Discuss the future of the planet. Include topics such as:
     a. What's the worst we can do to the planet?
     b. Will humans become extinct?
     c. What can we do to reverse or ameliorate anthropogenic changes?
     d. What will the continents look like in the future?

VII. Major Instructional Strategies Employed
  A. Problem solving

     The laboratory sections of the course emphasize problem solving, as do hypothetical questions the teacher poses during class discussions.

  B. Inquiry

     The laboratory sections of the course emphasize use of the scientific method to examine various natural phenomena. Much of the material discussed in class is the direct result of scientific inquiry; the evidence for the assertions made in class will be discussed so students can get a better feeling for the strategies scientists use to inquire into natural phenomena. In addition, extensive reading lists are provided at each session, and students are encouraged to pursue more information on topics of interest outside of class.

C. Grouping approaches

For the most part, activities were pursued either as a whole class or individually. Small-group activities didn't seem to be needed as the class consisted only of nine students.

D. Questioning techniques

Teacher-led class discussions emphasized student participation. Students were encouraged to volunteer information that helped build a better picture of the topic under discussion and to answer (and pose) hypothetical questions. Their opinions and judgment were elicited repeatedly, and they were required to support their statements with logical arguments. Many questions required them to propose an experiment to elucidate a scientific point.

VIII. Evaluation procedures

Evaluation of student performance was primarily anecdotal: I tried to see that all of them got a chance to participate in class discussions so I could tell whether they had understood the point under discussion. In addition to anecdotal assessment, the thought experiment in Session VIII provided a post-course assessment opportunity, as many of the concepts required for sophisticated answers to the questions posed in the experiment required application of the concepts covered in class.

IX. Materials/Resources

A. Teacher bibliography

1. For current information on scientific topics, see:
   — Tuesday Science section of *The New York Times*.
   — News and Views section of *Nature*.
   — News and Comment and Research News sections of *Science*.
   — Recent issues of *Scientific American*.

2. Bibliography of materials used to prepare the unit:

Bakker, R. T. (1986). *The dinosaur heresies: New theories unlocking the mystery of the dinosaurs and their extinction*. New York: Morrow.

Birdsell, J. B. (1975). *Human evolution*. Chicago: Rand McNally.

Dickerson, R. E., and Geis, I. (1969). *The structure and action of proteins*. Menlo Park, CA: W. A. Benjamin, Inc.

Eiger, M. S., and Olds, S. W. (1987). *The complete book of breast-feeding*. New York: Workman Publishing.

Frye, K. (1986). *Roadside geology of Virginia*. Missoula, MT: Mountain Press Publishing.

Gould, S. J. (1989). *Wonderful life: The Burgess shale and the nature of history*. New York: W. W. Norton.

Johanson, D., and Edey, M. (1981). *Lucy: The beginnings of human-kind*. New York: Simon and Schuster.

Keeton, W. T. (1972). *Biological science* (2nd ed.). New York: W. W. Norton.

Lehninger, A. L. (1975). *Biochemistry* (2nd ed.). New York: Worth Publishers.

Mahan, B. H. (1975). *University chemistry* (3rd ed.). Reading, MA: Addison-Wesley.

Pelzcar, M. J., Reid, R. D., and Chan, E. C. S. (1977). *Microbiology* (4th ed.). New York: McGraw-Hill.

Pyle, R. M. (1984). *The Audubon Society handbook for butterfly watchers*. New York: Charles Scribners' Sons.

Raup, D. M. (1986). *The nemesis affair: A story of the death of dinosaurs and the ways of science*.

Redfern, R. (1983). *The making of a continent*. New York: Times Books.

Scott, J. A. (1986). *The butterflies of North America*. Stanford, CA: Stanford University Press.

Silver, D. M. (1989). *Earth: The ever-changing planet* (Random House Library of Knowledge). New York: Random House.

Stein, S. (1986). *The evolution book*. New York: Workman Publishing.

Strickberger, M. W. (1976). *Genetics* (2nd ed.). New York: Macmillan.

Watson, J. D. (1976). *The molecular biology of the gene*. Menlo Park, CA: W. A. Benjamin, Inc.

Videotapes:

Planet Earth. (1989). John D. and Catherine T. MacArthur Foundation Library Video Classics Project. New York: BBC/Time-Life Films.

The Living Planet. (1984). John D. and Catherine T. MacArthur Foundation Video Classics Project. London: BBC/Time-Life Films.

Nova: Signs of the Apes, Songs of the Whales. (1984). John D. and Catherine T. MacArthur Foundation Video Classics Project. Boston: WGBH.

Lorne Greene's New Wilderness: Pretty Poison. (1987). A Greene and Dewar New Wilderness Production. Los Angeles: Prism Entertainment.

B. Student bibliography
For appropriate readings for students, please see the "Recommended Reading" section of the Weekly Planet handouts.

C. Handout material

X. Extension Ideas

In addition to the suggested reading material, you could suggest appropriate museums to visit (for example, the Smithsonian Institution and the Virginia Living Museum). It also would be worth watching the television schedule for appropriate nature and science programs.

Investigating Weather Folklore
Fourth Grade

William Chapman
Superintendent, Lancaster County School
Kilmarnock, Virginia

I. Curriculum Description

Rationale and purpose: The ability to predict weather accurately has long been of economic and social importance. We may have progressed from weather folklore through weather balloons to satellites, but an understanding of the causes and indicators of weather change still has the power to enrich our lives and contribute to our understanding of the world surrounding us. The purpose of this unit is to study and evaluate the accuracy of selected weather folklore, which will require learning the causes and physics of weather and an understanding of tools for measurement and prediction.

II. Nature of Differentiation

A. How has the unit been accelerated, compressed, and/or reorganized to accommodate gifted learner needs?

A process/product approach will allow and provide for extensions of basic content through opportunities for student selection of projects and group activities. A pretest will determine which learners may advance beyond the basic approach (reading and discussion), which ones need a brief review, and which students may be accelerated and placed in individual and cooperative learning group projects. Teacher-directed activities will involve all students.

B. How has the unit focused on higher-level process skills?

The unit focuses on a body of knowledge (weather physics) as a means of enabling students to analyze and evaluate weather folklore. Emphasis is on problem solving requiring critical-thinking skills such as clarifying (identifying central issues, reasons, assumptions), judging information (determining relevance), and making inferences to solve problems (judging inductive conclusions, judging deductive validity, and predicting consequences of various weather elements).

C. How has the unit engaged learners in meaningful product development?

The unit emphasizes student projects and activities. Fourteen of the activities result in a product.

D. How has the unit addressed key themes and ideas and related them to several domains of inquiry?

Students will interact cognitively with the subject matter through problem-solving activities. Through solving problems, exploring concepts, conducting experiments, and discovering relationships, students will be involved in science, history, and language arts domains.

III. Content Outline (9 weeks)
  A. Major content topics.
    1. Elements of weather
       a. Temperature
       b. Water in the air (humidity, dew, frost, precipitation, clouds)
       c. Air pressure
       d. Wind
       e. Air masses, fronts, tracking weather formations
    2. Forecasting weather
       a. History of the Weather Bureau
       b. Weather instruments
       c. Weather maps
    3. Weather folklore
       a. Valid
       b. Invalid
  B. Organizational structure and order.

IV. Prerequisites
    The whole class will be involved in the pretest. Those who score 80% or better on the pretest will advance immediately to independent reading and student-directed activities.
    The whole class will be involved in the teacher-directed activities.
    Students will choose one activity from each of the four objectives. Students may volunteer for additional activities. Identified gifted students will be assigned to work together on activities demanding a superior amount/level of production and a high degree of challenge in terms of mastery of knowledge of content. (Gifted students will also be assigned the most challenging individual assignments.)

V. Objectives
    1. Students will understand the causes of weather change (physics of the atmosphere).

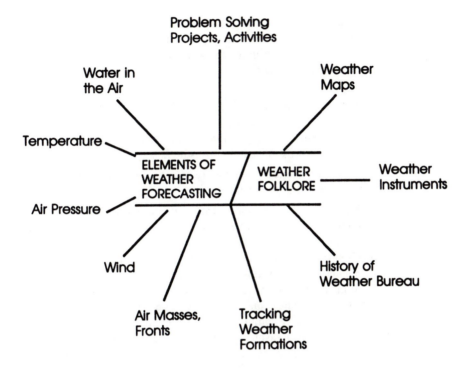

2. Students will develop a knowledge of basic weather instruments and how they help measure and predict weather.
3. Students will become familiar with weather-predicting technology in use today.
4. Students will attempt to prove or disprove the accuracy of selected weather folklore through observation and discussion, projects, and experiments.

VI. Sample Activities
Objective 1: Students will understand the causes of weather change (physics of the atmosphere).

A. Teacher-directed.
1. The teacher will show films and videotapes illustrating the causes of weather changes.
2. The teacher will invite a meteorologist to visit the class to explain how he or she predicts weather.
3. The teacher will take the class on a field trip to visit a meteorologist at work and to see how weather maps are used to chart weather.

B. Student-directed.
　　1. The teacher will provide a variety of materials for each group of four students and ask each group to use the materials to demonstrate one or more of the following:
　　　　a. Air has weight.
　　　　b. Water vapor in the air changes to a liquid and forms tiny drops at a certain temperature (dew point).
　　　　c. Temperature causes differences in air pressure (weight).
　　　　d. Moisture in the air can be measured.
　　2. Students may choose one or more of the following individual projects to present to the class:
　　　　a. Next-day and long-range weather forecasts will be collected and compared to actual weather, and reasons for errors will be proposed (3-week project).
　　　　b. Cloud formations will be videotaped and compared with weather data collected for a 3-week period.
　　　　c. Students will compete against each other in forecasting various weather features such as temperature, precipitation, types of clouds, relative humidity, and barometric pressure for the next day at noon. Reasons for hypotheses must be explained.
　　　　d. After researching weather maps and symbols, students will construct a weather map and explain how a cold front can travel across the country in several days and how the weather is affected in each area.

Objective 2: Students will develop a knowledge of basic weather instruments and how they help measure and predict weather.

A. Teacher-directed.
　　1. The teacher will display and explain real weather instruments, including a barometer, hygrometer, thermometer, rain gauge, and anemometer.
　　2. The teacher will take the class on a field trip to visit a meteorologist at work to see weather instruments and communication devices used for predicting and recording weather (same trip as described in Activity 1).

B. Student-directed. Students may choose one or more of the following projects:
　　1. Students will research, construct, and attempt to calibrate weather instruments, including a hygrometer, rain gauge, barometer, and anemometer. Students may combine their instruments to form a weather station and to attempt weather predictions and measurement.

2. Students will use their weather stations to issue "school weather forecasts" over the PA system during morning announcements for several weeks.
3. Students will research and present an oral or a written report on the history of weather prediction efforts.

Objective 3: Students will become familiar with weather-predicting technology in use today.

A. Teacher-directed.
   See Objective 2, A.2.

B. Student-directed. Students may choose to participate in a mentorship with a meteorologist, designed to provide in-depth knowledge of weather-prediction technology in use today.

Objective 4: Students will attempt to prove or disprove the accuracy of selected weather folklore through observation and discussion, projects, and experiments.

A. Teacher-directed.
   1. The teacher will provide a collection of weather folklore and will discuss samples representing scientifically valid and invalid lore, and the reasons why and why not.

      Example of valid folklore: "If the woolen fleece spread the heavenly ways, be sure no rain disturbs the summer day."

      Example of invalid folklore: "If the cat washes her face over her ear, 'tis a sign the weather will be fine and clear."

B. Student-directed.
   1. Students may choose to form a team to interview residents of nearby retirement homes, farmers, and meteorologists in order to develop and publish an article on weather folklore for the local newspaper (showing respect for all viewpoints).
   2. Students may choose to form a cooperative learning team to attempt to prove or disprove the accuracy of selected weather folklore through analysis of the elements of the folklore and modern knowledge of weather, including knowledge of the physics of the air.
   3. Students may choose to form a cooperative learning group to research and present oral reports on the history and importance of weather prediction efforts and beliefs since pioneer days.
   4. Students may choose to attempt to prove or disprove the accuracy of weather folklore by participating in a debate presented to the student body as a culminating activity of the unit.

5. Student teams may choose to document examples of valid and invalid weather folklore by preparing projects for the Science Fair.
6. Using knowledge gained earlier from the unit, student teams may choose to create valid and invalid "modern" (funny) weather folklore to be published in the school newspaper.
7. Students may choose to form a cooperative learning group to demonstrate weather phenomena (physics of air) involved in selected weather folklore, using self-made and professional weather instruments as a focus.

VII. Major Instructional Strategies Employed
    A. Problem solving.

The focus of the unit is to solve the problem of how to differentiate between valid and invalid weather folklore. Proving and/or disproving the accuracy of selected weather folklore will require problem solving through observation, discussion, experiments, and projects.

    B. Inquiry.

The unit emphasizes inquiry-based activities relative to predicting weather and proving/disproving the validity of weather folklore. A certain amount of research methodology (the scientific method) is required in order to reach such conclusions.

Meteorologists will interact with students as practicing scientists and mentors. The latest technology having to do with weather prediction and tracking will be shared with gifted students to provide challenge and depth of knowledge for further study and research.

    C. Grouping approaches.

The unit will be taught to a heterogeneously grouped class, with a cluster group of six gifted students. All students will be involved in the pretest and all teacher-directed activities.

Students who score 70% or higher on the pretest will advance immediately to independent reading and student-directed activities. Others will be grouped for teacher-directed study in the science text, featuring more traditional reading assignments, discussion, tests, and re-teaching, prior to moving into student-directed activities.

Identified gifted students will be grouped together for student-directed activities. Highly challenging activities are identified for choice-selections by gifted students/group.

Gifted students may opt to participate in more than the one-activity-per-objective, for extra credit, or may opt to create their own activity, with teacher approval.

D. Questioning techniques.

Teacher-directed activities will emphasize discussion and the use of questioning techniques. To challenge and motivate gifted students, memory/cognition-type questions will be deemphasized in favor of the following types:

(1) Convergent: analytical in nature, tend to begin with "why" or "how." Examples: "Why did people formerly think that 'lightning sours milk,' or 'thunder curdles cream'?" "How does a barometer help predict weather?"

(2) Divergent: hypothetical in nature, no right answer, frequently begin with "What if" or "Pretend." Examples: "What if there were no clouds?" "Pretend you are a meteorologist the day before the Fourth of July. How important would you be? What other occasions would be especially crucial for a meteorologist?"

(3) Evaluative: calls for judgment or opinion, begins with "In your opinion . . ." or "Which is best?" Examples: "In your opinion, what will our weather be tomorrow if the cold front passes through tonight?" "Which weather instrument is best for predicting long-range weather change?" "Which weather folklore was the most commonly accepted and yet without scientific basis?"

VIII. Evaluation Procedures
   A. Pre/post assessments.

A pretest will be used for initial teaching decisions for the unit. A posttest will be given to assess unit learning. The posttest grade will be averaged with the project grade 50-50. Projects will be evaluated according to teacher and student-developed criteria.

   B. Observational approaches.

The teacher will monitor the activities, observing and recording anecdotally the levels of effort, creativity, critical thinking, and mastery of concepts and understandings. Anecdotal records will be shared with students and student teams during a post-unit evaluation discussion session. Difficulty level of activities will be taken into consideration when deciding grades, as well extra-credit activities.

INVESTIGATING WEATHER FOLKLORE

Pretest

1. What causes weather to change?
2. What is meant by the term "dew point?"

3. Define the term "relative humidity."
4. What causes dew to form?
5. What is the purpose of a "hygrometer?"
6. Name and describe three types of clouds.
7. How is hail formed?
8. Describe briefly the way a barometer measures air pressure.
9. What causes wind to blow?
10. Define the following terms:
    a. Air mass
    b. Front

Posttest

Analyze the validity of the following weather folklore in terms of your scientific knowledge of weather physics:

1. "If the sun sets clear on Friday, it will storm on Sunday."
2. "When the leaves show their backs, it will rain."
3. "Rain long foretold, long last;
   Short notice, soon past."
4. "Evening red and morning gray
   Sets the traveler on his way;
   Evening gray and morning red
   Brings down rain upon his head."
5. "Lightning is attracted to mirrors."

What factors cause weather to change?

Which weather instruments are most helpful in *predicting* weather?

Which weather instruments are most helpful in *measuring* weather?

How has modern technology made weather prediction more accurate?

MATERIALS/RESOURCES

Biblliography of Teacher Materials Used in Preparation and Execution of the Unit

Books

Bates, D. (1959). *The earth and its atmosphere*. New York: Basic Books.
Cable, G. K., & Crull, P. (1959). *The physical sciences*. Englewood Cliffs, NJ: Prentice Hall.
Forsdyke, A. (1970). *Weather and weather forecasting*. New York: Grosset & Dunlap.
Sloane, E. (1963). *Folklore of American weather*. New York: Hawthorne Books.

Other Media

Films: "Synoptic Weather, Earth Science for Teachers," Virginia State Film Library, Richmond, VA.

Audiovisual instructional materials for Virginia's public schools: No. 22170, Richmond, VA: "Weather Forecasting;" 39605 "Weather — Understanding Storms;" 64190, "What Makes the Weather;" 67008, "Weather Scientists."

Computer Software: Carolina Biological Supply, Burlington, NC: "Water and Weather Services," "Forecast," and "Weather or Not."

Videotapes: "Understanding Weather and Climate," Educational Audiovisual, Pleasantville, NY. "Weather: Come Rain or Shine," National Geographic, Washington, DC.

Filmstrips: "Rain and Clouds," "The Atmosphere, Climate, and the Weather," Clearview Company, J. S. Latta, Distributor, Huntington, WV.

"Forecasting the Weather," National Geographic Society, Washington, DC.

Kits: "What Air Can Do," "Why Does It Rain?" National Geographic Society, Washington, DC.

Student Bibliography

Barufaldi, L., & Moses, A. (1981). *Health science*. Lexington, MA: D. C. Heath & Co.

Bodin, S. (1978). *Weather and climate in color*. Dorset, England: Blandford Press.

Hardy, R. (1982). *Weather Book*. Boston: Little, Brown.

"How to Make Weather Instruments." Santa Barbara, CA: Learning Works Enrichment Series.

Lambert, D., & Hardy, R. (1987). *Weather and its work*. New York: Macdonald and Company.

Lehr, P., Burnt, R., & Zim, H. (1957). *Weather*. New York: Golden Press.

Ross, F. (1965). *Weather*. New York: Lothrop, Lee, & Shepard, Inc.

Rubin, L. (1970). *The weather wizard's cloud book*. Chapel Hill, NC: Algonquin Books.

Thompson, P. (1968). *Weather book*. Boston: Little, Brown.

Whipple, A. (1968). *Planet earth — Storm*. New York: Time-Life Books.

Wigginton, E. (1972). *The foxfire book*. New York: Anchor Books.

Author Index

388   *Author Index*

Bristol, M. M., 286
Brody, L., 171, 172, 184, 209, 262,
    267, 268, 272
Brolin, D. E., 257
Bronfenbrenner, U., 286
Brooks, T. I., 217
Brower, P., 289, 291
Brown, A. L., 277
Brown, D., 215
Brown, V. L., 218
Brownowski, J., 103
Bruch, C. B., 162, 166
Bruner, J., 104, 226, 227, 229, 230
Bryan, J., 174
Bryan, T., 174, 265
Bryan, T. H., 174
Burger, D., 103
Burke, J., 103
Burningham, John, 94

C

Caldwell, M., 130-131
Callahan, C., 130-131, 169
Cariglia-Bull, T., 8
Carman, R. A., 278
Carter, K. R., 131
Chalfant, J. C., 170
Chapman, William, 377
Charles, C. M., 245
Charters, W., 225
Christenson, S. L., 269
Circirelli, V. G., 291
Clements, S., 267
Clift, R. T., 10
Cobb, J., 183
Cohn, S., 6
Colangelo, N., 166, 167, 289, 291
Coleman, J., 169
Colson, S. E., 256, 269
Combs, Arthur, 232
Comer, J., 157, 199
Conant, J. B., 229
Conlan, J., 230
Connell, J. P., 166
Cornell, D. G., 288, 289, 291
Counts, George, 231
Covington, M., 168
Cox, J., 184, 227
Csikszentmihalyi, M., 7
Cuban, L., 4
Curry, J., 81
Curtis, M. J., 216

Cutler, R. L., 216

D

Dahlstrom, M., 290
Daniels, N., 184, 227
Daniels, P. R., 157, 172, 262, 264, 265,
    272
Darling-Hammond, L., 5
Davids, A., 167
Davis, G., 184
Davis, H. P., 166
Davis, J., 169
Delaney, H. D., 278
Dember, C., 166
Denny, T., 169, 170
Deno, S. L., 268
Deshler, D., 278
Deshler, D. D., 251, 253, 256, 277
Dettman, D. F., 167
DeVore, Irven, 230
Dewey, J., 225, 229
Di Gang, S. A., 253
Diener, C., 168
Dillard, A., 104
Dinkmeyer, D., 216
DiNunno, L., 65
Dixon, J., 266
Donahoe, K. A., 251
Dow, P., 230
Downing, M. R., 216
Driver, R., 231
Dunham, G., 166
Dunkin, M. J., 226
Dweck, C., 7, 8, 168, 170
Dykstra, L., 173, 210

E

Eccles, J. S., 170
Eisendorfer, C., 216
Eisner, E. W., 226
Elder, J., 220
Ellis, A., 168
Ellis, E. S., 251, 256
Ellis, J., 292
Emerick, L. J., 266
Ennis, R. H., 305
Entwisle, D. R., 164
Epstein, M. H., 251, 271
Erickson, G., 231
Erlanger, W. J., 164
Escher, M. C., 323-324, 326
Evahn, C., 168

Subject Index